F. B. (Frank Byron) Jevons

An Introduction to the History of Religion

F. B. (Frank Byron) Jevons

An Introduction to the History of Religion

ISBN/EAN: 9783337130237

Printed in Europe, USA, Canada, Australia, Japan

Cover: Foto ©Lupo / pixelio.de

More available books at **www.hansebooks.com**

AN INTRODUCTION

TO THE

HISTORY OF RELIGION

BY

FRANK BYRON JEVONS, M.A., LITT.D.

CLASSICAL TUTOR IN THE UNIVERSITY OF DURHAM

METHUEN & CO.

36 ESSEX STREET, W.C.

LONDON

1896

PREFACE

In this book the history of early religion is investigated on the principles and methods of anthropology, and in the belief that the interests of truth and religion are fundamentally identical.

The work is intended primarily for students who require an introduction to the history of religion, but will also, it is hoped, prove interesting to students of folk-lore and anthropology, and to the wider circle of general readers.

As far as I am aware, there is no other book which covers exactly the same ground as this does, or which attempts to summarise the results of recent anthropology, to estimate their bearing upon religious problems, and to weave the whole into a connected history of early religion.

Thus far, then, this book is original, namely, as far as regards the use to which its materials are put; but the materials themselves are largely, though not wholly, derived from the writings of others. In all cases I have endeavoured to express my obligations in the footnotes. I am, however, more especially bound to mention here the name of the late Professor Robertson Smith, to whose *Religion of the Semites* my obligations are too great for their expression to be confined to footnotes. My indebtedness to the works of Messrs. E. B. Tylor, A. Lang, and Frazer is here gratefully acknowledged.

CONTENTS

AN INTRODUCTION

TO

THE HISTORY OF RELIGION

CHAPTER I

INTRODUCTORY

THE book now before the reader is not a History of Religion, but an Introduction to the History of Religion: its object is not to place a history of religion before the student, but to prepare him for the study of that history, to familiarise him with some of the elementary ideas and some of the commonest topics of the subject. Much which would fill a large part of a history of religion finds no place in this Introduction: thus, for instance, religions such as Christianity, Mohammedanism, Buddhism, which are the outcome of the teaching of their individual founders, are not included within the scope of this book. But these religions—which, on the analogy of "positive" law, *i.e.* law enacted by a sovereign, have been termed Positive religions—were all designed by their founders to supersede certain existing religions, which, not being enacted by the authority of any single founder, but being practised as a matter of custom and tradition, may be called customary religions. It is with these religions, their customs and institutions, that this Introduction deals.

Now, religious institutions are not the only institutions which an early people possesses: it has also social institutions, such as those which regulate marriage, the organisation of the family, the vengeance to be taken for the murder of a kinsman, the holding of property, the government of the community, etc.; and the study of these social institutions forms one branch of the science of anthropology. But religious institutions also all have their social side: religious worship is a public institution; the gods are the gods of the community as a whole, and all the members of the community are required by custom to unite in the performance of the rites and sacrifices with which it is the custom of that particular society to approach its gods. Thus, religious customs and institutions seem, on their social side, to require to be studied, like other social institutions, on the principles and methods of anthropology. Of late years they have been largely so studied; and in this book it is proposed to collect together the principal results of these recent investigations — an undertaking the more necessary because the studies in question are at present scattered and on single topics, and have not yet been focussed in such a way as to show what their total bearing on the history of religion is.

But the proposal thus to apply the methods of science and the principles of anthropology to the study of religion, meets in some quarters with not unnatural and certainly not unreasonable objections. We must therefore at the outset make a brief statement of the methods in question, and consider the objections that may be made to them. To begin with, anthropology employs the Comparative Method: the customs of some one uncivilised or semi-civilised people are compared with the customs of another people in the same stage of culture, and considerable resemblance is found to exist between them, just as the flint arrow-heads made by man bear always a striking likeness to each other, whether they come from Europe or from Mexico, and the rudest pottery from Greece cannot be distinguished from the pottery of the ancient Peruvians. These resemblances enable us to extend our knowledge considerably; thus the way in which cave-men contrived to fasten their stone axe-heads to wooden handles becomes clear when they are placed side by side with the axes, having stone heads fastened on to wooden handles, which are used by some savages at the present day. The purpose for which a stone implement was used by primitive man may be very doubtful until it is compared with the use made by living savages of some similiar implement. So, too, the purpose of some rite or custom practised by one people may be doubtful or unknown until it is compared with the same or a similar rite performed elsewhere under circumstances which clearly show its object. Again, the Comparative Method is used in anthropology in the same way as it is employed in deciphering fragmentary ancient inscriptions: in inscriptions of a similar kind similar formulæ recur, thus in decrees of the Athenian people the formula "resolved by the people" constantly recurs; so, if only a few letters of the formula can be traced in what is plainly a decree, we can restore the missing letters with confidence. In the same way, a custom consisting in the performance of a series of acts may be found amongst several peoples in its entirety, and may amongst another people only survive in a multilated form, and then we can infer with confidence that the missing acts also once formed part of this now fragmentary custom.

It is clear, therefore, that the Comparative Method can only be properly employed where the things compared resemble each other. If, then, we apply the Comparative Method to religion, we seem to be committed to the assumption that all religions are alike—and that is a proposition to which no religious-minded person can be expected to assent, especially when some writers apparently take it as self-evident that all religion is fetishism or animism or what not. Now, it is clear that the application of the Comparative Method to religion does imply that religions resemble one another, otherwise it would be useless to compare them. But it is also equally clear that the use of the Comparative Method implies that religions differ from one another, otherwise it would be unnecessary to compare them. A bilingual inscription (of sufficient length) in both Etruscan and some known language would settle the problem of Etruscan: the resemblance in meaning would enable us to compare the two languages together; it is the differences which make it necessary to have some such means of comparison. Comparative anatomy would have no object if the structure of all animals were exactly alike. If there were no differences between languages, there would be no need of Comparative

Philology. And so it is precisely because religions do differ that the Comparative Method can be applied to them; and the use of the method is a standing disproof of the idea that all religions are alike.

The Comparative Method, then, can only be used where there are differences in the things compared. Indeed, we may go further, and say that it is for the sake of ascertaining these differences that the method is brought into use. Thus it is not the recurring formulæ, the stereotyped official phrases, which are the interesting points in Athenian inscriptions, but their subject-matter in which they differ from each other and which is studied for the light it throws on the history of Athens. The various Indo-European languages both resemble and differ from one another; the resemblances are studied for the light which they throw on the differences, the differences are studied because in their explanation lies the key to the process by which the various languages all grew out of the common, original Aryan tongue. All growth consists in a series of changes, and the record of the successive differences is the history of the thing's growth. It was by a succession of changes in one direction that Italian was evolved out of Latin; in another French, in another Spanish. The primitive custom which required vengeance to be taken for the murder of a kinsman appears in one form in the Corsican vendetta, in a more developed form in the Saxon demand for wer-geld, in a yet more developed form in the Athenian laws against murder, while in English law the prosecution has been taken entirely out of the hands of the kin. Now, the stages by which the final form of this or any other institution was reached in any given country may all be recorded in the annals of that country, but if some are missing the Comparative Method warrants us in inferring that they were the same as those by which the same institution reached its final form in other countries. Thus by the Comparative Method we are enabled to apply the theory of evolution to the study of social institutions, and amongst others to the study of religious customs and institutions, on their social side.

Here again, however, we are met with serious objections: evolution is the development of higher forms of life and thought out of lower, monotheism is the highest form of religion, and therefore, on the general principles of evolution, must have been the final form reached by a slow evolution from such lower stages as polytheism, fetishism, ancestor-worship, etc. They, therefore, who believe in the Bible must consider the very notion of evolution as essentially inapplicable to religion. Monotheism, according to Genesis, was revealed to begin with, and therefore cannot have been reached by a process of development. The truth was given to man at the beginning, and therefore cannot be the outcome of evolution. Every step taken in religion by man since Adam, if it was not in the right line of monotheism, must have been away from the truth of revealed religion; the only evolution, the evolution of error. Man's imagination, when once it abandons the one guide, becomes the prey of all sorts of perversion, of the monstrous customs of heathendom, which it is useless to trace, as they lead only away from the truth, and are as irrational and as little to be heeded as the ravings of a mind distraught.

The validity of this reasoning all depends upon the tacit assumption that evolution is the same thing as progress, whereas in point of fact evolution is universal, but progress is very rare—the civilised peoples of the earth are less numerous than the semi-civilised and uncivilised; and of the civilised themselves the progressive peoples are a minority. Institutions not only grow but decay also, and decay as well as growth is a process of evolution. Florid art is evolved out of something simpler, but is not therefore superior to it. The Roman Empire was evolved out of the Roman Republic, and was morally a degeneration from it. The polytheism of Virgil is not better, as religion, than that of Homer; the polytheism of late Brahminism is certainly worse than that of the earlier periods. Therefore, to say that the only evolution in religion—except that which is on the lines of the Bible—is an evolution of error, may be quite true and yet not show that the idea of evolution is inapplicable to heathen religions. Their evolution may well have been, from the religious point of view, one long process of degeneration. Progress is certainly as exceptional in religion as in other things, and where it takes place must be due to exceptional causes. The study of heathen religions, therefore, on evolutionary principles, may throw some light on true religion; if we can ascertain the reasons why they have failed to advance, we shall be able better to appreciate the causes to which progress is really due. This, however, assumes that it is possible scientifically to ascertain the law of growth in the case of pagan religions; and it may seem that they are too hopelessly fallacious, almost insane, in their perversions of the truth. But the study of fallacies is a part, and a very valuable part of logic. Even insanity has its laws, and it is only by their discovery that the medical man can hope to cure the mind diseased. And though the missionary has resources which the physician has not, still it cannot but help him if he starts with a knowledge of the savage's point of view. To the necessity of such knowledge for the missionary, no more eloquent testimony could be given than is afforded by the labour which missionaries have bestowed on the study of native religions, and which provides most of the material for the history of early forms of religion.

To accept the principle, therefore, that religion is evolved, by no means pledges us to reject *à priori* and without examination the possibility that monotheism may have been the original religion. Nor shall we so reject it here. On the other hand, a writer who approaches the history of religion from the anthropological standpoint cannot start by assuming that monotheism was the original religion. He must start from the facts provided by his science, namely, the religious customs and institutions of the various peoples of the world. And even so, he will not be able to work back to the time of our first parents; anthropology carries us no further back than the period just before the civilised races appear to our view. It is to this period, therefore, that "primitive man," as he appears in these pages hereafter, belongs; and, let it be borne in mind, he is a hypothesis, like the creatures which have left only a single bone, or a foot-print, behind—he is reconstructed from the traces he has left. He is invented to account for the features common to both civilised man and existing savages, or rather to their ancestors. He is not purely identical with the savage as he now exists, for the savage has existed for a long time, and we cannot suppose without change—indeed, he can be shown to have retrograded in many cases. Thus between "primitive man" and our first parents there is a wide gap; and the anthropologist standing on primitive man's side of the gulf cannot pretend to see or say with certainty what did or did not happen on the other side. Science has not yet even settled the question whether man's origin was monogenetic or polygenetic—though the balance of opinion seems inclined to settle in favour of the former theory.

Whether the anthropologist will fall back upon the Book of Genesis to assist him in his conjectures as to what happened before the earliest times on which his science has any clear light to throw, will depend upon the value he assigns to Genesis, and the interpretation he puts upon it. Some writers argue that Genesis may be literally true, but it never says that religion was revealed. But it seems to me that the account in Genesis could never have been written except by one who believed (1) that monotheism was the original religion, (2) that there never was a time in the history of man when he was without religion, (3) that the revelation of God to man's consciousness was immediate, direct, and carried conviction with it. Now, the first of these three tenets is a point on which we have already touched, and the discussion of which we shall take up again in its proper place. The second is a proposition the falsity of which some writers have endeavoured to demonstrate by producing savage peoples alleged to have no religious ideas whatever. This point we have no intention of discussing, because, as every anthropologist knows, it has now gone to the limbo of dead controversies. Writers approaching the subject from such different points of view as Professor Tylor, Max Müller, Ratzel, de Quatrefages, Tiele, Waitz, Gerland, Peschel, all agree that there are no races, however rude, which are destitute of all idea of religion.

The third is a point which must receive rather fuller treatment here. To the religious-minded man, the existence, the personality of God and communion with Him, are facts of internal but immediate consciousness: he has as direct perception of the light of the soul as he has of the light of the eye. To him, therefore, since God has never at any time left Himself without a witness, it is perfectly natural that the same revelation, carrying conviction with it, should have been made to all men in all times. It is this revelation, this element in the common consciousness of all generations of men, which for him constitutes the continuity of religion. He is aware that the facts of consciousness receive very unequal degrees of attention; the mind's eye can only be focussed on one spot in the field of consciousness at the same time, it is but on a chosen few of the mass of presentations flowing in upon the mind that attention can at any one time be concentrated. Indeed, the art of life consists in paying attention to the right things and neglecting the rest; and systematic inattention may be carried to such a point that in course of time the very roar of Niagara becomes, if not inaudible, at anyrate unnoticed. Here, then, we have the explanation of that slow process of religious degeneration—due to prolonged and increasing distraction of attention—which is, as we have seen, one form of evolution. But as long as religion exists at all, in however degenerate a form, some faint consciousness of the fundamental facts must linger on—and it is that consciousness, attenuated as it may be, which constitutes that continuity without which there could be no evolution. If evolution takes place, something must be evolved; and that something, as being continuously present in all the different stages, may be called the *continuum* of religion. Whether the movement of religion be upwards or downwards, whether its evolution in any given case be a process of progress or of degeneration, it is by the *continuum* running through all its forms that the highest stages and the lowest are linked together.

Now the existence of this *continuum* the historian of religion, if he is an evolutionist, has to accept. He is bound to assume its presence from the very beginning of the process of evolution—the process cannot begin without it. The belief that the course of the world is directed by divine agency and personal will, is one the existence of which the historian, even if he could not explain it, would still be bound to assume. He is in exactly the same position as the physicist is. The physicist has to assume the reality of the external world before he can show what consequences his science can trace from the assumption; but he knows that some philosophers, *e.g.* Hume and Mill, deny its reality; and that no proof of its reality has been discovered which all philosophers accept. So, too, the historian of religion must assume the reality of the facts of the religious consciousness to begin with, else he cannot explain the various forms they take in the course of their evolution, nor the various customs and institutions in which they find outward expression. But he knows that their reality is confidently denied as well as stoutly asserted. Further, it is clear that physical science cannot prove the existence of the external world; if a physicist were to undertake to devise a chemical experiment which should prove or disprove the existence of matter, he would show thereby that he had not got beyond the Johnsonian stage of the discussion. Physical science, being a body of inferences which flow from the assumption, cannot prove the assumption except by arguing in a vicious circle. So, too, the history of religion has to assume, it cannot prove or disprove, the reality of the facts of the religious consciousness. Perhaps another analogy may make this clearer.

It is only by a slow process of accumulation that human knowledge has reached its present dimensions; the science of the modern *savant* has been evolved out of the errors of the simple savage. But it would be obviously absurd, therefore, contemptuously to pooh-pooh the discoveries of modern science as merely survivals of the old erroneous way of looking at the world. And it is equally fallacious to talk, as both friends and foes of religion do sometimes talk, as though the application of the theory of evolution to religion would reduce the higher forms of it to mere survivals of barbarism, animism, and so on. The art of Phidias was evolved out of something of which we may almost say that it was artistic only in intention; but the man would be to be pitied who could see nothing in the highest art of Greece but survivals of a barbaric stage of carving. Art is a mode of expression, whereby the artist delivers himself of his message. It is common to both barbaric and civilised man; and the inference is that it is neither peculiarly barbaric nor specifically civilised, but universally human. So, too, with religion as a form of thought, the perception of "the invisible things of Him through the things that are made"; it is common both to barbaric and civilised man, but it is not therefore a barbaric form of thought—rather it is a mode of cognition which is part of human nature. The perfect beauty of fully-developed art is of course not present in its rude beginnings; but even the barbaric artist is feeling after the ideal if peradventure he may find it.

In the case of science, the *continuum* which, however fine and long drawn out, yet links the *savant* to the savage, is their common belief in the uniformity of Nature. Now, the savage doubtless often wrongly applies this belief. He sees uniformities where they do not exist, but we do not regard this as a proof that Nature is not uniform. He ascribes events to their wrong causes, but this does not shake our faith in the proposition that every event has a cause. So, too, the belief that all things are ruled by supernatural will is not proved to be false because it is often wrongly applied. When the history of religion has recorded all the wrong applications of the belief, the validity of the belief has still to be tested on quite other grounds and with quite other tests by the philosophy of religion. The validity of the belief in the uniformity of Nature is in nowise affected by the vast array of errors contained in the history of science. Unfortunately, though we all believe in the uniformity of Nature, as we all believe in the reality of the external world, there is no satisfactory way of proving either to be true. The average man of science simply walks, and wisely walks, by faith in these matters; he takes it for granted that Nature is uniform and that the external world is real. And in religion the average man may do worse than imitate the example given him in science. It is the boast of science that it deals with things, not names; that it proves everything by experience, brings every proposition to the test of immediate consciousness. Religion has no other proof, no other test for its truths; it is by his own experience a man proves the truth that "blessed are the humble and meek"; it is by the test of immediate consciousness that he learns—if he does learn—that God "is not far from each one of us."

CHAPTER II

OUTLINE OF THE ARGUMENT

THE savage imagines that even lifeless things are animated by a will, a personality, a spirit, like his own; and, wherever he gets his conception of the supernatural from, to some at least of the objects which surround him, and which are supposed by him to be personal agents, he ascribes supernatural power (ch. iii. "The Supernatural"). Some writers have imagined that there was a time in the "prehistory" of man, when he could not tell the natural from the supernatural, and that consequently magic existed first and religion was developed out of it. But this view seems to proceed on a misconception of the nature of Sympathetic Magic (ch. iv.). Be this as it may, it was natural that man should wish to establish friendly relations with some of these supernatural powers; and the wish seemed one quite possible to carry out, because he was in the habit of communicating with certain beings, who, whether they possessed supernatural powers or not, at anyrate were spirits, namely, the souls of the departed (ch. v. "Life and Death"). But this assumes that ghosts, or at anyrate some ghosts, were friendly to the living, and were loved by them; whereas it is sometimes maintained that all ghosts are malevolent, and that the corpse-taboo is a proof of the universal dread of the ghost. But when we examine the institution of taboo generally, we find, first, that taboo is transmissible (*e.g.* the mourner is as dangerous as the corpse he has touched), and next, that its transmissibility implies no hostility—the mourner is as dangerous to those he loves as to those he hates (ch. vi. "Taboo: its Transmissibility"). Taboo is not fear of "the clinging ghost" nor of any physical emanation, but is the conviction that there are certain things which must—absolutely, and not on grounds of experience or "unconscious utility"—be avoided (ch. vii. "Things Taboo"). It is the categorical imperative "Thou shalt not—" which is the first form assumed by the sense of social and moral obligation and by religious commandments (ch. viii. "Taboo, Morality and Religion").

Primitive man, then, feeling it both necessary and possible to establish permanent friendly relations with some of the supernatural powers by which he was surrounded, proceeded to do so. He not only ascribed to natural objects a personality like his own; he also noticed that, as men were organised in kins (clans and families), so natural objects grouped themselves in natural kinds (genera and species). And as alliances between human kins were formed by means of the blood-covenant which made all the members of the two contracting tribes blood-brothers, so he proceeded to make a blood-covenant between a human kind and an animal species. This is Totemism (ch. ix.). We may not be able to say *à priori* why he chose animals first rather than any other natural kind, but the hypothesis that he did so is the one which alone, or best, accounts for the facts to be explained, and therefore may be taken as a working hypothesis. It accounts for animal worship, for the animal or semi-animal form of many gods, for the "association" of certain animals with certain gods, for "sacred" and for "unclean" animals, and for the domestication of animals (ch. x. "Survivals of Totemism"). It also accounts for the altar and for the idol (ch. xi. "Animal Sacrifice: The Altar"), and for animal sacrifice and for the sacramental meal (ch. xii. "Animal Sacrifice: The Sacramental Meal").

Thus far we have been dealing with public worship, to which the individual was admitted, not on his private merits, but because he was a member of the tribe which had a blood-covenant with a totem-species. If the individual, however, wished to commend himself specially to supernatural protection, there were two ways in which he might do so, one illicit and one licit. He might address himself to one of the supernatural powers which had no friendly relations with his own tribe or any other—which was no "god"—and this was in itself a suspicious way of proceeding, which the community resented, and if harm came of it, visited with punishment (ch. xiii. "Fetishism"). Or he might, with the approval of the community, and by the intermediation of the priest, place his family or himself under the immediate protection of one of the community's gods. In any case, however, licit or illicit, the ritual adopted was copied from that observed by the community in approaching its gods (ch. xiv. "Family Gods and Guardian Spirits"). Like all other private cults, the worship of ancestors was modelled on the public worship of the community; and as the family is an institution of later growth than the tribe or clan, the worship of family ancestors is a later institution than the worship of the tribal god (ch. xv. "Ancestor Worship").

We now return to public worship. Species of trees and plants might be, and were, taken for totems, as well as species of animals. This led to the domestication of plants. Another result was that bread (or maize) and wine came to furnish forth the sacramental meal in the place of the body and blood of the animal victim hitherto sacrificed (ch. xvi. "Tree and Plant Worship"). The breeding of cattle and cultivation of cereals made man more dependent than heretofore on the forces of nature (conceived by him as supernatural powers), and led him to worship them with the same ritual as he had worshipped his plant or animal totems (ch. xvii. "Nature Worship"). Agriculture made it possible to relinquish a wandering mode of existence for settled life; and settled life made it possible for neighbouring tribes to unite in a larger political whole, or "state." But this political union involved a fusion of cults, and that fusion might take one of two forms: if the resemblance between the gods worshipped by the two tribes was close, the two gods might come to be regarded as one and the same god; if not, the result was polytheism (ch. xviii. "Syncretism and Polytheism"). In either case the resulting modifications in the tribal worship required explanation, and was explained, as all things were explained by primitive man, by means of a myth (ch. xix. "Mythology"). Myths were not the work of priests—that is but a form of the fallacy that the priest made religion, the truth being that religion made the priest (ch. xx. "Priesthood").

Sometimes the next life was conceived as a continuance of this life, under slightly changed and less favourable conditions (ch. xxi. "The Next Life"). Sometimes, by a development of the belief that man after death assumed the form of his totem, it was conceived as a transmigration of the soul (ch. xxii. "The Transmigration of Souls"). Neither belief, however, proved permanently satisfactory to the religious consciousness; and in the sixth century B.C. the conviction spread from Semitic peoples to Greece, that future happiness depended on communion with (some) God in this life by means of a sacrament, and consisted in continued communion after death (ch. xxiii. "The Mysteries"). In Greece this belief was diffused especially by the Eleusinian Mysteries (ch. xxiv. "The Eleusinia").

There remains the question, what we are to suppose to have been the origin of Monotheism (the subject of ch. xxv.), on which will depend largely our theory of the Evolution of Belief (discussed in ch. xxvi.).

CHAPTER III

THE SUPERNATURAL

THERE are no savages in existence to whom the use of implements and the art of making fire are unknown; and vast as is the antiquity of the earliest remains of man, they do not take us back to a time when he was ignorant of the art of making either fire or stone-implements. It is therefore mere matter of speculation whether there ever was such a period of ignorance. It was man's physical inferiority to his animal competitors in the struggle for existence which made it necessary that he should equip himself with artificial weapons, if he was to survive; and the difficulty of maintaining existence under the most favourable natural conditions is so great for the savage even now, when he has fire and tools at his command, that we may imagine he could not, in the beginning, have long survived without them, if at all. But as there must have been one weapon which was the first to be made, one fire which was the first ever kindled, we must either infer that for a time man was without fire and without implements, or else we must assign this discovery to some hypothetical, half-human ancestor of man. Whichever was the case, whether there was ever or never such a period of human ignorance, the object of this chapter is to argue that from the beginning man believed in a supernatural spirit (or spirits) having affinity with his own spirit and having power over him. It is of course only with the existence of this belief that a history of religion has to do. Its validity falls to be discussed by the philosophy of religion.

Thanks to the assiduous labours of a long line of men of science, the laws of nature have been so exactly laid down, and the universe works with such regularity nowadays, that it is difficult even to conceive a time when there were no natural laws. And yet to him who knows not the law of a thing's movements, the thing's behaviour is as though it had no law, for *ex hypothesi* he does not know what it will do next. If, then, we suppose a time when no natural laws had as yet been discovered, all things then must have appeared to happen at haphazard; and primitive man's experience must have consisted of a stream of events as disjointed and disconnected as the successive incidents in a dream. So Æschylus describes the condition of men before Prometheus:

> *οἳ πρῶτα μὲν βλέποντες ἔβλεπον μάτην,*
> *κλύοντες οὐκ ἤκουον, ἀλλ' ὀνειράτων*
> *ἀλίγκιοι μορφαῖσι τὸν μακρὸν βίον*
> *ἔφυρον εἰκῇ πάντα.*

Of what might happen in those early days, when nature had but few laws to obey and obeyed them by no means uniformly, we have fortunately plenty of contemporary evidence: the fairy tales which were composed in the infancy of the human race, and are still the delight of childhood, faithfully reflect what actually happened in the daily life of primitive man. The proof of this statement is the fact that for savages now existing the incidents of which fairy tales are made up, and which seem to us most extravagant and supernatural, are matters of ordinary if not everyday occurrence. The transformation of men into beasts and *vice versâ* is not only believed to take place, but is actually witnessed by savages, and in the case of witches has been proved in many an English court of law. "The Jacoons believe that a tiger in their path is invariably a human enemy who assumes by sorcery the shape of the beast to execute his vengeance or malignity. They assert that, invariably before a tiger is met, a man has been seen or might have been seen to disappear in the direction from which the animal springs. In many cases the metamorphosis they assert has plainly been seen to take place" (Cameron). The Bushmans say their wives can change themselves into lions and so get food for the family (Anderson). Even in Europe, a woman still (1860) living in Kirchhain changed herself not long ago into a wolf, and scratched and tore a girl going across the fields (Mühlhausen). The giant "who had no heart in his body," and was invulnerable and immortal because he had deposited his heart or soul in a safe place, was but doing what the Minahassa of Celebes do whenever they move into a new house: "A priest collects the souls of the whole family in a bag, and afterwards restores them to their owners, because the moment of entering a new house is supposed to be fraught with supernatural danger."[1]

The helplessness of primitive man set down in the midst of a universe of which he knew not the laws, may perhaps be brought home to the mind of modern man, if we compare the universe to a vast workshop full of the most various and highly-complicated machinery working at full speed. The machinery, if properly handled, is capable of producing everything that the heart of primitive man can wish for, but also, if he sets hand to the wrong part of the machinery, is capable of whirling him off between its wheels, and crushing and killing him in its inexorable and ruthless movement. Further, primitive man cannot decline to submit himself to the perilous test: he must make his experiments or perish, and even so his survival is conditional on his selecting the right part of the machine to handle. Nor can he take his own time and study the dangerous mechanism long and carefully before setting his hand to it: his needs are pressing and his action must be immediate.

It was therefore often at the actual cost and always at the danger of his life that primitive man purchased that working knowledge of the laws of nature and the properties of matter, without which modern man could never have acquired either the theoretic science or the material comfort which he now enjoys. But if modern man owes his science and his comfort to primitive man, primitive man in his turn owes his preservation in his perilous quest to a gift by the power of which mankind has conquered the material universe; that gift is the faith in the uniformity of nature, the belief that what has once happened will in similar circumstances happen again. The existence of this belief in the earliest times is a matter susceptible of easy demonstration, and is of some importance for the history of religion. It is important, because when it

[1] Frazer, *G. B.* ii. 327.

is overlooked we are liable to fall into the error of imagining that there was a time when man did not distinguish between the natural and the supernatural. This error may take the form of saying either that to primitive man nothing was supernatural or that everything was supernatural. Nothing, it may be said, was supernatural, for, as in a dream the most incongruous and impossible incidents are accepted by the dreamer as perfectly natural, and are only recognised as surprising and impossible when we wake and reflect on them, so events which are seen by civilised man to be incredible and impossible are to primitive man matters of everyday occurrence, and are perfectly natural. On the other hand, it is said that, when no natural laws are known there can be no natural and necessary sequences of events, and everything therefore is supernatural. According to this view, primitive man lived in a state of perpetual surprise: he marvelled every time he found that water was wet, he was racked with anxiety every time he went to bed lest the sun should not rise the next day, and he was filled with grateful astonishment when he found that it did rise. But this view, sufficiently improbable in itself, must be rejected for two reasons: first, the very animals have, for instance, their lairs and their customary drinking-places to which they resort in full confidence that they will find them where they were before; and we cannot rate the intelligence of primitive man so far below that of the animals, as to imagine that he was ever in doubt whether, for instance, water would slake his thirst, or food appease his appetite. Next, it is a fact of psychology that the native tendency of the human mind to believe that what has once happened will happen again is so strong that, until experience has corrected it, a single occurrence is sufficient to create an expectation of recurrence: the child to whom you have given sweetmeats once, fully expects sweetmeats from you at your next meeting.

We may then regard it as certain that from the beginning there were some sequences of phenomena, some laws which man had observed, and the occurrence of which he took as a matter of course and regarded as natural. Or putting ourselves at the practical point of view—the only point of view which could exist for primitive man in his strenuous and unrelaxing struggle for existence—we may say that he discovered early how to set going certain portions of the mechanism of nature to further his own private ends, and that he felt neither surprise nor gratitude when the machinery produced its usual results. It was when the machinery did not produce its usual results that he was astonished—when it produced nothing or produced something the opposite of what he expected—when, for instance, the cool water which aforetimes had refreshed his limbs gave him, in his heated condition, erysipelas. And as at the present day man takes to himself the credit of his good actions and throws the blame of the bad on circumstances—over which he had no control—so we may be sure that primitive man took to himself the credit of his successful attempts to work the mechanism of nature for his own advantage, but when the machinery did not work he ascribed the fault to some overruling, *super*natural power. In fine, where the natural ended, the supernatural began. Laws on which man could count and sequences which he habitually initiated and controlled were natural. It was the violation of these sequences and the frustration of his expectations by which the belief in supernatural power was not created but was first called forth.[1] That this was the first and earliest way in which man's attention was directed to the supernatural is probable, because his earliest inductions were necessarily framed on a narrow basis of experience, and consequently must soon have broken down. He must therefore from the beginning have been brought to confront a mysterious power which was beyond both his calculation and his control. In the next place, the shock of surprise with which he witnessed the violation of his expectations

[1] Since writing the above, I find Waitz says (*Introduction to Anthropology*, p. 368) "that which regularly and periodically recurs passes by unheeded, because, being expected and anticipated, he (primitive man) is not obstructed in his path"; and that Major Ellis (*Tshi-speaking Peoples*, p. 21), quoting this passage from Waitz, says: "Hence the rising and the setting of the sun and moon, the periodical recurrence of the latter, the succession of day by night, etc., have excited no speculation in the mind of the Negro of the Gold Coast. None of the heavenly bodies are worshipped; they are too distant to be selected as objects of veneration; and the very regularity of their appearance impresses him less than the evidences of power and motion exhibited by rivers, the sea, storms, landslips, etc."

was as great as that with which civilised man would witness the unaccountable suspension or inversion of what he considered a law of nature; for the tenacity with which a belief is held does not vary with the reasonableness of the belief or the amount of evidence for it; but, on the contrary, those people are usually most confident in their opinions who have the least reason to be so. Again, it will hardly be doubted that, when primitive man found his most reasonable and justifiable expectations (as they appeared to him) frustrated in a manner for which he could not account or find any assignable cause, the feeling thus aroused in him would be that which men have always experienced when they have found themselves confronted by what they deemed to be supernatural. At all times the supernatural has been the miraculous, and the essence of miracle has been thought to be the violation of natural law. Even where there is no violation of natural laws, men may be profoundly impressed with the conviction that they are in the hands of an inscrutable, overruling, and supernatural power. To awaken this conviction it is only necessary that their "reasonable" expectations should be disappointed in some striking way, as, for instance, by the triumph of the ungodly or the undeserved suffering of the innocent. In fine, to be convinced of the existence of the supernatural, it is sufficient that man should realise his helplessness.

When, however, primitive man realised that he was in the hands, at anyrate occasionally, of a mysterious and supernatural power, it was inevitable that he should cast about for some means of entering into satisfactory relations with that power. We shall have to consider hereafter what were the conditions which governed and directed his first attempts; here, however, we may note two things. The first is, that it is not always necessarily to the disadvantage but sometimes to the advantage of man that his reasonable expectations may be miraculously disappointed—in other words, the belief in the supernatural is not necessarily or exclusively the outcome of fear. Thus "tradition says that the people of Cape Coast first discovered the existence of Djwi-j'ahnu [the local deity of Connor's Hill] from the great loss which the Ashantis experienced at this spot during their attack on Cape Coast on the 11th of July 1824. The slaughter was so great and the repulse of the Ashantis so complete, that the Fantis, accustomed to see their foes carry everything before them, attributed the unusual result of the engagement to the assistance of a powerful local god," and they set up a cult accordingly.[1] The Kaffirs of Natal make thankofferings and express gratitude to the spirits for blessings received thus: "This kraal of yours is good; you have made it great. I see around me many children; you have given me them. You have given me many cattle. You have blessed me greatly. Every year I wish to be thus blessed. Make right everything at the kraal. I do not wish any omens to come. Grant that no one may be sick all the year."[2] In fine, as Mr. Clodd says, in primitive religion there is "an adoration of the great and bountiful as well as a sense of the maleficent and fateful."[3]

The second thing to notice is that, as it was owing to man's physical helplessness in his competition with his animal rivals that he was compelled to exercise his intellect in order to survive in the struggle for existence, so it was his intellectual helplessness in grappling with the forces of nature which led him into the way of religion; and as it was his intellectual faculties which gave him the victory over his animal competitors, so it was the strength drawn by him from his religious beliefs that gave him the courage to face and conquer the mysterious forces which beset him.

Assuming, then, that from the beginning man was compelled from time to time to recognise the existence of a supernatural power intervening unaccountably in his affairs and exercising a mysterious control over his destinies, we have yet to inquire how he came to ascribe this supernatural power to a spirit having affinity with his own. Now, savages all the world over believe that not only animals and plants but inanimate things also possess life; and the inference that whatever moves has life, though mistaken, is so natural, that we have no difficulty in understanding how the gliding stream and the leaping flame may be considered to be veritably living things. But savages also regard motionless

[1] Ellis, *Tshi-speaking Peoples*, 40. [2] Shooter, *Kafirs of Natal*, 166.
[3] Clodd, *Myths and Dreams*, 114.

objects as possessing life; and this, too, is not hard to understand: the savage who falls and cuts himself on a jagged rock ascribes the wound to the action of the rock, which he therefore regards as a living thing. In this case there is actual physical motion, though the motion is the man's. In other cases the mere "movement of attention" by which an object was brought within the field of consciousness would suffice to lend the thing that appearance of activity which alone was required to make it a thing of life. Then, by a later process of reasoning, all things would be credited with life; we talk of a rock "growing" (*i.e.* projecting) out of the ground, the peasant believes that stones actually "grow" (*i.e.* increase), and as it is from the earth that all things proceed, the earth must be the source of all life, and therefore herself the living mother. In fine, all changes whatever in the universe may be divided into two classes, those which are initiated by man and those which are not; and it was inevitable from the first that man should believe the source and cause of the one class to be Will, as he knew it to be the cause and source of the other class of changes.

All the many movements, then, and changes which are perpetually taking place in the world of things, were explained by primitive man on the theory that every object which had activity enough to affect him in any way was animated by a life and will like his own—in a word (Dr. Tylor's word), on the theory of animism. But the activity of natural phenomena as thus explained neither proceeds from nor implies nor accounts for belief in the supernatural. This may easily be made clear. Primitive man's theory, his animism, consists of two parts: the facts explained and the explanation given—and in neither is anything supernatural involved. Not in the facts explained, for the never-hasting, never-resting flow of the stream, for instance, was just as familiar and must have seemed just as "natural" to primitive as to civilised man: there was nothing *super*natural in such activity. But neither was the cause to which he ascribed this activity supernatural; for the cause assigned was a will which, being exactly like his own, had nothing unusual, mysterious, or supernatural about it; for we must remember two things, first, that for the average mind "explanation" means likening the thing to be explained to something already familiar, and next, that the familiar, which often most needs to be explained, is usually supposed to require no explanation and to have nothing miraculous in it.

If, then, for the phrase "life and will" we substitute the word "spirit," and say that in the view of primitive man all things which possessed (or seemed to him to possess) activity were animated by spirits, we must also add that those spirits were not in themselves supernatural spirits. They only became so when man was led to ascribe to them that supernatural power which he had already found to exercise an unexpected and irresistible control over his destiny. The immediate causes of this identification are easily conjectured. When a startling frustration of man's calculations brought home to him the existence of an overruling power, man would, as has been already said, eventually cast about for means of entering into relations with that power. The first thing to do for this purpose necessarily was to locate the power; and when primitive man was on the look-out for some indication as to the place of origin whence this power emanated, it would not be long before he found what he was on the watch for. In some cases the indications would be so clear that the identification would be immediate and indubitable; the erysipelas which was the result of bathing when overheated would be regarded as due to the supernatural power of the water-spirit, and was so interpreted by an Australian black-man. In other cases a longer process of induction would be required; the Peruvian mountaineer of the time of the Incas, who fell ill when he had to descend into the unhealthy valleys, ascribed his sickness to the supernatural power of the sea, for it was only when he was in sight of the sea that he was ill.

In this way the notion of supernatural power, which originally was purely negative and manifested itself merely in suspending or counteracting the uniformity of nature, came to have a positive content. A natural agent, such as the river-spirit, which at first confined its energies to the production of its ordinary operations, namely, the ceaseless, pauseless motion of the river, was eventually invested with the supernatural power, transcending its natural sphere of operation, of violating the laws of nature, and producing, say, sickness. But when once one exceptional action of the river-spirit had been put down as the outcome of supernatural power, then in course of time even its ordinary operation and the customary flow of the water would also come to be regarded as having a supernatural cause, and as being the manifestation, not merely of a spirit, but of a supernatural spirit. Thus in course of time all the phenomena of nature, even the discharge of the storm-cloud and the movement of the stars in their courses, came to be regarded as due to supernatural power.

To some readers this account of the conception of the supernatural may, perhaps, seem to be an inversion of the real process by which the conception was developed. Surely, it will be said, the characteristic mark of things supernatural is that they are things which it is beyond the power of man to perform or to control, and from the very beginning he must have learnt, by painful experience of the elements, that he could not control the drenching tempest or command the scorching sun. To this the reply is that primitive man for long did not believe that these elemental phenomena were beyond his control; of which the proof is that at the present day many savages are in the habit of making rain to fall, the wind to blow, or the sun to stand still; and they do not consider the power of producing these results to be supernatural. In Africa rain-makers are to be found in most negro villages, and their reputation and even their lives depend upon their success in making it. In the Isle of Man there were, and in the Shetlands there still are, old women who make a livelihood by selling winds to seamen. The Australian black-fellow, in order that he may not be late for supper, will delay you the setting of the sun. These results are admittedly obtained by means of Sympathetic Magic. But whether sympathetic "magic"—a question-begging epithet—has anything supernatural about it, we have to inquire.

The inquiry has a special interest for the history of religion, because, according to a not uncommon view, all religion has been developed out of magic; the priest has been evolved out of the sorcerer, the idol is but an elaborated fetish. On this theory the distinction between the natural and the supernatural was known to primitive man; things natural were things which men did, things supernatural were things which the gods did, *e.g.* causing rain or sunshine. But the distinction between men and gods, according to this theory, was somewhat blurred, because man also by means of magic art could do things supernatural, and even constrain the gods to work his will. Gradually, however, he learned that his powers were not supernatural, and that he could not use force to the gods, but must persuade them by prayer and sacrifice to grant his wishes. Then to attempt the supernatural by means of magic became an invasion of the divine prerogative, and the priest was differentiated by his orthodoxy from the sorcerer. Thus, according to this view, divine power and magic were originally identical, and the early history of religion consists in the differentiation of the two, and the partial triumph of the former.

But there are reasons for hesitating to accept this view, and for believing, first, that religion and magic had different origins, and were always essentially distinct from one another; next, that the belief in the supernatural was prior to the belief in magic, and that the latter whenever it sprang up was a degradation or relapse in the evolution of religion. In this discussion everything turns on the recognition of the difference between the negative and the positive aspects of the supernatural: the negative aspect of supernatural power becomes manifest to the mind of man in any striking violation of that uniformity in nature which it is the inherent tendency of man to count upon with confidence; the positive aspect of supernatural power is later displayed to man's consciousness as the cause of the ordinary and familiar phenomena of nature. Now, the very essence of the conception of the supernatural in its negative aspect is that it is a power which mysteriously overrides and overturns the best founded human expectations, sometimes to man's disappointment, sometimes to his more agreeable surprise.

πολλαὶ μορφαὶ τῶν δαιμονίων,
πολλὰ δ' ἀέλπτως κραίνουσι θεοί·
καὶ τὰ δοκηθέντ' οὐκ ἐτελέσθη,
τῶν δ' ἀδοκήτων πόρον ηὗρε θεός.

So far, then, as man was under the dominion of this conception of the supernatural, he could not possibly believe that he himself was in possession of supernatural power, or that he was on a level with the wielders of it. And if, as we have seen reason to believe, this the negative phase of the supernatural dawned upon the mind of man before the positive, then man could not have begun by thinking himself equal to or more powerful than his gods. In fine, the power of the supernatural was from the beginning conceived as something different in kind from any power exercised by man.

Next, as has already been urged, the regular and familiar phenomena of nature, such as the shining of the sun and the descent of rain, were not at first regarded as supernatural, nor was it the observation of such familiar facts which could have stimulated the sentiment of the supernatural into activity. Even when these phenomena were attributed (as probably from the beginning they were attributed) to the agency of indwelling spirits, and when material objects were regarded as living things, those living things and those indwelling spirits were not at first regarded as *super*natural beings. Consequently, when man attempted, as undoubtedly at first he did attempt, to make rain or sunshine, he was not conscious, of attempting anything supernatural. He could not know *à priori* and at the beginning what series of changes it was possible for man to initiate and what not, what effects in nature it was and what it was not possible for man to produce. It was only by trying all things that he could learn that not all things were possible for man; and it was only when he had learned that lesson that he could extend the denotation of the term "supernatural" so as to include in it "things impossible for man." It was only after making many experiments that he learned that the power to stay the sun or to make the wind to cease was supernatural. He could not therefore have known whilst making his experiments, that he was attempting the supernatural. The conclusion that the things attempted were supernatural was the consequence of his attempts, and was the very opposite of the idea with which he started.

Finally, the means by which the savage attempts to produce results which we should but which he does not consider to be superhuman, are not regarded by him as supernatural. He does not imagine that he possesses supernatural power. His sympathetic magic is but one branch of his science, and is not different in kind from the rest. He neither produces, in his opinion, supernatural results nor uses supernatural means to produce what he effects. Sympathetic magic was not in the beginning identical with the supernatural, nor was the conception of the latter evolved out of or differentiated from the latter. But perhaps we had better devote a separate chapter to the establishment of this point.

CHAPTER IV

SYMPATHETIC MAGIC

THE law of continuity holds not only in science but of science. It is true not only of the subject-matter with which science deals, but of the evolution of science itself. The assured triumphs of modern science are linked to the despised speculations of the savage by a chain which may be ignored but cannot be snapped; for, in the first place, though the mass of observed facts which the modern investigator has at his command is greater than that which was at the disposal of the ancient student of nature, the accumulation has been gradual; and, in the next place, the foundation, the principle, and the methods of savage logic and scientific logic are identical.[1]

The foundation of both logics is the same, for it is the uniformity of nature. What reason we have for believing that nature is uniform is a matter much disputed by philosophers. The cause of the belief, the inherent tendency of the human mind to expect similar sequences or coexistences in similar conditions, was as strong in primitive man as in the modern *savant*; and the savage not only expects a cause to produce its effect, but also holds with Mill that a single instance of the production of a phenomenon by a given antecedent is enough to warrant the belief that it will always tend to be produced by that antecedent. Thus, "the king of the Koussa Kaffirs having broken off a piece of a stranded anchor died soon afterwards, upon which all the Kaffirs looked upon the anchor as alive, and saluted it respectfully whenever they passed near it."[2]

[1] See *Folk-Lore*, ii. 2. 220, F. B. Jevons, "Report on Greek Mythology" (June 1891).

[2] Lubbock, *Origin of Civilisation*, 188.

Here the Kaffirs' error consisted in jumping to the conclusion that the molestation of the anchor was the cause of the king's death; and as it is against this class of error that the inductive methods are designed to guard, the reader may be tempted to imagine that it is in the ignorance of those methods that the difference between savage and scientific logic consists. But the reader would be mistaken. The savage has not indeed formulated the methods, but he uses them all to distinguish the antecedent which is the cause from the other antecedents which have nothing to do with the effect under investigation. Thus the Peruvian mountaineers mentioned in the last chapter, who observed that a certain kind of illness befell them whenever they were in sight of the sea, were using the Method of Agreement in inferring that the sea-spirit was the cause of that particular kind of illness. The Method of Difference, according to which, if the introduction of a new antecedent into a set of conditions already known is immediately followed by the emergence of a new effect, the new antecedent may be regarded as the cause of the new effect, is employed by the Dusuns in Borneo, who, according to Mr. Hatton (*North Borneo*, 233[1]), "attribute anything—whether good or bad, lucky or unlucky—that happens to them to something novel which has arrived in their country. For instance, my living in Kindram has caused the intensely hot weather we have experienced of late." The Method of Concomitant Variations again plays a large part in savage logic. According to this method, things which vary together are causally related to one another, or, *vice versâ*, things which are related together vary together. Hence the world-wide belief that, if the nail-parings or the cut hair of a man pass into the possession of an enemy, the enemy can injure the man; and hence, too, the equally wide-spread custom of burying hair or nail-parings, or otherwise placing them beyond reach of an enemy. The shadow, the image, the picture, and the name of a man are closely related to him; and therefore as they are treated so will he suffer. Hence the witch could torture her victim by roasting or wounding a waxen image of him. The savage declines to be sketched or photographed for the same

[1] Quoted in *G. B.* i. 174.

reason;[1] the ancient Egyptian secured happiness hereafter by having his tomb filled with pictures representing him engaged in his favourite occupations and surrounded by luxury; wounds inflicted on the shadow or the foot-prints of a man will take effect on him; savages frequently keep their names a profound secret, and the safety and inviolability of the city of Rome depended on the secrecy observed as to the name of its tutelary deity. If the connection required by the method does not exist, then it must be artificially created, as it easily may be: the Ephesians placed their city under the protection of Artemis by connecting the city and the temple with a rope seven furlongs long. But the best exemplification of the savage application of the Method of Concomitant Variations is the waxing and the waning of the moon, with which the growth and decay of all sorts of sub-lunar objects, plants, and animals, things animate and inanimate, are associated; and if the reader is inclined to smile at the obvious folly and puerility of the savage, let him remember that the weather is still supposed, by educated people, to vary with the changes of the moon; and that as to the influence of her phases on vegetation and the advisability of sowing on a waxing moon, the founder of inductive logic, Bacon himself, thought there was something in it: "videmus enim in plantationibus et insitionibus ætatum lunæ observationes non esse res omnino frivolas" (*De Aug. Scient.* iii. 4). So thin are the partitions between savage and scientific logic.

The principle of induction, again, is the same in the logic of the savage and the *savant*. That principle is the principle of similarity in difference. Whether the induction be an inference from particulars to particulars or to universals, it proceeds from similars to similars, and would be impossible if similar cases did not recur in experience. In such an induc-

[1] "When Dr. Catat and his companions, MM. Maistre and Foncart, were exploring the Bara country on the west coast of Madagascar, the people suddenly became hostile. On the previous day, the travellers, not without difficulty, had photographed the royal family, and now found themselves accused of taking the souls of the natives with the object of selling them when they returned to France. Denial was of no avail; following the custom of the Malagasays, they were compelled to catch the souls, which were then put into a basket and ordered by Dr. Catat to return to their respective owners."[1]

[1] *Folk-Lore*, vi. 1. 75, from the *Times* of March 24, 1891.

tion, for instance, as that Socrates and Plato are mortal, therefore Aristotle is mortal, it is because Socrates, Plato, and Aristotle resemble each other in being men that we can infer that they also resemble each other in being mortal. They also resemble each other in other points, *e.g.* in being Greeks and philosophers, etc., and differ from each other, *e.g.* in size and weight; but these points of resemblance and difference do not affect the question: it is not because they were Greeks that they died, and their differences in physical characteristics did not exempt any of them from the common doom. These irrelevant points, therefore, have to be set aside, or, in technical language, "abstracted," and the result of the abstraction is that we are enabled to assert the coexistence of the two qualities of humanity and mortality. Now the savage also is capable of abstract ideas and of asserting their coexistence. He recognises the hardness of some substances and the scent of others, and he wears a ring of iron in order that it may impart its quality of hardness to his body, as he might wear a flower for the sake of its scent; or when he is bargaining for a cow or asking a woman for wife, he chews a piece of wood to soften the heart of the person he is dealing with. In the same way, having discovered in the lion the quality of courage, or in the deer that of swiftness, he eats the former that he may become bold and the latter that he may run well. So also he will eat an enemy to acquire his boldness, or a kinsman to prevent his virtues from going out of the family. The points of resemblance between what he does and what he wishes to effect seem to the savage to be the essential points for his purpose: the man of science deems otherwise. Doubtless the man of science is right; but the savage is not therefore superstitious in this matter. He applies a principle of logic—to the wrong things perhaps, but still the process is one of logic, savage if you like, but not superstitious.

The savage theory of causation, again, is not fundamentally different from the scientific: it is only incomplete and exaggerated. The effect is the offspring of the cause, and resembles its parent; to produce motion in a body you must impart motion, to moisten a thing you must communicate moisture to it. Hence the savage makes the generalisation that like produces like; and then he is provided with the means of bringing about anything he wishes, for to produce an effect he has only to imitate it. To cause a wind to blow, he flaps a blanket, as the sailor still whistles to bring a whistling gale. Before going on the warpath or the chase, a mimetic dance, in which the quarry or the foe are represented as falling before his weapon, will secure him success. If the vegetation requires rain, all that is needed is to dip a branch in water and with it to sprinkle the ground. Or a spray of water squirted from the mouth will produce a mist sufficiently like the mist required to produce the desired effect; or black clouds of smoke will be followed by black clouds of rain. If the moon's light threatens to fail, fire-tipped arrows are shot up to it by the Hottentots; and the same remedy is applied by the Ojibways to the sun when eclipsed.

To complete these outlines of savage logic, it is only necessary to point out that hypothesis is an instrument of thought which is of great service in primitive speculation. A hypothesis is any assumption made for the purpose of explaining a fact or facts already known to be true. But whereas the assumptions of the *savant* are hypotheses, those of the savage are called myths. Thus, when it is sought to account for the observed fact that the moon periodically decreases in size and that her appearance in the sky is the signal for the departure of the sun, a savage hypothesis accounting for the facts is that sun and moon are husband and wife who have quarrelled and separated; periodically the moon makes overtures of reconciliation and periodically wastes away before our eyes in grief at their rejection. Or the observed facts of thunderstorms are accounted for on the supposition that a jar of rain is carried by one spirit and is smashed by the mace of another; whence the crash of the thunder and the descent of the rain. The importance of hypothesis as a savage instrument of thought may be judged by the fact that it is a quite tenable position that all the countless myths in the world were originally explanatory (ætiological) myths, primitive hypotheses.

It should now be clear that there is no fundamental difference between savage and scientific logic, but that, on the contrary, they are fundamentally identical. The uniformity of nature, the principle of induction, the theory of causation, the inductive methods, form the common framework of both logics: the savage would probably be able to give his assent to all the principles of Mill's logic. In other words, the differences are not formal but material. The errors of the early logician were extra-logical, and therefore were such as could be remedied by no process of logic but only by wider experience. The problem of induction is to ascertain the cause (or effect) of a given phenomenon; and the cause (or effect) is to be looked for amongst the immediate antecedents (or consequents) of that phenomenon. But the antecedents (or consequents) comprise every single one of the countless changes which take place in any part of the universe the moment before (or after) the occurrence of the phenomenon under investigation: any one of these antecedents (or consequents) may be the cause (or effect), and there is nothing *à priori* or in logic to make us select one rather than another. It is plain, therefore, that as long as man is turned loose as it were amongst these innumerable possible causes with nothing to guide his choice, the chances against his making the right selection are considerable, and that to speak of the savage's choice as haphazard and illogical is to misconceive the nature of logic. It should also be clear that no progress could be made in science until man had distinguished, at anyrate roughly, possible from absolutely impossible effects (or causes), and had learned to dismiss from consideration the impossible. Now it might be expected that, as it was only experience which could show what was impossible, so experience would suffice of itself to teach man this essential distinction. But, as a matter of fact, experience by itself has done no such thing, as is shown by the simple fact that great as is the age and long as is the experience of the human race, the vast majority of its members have not yet learnt from experience that like does not necessarily produce like: four-fifths of mankind, probably, believe in sympathetic magic, and therefore neither need nor can make any intellectual progress, whilst the progressive minority are precisely those from amongst whom magic has been uprooted by its relentless foe, religion. The reason why the real order and sequence of natural events does not mechanically impress itself in its correct form upon the human mind, is that the mind is not the passive recipient of external impressions, but reacts upon them and remodels them, so that the ultimate shape taken by them depends as much on the form of the mental mould, so to speak, into which they are poured, as it does upon their own nature. In other words, the mind does not pay equal attention to everything which is presented to it: it only sees what it is prepared to see. Thus the preconception that things causally related to one another must be similar and *vice versâ*—a preconception due to the mental law by which similar ideas suggest one another—is so strong as to prevent the savage from seeing facts which are at variance with it, and thus the experience which might be expected automatically to correct the error serves but to strengthen it. But when the consequences of that error came in conflict with the religious sentiment, that hostility between magic and religion was aroused of which the existence is universally admitted though differently explained.

Now the fallacy that things causally related must be similar to one another, is one that the human mind, from its very constitution, must have fallen into in its very first attempts to interpret the complex manifold of nature. It is also a fallacy from which most savages, who in this may be taken as representing primitive man, have not yet escaped. But the fallacy, though primeval, has nothing to do with magic or the supernatural: it requires for its existence no belief in supernatural powers or even in spirits, it might perfectly well flourish in a region where neither religion nor magic had been heard of. Thus the fact of a man's using this fallacious mode of procedure to produce or forecast certain desired results does not in the least tend to show that he considers the process itself to be magical or supernatural; the savage who wears an iron ring to give strength to his body has not advanced so far in science as the man who takes iron in a tonic, but he no more believes himself to be dealing in magic and spells than the educated persons of to-day do who forecast the weather by the changes of the moon.

This will perhaps be made clearer if it be pointed out that it is not merely the fallacy of "like produces like," but the inductive methods themselves which the savage uses in order to work his wonders. Most of the examples of savage logic already given in this chapter are instances of "sympathetic magic"; but as the means which the savage employs for this purpose are precisely those used for the ordinary commonplace purposes of life both by him and by civilised man, it cannot be argued that those means are in themselves considered magical or supernatural.

These, then, are the grounds on which it is here maintained that sympathetic magic, which is the germ of all magic, does not involve in itself the idea of the supernatural, but was simply the applied science of the savage. Yet out of the theory of causation and the methods of induction, which under certain rare, favouring conditions, and with the assistance of the religious sentiment, developed into modern science, elsewhere the process of evolution produced "one of the most pernicious delusions that ever vexed mankind, the belief in magic." It remains for us to inquire how this came about.

Art magic is the exercise by man of powers which are supernatural, *i.e.* of powers which by their definition it is beyond man to exercise. Thus the very conception of magic is one which is essentially inconsistent with itself; and, being such, the belief in it seems to be thought by many writers to require no further explanation. Now, doubtless it is the conception's very inconsistency with itself which gives it its fascination; the prospect of being able to do the impossible is singularly attractive. At anyrate the hold which the idea, when once introduced, has over the mind of man is so familiar a fact that it does not need to be proved. But all this does not show how the idea ever could have occurred to the human mind in the first instance; it only proves what a very suitable nidus was ready for the germ when it should come. To read some writers, who derive the powers of priests (and even of the gods) from those of the magician, and who consider apparently that magic requires no explanation, one would imagine that the savage, surrounded by supernatural powers and a prey to supernatural terrors, one day conceived the happy idea that he too would himself exercise supernatural power — and the thing was done;

sorcery was invented, and the rest of the evolution of religion follows without difficulty; or, if any further explanation is required, it is to be found in the fact that the imagination of the savage is unbridled. Now, though the savage, if the idea that he too should have supernatural powers had been suggested to him, would doubtless have thought the suggestion excellent if it could be carried out, he would also have inquired how the thing was to be done. It is one thing to wish you had a certain power; it is quite another thing to imagine you have it—something, be it what it may, is required to set the imagination to work, to start the idea that it is possible to work impossibilities. The suggestion that the savage fancy is so unbridled that it is capable of believing anything, does not help us much here, for several reasons. One is that, as Mr. Andrew Lang has conclusively shown,[1] the incredulity of the savage is quite as strong and as marked as his credulity: he is proof against the invasion of unfamiliar ideas. Another is that, according to the best observers, the imagination of the savage is not unbridled but is singularly sterile, and moves within remarkably narrow limits. A third is that the savage's thought is subject to mental laws as much as is civilised man's; and that the conception of art magic could not possibly have sprung up uncaused and without a reason. If the conception were confined to some one region, it might possibly be due to a fortuitous combination of ideas or a fancied resemblance in particular things which no general laws could assist us to divine. But the belief in magic is world-wide, and should be due to some widely working cause.

Dr. E. B. Tylor[2] has pointed out that "nations whose education has not advanced far enough to destroy their belief in magic itself" yet "cannot shut their eyes to the fact that it more essentially belongs to, and is more thoroughly at home among, races less civilised than themselves." "In any country an isolated or outlying race, the lingering survivor of an older nationality, is liable to the reputation of sorcery." It is from this fact that the explanation of magic here advanced takes its start. In historic times the belief in magic is fostered by the juxtaposition of two races, the

[1] *Myth, Ritual, and Religion*, i. 91. [2] *Primitive Culture*, ch. iv.

one more and the other less civilised. The one race, being the more civilised, has learnt (whether in the way suggested in the last chapter or otherwise) that certain natural phenomena are due to divine agency and are beyond the power of man to influence or control. The other race, being less civilised, has not yet learnt this lesson, has not yet learnt to distinguish between what it is and what it is not possible for man to effect, but still employs for the production of both classes of effects indiscriminately those principles of induction which are common both to savage and scientific logic. Hence the more civilised race find themselves face to face with this extraordinary fact, namely, that things which they know to be supernatural are commonly and deliberately brought about by members of the other race. But this is what is meant by magic.

Now, if this be the correct account of the origin of the idea of magic, it follows, first, that the idea was not due to any freak of savage fancy, that it was not anybody's invention nor the outcome of research, but was, like most other ideas, simply and directly suggested by actual facts; and, in the next place, that the cause which suggested it is not local or transient, but is the necessary and inevitable outcome of the fact that some men progress more rapidly than others, and consequently is, what we are in search of, namely, a world-wide cause.

It is, however, not essential to the production of the idea of magic that there should be a difference of race between those who are credited with magical power and those who credit them with it. They may be members of the same community. All that is requisite is the juxtaposition, the coexistence of the more and the less enlightened views of what man can effect in different sections of the community, and the survival amongst the more backward members of the belief in the power of certain processes to produce effects which are deemed by the more advanced section to be supernatural. Wherever these conditions were to be found, that is everywhere, causes were at work which must inevitably produce in the more (but by no means fully) advanced members a belief that the lower possessed magical powers. That the lower section or race readily accepted the reputation thus put upon them, is the more intelligible because sometimes it is practically the only thing which saves them from extinction at the hands of their more advanced neighbours or conquerors; and at all times it is gratifying to the despised "nigger" or "barbarian" to excite the terror of his owner or his superior in civilisation. The privilege thus conferred upon the lower race or section would be jealously preserved and handed down; and hence probably nowadays all those who are credited by their neighbours with this power firmly believe themselves that they possess it.

We may now proceed to consider the conditions under which was waged that struggle for existence between magic and religion, on the issues of which the future progress, scientific as well as religious, of mankind depended. And first let it be observed that, though evolution is universal, progress, whether in religion, morality, science, or art, is exceptional. The law of the survival of the fittest works inexorably; the fittest form of belief—be it the belief in magic or the belief in religion—inevitably survives, only the "fittest" is not necessarily or usually the highest; it is that which the particular race under its special conditions is fittest for.

The hostility from the beginning between religion and magic is, as has already been said, universally admitted; its origin is disputed. The suggestion made by those who regard sorcery as the primeval fact of which religion was an offshoot, that it is due to the priest's jealousy of the sorcerer, once his *confrère* and then his professional rival, does not carry us very far. To say nothing of the fact that he who says priest says religion, *i.e.* of the fact that to assume without explanation the existence of the priest is to leave the origin of religion unexplained, the jealousy of the priest is not the fact of real importance in the discussion. What we want to know is why the jealousy of the priest woke an answering chord in the heart of the average man, for without that response the priest's jealousy would be powerless for good or for evil. The probable answer is that the sentiment of the supernatural, the conviction of the existence of an overruling supernatural power, whatever the occasion under which man first became aware of its existence as one of the facts of his internal experience, was offended by the pretension of any merely human being to wield supernatural power; such a pretension was irreconcilable with the existence of the sentiment, and the shock which ensued from the collision of the two resulted in the feeling, or rather was the feeling, that the pretension was impious. But it is obvious that the violence of the shock and the vigour of the consequent reaction would depend considerably on the strength of the sentiment and conviction of the supernatural. This brings us to note that in the historical instances given by Dr. Tylor of the existence in civilised races of the belief in magic, those races have not yet reached the stage of development in which sorcery is seen to be an absolute impossibility, both from the religious and the scientific point of view. Probably even their present stage of development is higher, however, than that in which they were when the belief first appeared amongst them. In fine, the triumph of magic, where it was complete, is itself a considerable presumption that the conflict began at a time when the religious sentiment was quite immature and incapable of successfully asserting itself. Where the sentiment of the supernatural succumbed, it did not cease to exist, but was modified or misinterpreted in accordance with the magical view of the universe. Progress in science and religion ceased, but the evolution and organisation of magic into a system went on apace, until, where a people is entirely given up to magic, the world is filled with supernatural terrors, and life with the rites prescribed to exorcise them. On the other hand, where we find religion in the ascendant but sorcery coexisting with it, we may infer that religion had become firmly established in the more progressive section of the community before the contrast between the beliefs of the more and the less enlightened members had produced that confusion of ideas which is the essential condition of the belief in magic. And here we may remark that, as sorcery, when it is victorious, does not kill the sentiment of the supernatural, but, on the contrary, lives on it and perverts it to its own uses, so there are few religions which succeed in entirely uprooting the belief in magic from the minds of the most backward members of their congregations; and that, owing to the vitality and tenacity of primitive modes of thought, no religion is free from the danger of relapse on the part of some of its believers and the recrudescence of a belief in magic. Hence it is that we find religion and magic sometimes acting and reacting on one another. Even a religion so comparatively developed as that of ancient Rome, sanctioned the resort in times of stress, such as an exceptional drought, to magic, and fell back on the *lapis manalis* as a rain-making charm. Sometimes religion will have a fixed *modus vivendi* with sorcery, and take magic into its own organisation, as in Chaldæa. On the other hand, magic, even where its relation to religion is one of avowed hostility, will implicitly recognise the superiority of its rival by borrowing from or travestying its ritual; the superstitious mind, incapable of understanding prayer, will recite the Lord's Prayer backwards as a spell more powerful than any of its own; and the Irish peasant uses holy water where simple water would have been considered by his pre-Christian ancestor as sufficiently efficacious.

Consequently, everywhere now we find either (1) magic surviving in countries where religion is dominant, or (2) magic practically in sole possession of the human mind. By the former fact some inquirers have been led to regard the two as originally identical; by the latter, to regard magic as that out of which religion has been evolved. But both inferences may be as erroneous as it would be to infer that, because in Southern Europe pagan practices are still sometimes tolerated under the sheltering shadow of the Church, therefore Christianity was evolved out of Aryan polytheism. At anyrate, whether the attempt made in this chapter and the last to offer a third explanation be accepted or rejected, it is well to recognise that the facts are not necessarily exclusive of the view that religion and magic had different origins, nor absolutely conclusive in favour of viewing religion as a mere variety or "sport" of sorcery.

CHAPTER V

LIFE AND DEATH

ACCORDING to the view advanced in the previous chapters, the belief that all natural phenomena have life, and that all the many changes in nature are due to a will or wills similar to man's, does not necessarily imply any belief in the supernatural. The sequences of events which this piece of primitive philosophy seeks to explain are themselves, *ex hypothesi*, uniform, familiar, in a word natural, not supernatural; and the explanation itself consists in assimilating the things explained not to anything supernatural or superhuman, but to something essentially characteristic of human nature. The sentiment of the supernatural is not aroused by events which happen as they were expected to happen, but by some mysterious and unaccountable deviation from the ordinary course of nature. It is specifically distinct also from the terror which dangers inspire, or the respect and admiration which the strength of the greater carnivora may have exacted from primitive man; and it seems psychologically inadmissible, on the one hand, to derive it from any of these feelings, and, on the other, to confound it either with fear or with gratitude; for though each of these latter two emotions may go with it, neither is indispensable to it.

But though no belief in the supernatural is necessarily implied in the view that all things which affect man possess life, still the two beliefs seem to have been universally combined in varying degrees. This combination is, I suggest, the first great step in or towards the evolution of religion. The second great step was that which settled the terms on which man was to live with the supernatural beings by whom he was surrounded. Those terms could only be terms either of hostility or of friendship; indifference towards the powers with whom it lay to thwart man's most cherished hopes, and even his efforts to effect his own self-preservation, was an impossible attitude. But permanent resistance to such powers was an attitude equally impossible. Primitive man in his struggle for existence must have suffered so many defeats, his generalisations must have been so often upset, his forecasts of the immediate future so often disappointed, as perpetually to strengthen the belief that amongst the forces against which he was contending there were many that were irresistible, supernatural. That, relying upon magic, he thought to combat and actually to coerce the supernatural beings that he had to deal with, is difficult to believe. Much that civilised man regards as magic is regarded by those who practise it not as sorcery but as science, and its practice implies no intention to put constraint upon supernatural beings. Of the practices which are in intention magical, some are in their origin "sympathetic" (*i.e.* pieces of savage science), and the rest are perversions or parodies of acts of true worship; but both classes presuppose the conception of the supernatural: the latter by the terms of its definition, the former because it could not be used to constrain supernatural beings until the beings to whom it was applied came to be thought supernatural. In fine, both classes are subsequent in development to the establishment of those permanent friendly relations between worshipper and God in which worship takes its rise. Again, in conjectures about primitive man, we argue back from existing savages; now, many of the cases in which savages have been reported to apply constraint to their gods and inflict punishment upon them, prove to be due to misunderstanding—as we shall see in a subsequent chapter on Fetishism—for the savage's terror of the supernatural is too great to allow him wantonly to provoke its anger. We may therefore reasonably doubt whether all the supposed cases of coercion are not due to error in observation; at anyrate we may confidently assert that there is no tribe existing whose attitude towards the supernatural is one of hostility pure and simple, and whose faith is placed in magic alone, as there must once have been, if they are right who hold that magic first existed and then religion was developed out of it. Be that as it may, even those who maintain that man started by considering himself and his own magical powers capable of coercing the gods, admit that finally facts corrected that vain opinion—in other words, that hostility towards the supernatural was not a permanently possible attitude for man.

Whether man's attitude towards the supernatural has or has not ever at any period been one of complete hostility, at anyrate there came a time when he established friendly relations with some of the supernatural powers by which he was surrounded; and the business of this chapter is to conjecture what may have suggested to him the idea of forming an alliance with the particular supernatural spirit whose help and favour he desired. For, desirable as such an alliance must have appeared, the question how to effect it cannot have been easy to answer. The idea of alliance at all, like most other ideas, is more likely to have been suggested to man by some fact in his experience than to have been manufactured by him either *à priori* or *ex nihilo.* We have therefore to seek amongst the familiar facts of primitive man's experience for something capable of suggesting to his mind the possibility and the mode of gaining the friendship and favour of a supernatural spirit. To do this, it will be well to examine his views on spirits.

Hitherto all that it has been necessary to assume for the purpose of the previous chapters has been that man believed the gliding streams, the swaying trees, etc., to be living things like himself, and having the same kind of personality as himself. How he conceived that personality we have not yet considered, but must consider now. As Professor Tylor has demonstrated with abundant illustrations in his *Primitive Culture*, dreams supply the principal factor in the formation of the savage's conception of his own spirit. His dream-experiences are to him real in exactly the same way and degree as anything he does or suffers in his waking moments: the places he visits are the real places, the persons he sees the real persons. Hence a dilemma and its solution. The dilemma is that at the time when he knows from actual experience (in a dream) that he was in a far country, his friends can testify that he was in his own bed. The solution is that both he and his friends were right: his body was in bed, but his spirit was away. As for the appearance of his spirit, it is the counterpart or double of himself (his body), for he has himself in dreams met the spirits of friends who (in the flesh) were far away, and has recognised them. As for the nature or constitution of the spirit, it is essentially unsubstantial, and hence it is commonly called by some word which means "breath" (*spirit*, *spiritus*, *animus*, *soul*, etc.), or "shade" (*umbra*, *σκιά*, etc.). Or, as its usual place of abode is inside the man, it may be identified with one of the internal organs and called the "heart" or "midriff." Or, again, it is the "life," because in its merely temporary absence the sleeping body presents the appearance of an almost lifeless body; or it is the blood, because "the blood is the life," and when blood is shed, life departs. Or, finally, it may at one and the same time be all these things; and so a man may have, as amongst the Romans, four souls, or, as amongst savages, even more.

The savage is thus equipped with an explanation of sleep, death, and disease. Sleep is due to the temporary absence of the spirit from the body—hence the belief that it is dangerous to wake a sleeper suddenly and before his spirit has had time to return to his body. Death is caused by, or consists in, the permanent absence from the body of the spirit. Illness is the threatened departure of the spirit. Hence the remedy for illness is to tempt the wavering, and as yet hesitating, spirit to return to its body. This may be done in various ways, as, for instance, by making a display of all the patient's best clothes, or by rehearsing the pains and penalties incurred by spirits who wilfully desert their true and lawful bodies. On the Congo, "health is identified with the word 'Moyo' (spirit, Lower Congo), and in cases of wasting sickness, the Moyo is supposed to have wandered away from the sufferer. In these cases a search party is sometimes led by a charm doctor, and branches, land-shells, or stones are collected. The charm doctor will then perform a series of passes between the sick man and the collected articles. This ceremony is called *vutulanga moyo* (the returning of the spirit)."[1]

[1] *Journal of the Anthropological Institute*, xxiv. 287. The method by which, among the Burats, a shaman restores a sick man his soul is described, *ibid.* 128.

In Celebes, the Topantunuasu whip the patient soundly, in order that the spirit may feel sorry for its poor body, and return to it to save it from further castigation. In Ambon and the Uliase Islands the medicine-man flaps a branch about, calling out the sick man's name, until he has caught the wandering soul in the branch; he then strikes the patient's body and head with the branch, and thus restores his soul to him. In Nias, the departing soul is visible to the medicine-man alone; he catches it with a cloth, then with the cloth rubs the forehead and breast of the patient, and thus saves him. The Haidah Indians have soul-catchers, bone implements for catching the patient's soul when it tries to fly away, specimens of which may be seen in the Berlin Museum für Völkerkunde.[1] Where, as in Sarawak, the spirit or life is believed to reside, not in the blood or the heart, but in the head or the hair, and the soul has deserted the patient, he is cured by the restoration of his soul in the shape of a bundle of hair. So, too, in Ceram, the hair may not be cut because it is the seat of the man's strength; the Gaboon negroes, for the same reason, will not allow any of their hair to pass into the possession of a stranger; and the same belief apparently prevailed in Rome, "unguium Dialis et capilli segmina subter arborem felicem terra operiuntur."[2]

Even when the sick man is really dead, there is uncertainty whether the soul is for ever fled; there is the possibility that it may return. "It is in consequence of the belief," amongst the Ewe-speaking peoples of the Slave Coast, "that the soul does occasionally return after leaving the body, that appeals to the dead to come back are always made immediately after death; and, generally speaking, it is only when the corpse begins to become corrupt, and the relatives thereby become certain that the soul does not intend to return, that it is buried."[3] So, too, on the Gold Coast, "all the most valuable articles belonging to the deceased are placed round the corpse, and the dish that was most preferred in life is prepared and placed before it; the wailing being interrupted every now and then, to allow the widows to

[1] Bartels, *Medicin der Naturvölker*, 201–3.

[2] Bastian, *Allerlei*, i. 401. Cf. Num. vi. 5, 18, and Judg. xvi. 17.

[3] Ellis, *Ewe-speaking Peoples*, 156.

entreat the deceased to eat or drink,"[1] the idea evidently being that the soul may be tempted by these delicacies to return. In Eastern Asia, again, the Arafuas tie the deceased to an upright ladder, and invite him to join in the funeral feast; and it is only when they have placed food in his mouth in vain that they bury him.[2] On the Slave Coast, too, "the corpse is washed, attired in the best clothes, bedecked with ornaments, and placed in a chair, before which a small table with food and drink is set out . . . the deceased is implored to eat, and portions of food are put to his lips."[3] In China, too, according to the Li Yun, "when one died they went upon the house-top and called out his name in a prolonged note, saying, 'Come back, So-and-So.' After this they filled the mouth (of the dead) with uncooked rice, and (set forth as offerings to him) packets of raw flesh."[4]

At this point perhaps it is fitting that I should frankly state to the reader what is my object in making these quotations and those which I am about to make. Many learned, and many unlearned, anthropologists hold that the original, and, so to speak, the "natural" sentiment of man towards his dead, is that of fear. So, too, many writers have seen in fear the sole source of religion. So, too, again, many moral philosophers, from the time of Thrasymachus or earlier, have regarded selfishness, the selfish desires, personal fear, and the baser passions, as the only natural impulses to action. In this book the opposite view—that of Bishop Butler—is maintained, namely, that love, gratitude, affection, are just as "natural" as their opposites. Now, as regards the family affections, there can be no possibility of doubt; the infancy of man is longer than that of any of the animals, most of which can walk and take care of themselves almost, if not quite, as soon as they are born. Man's infancy, on the other hand, is so long that the human race could not have survived in the struggle for existence, had not the parental instincts and family affections been strong in primitive man. Existing savages are in this respect "men, so to speak." In Samoa, for instance, "whenever the eye is fixed in death, the house

[1] Ellis, *Tshi-speaking Peoples*, 238. [2] Bastian, *Oest. Asien*, v. 83.
[3] *Ewe-speaking Peoples*, 157–8.
[4] Legge, *The Li Ki*, 369 (*Sacred Books of the East*).

becomes an indescribable scene of lamentation and wailing. 'Oh, my father, why did you not let me die, and you live here still!' 'Oh, my child, had I known you were going to die! of what use is it for me to survive you? would that I had died for you!' . . . These and other doleful cries . . . are accompanied by the most frantic expressions of grief."[1] Among the negroes of the Slave Coast, "the widows and daughters lament their lonely and unprotected state, somewhat as follows:—'I go to the market, it is crowded. There are many people there, but he is not among them. I wait, but he comes not. Ah me! I am alone. Never more shall I see him. It is over; he is gone. I shall see him no more. Ah me! I am alone. I go into the street. The people pass, but he is not there. Night falls, but he comes not. Ah me! I am alone. Alas! I am alone. Alone in the day—alone in the darkness of the night. Alas! my father (or husband) is dead. Who will take care of me?'"[2] Amongst the negroes of the Gold Coast, "no sooner has the breath left the body than a loud wailing cry bursts forth from the house, and the women rush into the streets with disordered clothes and dishevelled hair, uttering the most acute and mournful cries."[3] Amongst the Ewe-speaking peoples of the Slave Coast, "a death in a family is announced by an outbreak of shrieks and lamentations on the part of the women, who throw themselves on the ground, strike their heads against the walls, and commit a variety of extravagances; calling upon the deceased meanwhile not to desert them, and endeavouring, by all kinds of supplications, to induce the soul to return and reanimate the body."[4] It not unfrequently happens that what, in its origin, was spontaneous, comes in time to be conventional; and in Bonny[5] (as in China) there is a regular ceremony entitled "recalling the soul to the house." Perhaps also in the feast which is spread with the dead man's favourite delicacies, to tempt his soul to return, we may have the origin of the funeral feasts and wakes, which are universal, and therefore need not be illustrated.

The natural affection which makes the relatives of the

[1] G. Turner, *Nineteen Years in Polynesia*, 227.
[2] Ellis, *Yoruba-speaking Peoples*, 157. [3] *Tshi-speaking Peoples*, 237.
[4] Ellis, 157. [5] Bastian, *Expedition an der Loango Küste*, i. 114.

deceased reluctant to believe that he can be dead, and which leads the negroes of the Loango Coast to try to induce him to eat, and makes them talk of his brave exploits, peradventure he may be beguiled into listening and returning, does not cease immediately, when it is ascertained that he is beyond doubt dead. "Thus we read of the Mandan women going year after year to take food to the skulls of their dead kinsfolk, and sitting by the hour to chat and jest in their most endearing strain with the relics of a husband or child; thus the Guinea negroes, who keep the bones of parents in chests, will go to talk with them in the little huts which serve for their tombs."[1] We cannot doubt the affection with which the Hos invite the soul to return to them when the body has been burned—

> "We never scolded you; never wronged you;
> Come to us back!
> We ever loved and cherished you; and have lived long together
> Under the same roof;
> Desert it not now!
> The rainy nights, and the cold blowing days, are coming on;
> Do not wander here!
> Do not stand by the burnt ashes; come to us again!
> You cannot find shelter under the peepul, when the rain comes down.
> The sœul will not shield you from the cold bitter wind.
> Come to your home!
> It is swept for you and clean; and we are there who loved you ever;
> And there is rice put for you; and water;
> Come home, come home, come to us again!"[2]

The natural reluctance to believe that the beloved one has gone from us for ever does not among savages limit itself merely to poetical invitations to the spirit to return. In the Marian Isles a basket is provided in the house for the soul to rest in when it revisits its friends;[3] and on the Congo the relatives abstain for a year from sweeping the house of the deceased, for fear they should unwittingly and involuntarily sweep out the soul.[4] In Hawai, where ghosts usually go to the next world, the spirit of a dear friend dead may be detained by preserving his bones or clothes.[5] The

[1] Tylor, *Prim. Cult.* ii. 150; Catlin, *N. A. Indians*, i. 90; J. L. Wilson, *W. Africa*, 394.

[2] Tylor, *loc. cit.* ii. 32.

[3] Bastian, *Oest. Asien*, v. 83.

[4] Bastian, *Der Mensch*, ii. 323.

[5] Bastian, *Allerlei*, i. 116.

belief that the spirit is attached to his former earthly tenement is common enough, and indeed is a necessary outcome of a very natural association of ideas; a modern graveyard is the haunt of ghosts, though the soul is in the next world; in ancient Rome—

"Terra tegit carnem, tumulum circumvolat umbra
Manes Orcus habet, spiritus astra petit";

the Fantees believed that the ghost remains in the neighbourhood of the corpse;[1] and this belief enables the savage to cheat his grief to some extent. In Fiji, "a child of rank died under the care of Marama, the queen of Somosomo. The body was placed in a box and hung from the tie-beam of the chief temple, and for some months the best of food was taken to it daily, the bearers approaching with the greatest respect, and, after having waited as long as a person would be in taking a meal, clapping their hands, as when a chief has done eating, and retiring."[2] The persistence, even amongst savages, of natural affection when the object of affection is dead, may be further illustrated by a similar example from a different quarter of the globe: "When a child dies among the Ojibways, they cut some of its hair and make a little doll, which they call the doll of sorrow. This lifeless object takes the place of the deceased child. This the mother carries for a year. She places it near her at the fire, and sighs often when gazing on it. She carries it wherever she goes. They think the child's spirit has entered this bundle, and can be helped by its mother. Presents and sacrificial gifts are made to it. Toys and useful implements are tied to the doll for its use."[3] In Guinea, so far from being afraid of the dead man, they keep him for a whole year or even several years in the house before burying him —which leads to a sort of mummification.[4] In Bonny, where also he is embalmed, they do not part with him even when buried, but bury him in the house,[5] as is customary on the Amazon[6] and was the custom amongst the early Romans,

[1] Bastian, *Der Mensch*, ii. 335.
[2] Williams, *Fiji and the Fijians*, i. 177.
[3] Dorman, *Primitive Superstitions*, 116 (Kohl's *Kitchi Gami*, 108).
[4] Bastian, *Loango Küste*, i. 232.
[5] *Der Mensch*, *loc. cit.*
[6] Wallace, *Amazon*, 346.

Greeks, Teutons, and other Aryan peoples. Even when the corpse is buried at a distance from the house, measures may be and are taken to facilitate the return of the spirit to his friends. Thus the Iroquois leave a small hole in the grave in order that the soul may pass freely in and out;[1] and Count Goblet d'Alviella[2] conjectures that this practice was known to Neolithic man: "There is a certain detail, frequently observed in these dolmens, which has not failed to exercise the minds of the archæologists, especially when the dolmens were supposed to be the work of one particular people. It is the presence in one of the walls—generally the one that closes the entrance—of a hole not more than large enough for the passage of a human head. In the Caucasus and on the coast of Malabar, these holes have given the dolmens the popular name of 'dwarf-houses.' The hole is too small to serve as a passage for living men or for the introduction of the skeleton; or even for inserting the sacrifices, which, moreover, would be found piled up against the interior wall. The most probable explanation seems to be that it was intended for the soul to pass through."

The belief that the soul cannot bring itself to desert its body leads some peoples, who wish the soul to stay with them, to burn the body, in order that the soul may be detached and free to revisit them. Thus in Serendyk the corpse is burnt to enable the soul to return, and the Catal (on the coast of Malayala) burn the good and bury the bad, for then the bad cannot return.[3] But the soul, when released, whether by burning or otherwise, from the body, is apt to lose its way when it seeks to come home; so to the present day in the Tirol the corpse is always conveyed to the cemetery by the high-road, in order that the souls may have no difficulty in retracing the route. Or care is taken to catch the soul as soon as possible, so that it may not get lost; the Tonquinese cover the dying man's face with a cloth, the Marian Islanders with a vessel, to catch the soul; the Payaguas (South America) do not cover the corpse's head

[1] Bastian, *Oest. Asien*, iii. 259. "The Ohio tribes bore holes in the coffin to let the spirit pass in and out," Dorman, *Prim. Sup.* 20.

[2] *Hibbert Lecture*, 24.

[3] Bastian, *Der Mensch*, ii. 331.

with earth, but with a vessel, and the Samoyeds put an inverted kettle over his head.[1]

That the presence of the spirit of the departed is desired, welcomed, and invited by many peoples, is shown by the feasts held in honour of the dead, not only before the funeral, but at intervals afterwards. Thus, "on the third, sixth, ninth, and fortieth days after the funeral, the old Prussians and Lithuanians used to prepare a meal, to which, standing at the door, they invited the soul of the deceased . . . if any morsels fell from the table they were left lying there for the lonely souls that had no living relations or friends to feed them."[2] Six weeks after the funeral, the Tscheremiss go to the grave, and invite the ghost to come to the house to a feast, at which a seat and food are provided for him.[3] Elsewhere this feast becomes an annual all-souls' festival, and as it is or was found amongst the Greeks (the Apaturia), the Romans (Parentalia or Feralia), the Zoroastrians, the Bulgarians, the Russians, the Icelanders, and other Aryan peoples, we may perhaps infer that the practice goes back to the earliest Indo-European times. It is, however, by no means confined to the Aryan area, but is found amongst the Mixteks, the Karens, the Kocch, the Barea, and in Tonquin and Dahomey, as well as amongst the Tschuwasch and the Tscherkess.[4] In Dabaiba, according to Hakluyt's *Historic of the West Indies* (Decade vii. ch. 10), "in the sepulchers they leave certayne trenches on high, whereinto euery yeere they poure a little of the graine Maizium and certayne suppinges or smal quantities of wine made after their manner, and they suppose these thinges will bee profitable to the ghosts of their departed friendes."

Where the dead are buried in the house, there is no need to issue a formal invitation to the spirit to come back and eat, for he can be and is fed as regularly as the living inmates. Thus in Bonny the dead are buried under the doorstep, a funnel communicates with the mouth of the deceased, and libations of blood are poured down the funnel

[1] Bastian, *Oest. Asien*, iv. 386.
[2] Frazer, *Golden Bough*, i. 177.
[3] Bastian, *Der Mensch*, ii. 336.
[4] Bastian, *loc. cit.*, and Tylor, *Prim. Cult.* ii. 36; cf. for Ashanti, *Tshi-speaking Peoples*, 167.

by the negro every time he leaves the house.[1] Even when the burial-place is away from the house, the same provision may be made for regularly tending the deceased. Thus in the Tenger Mountains (in Java) a hollow bamboo is inserted in the grave at burial, in order that offerings of drink and food may be poured down it.[2] In the houses in which the bones of the chiefs of the Timmanees are kept there are small openings through which food can be given to the dead.[3] In ancient Mycenæ an altar over one of the shaft-graves has been discovered, with a tube leading into the grave; the altar is evidently not intended for the worship of the gods, but is an *ἐσχάρα*,[4] and the tube fulfils the same purpose as the bamboo in Java and the funnel in Bonny;[5] while the trench dug in Dabaiba has its exact parallel in the Greek *βόθρος*, into which Odysseus, for instance, poured the blood of which the spirits were to drink. In historic times, in Greece blood was daily offered in Tronis of Daulia to the spirit of the hero-founder in the Mycenæan mode: *τὸ μὲν αἷμα δι' ὀπῆς ἐσχέουσιν ἐς τὸν τάφον*.[6] In Peru "the relations of the deceased used to pour some of the liquor named *Chica* into the grave, of which a portion was conveyed by some hollow canes into the mouth of the dead person."[7]

Blood, which is the life, is the food frequently offered to the dead. The priests of the Batta pour the blood of a fowl on the corpse.[8] In Ashanti the skeletons of deceased kings, carefully preserved and mounted on gold wire, are seated each on his own stool, and the living king washes each with blood.[9] The Marian Islanders anoint the bones of their dead.[10] Then by a substitution of similars, it is considered sufficient to colour the corpse, or some part thereof, with some red substance taking the place of blood. Thus in Tanna, "the face is kept exposed and painted red, and on the following day the grave is dug and the body buried."[11] The

[1] Bastian, *Rechtsverhältnisse*, 296, and *Der Mensch*, ii. 335; cf. Liebrecht, *Zur Volkskunde*, 399.

[2] Bastian, *Der Mensch*, ii. 336.

[3] Bastian, *loc. cit.*

[4] *ἐφ' ἧς τοῖς ἥρωσιν ἀποθύομεν*, Poll. i. 8.

[5] Rohde, *Psyche*, 33.

[6] Pausanias, x. 4.

[7] Zarate, *Conquest of Peru* (translated in Kerr, *Voyages and Travels*, iv. 362).

[8] Bastian, *Oest. Asien*, v. 365.

[9] Ellis, *Tshi-speaking Peoples*, 168.

[10] Bastian, *Oest. Asien*, v. 281.

[11] Turner, *Nineteen Years in Polynesia*, 93.

Kalmucks are content to cover the corpse with something red whilst it is awaiting burial.[1] And, according to Count Goblet d'Alviella,[2] "in certain graves, the earliest of which go back to the reindeer age (those of Mentone, for example), the bones of the dead are painted red with oligist or cinnabar; and in our own day some of the North American tribes, who expose their dead on trees, collect the naked bones and paint them red before finally burying them. An analogous custom has been observed amongst the Mincopies of the Andaman Islands and the Niams of Central Africa."

The feeling towards the dead in all these examples—examples which a learned anthropologist would with ease, I am convinced, have made many times as numerous—is or in all cases may be that prompted by the affection, parental, filial, conjugal, which was even more necessary for the self-preservation of the human race in the earliest days than it is in civilised times. But it is not here suggested that love was the only feeling ever felt for the deceased. On the contrary, it is admitted that fear of the dead was and is equally widespread, and is equally "natural." What inference, then, is to be drawn from these two sets of apparently opposed facts, or what explanation is to be given of them? To this question the right answer is given both by savages themselves and by careful observers of savage modes of thought. Kubary, long a resident in the Pelew Islands, says[3] the islanders "are only afraid of ghosts of strangers, as they are safe from the ghosts of their own people because of the good understanding which exists between the family and its own ghosts." So on the Gold Coast, though the spirit of the dead man wanders about, if homeless, doing good or evil according to his disposition, it is to his own family that he does good.[4] "Black people," said a Zulu, "do not worship all Amatongo indifferently, that is, all the dead of their tribe. But their father whom they knew is the head by whom they begin and end in their prayer, for they know him best, and his love for his children;

[1] Bastian, *Oest. Asien*, vi. 607.
[2] *Hibbert Lecture*, 17, referring to Castailhac, *La France prehistorique*, 292.
[3] In *Allerlei aus Volks und Menschenkunde*, i. 10.
[4] Ellis, *Ewe-speaking Peoples*, 102.

they remember his kindness to them whilst he was living; they compare his treatment of them whilst he was living, support themselves by it, and say, 'He will still treat us in the same way now he is dead. We do not know why he should regard others beside us; he will regard us only.'"[1] In fine, as we might reasonably expect, the man who was loved during his lifetime did not immediately cease to be loved even by savages, when he died, nor was he who was feared in life less feared when dead.

In primitive societies there is no state or central power administering justice between its members and protecting them from external aggression. The only bond which unites the society is the tie of blood. The individual exists only as a member of a family or clan, and only so far as it supports and protects him. The survival of the race thus depends on the ready and effective aid rendered by the clan to its members. Consequently the individual's only friends are his clansmen, and "stranger" means "enemy"—*guest* and *hostis* are philologically the same word. Nor does a man cease to be a member of his clan when or because he dies. On the contrary, his claims on his clansmen may then become more sacred and more exacting than ever, for if he has been murdered they must avenge him at all costs. It is then quite intelligible that strangers, who as strangers were enemies while alive, should continue to be hostile after death; and that clansmen, especially "the father whom they knew," should both show and receive the loving-kindness which during their lifetime marked their relations with their fellow-members.

The object of this chapter was to conjecture what there was in the daily experience of the earliest form of society which may have suggested the possibility of maintaining permanently friendly relations with some of the spirits by which primitive man was surrounded and by which his fortunes were influenced. The conjecture offered is that he was ordinarily and naturally engaged in maintaining such relations with the spirits of his deceased clansmen; that he was necessarily led to such relations by the operation of

[1] Callaway, *Religious System of Amazulu*, part ii., quoted by Tylor, *Prim. Cult.* ii. 116.

those natural affections which, owing to the prolonged, helpless infancy of the human being, were indispensable to the survival of the human race; and that the relations of the living clansman with the dead offered the type and pattern, in part, though only in part, of the relations to be established with other, more powerful, spirits.

The reader will already have noticed — if not, his attention is now drawn to the fact—that hitherto, with the exception of the last quotation (that referring to the Zulus) no mention has been made of ancestor-worship. The reason is not merely that ancestor-worship may be and is explained —erroneously, in the opinion of the writer of these lines—as due in its origin solely to fear, like all worship; but that ancestor-worship implies a belief on the part of the worshipper that the spirit worshipped is a supernatural spirit. Now, according to the thesis set forth in the previous chapters, not all spirits are necessarily supernatural spirits; the man who believes the bowing tree or the leaping flame to be a living thing like himself, does not therefore believe it to be a supernatural being—rather, so far as it is like himself, it, like himself, is not supernatural, for we have seen reason to reject the conjecture that man began by thinking he himself possessed supernatural powers. With this distinction between spirits and supernatural spirits, it has not been necessary for the purpose of this chapter to assume that the spirits of the dead possessed in the earliest form of society that power of thwarting man's best-grounded anticipations, which is of the essence of supernatural power. There may indeed be no *à priori* reason why man, when casting round for the source of this mysterious, supernatural interference with natural laws, should not have found it in the action of the spirits of the dead as well as in that of any other class of spirits. And, as a matter of fact, in some religious systems the spirits of the dead are credited with supernatural powers, though, it must be remarked, their powers are not by any means so great as those of the national or local gods, and the general feeling is that it is the dead who are dependent on the living for their comfort and even for their continued existence, rather than *vice versâ*; in Egypt the *ka* was annihilated, if the survivors did not embalm the body of the deceased and make images of the dead man; in Greece and Aryan India the main motive for marriage was, and in China is, anxiety to provide descendants competent to continue the rites on which the *post-mortem* welfare of the deceased depends; and amongst savages generally the belief is that the dead stand in actual need of the food that is offered to them. But, as a matter of fact, there are grounds for believing that it was to another quarter altogether than ancestral spirits that man looked in his attempts to locate the supernatural in the external world. This point will be fully discussed in a later chapter.

In the next place, if, as is here argued, man's communion with the spirits of his dead suggested the possibility of communication with other and supernatural spirits, then it is intelligible that, if ever the ritual for approaching both classes of spirits came to be the same, the similarity would eventually react to the advantage and increased honour of the spirits of the dead. The acts which constituted worship in the case of the supernatural spirit would not differ from those in which affection for a deceased father found its natural expression; and consequently, not differing, would come to be worship in the case of the deceased ancestor also. Thus, on this guess, ancestor-worship is secondary on and a by-product of the act of worship in the proper sense (*i.e.* the worship of a god).

To restate the argument: (1) The family-feast held immediately after the death of the deceased and repeated at intervals afterwards, and the other offerings of food to the deceased, are not originally acts of worship; (2) the same sort of offerings and festivals come to be employed in the case of supernatural spirits and to constitute the (external) worship of those spirits; (3) the offerings to the spirits of the dead then become ancestor-worship. This argument depends for its validity largely on the identity, here alleged, of the ritual for approaching spirits of the dead and supernatural spirits. The identity cannot be exhibited fully until the act of "worship" in the proper sense has been—as in a later chapter it will be—fully set forth; and the reader is accordingly requested to suspend his final judgment on the question till the full evidence is before him. There are, however, some outstanding points to consider before we can proceed to consider this evidence. For instance, it will have struck some readers as a serious omission that no reference has been made in this discussion to the "uncleanness" which is very generally, if not universally, considered to attach to a corpse and to all who come in contact with it—an omission all the more serious because this "taboo" has been explained as due to fear lest the spirit of the deceased should lodge on the person who touches the dead body.[1] The omission, however, has been intentional, and the reasons for it are twofold. First, whatever the theory of this taboo, in practice the taboo may and does coexist with love for and confidence in the spirit of the deceased. Thus amongst the Pelew Islanders, who, as has been said already, have no fear of the ghosts of their own people, "because of the good understanding which exists between the family and its own ghosts," the relatives of the deceased are "unclean" for several days.[2] In Samoa, where the natural affection for the deceased finds touching expression, "those who attended the deceased were most careful not to handle food, and for days were fed by others as if they were helpless infants . . . fasting was common at such times, and they who did so ate nothing during the day, but had a meal at night; reminding us," says the Rev. G. Turner,[3] "of what David said when mourning the death of Abner: 'So do God to me and more also, if I taste bread or ought else till the sun be down.' The fifth day was a day of 'purification.' They bathed the face and hands with hot water, and then they were 'clean,' and resumed the usual time and mode of eating." On the Gold Coast, where the wives of the deceased try to tempt his soul to return by offering him his favourite dish, "those persons who have touched the corpse are considered unclean; and after the interment, they go in procession to the nearest well or brook, and sprinkle themselves with water, which is the ordinary native mode of purification."[4] In ancient Greece, also, where ancestors were worshipped, the relatives were tabooed.[5] In

[1] I have not been able to see the paper in which this explanation is put forth; but cf. Frazer, *Golden Bough*, i. 154.

[2] Kubary in *Allerlei*, i. 6.

[3] *Nineteen Years in Polynesia*, 228.

[4] Ellis, *Tshi-speaking Peoples*, 241.

[5] See my paper, "Funeral Laws and Folk-Lore in Greece," in the *Classical Review* for June 1895, for instances.

China, too, where the spirit, so far from being feared, was, as in Bonny, invited to return, the corpse is or was taboo; for we may infer from the question in *The Li Ki*,[1] "Whoever being engaged with the mourning rites for a parent bathed his head or body?" that the period of the mourning rites was a time of "uncleanness" for the son.

It seems, therefore, that even if we were to admit that this species of "uncleanness" originated in a savage theory that the soul might settle on the "unclean," we could not infer that deceased spirits were feared wherever this taboo was found to exist. Next—and this is the second reason why no reference has been previously made to this important set of facts—there are several kinds of taboo, of which the corpse-taboo is only one, and it seems proper to employ the comparative method and consider the various kinds together. We may thus perhaps avoid one-sided conclusions, and get a general view, if not a general theory, of the subject. The next chapter, therefore, deals with taboo.

[1] Legge's translation (*Sacred Books of the East*), 181.

CHAPTER VI

TABOO: ITS TRANSMISSIBILITY

TABOO is a Polynesian word, said to mean "strongly marked"; but though the word is Polynesian, the institution is universal.[1] Things are taboo which are thought to be dangerous to handle or to have to do with: things "holy" and things "unclean" are alike taboo; the dead body, the new-born child; blood and the shedder of blood; the divine king as well as the criminal; the sick, outcasts, and foreigners; animals as well as men; women especially, the married woman as well as the sacred virgin; food, clothes, vessels, property, house, bed, canoes, the threshing-floor, the winnowing fan; a name, a word, a day; all are or may be taboo because dangerous. This short list does not contain one-hundredth part of the things which are supposed to be dangerous; but even if it were filled out and made tolerably complete, it would, by itself, fail to give any idea of the actual extent and importance of the institution of taboo. If it were merely bodily contact with the person or thing tabooed which entailed danger, it would be sufficiently difficult for the savage to avoid unintentionally touching some of all the many things taboo. But the difficulty and danger are multiplied by the fact that involuntarily to catch sight of the tabooed object, or to be seen by the tabooed person, is as dangerous as to

[1] The best collections of facts are, for Polynesia, Waitz-Gerland, *Anthropologie*, vi. 343 ff.; for food-taboos, A. E. Crawley in *Folk-Lore*, vi. 2 (June 1895), 130 ff.; for taboos on women, A. E. Crawley in the *Journal of the Anthropological Institute*, xxiv. Nos. 2, 3, 4 (Nov. 1894, Feb. and May 1895), 116 ff., 219 ff., 430 ff.; Frazer in the *Encyclopædia Britannica*, s.v. "Taboo," and in the *Golden Bough*, i. 109 ff.; cf. also Robertson Smith, *Religion of the Semites*, 152 ff., 446 ff., 481. For instances not drawn from the above collections, the special references will be given in each case below.

touch, taste, or handle. Thus in Samoa, "Tupai was the name of the high priest and prophet. He was greatly dreaded. His very look was poison. If he looked at a cocoa-nut tree it died, and if he glanced at a bread-fruit tree it also withered away."[1] The king of Loango may not, for the same reason, see a river or tree, and he has to make many long detours in consequence when he goes visiting.[2] In some places girls when taboo have an equally poisonous glance, and are made to wear very broad-brimmed hats, in order that they may not infect the sun. The custom common amongst savage royalties, of holding a state umbrella over the king, may be, I conjecture, a survival from times when the king was a divine king, and, like Tupai or a tabooed woman, might do mischief with his eyes. In Whydah, "in former times, on the eve of the day for the public procession [of the sacred python], the priests and Dañh-si went round the town, announcing the approach of the festival, and warning all the inhabitants, white and black, to close their doors and windows, and to abstain from looking into the streets."[3] In ancient Greece the same belief manifests itself in the tale that Euryphylus was stricken with madness, when he ventured to open the λάρναξ or tabernacle, and look upon the image of Dionysus Æsymnetes.[4] In the mysteries, the secret objects of worship were so taboo that it was only after a long course of preparatory purification and communion that it became safe for the worshipper to see them: "the ἐποπτεία was the last and highest grade of initiation."[5] In modern folk-lore it is held to be fatal to see "the good people"— "they are fairies: he who looks on them shall die."

On the same principle that seeing or being seen is dangerous, mere proximity also is forbidden; and amongst the Basutos, during harvest-time, the "unclean" may not even approach the crop.[6] In the same way, too, to hear is as dangerous as to see; thus amongst the Zulus, on receipt of the news that a relative is dead, the hearer must sprinkle himself with the blood of sacrifice, "to purify himself from

[1] Turner, *Samoa*, 23.
[2] Bastian, *Loango Küste*, i. 263-8.
[3] Ellis, *Ewe-speaking Peoples*, 61.
[4] Pausanias, viii. c. 19.
[5] Gardner and Jevons, *Greek Antiquities*, 278.
[6] Casalis, *Les Bassoutos*, 266.

the mourning,"[1] though obviously from the nature of the case there can have been no bodily or even visual contact with the corpse to defile the mourner. Even the name of the deceased, as well as the news of his death, is dangerous to hear, and may not be pronounced. Thus the native tribes of Tasmania, now extinct, "never mentioned the dead";[2] and the same reticence is observed by the Ainos,[3] and the Australian black-men.[4] The Ostiaks avoid mentioning the name of the deceased;[5] the Caribs do not like to pronounce the names of their dead.[6] The same dislike is found in Tierra del Fuego.[7] The Guaycorous never utter the name of a deceased chief,[8] and the Abipones[9] abstain not only from the name of the deceased, but from any word of which the name may happen to form part. It would, however, be an error to suppose that it is only the names of things "unclean" and defiling, such as the name of one who is now a corpse, are dangerous to hear; in Polynesia, chiefs are so sacred that their names are strictly taboo, and the component syllables may not be used in common conversation. In Sumatra, the name of the tiger is taboo, and when a reference to him is unavoidable, euphemisms are employed, and he is called "Grandfather," "Ancient One," "The Free," etc.[10] The later Jews shrank from pronouncing the actual name of God, and made substitutions, to avoid unnecessary contact even of this indirect kind with the consuming holiness of the Lord. In ancient Greece, the rites to which the initiated alone were admitted were so sacred that all mention of them to the profane was tabooed—hence our uncertainty as to what those rites really were.

We have, however, yet to mention the peculiar characteristic of the institution of taboo, and that which gives it its widest range and greatest power. That is the transmissibility, the infection or contagion of taboo. Everything which comes in

[1] Bastian, *Der Mensch*, iii. 24.
[2] *Journal of the Anthropological Institute*, 238.
[3] *Ibid.* 238.
[4] Bastian, *Oest. Asien*, v. 86.
[5] Bastian, *Der Mensch*, ii. 362.
[6] Père Delaborde in the *Recueil de divers voyages* (A.D. 1684), 8.
[7] Réville, *Religions des peuples non-civilisés*, i. 398.
[8] *Ibid.* 384.
[9] *Ibid.* 386.
[10] Bastian, *Oest. Asien*, v. 51.

contact with a tabooed person or thing becomes itself as dangerous as the original object, becomes a fresh centre of infection, a fresh source of danger to the community. In the case of things "unclean," the modern mind can without difficulty understand that, granted the original object is really polluted, it communicates its pollution to whatever touches it. It requires no great exercise of the imagination to comprehend that in ancient Greece the offerings used for the purification of a murderer, became, in the very process of purifying him, themselves polluted and had to be buried.[1] The rules about the uncleanness produced by the carcases of vermin in Leviticus xi. 32 ff., are also intelligible from this point of view: "Whatever they touch must be washed; the water itself is then unclean, and can propagate the contagion; nay, if the defilement affect an (unglazed) earthen pot, it is supposed to sink into the pores, and cannot be washed out, so that the pot must be broken."[2] It is, however, strange to find that the "infection of holiness" produces exactly the same results as the pollution of uncleanness, that is to say, it renders the thing touched taboo and therefore unusable. But in Tahiti if a chief's foot touches the earth, the spot which it touches becomes taboo thenceforth, and none may approach it—chiefs are therefore carried in Tahiti when they go out. If he enters a house, it becomes taboo; no one else may go into it ever after. No one may touch him, or eat and drink out of a vessel which he has touched. In New Zealand it is fatal to touch anything that is his or that he has used; none may use a bed that he has slept in. If a drop of his blood happens to fall on anything, the thing on which it falls becomes his property. When a missionary had saved a choking Maori from death by extracting a bone from his throat by means of a pair of tweezers, the first thing the Maori did on recovering his breath was to claim the tweezers: they had touched him and were taboo, and thereby appropriated to him. In ancient Greece the priest and priestess of Artemis Hymnia amongst the Orchomenians, and the Rechabites amongst the Jews, might not enter a private house,[3] for the same reason as the Polynesian chief.

[1] Pausanias, ii. 31. [2] Robertson Smith, *Religion of the Semites*, 447.
[3] Pausanias, viii. 13, and Jer. xxv. 9 ff.

The clothes as well as the drinking vessels of the Mikado were fatal to those who touched them.[1] Amongst the Tshi-speaking peoples of the Gold Coast, "all the commoner utensils that have been used during the festival [a general remembrance of the dead], such as calabashes and earthen pots, are carried out at daybreak on the ninth day, and thrown away."[2] The Selli at Dodona were χαμαιεῦναι, *i.e.* abstained from sleeping in a bed, probably for the reason that the bed would become too holy for anyone else to occupy afterwards. They were also ἀνιπτόποδες, and the priest and priestess of Artemis Hymnia did not wash like other people,[3] doubtless because of the excessive sanctity of their persons, just as the Arabians of old might not wash or anoint the head; and the head of a Maori chief was so sacred that "if he only touched it with his fingers, he was obliged immediately to apply them to his nose, and snuff up the sanctity which they had acquired by the touch, and thus restore it to the part from whence it was taken."[4]

As tabooed persons render everything taboo with which they come in contact, so holy places make everything in them taboo. The fish in the sacred river Reiti in Attica were themselves, like the stream, sacred to Demeter,[5] and might be caught by her priests alone. In Pharæ (a town of Achæa) there was a stream sacred to Hermes, the fish of which, as being sacred to the god, were taboo and might not be caught at all.[6] In Yabe there is a certain deity's hut which is so taboo, that whoso enters it, except on business, becomes the slave of the priest.[7] On the Slave Coast any person accidentally touched by the sacred python is thereby made dedicate to the god and has to serve it for the rest of his life.[8] By an extension of the same principle, in Polynesia the holy places of the gods and the houses of the most sacred chiefs became asylums for fugitives. The very soil of holy places is sacred, and communicates its sanctity to that which touches it: hence in Peru, "none came within where the idol was, save

[1] Bastian, *Oest. Asien*, v. 282.
[2] Ellis, *Tshi-speaking Peoples*, 228.
[3] Pausanias, viii. 14.
[4] Frazer, *Golden Bough*, i. 191, quoting R. Taylor.
[5] Pausanias, i. 38.
[6] *Ibid.* viii. 22.
[7] Bastian, *Loango Küste*, i. 219.
[8] Ellis, *Ewe-speaking Peoples*, 57.

the principal chiefs, who entered with much reverence and veneration, having removed their sandals,"[1] doubtless because the sandals by contact with the sacred soil would become taboo and unfit thereafter for daily use. In the same way in Tonga, the upper garment was removed in the presence of the king, because his glance would render it taboo, and therefore useless afterwards.

The sanctity of the soil of sacred places gives rise to a remarkable coincidence in the practices of two races so widely separated as the ancient Mexicans and the negroes of the Gold Coast. The former practised "eating earth in honour of the god," the latter still "eat fetish." The Mexicans on entering any sacred place, or by way of taking oath, touched the soil with their finger and then placed the finger in the mouth.[2] Amongst the negroes, "to make an oath binding on a person who takes it, it is usual to give him something to eat or drink which in some way appertains to a deity . . . the ordinary plan is to take something from the spot in which the deity resides . . . a little earth, or some leaves or berries . . . this is (incorrectly) called 'eating fetish.'"[3] That this procedure somehow gives the deity of the place a greater hold over the person taking oath than he would have if the ceremony was omitted, is clear. How or why this should be, may be difficult for the enlightened reader to imagine, but it would be intelligible enough to the intending perjurer, who at the present day in an English court of justice kisses his thumb instead of "the book," and thinks thereby to escape the consequences of his perjury. The mediæval practice of swearing by or on the relics of a saint, and the classical custom of swearing or conjuring by the beard (which partakes of the peculiar sanctity of the head), though they do not involve eating or kissing, are inspired by the same feeling; indeed, we may say generally that the practice of swearing "by" anything, and therefore the very conception of an oath, is due in its origin to the feeling that the sacredness of the object held or kissed communicates itself and gives sacredness to the oath. Probably the earliest oaths are those of "compurgation," and the person thus freeing

[1] Payne, *The New World called America*, i. 513, quoting Juan de Betanzos.
[2] Sahagun, Appendix to bk. ii.
[3] Ellis, *Tshi-speaking Peoples*, 196.

himself from the charge made against him does so by voluntarily making himself taboo, by "eating fetish" or otherwise devoting himself to the god. Thus his enemy no longer can touch him, for he is taboo, nor is it necessary that his enemy should touch him; it is now the god's affair. Oaths of witness then follow the analogy of purgatory oaths.

But perhaps the most remarkable instance of the "contagion" of taboo is to be found in the fact that it is capable of infecting not only things but actions, and even time itself. Thus amongst the Basutos, on the day of a chief's decease work is tabooed:[1] the corpse "defiles" not only those who come in contact with it, but all work done on the fatal day. In Madagascar, work is taboo to the relatives of the deceased for a longer or shorter time according to his rank.[2] The Tshi-speaking negroes celebrate an annual feast for the dead generally, and "the whole eight days are termed *egwah awotchwi*, 'Eight Seats,' because it is a period of rest, during which no work may be performed."[3] In the New World, the funeral ceremonies of the kings of Mechoacan "lasted five days, and in all that time no Fire was permitted to be kindled in the City, except in the King's house and Temples, nor yet any Corn was ground, or Market kept, nor durst any go out of their houses."[4] And it is not only in the case of things "unclean" that time itself becomes a channel of infection: the "infection of holiness" is transmitted in the same way. On the Gold Coast, "on the day sacred to or set apart for the offering of sacrifice to a local god, the inhabitants abstain from all work, smear their bodies with white clay, and wear white cloths in sign of rejoicing."[5] On the Slave Coast, "every general, tribal, and local god, with the exception of Mawu, has his holy day."[6] Amongst the Tshi-speaking peoples, "on the day sacred to it [the tutelary deity] all the members of the family wear white or light-coloured cloths and mark themselves with white . . . . no work of any kind may be done, and should one of the members of the family

[1] Casalis, *Les Bassoutos*, 275. [2] Réville, *Rel. des peup. non-civ.* ii. 167.
[3] Ellis, *Tshi-speaking Peoples*, 228.
[4] Gage, *A New Survey of the West Indies*, 160.
[5] Ellis, *Tshi-speaking Peoples*, 74. [6] Ellis, *Ewe-speaking Peoples*, 79.

be absent on a journey, he must on that day make a halt."[1] In Polynesia, not only on the death of Tuitonga, or in time of general mourning or of sickness in the royal family, but before war (a sacred function), or before a great feast, a taboo-day or days are proclaimed; no one may cook food, no fire or light may be kindled, no one may go outside of his house, no domestic animal may utter a sound (dogs are muzzled, cocks put under a calabash). In Mexico, too, the principal feasts of the two chief deities, Tezcatlipoca and Huitzilopochtli, were preceded by a taboo period, "notice of which was solemnly given by the officials."[2] In Madagascar there are days on which it is taboo to go outside the house or begin any business; "the child who comes into the world on one of those days is drowned, exposed, or buried alive, for it belongs to the gods, and therefore may not be kept from them."[3]

This last quotation may make it easier to understand why work is taboo on a holy day; anything begun or done on such a day belongs to the god, and is not for common use. But the reference to a god is not indispensable; work done or begun on an "unclean" day is equally unfit for every-day use, though there is no god for it to belong to. An exact parallel may be found in the matter of raiment, of "best clothes" and "mourning." The clothes which a mourner wears become "defiled" by his contact with the deceased; and, when the days of his "impurity" are over, they are cast aside; they can no longer be used in his ordinary avocations, for they would communicate to all that he touched and to everything that he did the pollution with which they are infected. He therefore confines himself to one set of garments, in order not to spoil too many; and if it is the custom in his country to mark tabooed objects by some special colour, he is expected to wear raiment of that colour, to warn off those who otherwise might unwittingly come in contact with him and become defiled. So, too, the clothes which a man wore in the worship of the gods acquired sanctity and could not be used in his ordinary avocations (just as "among the later Jews the contact of a sacred volume or a phylactery 'defiled the hands' and called for an

[1] Ellis, *Tshi-speaking Peoples*, 93. [2] Payne, *New World*, i. 486.
[3] Réville, *Rel. des peup. non-civ.* i. 167.

ablution"[1]). A special set of garments therefore was reserved for this purpose exclusively; these were presumably the best that the wearer possessed, and so "in early times best clothes meant clothes that were taboo for the purposes of ordinary life."[2] On the Gold Coast there is a special colour (white) for holy days, distinguished from that distinctive of mourning (red).[3]

Intermediate between the taboo on "best clothes" and that on "mourning" is the New Zealand taboo already mentioned on a garment on which the glance of a chief has rested. Intermediate, too, between "holy days" and days of mourning are the *dies nefasti* of the Romans and the ἡμέραι ἀποφράδες of the Greeks, which were neither dedicated to any god nor "unclean," but were certainly taboo days.

To a certain extent, it is plain, the transmissibility or infection of taboo can be explained by the laws of the Association of Ideas: the sentiment with which a person or thing is regarded colours all that is associated with that person or thing, and may be revived by anything which reminds us of it or him. "The glove upon that hand" has for the lover some of the glamour which surrounds his mistress; to all, the scene of former misery is painful. So, too, the terror which attaches to a thing taboo may be reawakened by anything which calls it to mind; of all things blood is most taboo; hence in Polynesia red berries are taboo, because of their colour; on the Gold Coast "every spot where the earth is of a red colour is believed to be or to have been the place of abode of a Sasabonsum,"[4] and is taboo; and in both countries red is the colour used to signify that a thing is tabooed. But whereas civilised man is aware that the association between such ideas is merely mental, to the savage the connection is real. The savage believes that the same terrible consequences—whatever they may be—which ensue on contact with blood, do actually and really follow on contact with things which by their colour or otherwise remind him thereof. That primitive man should mistake the mental association for a real connection was inevitable; he could not do otherwise. The reality of the connection was not for him matter of

[1] Robertson Smith, *Religion of the Semites*, 452. [2] *Ibid.* 453.
[3] See Ellis, *Tshi-speaking Peoples*, 88, 89, 93, 156. [4] *Ibid.* 35.

argument; it was a self-evident fact, of which he had direct consciousness and immediate certitude. But if this is so, if man began with this belief, and did not infer or deduce it from anything, then we must reject those theories which represent taboo as being the consequence of some other belief, such as that things taboo transmit a material, physical pollution, or that some supernatural influence is transmitted, or that the dead man's spirit adheres to those who touch the corpse. The material, physical theory (implied in the use of the terms "contagion," "infection" of taboo) is untenable, because the belief in taboo is not an induction based upon observation, experience, and experiment, but an *à priori* conviction: it is not an inference from such facts of observation as that pitch, mud, etc., defile, but a belief prior to, independent of, indeed, irreconcilable with the facts of experience. The theory of a supernatural cause is simply superfluous; the connection between the two associated ideas was a self-evident fact, which for the savage required no explanation—supernatural or other—but was rather itself the explanation of other things.

But though the laws of the Association of Ideas explain the transmissibility of taboo and account for the fact that whatever is mentally associated with the thing taboo awakens the same terror as the thing itself, still they obviously cannot explain why the thing itself is terrible to begin with. To learn that, we must examine the things themselves.

CHAPTER VII

THINGS TABOO

Before beginning to examine things taboo, with a view to seeing whether they possess any common quality, whether any general statement can be made with regard to them, whether, in fine, it is possible to frame any induction from them, it is plain that we must discriminate between things which I will venture henceforth to distinguish as things taboo and things tabooed. Both classes are "infectious" and communicate their mysterious and dangerous qualities to whatever they come in contact with; but things tabooed are those which would not possess the taboo-infection, if they had not derived it from contact with something else taboo or tabooed, whereas things taboo are those which do not derive the contagion from anything else, but have it inherent in themselves. A single thing taboo might infect the whole universe; on the Loango Coast, a divine king's glance would infect a river and the river infect all in its course;[1] in modern Polish folklore a corpse may not be carried over a stream,[2] for the same reason; taboo persons are generally not allowed to be seen by the sun, for they would infect him, and he the universe.

For the purpose of this chapter, therefore, we must set aside things tabooed. Food, for instance, is not inherently taboo, though it may become tabooed in many ways—if it is touched, intentionally or unintentionally, by a sorcerer (in the Mulgrave Islands), or by an Amatonga (amongst the Zulus), or by a "tapued person" (in New Zealand), or by the Mikado, or by the sick (in Fiji), or by mourners (Tahiti, New Zealand, Samoa), or by a superior chief (Fiji and Tonga), or by an outcast (Burma and the Brahmins); and as the hands are

[1] Bastian, *Loango Küste*, i. 263.

[2] *Am Urquell*, iii. 51.

used for all sorts of things and are specially liable therefore to become "unclean," not only are mourners not allowed in Tahiti to feed themselves "lest the food, defiled by the touch of their polluted hands, should cause their own death,"[1] not only has the tabooed person in Timor to be fed like a little child, for the same reason,[2] not only was sacred food consumed in Mexico by a sort of "bob-cherry" performance without the use of the hands,[3] but in Tanna no food whatever might be offered with the bare hands, as such contact might give the food a potency for evil; finally, as a taboo person can infect things by his mere glance, it is a common precaution to allow no one to see you take your food.[4]

Tabooed persons, too, must be distinguished from persons taboo; and under the former head must probably be placed criminals and the sick. There is reason to think that in primitive society the only criminals are the violators of taboo; and this crime carries its own punishment with it, for in the act of breaking taboo the offender himself becomes tabooed, and no one in the community will touch him or have anything to do with him. In fine, as the only offence known to primitive society is taboo-breaking, so the only punishment is excommunication. As far as the early Indo-Europeans are concerned, the evidence of linguistic palæontology is clear upon the latter point: "wretch" is a word which goes back to the earliest Aryan times, and it means an outlaw.[5] Even in historic times the Roman community continued to protect itself by the interdict from fire and water, the object of which was probably in its origin rather to save those necessaries of life from pollution than to punish the offender.[6] As for the sick, the taboo on them is, I think, confined to Polynesia, and is expressly explained as due to the fact that an *atua* or spirit enters them: they are thereby tabooed, but they are not taboo.

[1] Wilkes, *U.S. Exploring Expedition*, iii. 115.

[2] Réville, *Rel. des peup. non-civ.* ii. 162.

[3] Payne, *New World*, i. 428.

[4] Mr. Crawley gives instances from Abyssinia, Nubia, Madagascar, the Aztecs, Cacongo, Cauna, Dahomey, Congo, the Monbuttoo, the Pongo Coast, Ashanti, Tonga, the Bakairi, the Karaja, Loango Coast, Celebes, Sandwich Islands. *Folk-Lore*, vi. 2. 140.

[5] Schrader, *Prehistoric Antiquities of the Aryan Peoples*, 350.

[6] Granger, *Worship of the Romans*, 266; cf. Cicero *pro S. Roscio*, § 71.

In the same way, it is clear that, for the purposes of this chapter, we must class as tabooed and not as taboo all persons, animals, and objects in which a supernatural spirit takes up his abode. But though all supernatural beings are inherently taboo, we are not yet in a position to convert the proposition simply and say that all things taboo are supernatural: we have to inquire without prejudice whether as a matter of fact there are things taboo and yet not supernatural. However this may turn out to be, a thing or person may undoubtedly become tabooed by contact with the supernatural. Hence strangers are not inherently taboo, but as belonging to strange gods bring with them strange supernatural influences. It is well, therefore, not to touch their food or eat with them—as the Yule Islanders hold and are supported by the Papuans of Humboldt Bay, the blackfellows of Victoria, and the Atiu Islanders,[1] as well as the inhabitants of Van Diemen's Land.[2] A common practice, also, is to fumigate strangers, to drive away their evil influences, or for the natives to offer blood to their own gods and so gain divine protection. The early explorers of the New World mistakenly regarded these proceedings as done in their honour: in Palmeria, "when they recieue straungers or newe guestes . . . in token of friendshippe, they drawe a little bloud from themselues either out of the tongue, hand, arme, or any other part of the bodie."[3]

Finally, to our list of things tabooed rather than taboo we must add two—if originally they were two and not one class—in which the institution of taboo has had marked effects on the progress of civilisation; they are property and wives. In Polynesia, women before marriage are *noa* (common, safe), afterwards tabooed. So, too, in Mayumbe it is death to touch another man's wife, whereas unmarried women are free to all;[4] and, elsewhere on the Loango Coast, married women are so taboo that things must not be handed directly to them by a man, but must be put down on the ground for them to pick up.[5] In the same way a Waliah making

[1] Crawley, *loc. cit.*

[2] Réville, *Rel. des peup. non-civ.* ii. 159.

[3] Hakluyt, *Historie of the West Indies*, Decade iv. ch. 4. Bernal Diaz repeatedly makes the same mistake.

[4] Bastian, *Loango Küste*, i. 244.

[5] *Ibid.* 168.

offerings to a Brahmin must not hand them but put them on the ground for him to pick up.[1] As for property generally, in Polynesia the owner protects himself in possession by tabooing it; where fishing is conducted co-operatively, the catch is tabooed until divided; when a diamond mine was supposed to have been found near Honolulu, King Tamehameha at once tabooed it, in order to appropriate it exclusively to himself; and European shipmasters who did not care for native visitors got their vessels tabooed by a native chief. In the Moluccas charms are used for the protection of property which have the power of bringing illness or misfortune on the thief.[2] And, according to Hakluyt, the Caribs cultivated the plant called by them *Hay*; each man had his own plot of ground, and "euery one incloseth his portion onely with a little cotton line and they account it a matter of sacriledge if any passe ouer the corde and treade on the possession of his neighbour, and holde it for certayne that whoso violateth this sacred thing shall shortly perish."[3] So, too, in Melanesia, "in the eastern islands, the tambu [taboo] sign is often two sticks crossed and placed in the ground. In such a manner, the St. Christoval native secures his patch of ground from intrusion."[4] In Eastern Central Africa, "the same word that is used for betrothing a girl is also applied to the selecting of a piece of ground for hoeing. A person who wants a new farm goes forth and makes his selection. After doing so he takes bunches of long grass and ties round the trees in that field. Everyone that passes knows by the grass put upon the trees that the field has been taken possession of. . . . In the same way the intending husband points to the cloth that he has given to the girl, and says, 'She is mine.'"[5]

But the distinction between things tabooed and things taboo is not the only distinction that it is necessary to draw. The very conception of taboo, based as it largely is on the association of ideas, is one peculiarly liable to extension by analogy. If, for instance, a species of things is taboo, then

[1] Bastian, *Oest. Asien*, v. 53. [2] Waitz-Gerland, *Anthropologie*, vi. 354.
[3] Hakluyt, *Historie of the West Indies*, Decade viii. ch. 6.
[4] Guppy, *The Solomon Islands*, 32.
[5] Duff Macdonald, *Africana*, i. 118.

ex abundantia cautelæ, in the supererogation of precaution, the whole genus to which the species belongs might well come to be taboo. Or an individual which originally was only taboo at certain periods of its existence might easily come to be considered taboo at all times. Or we might expect *à priori* that new social institutions would, on the analogy of old ones, come to be protected by the power of taboo. And, as a matter of fact, unless we are going to ascribe division into castes to primitive society, we have in them a clear case of the growth of a taboo, and of its extension by analogy: the members of an inferior caste are treated by the superior castes as criminals were treated by primitive society; outcasts are, like outlaws, taboo—eating, especially, must be avoided "with publicans and sinners."

It was not, however, specially for the benefit of outcasts that the last paragraph was penned. Of persons or things inherently taboo we have now two classes left: one consists of supernatural beings, the other includes blood, new-born children with their mothers, and corpses; and it is conceivable that the taboo on one class was extended by analogy to the other class. That is a question to be considered hereafter. At present our business is to show that blood, etc., are as a matter of fact taboo.

As for blood, its taboo character has been so fully demonstrated by Mr. Frazer[1] as to be beyond possibility of doubt. Here it will suffice to add one or two instances to his collection. Blood, as we have already seen, tabooes whatever it falls on, and renders the object or spot useless for all common purposes. Hence the very general precautions taken to prevent royal or sacred blood from being spilled on the ground. Thus in Angoy the blood of royal women may not be shed, and if they have to be put to death, their ribs must be broken.[2] In Dahomi, in 1818, Gezo dethroned Adanlosan, and "as the royal blood may not be shed, Adanloṣan, bound hand and foot, was walled up in a small room, and left to die of starvation."[3] In Dabaiba it was ordained that a priest who has offended "shall eyther

[1] *Golden Bough*, i. 178 ff. [2] Bastian, *Loango Küste*, i. 216.
[3] Ellis, *Ewe-speaking Peoples*, 89.

be stoned to death or burned."[1] So, too, the blood of sacrifice was not allowed to be spilled on the ground either in ancient Egypt or in ancient India; according to the Grihya Sutra,[2] "the effused blood, which at the time of immolation was held in a vessel, should be thrown on bundles of kúśa grass." Strabo,[3] too, says of an Indian tribe that they do not shed the blood of the victims they offer to the gods, but strangle the animals. And in ancient Egypt, "when an ox was sacrificed at the grave, a priestly official caught in a vessel the blood which flowed from the throat when cut (cf. Pyramid text, Teta, line 144)."[4] Even to see a thing taboo is dangerous. Blood therefore must not be seen, and in ancient India, it appears from a Prayoga,[5] "the institutor of the sacrifice and the priests should sit during the operation with their faces averted, so as not to behold the sanguinary work." Naturally, therefore, the shedder of blood is regarded as taboo. Amongst the Yumos of Colorado the man-slayer is taboo for a month, during which time he must fast;[6] and the Kaffir is "unclean" after a battle.[7] Animal blood produces the same effects. The Hottentot after a hunt must purify himself from the blood of the animals he has slain.[8]

The "sanctity" or "uncleanness" of the new-born child and its mother may next be illustrated. In West Africa, "after childbirth, the mother is considered unclean for seven days."[9] The Leaf-Wearers of Orissa also seclude a woman after childbirth for seven days.[10] On the Loango Coast the mother is taboo for as long as six months.[11] In Celebes she is *pamali* (= taboo) for a period the length of which is not stated.[12] Amongst the Australian tribes of lat. 31° 0′ S., long. 138° 55′ E., "for a short time after birth of child she

[1] Hakluyt, *Historie of the West Indies*, Decade vii. ch. 10.

[2] Quoted by Rajendralála Mitra, *Indo-Aryans*, i. 365.

[3] P. 710.

[4] A. Wiedemann in *Am Urquell*, iii. 114.

[5] MS. No. 1552, Sanskrit College of Calcutta, quoted by Rajendralála Mitra, *Indo-Aryans*, i. 372.

[6] Bastian, *Der Mensch*, iii. 24.

[7] *Ibid.*

[8] *Ibid.*

[9] Ellis, *Tshi-speaking Peoples*, 233.

[10] *Journal of the Anthropological Society*, III. cxxxvi.

[11] Bastian, *Loango Küste*, i. 184.

[12] Waitz-Gerland, *Anthropologie*, vi. 355.

is considered unclean."[1] In Central Australia "the mother is isolated until she is able to leave her seclusion with the baby."[2] For the Australians generally, one moon is the length of time stated.[3] Being herself taboo, she tabooes everything with which she comes in contact; therefore, on the Amazon, "when a birth takes place in the house, everything is taken out of it, even the pans and pots, and bows and arrows, till next day";[4] and in Western Africa the mother "can touch nothing without rendering it also unclean."[5] The vessels she has used must therefore, like those of the Mikado, be burned; and her hair—for it conveys the infection of taboo—be likewise burned. Persons taboo cannot take food into their hands without "infecting" it and rendering it unfit for consumption. The Kaniagmut mother therefore must be fed by others, and they, to avoid the contagion, must not touch her but offer the food on a stick. In Travancore the Veddah father shares the taboo, and dare not eat anything but roots. Among the Piojés of Putumayo, both parents fast for days after the birth of a child.[6] The Caribs, too, fasted on the occasion.[7] Finally, the taboo is removed by some mode of purification: amongst the Leaf-Wearers of Orissa the woman bathes and a feast is made.[8] Amongst the Alfoers, not only must the mother be purified in running water, but, on the return from the stream, the whole village must beat the father with sticks, wishing good-luck to the new-born child.[9] On the Gold Coast, when three months have elapsed, the mother "makes offerings to the tutelary deity of the family; and then, attired in her best clothes, and covered with gold ornaments, she pays visits to her friends and neighbours, accompanied by a band of singing women, who sing songs of thanksgiving for her safe delivery."[10]

The new-born child also possesses the taboo-infection in a high degree. Just as the Polynesian chief rendered the

[1] *Journal of the Anthropological Institute*, xxiv. 2. 168. [2] *Ibid.* 183.
[3] *Ibid.* 187. [4] Wallace, *Travels on the Amazon*, 345.
[5] Ellis, *loc. cit.* [6] *Journal of the Anthropological Institute*, viii. 222.
[7] Müller, *Geschichte der Amerikanischen Ur-religionen*, 212.
[8] *Journal of the Anthropological Society*, III. cxxxvi.
[9] Bastian, *Oest. Asien*, v. 270.
[10] Ellis, *Tshi-speaking Peoples*, 233.

ground on which he trod taboo, so amongst the Mexicans children on the day of birth were so taboo they might not be put upon the ground.[1] Amongst the Dyaks, as commonly in modern European folk-lore, new-born children are the especial prey of evil spirits,[2] that is to say are taboo, for the restrictions of taboo are frequently thus explained, when the institution itself has otherwise perished. The child, like the mother, being thus "infectious," must be purified. Amongst the Caribs, the purification was effected by sprinkling the child with some of the father's blood.[3] Amongst the Alfoers, the child was washed in swine's blood.[4] On the Gold Coast rum is squirted over the child by the father.[5] The rum is a substitute or surrogate for blood. Finally, in Polynesia, the Tohunga or priest dips a green twig into water and sprinkles the child's head, or else immerses the infant totally.[6] The common custom of washing the new-born child is probably to be regarded as originally ceremonial rather than cleanly in intent. Amongst the Damaras, "a new-born child is washed —the only time he is ever washed in his life—then dried and greased, and the ceremony is over."[7]

The perfect parallel between the three notions of "uncleanness," "holiness," and taboo pure and simple, is well marked in the case of corpses—with which our list of things inherently taboo concludes. As contact with what is holy or taboo makes a thing holy or taboo, so in West Africa—and indeed we may say universally—"those persons who have touched the corpse are considered unclean."[8] As the new-born child or a "tapued person" tabooes the ground he touches, so amongst the Buryats the corpse of a Shaman is placed "on a felt carpet, so that it be not defiled by contract with the ground";[9] and a lingering survival of this feeling is probably the explanation of some modern European folk-lore, *e.g.* in the Tirol a corpse must be conveyed by the high-road;[10] in some parts of England the conveyance of a corpse

[1] Bastian, *Oest. Asien*, v. 41. [2] *Ibid.* 47.
[3] Müller, *loc. cit.* [4] Bastian, *op. cit.* v. 270.
[5] Ellis, *loc. cit.* [6] Waitz-Gerland, *Anthropologie*, vi. 132 and 362.
[7] Galton, *South Africa*, 190.
[8] Ellis, *Tshi-speaking Peoples*, 241.
[9] *Journal of the Anthropological Institute*, xxiv. 2. 135.
[10] Bastian, *Der Mensch*, ii. 329.

over private property is supposed to give a right of way. That contact with a corpse, like contact with things holy or taboo, renders special vestments necessary, has been already mentioned. Here we need only add one quotation to show that the reason is that the garments are rendered useless, and therefore, sometimes at least, must be destroyed. On the Slave Coast, "at the end of the period of mourning the widows put on clean cloths, the old cloths being burned. At Agweh, men who have lost their head wives do this also."[1] Not only are clothes taboo but the house also, either for a certain period (eight days amongst the Hill Dyaks,[2] one according to the funeral law of Ceos[3]), or altogether, in which case the house is deserted or destroyed ("usually the apartment in which the deceased is buried is closed, and never used again, and sometimes the roof is removed"[4]), just as amongst the Ewe-speaking peoples the house of a person struck by the lightning-god is plundered, and even in the Middle Ages a murderer's house was formally and solemnly pulled down.[5] That death, like the service of the gods, makes the day on which it takes place taboo for other purposes, has been already pointed out, as also that the very name of the deceased or of a god may be tabooed. Again, those who have touched holy things, or are—like the priest and priestess of Artemis Hymnia[6]—themselves holy, may not eat like other people, *i.e.* may not touch food with their hands, and on the same ground, namely, that they would taboo their own food; "those who attended the deceased were most careful not to handle food, and for days were fed by others as if they were helpless infants."[7] Hence some peoples, pushing things to their logical conclusion, fast altogether in mourning, as also in the case of vows (for persons under a vow are dedicate and sacred to the god

[1] Ellis, *Ewe-speaking Peoples*, 160.

[2] Waitz-Gerland, *Anthropologie*, vi. 355. [3] Roehl, *Inscr. Ant.* 395.

[4] Ellis, *Yoruba-speaking Peoples*, 160. Cf. Dobrizhoffer, *History of the Abipones*, ii. 273, "the house which he (the deceased) inhabited they pull entirely to pieces"; Im Thurn, *Indians of Guiana*, 225, "a feast is celebrated, and the house is then deserted for ever"; Dorman, *Primitive Superstitions*, "the Ojibways pulled down the house in which anyone had died"; so, too, the Navajos, Seminoles, Arkansas, and New English tribes.

[5] Post, *Geschlechtsgenossenschaft*, 113. [6] Pausanias, viii. 13.

[7] Turner, *Nineteen Years in Polynesia*, 228.

to whom the vow is made). "Fasting was common at such times (*i.e.* mourning), and they who did so ate nothing during the day, but had a meal at night; reminding us of what David said when mourning the death of Abner: *So do God to me and more also, if I taste bread or ought else till the sun be down.*"[1] Amongst the Ewe-speaking peoples, "the relatives must fast."[2] Amongst the Tshi-speaking peoples, "from the moment of death, the relatives of the deceased, and the members of the household, abstain from food and continue fasting as long as their strength permits."[3] Amongst the Yoruba-speaking peoples, "usage requires them to refuse all food, at least for the first twenty-four hours, after which they usually allow themselves to be persuaded to take some nourishment."[4] The Caribs also fasted during mourning.[5]

Holy persons, such as the Selli, and tabooed persons, *e.g.* candidates prepared for initiation in the Eleusinia, generally may not wash, for fear, probably, lest the sanctity should be communicated by the water to other persons or things, in the same way as the impurity of the murderer in Greece might be conveyed by the offerings used in his purification. The hair and nail-parings of holy persons are also capable of conveying the taboo-infection. Hence they either remove their hair before entering into the taboo-state, or else allow it to grow during that period and remove and dispose of it carefully afterwards. These restrictions are common to mourners, as well as to persons under a vow, or otherwise sacred. In Central Africa, "while a woman's husband is absent, she goes without anointing her head or washing her face";[6] and amongst the ancient Mexicans the relatives of a merchant abroad did not wash their heads or faces[7]—a restriction which was probably part of a vow for the safety of the absent one. In the Miaotze tribe, at a parent's death the son remains in the house forty-nine days without washing his face;[8] and when it is said of the Leaf-Wearers of Orissa that the only death ceremonies known to them are

[1] Turner, *Nineteen Years in Polynesia*, 228.
[2] Ellis, 158.
[3] Ellis, 230.
[4] Ellis, 157.
[5] Bastian, *Der Mensch*, ii. 328.
[6] Macdonald, *Africana*, i. 81.
[7] Sahagun, bk. iv. c. 19.
[8] Bastian, *Der Mensch*, ii. 111.

bathing and fasting, this probably implies a previous (ceremonial) unwashen state. Amongst the negroes of the Gold Coast "the relations may not wash themselves or comb their hair during the funeral ceremonies, in consequence of which the rites themselves are sometimes styled *Ofo*, 'unwashed.'"[1] "In Agweh a widow is supposed to remain shut up for six months in the room in which her husband is buried, during which time she may not wash or change her clothes. . . . At the end of the period of mourning the widows wash, shave the head, pare the nails, and put on clean cloths, the old cloths, the hair, and the nail-parings being burned."[2] Amongst the Crow Indians the widow shaves her head and her mourning ceases when the hair has grown again.[3] In the Tonga Islands, at the death of a Tooitonga the whole population shaved their heads.[4] In Savage Island "the women singed off the hair of their heads as a token of mourning on the death of their husbands."[5] In Siam the head is shaved as a sign of mourning.[6] The classical reader will be reminded of the Greek and Roman funeral custom. On the Gold Coast "the nearest relations of the deceased, of both sexes, shave the head and all hair from their bodies. This has commonly been regarded as a sign of grief; but, having in view the shaving of the head by women on the sacred days of deities, which are days of rejoicing, it appears rather to be a sign of respect."[7] Amongst the Ewe-speaking and the Yoruba-speaking peoples also, shaving marks the termination of the period of mourning.[8] Amongst the Soumoo or Woolwa Indians of the New World, "the hair is cropped in sign of mourning";[9] and the Australian blacks "usually shave the head and plaster themselves with white copi or pipe-clay."[10] Amongst the Bakongo, on the death of a chief, "all his followers shaved their heads in token of mourning."[11] Of the Abipones, last century it was noted

[1] Ellis, *Yoruba-speaking Peoples*, 160.
[2] Ellis, *Ewe-speaking Peoples*, 160.
[3] Bastian, *Der Mensch*, ii. 328.
[4] Mariner, *Tonga Islands*, 214.
[5] Turner, *Samoa*, 306.
[6] Bastian, *Oest. Asien*, iii. 320.
[7] Ellis, *Tshi-speaking Peoples*, 241.
[8] Ellis, *Ewe*, 160; *Yoruba*, 160.
[9] *Journal of the Anthropological Institute*, xxiv. 2. 207.
[10] *Ibid.* 188.
[11] Ward, *Congo Cannibals*, 43.

that "it is also a custom to shave the heads of widows . . . and to cover them with a grey and black hood . . . which it is reckoned a crime for her to take off till she marries again. A widower has his hair cropped, with many ceremonies, and his head covered with a little net-shaped hat, which is not taken off till the hair grows again."[1] Of the Indians of Guiana it still holds good that "the survivors crop their hair,"[2] and of the Fijians "many make themselves 'bald for the dead.'"[3]

Purification, again, is required not only of the mourners, but of all who may have touched the dead, just as contact with a holy volume "defiled the hands" of the later Jews and entailed ablution. "Contact with a corpse renders a person unclean, and he must purify himself by washing in water from head to foot."[4] "Those persons who have touched the corpse are considered unclean; and, after the interment, they proceed in procession to the nearest well or brook, and sprinkle themselves with water, which is the ordinary native mode of purification."[5] In Samoa "the fifth day (of mourning) was a day of 'purification.' They bathed the face and hands with hot water, and then they were 'clean,' and resumed the usual time and mode of eating."[6] In Peru "certain springs were assigned as places for ablution after performing funeral rites."[7] In ancient Greece a basin of lustral water was placed at the door of the house of mourning for purposes of purification.[8]

Since, then, the reluctance to come in contact with a corpse and the precautions taken by those who have to come or have come into such contact are identical with the reluctance and precaution observed in the case of other things taboo or tabooed, it is reasonable to look for an identical cause. Now, the supposed hostility or malevolence of the spirit of the deceased will not serve as a common cause: the phylacteries and the sacred volume of the Jews were not

[1] Dobrizhoffer, *History of the Abipones*, ii. 18.

[2] Im Thurn, *Indians of Guiana*, 224.

[3] Williams, *Fiji and the Fijians*, i. 177.

[4] Ellis, *Ewe*, 160.

[5] Ellis, *Tshi-speaking Peoples*, 241.

[6] Turner, *Nineteen Years in Polynesia*, 228.

[7] Payne, *New World*, i. 445; Markham, *Rites and Laws of the Incas*, 12.

[8] Eur. *Alc.* 100.

the seat of any hostile spiritual influence, the Mikado was not malevolent towards his own people, and yet contact, direct or indirect, with him or them was avoided as scrupulously as contact with a corpse. Besides, the rites for driving away the spirit of the deceased—and there are many such rites[1]—are altogether distinct from and have nothing in common with the precautions taken to prevent contact with the corpse. Fear of evil spirits, therefore, cannot be the source of the world-wide institution of taboo. What the source was, we have yet to consider—in our next chapter.

[1] For some Indo-European rites, see my paper in the *Classical Review* for June 1895.

CHAPTER VIII

TABOO, MORALITY, AND RELIGION

In Polynesia the institution of taboo was closely entwined with the social and political constitutions of the various states; taboos were imposed by the priests and the nobility, and the unwritten code of taboo corresponded in many important respects with the legal and social codes of more advanced civilisations. It is not, therefore, surprising that the earlier students of the system regarded it as an artificial invention, a piece of state-craft, cunningly devised in the interests of the nobility and priests. This view is, however, now generally abandoned. Wider researches have shown that the institution is not due to state-enactment or to priest-craft, for the simple reason that it is most at home in communities which have no state-organisation, and flourishes where there are no priests or no priesthood. Above all, the belief is not artificial and imposed, but spontaneous and universal.

Taboo was next explained, and is still explained, as a religious observance; everything belonging to or connected with a god is forbidden or taboo to man. This explanation, however, has the fault, fatal to a hypothesis, of not accounting for all the facts. It is true that everything sacred is taboo; it is not true that everything taboo is sacred. Temples and all the apparatus of ritual belong to the god, and therefore are taboo; and even the corpse-taboo may be brought into a sort of harmony with this theory, if we assume that the spirit which has left the corpse becomes a god, and if we also further assume that the spirit is regarded as hostile by the mourners. With a little more strain upon the theory, it can be made also to explain the blood-taboo; for the blood is commonly regarded as the seat of, or as itself being the life and the spirit. But it seems too great a strain to say that "new-born children belonged also to the god, and therefore were strictly taboo, together with their mothers."[1] In fine, it is impossible to make out that all things "unclean" were originally "sacred," or to show that the carcases of vermin[2] ever "belonged" to any god.

The latest theory of taboo is that put forward by Mr. Crawley. In his own words, "the principle of Social Taboo is an idea . . . that the attributes assigned to the individual who is feared, loathed, or despised are materially transmissible by contact of any sort."[3] The expression "Social Taboo" seems to imply that its author does not claim for his principle that it explains religious taboo. Anyhow, the gods are not "loathed or despised," and their "attributes" would seem rather to be desirable than things to be shunned. But, without labouring the argument that no explanation is satisfactory which does not account for all the facts, religious as well as social; and without denying that savages think "qualities" are transmissible by physical contact; we may still point out that it is not the transmission of loathed or despised attributes —such as the weakness and timidity of women—that savages fear. "An Australian black-fellow, who discovered that his wife had lain on his blanket . . . died of terror in a fortnight."[4] There was something more here than fear of becoming weak and timid. Again, it is surely a "social" taboo which forbids a slave from touching a chieftain's food; but the sanction of the taboo is no mere fear of contracting the chief's "qualities," as the following instance shows:—"It happened that a New Zealand chief of high rank and great sanctity had left the remains of his dinner by the wayside. A slave, a stout, hungry fellow, coming up after the chief had gone, saw the unfinished dinner, and ate it up without asking questions. Hardly had he finished, when he was informed by a horror-stricken spectator that the food of which he had eaten was the chief's. 'I knew the unfortunate delinquent well. He was remarkable for courage, and had signalised

[1] Gerland, *Anthropologie*, vi. 346.

[2] Lev. xi. 32 ff.

[3] *Folk-Lore* (June 1895), vi. 2. 130.

[4] Frazer, *Golden Bough*, i. 170, referring to *Journ. Anthrop. Inst.* ix. 458.

himself in the wars of the tribe. . . . No sooner did he hear the fatal news than he was seized by the most extraordinary convulsions and cramp in the stomach, which never ceased till he died, about sun-down the same day.' "[1] Contact with the Mikado's clothes or drinking vessels was avoided, not from fear of contracting any of his qualities, but because the clothes would cause swellings and pains all over the body, and the vessels would burn up the throat. Contact with a corpse, which might, one would have thought, lead to contracting the "quality" of death, produces loss of hair and teeth.[2] In Whydah the negroes may not look upon the sacred python, when it goes in procession, because, if they did, "their bodies would at once become the prey of loathsome maggots."[3] Fear of contracting the qualities of the thing loathed does not, as far as appears, seem to be alleged by the savage as his reason for avoiding persons or things taboo. He is not commonly explicit as to the consequences of breaking taboo; he only gets so far as something plainly suggested by the association of ideas, *e.g.* tabooed food will disagree with him more or less seriously; clothes be, like the robe steeped in the blood of Nessus, more or less uncomfortable. But as a rule the consequences are left in the vague; they are matter for private and divers conjectures — the one thing about which the savage has no doubt is that the taboo must not be broken. In fine, the imperative of taboo is categorical, not hypothetical.

The last sentence will have reminded the reader that, according to the Intuitionist school of moral philosophers, what distinguishes the Moral Sentiment and Ethical Laws from all others is precisely the fact that their commands are categorical, and that they require unconditional obedience without regard to the consequences. The man who is honest because to be honest is the best policy, is not actuated by a moral motive, for if dishonesty were a better policy, he would, for the same reason, pursue it; whereas the truly good man is he who does what is right because it is right, no matter what the consequences. That there is further a real connection between taboo and morality has been noticed by Mr.

[1] Frazer, *op. cit.* 168, and A Pakeha Maori, *Old New Zealand*, 96.

[2] Crawley, *Folk-Lore*, *loc. cit.*

[3] Ellis, *Ewe-speaking Peoples*, 61.

Frazer, who says taboo "subserved the progress of civilisation by fostering conceptions of the rights of property and the sanctity of the marriage tie. . . . We shall scarcely err in believing that even in advanced societies the moral sentiments, in so far as they are merely sentiments, and are not based on an induction from experience, derive much of their force from an original system of taboo."[1]

We may now, taking leave of previous theories of taboo, go on our own way; and, as our starting-point, we will take the fact that among savages universally there are some things which categorically and unconditionally must not be done. That this feeling is a "primitive" sentiment, a tendency inherent in the mind of man, the following considerations will, I hope, incline the reader to believe. Though all things taboo are dangerous, not all dangerous things are taboo; for instance, it is not taboo to eat poisonous plants, handle venomous serpents, jump over a precipice, beard the lion, or, in fine, to do anything the danger of which you can discover for yourself, either by your own experience or that of others. On the contrary, it is things which experience could never teach you to be dangerous that are taboo, such as touching a new-born child, or the water in which a holy person has washed. Indeed, experience, so far from being able to generate the belief that these things are dangerous, would have shown that there was no danger in them, and would not have given rise to but have destroyed the belief—the proof of which is that, in Polynesia, the belief in taboo has been broken down chiefly by the fact that Europeans violated taboos innumerable, and were, as the natives saw, none the worse. The sentiment, then, as it appears even in its earliest and lowest manifestations, cannot have been derived from experience; it is prior to and even contradictory to experience. In fine, it is an inherent tendency of the human mind; and as such it does not stand isolated and alone, for in a previous chapter we have seen that the belief in the uniformity of nature, the tendency to expect what has once happened to happen again, is independent of, as it is often disappointed by experience. Between these two sentiments, namely, the positive belief that what you have done

[1] *Encyclopædia Britannica*, s.v. "Taboo."

once you can do again, and the negative belief that there are some things which you must not do, there are other points of contact, as we shall have occasion to note, besides their common origin.

The next point in our theory of taboo is that, though the moral sentiment undoubtedly does "derive much of its force from an original system of taboo," it is not merely in the *morality* of advanced societies that taboo continues to display its force, nor is taboo in its origin specifically moral. In advanced societies there are other things which must not be done, besides immoral acts, *e.g.* irreligious acts, breaches of the code of honour, violations of etiquette, etc. And in savage communities there are things taboo which are not irreligious or immoral, but rather non-moral. But the sentiment, merely as a sentiment and apart from the reason or justification of it, is the same in all cases, namely, that the thing must not be done. The sentiment in itself, therefore, is neither exclusively moral, religious, nor social. In other words, the sentiment is purely formal and without content; the conviction that there are some things which must not be done does not help us at all to know what things they are which must not be done, just as the conviction that what has happened once will happen again under similar circumstances does not tell us whether the circumstances of the second occasion of a given experience are similar to those of the first—whether the a we have before us is really similar to the *a* which was followed by *b*.

How primitive man settled what things were not to be done there is no evidence to show. We will therefore content ourselves with the fact that as far back as we can see in the history—or rather the prehistory—of man, taboo was never grossly material. It marked the awe of man in the presence of what he conceived—often mistakenly—to be the supernatural; and if his dread of contact with blood, babes, and corpses appears at first sight irrational, let us remember that in these, the three classes of objects which are inherently taboo, we have man in relation to the mystery of life and death, and in his affinity to that supernatural power which he conceived to be a spirit like himself. The danger of contact with these objects is "imaginary," if you like, but it is spiritual, *i.e.* it is the feeling that experience, sense-experience, is not the sole source or final test of truth; and that the things which are seen bring man daily into relation with things unseen. For, once more, the essence of taboo is that it is, *à priori*, that without consulting experience it pronounces certain things to be dangerous. Those things, as a matter of fact, were in a sense not dangerous, and the belief in their danger was irrational. Yet had not that belief existed, there would be now no morality, and consequently no civilisation. The things were indeed dangerous, but the danger was for us men of to-day, not for those who obeyed the taboo—for civilisation and not for the savage. It was a danger which no experience at the time could have discovered, so remote was it—and so great.

If the savage appears irrational in his choice of objects to be taboo, his belief in the transmissibility of taboo was equally irrational—and equally essential to the progress of mankind. The belief that every person who touched a thing taboo became himself tabooed, and was a fresh centre of infection to everyone and everything around him, is obviously an *à priori* belief, which is due not to experience at all, but to the association of ideas. The terror of the original taboo spread to all associated with it, and everything that suggested it. This belief was a fallacy, as experience would at once have demonstrated, had the savage dared to make the experiment. But this fallacy was the sheath which enclosed and protected a conception that was to blossom and bear a priceless fruit—the conception of Social Obligation. To respect taboo was a duty towards society, because the man who broke it caught the taboo contagion, and transmitted it to everyone and everything that he came in contact with. Thus the community had a direct and lively interest in requiring that every member should respect taboo. On the other hand, it was equally the interest of the individual to avoid contact with things taboo, because the infection fell first and most fatally on him. Thus private interest and public good coïncided exactly; and the problem that puzzles modern moral philosophers so much, namely, which of the two, if they do not coincide, can a man reasonably be expected to follow, was and would be still absolutely inconceivable in a community where taboo is an institution. It seems, therefore, that those philosophers who regard selfishness as alone "natural" and primitive, have neglected the actual facts of the case, for from the beginning the sense of duty towards society has been necessarily present as a restraining influence on the individual. He has shrunk from violation of taboo not merely as an individual, but also and always as a member of society. The terror with which he viewed the prospect of coming into personal contact with things taboo was identically the same feeling with which he viewed the taboo-breaker. Nor could he, if he broke taboo, hope by secrecy to conceal his offence and escape his punishment, for the taboo contagion infects, as we have seen, even those who unwittingly come in contact with the thing taboo.

That society would not exist, if the individual members thereof did not find their account in supporting it, is undeniable; but it is equally true that no society could exist unless the feeling of social obligation held it together. Now, it is clear that the conviction that a man's own private interest requires him to perform his duty towards the community must have done much to bind society together. It is also obvious that a man must have been powerfully stimulated to do his duty by the further conviction that it was impossible for any violation of duty to be hid. The belief, therefore, in the transmissibility of taboo effected two things. First, by rendering it impossible even to imagine a divergence between private and public good, it protected the growth of the feeling of social obligation until it was strong enough to stand to some extent alone. Next, by inspiring the conviction that all breaches of taboo must inevitably be promptly discovered, it prepared the way for the higher feeling that, whether likely to be discovered or not, wrong must not be done.

But though there were all these possibilities of good in the institution of taboo, it was only amongst the minority of mankind, and there only under exceptional circumstances, that the institution bore its best fruit. For evolution and progress are not identical. Everywhere there has been evolution, but progress has been rare. Indeed, in many respects the evolution of taboo has been fatal to the progress of humanity. The belief in the transmissibility of taboo led, for instance in Polynesia, to the desertion and inhuman abandonment of the sick, who were regarded as taboo, and therefore could not be ministered to, because those who tended them would themselves become taboo. Again, the taboo contagion spread so widely as to check man with its iron hand in every attempt which he might make to subdue nature and utilise her gifts. With its arbitrary and senseless restrictions it overgrows healthy social tendencies and kills them, as moss kills off grass or ivy strangles the tree. The taboo laid on young mothers is extended to all women; hence the separation of man and wife ("I have scarcely ever seen anything like social intercourse between husband and wife," says the Ojibway, Peter Jones), the degradation of women and the destruction of natural affection ("the wife beheld unmoved the sufferings of her husband, and the amusement of the mother was undisturbed by the painful crying of her languishing child"[1]). In religion the institution also had a baneful effect; the irrational restrictions, touch not, taste not, handle not, which constitute formalism, are essentially taboos—indispensable to the education of man at one period of his development, but a bar to his progress later.

The growth of taboo, then, need not detain us. It is amply accounted for by the fatal rapidity with which, thanks to the association of ideas, it spreads over the whole of savage and even semi-civilised life. But the process by which taboo has been converted into an element of civilisation calls for some explanation. The facts with which we have to reckon in our attempt are these: on the one hand, we have a network of innumerable taboos covering the whole life of the savage, restricting in the most irrational and injurious manner his incomings and outgoings, his mode of eating, his family life, his whole existence, from the time when he is taboo as a new-born child to the time when he is a corpse, and as such is equally taboo. On the other, in modern civilisation we have all these taboos cast aside, except those which subserve the cause of morality and religion, and those which lend their force to the code of honour, social etiquette, and minor morals generally. Evidently a process of selection—"natural" or otherwise—has been at work, and the problem is to discover

[1] Ellis, *Polynesian Researches*, iv. 126.

the nature of that process. We might surmise that the selective agency has been experience. Mankind has discovered by experience the baleful consequences of certain taboos, the beneficial effects of others, and has retained the latter while rejecting the former. Not all communities have been equally alert in the work of discrimination; the most discriminating, the quickest to learn by experience, have fared best, the fittest have survived. This theory has its recognised place in moral philosophy under the title of "the Unconscious Utilitarianism of Common Sense"; unconsciously, but none the less effectively, mankind has selected for condemnation as immoral those actions which militate against utility, and has exacted as a moral duty the performance of those which tend to the general good.

The difficulty I have in accepting this theory is that it fails to take into account one of the most marked features of taboo. The very life of taboo as an institution depends on the success with which it forbids the appeal to experience and prevents experiments from being made. If the field of experience were open freely to the savage, doubtless repeated experiment would in course of time teach him, as the theory of unconscious utilitarianism requires that it should. But taboo closes the field to him. He dare not make the experiments which, if made, would enlighten him. Even if accidentally and unintentionally he is led to make such an experiment, instead of profiting by the experience, he dies of fright, as did the Australian slave who ate his master's dinner; or if he does not die, he is tabooed, excommunicated, outlawed; and his fate in either case strengthens the original respect for taboo. The vicious circle with which taboo surrounds the savage is exactly like that which "sympathetic magic" weaves round him. The belief that "like produces like"—which is the foundation of sympathetic magic—blinds his eyes to the facts which should undeceive him, and the teachings of experience fall consequently in vain on ears which will not hear.

Now, the fallacy that like produces like stands in the same relation to the positive belief in the uniformity of nature that the transmissibility of taboo stands in to the negative belief that some things there are which must not be done.

Each belief, the positive and the negative, is inherent in man's mind and indispensable to his welfare. Each, however, is rendered barren or misleading by a fallacy due solely to the association of ideas. From the fallacy of magic man was delivered by religion; and there are reasons, I submit, for believing that it was by the same aid he escaped from the irrational restrictions of taboo.

The reader will have noticed for himself that the action of taboo is always mechanical; contact with the tabooed object communicates the taboo infection as certainly as contact with water communicates moisture, or an electric current an electric shock. The intentions of the taboo-breaker have no effect upon the action of the taboo; he may touch in ignorance, or for the benefit of the person he touches, but he is tabooed as surely as if his motive were irreverent or his action hostile. Nor does the mood of the sacred persons, the Mikado, the Polynesian chief, the priestess of Artemis Hymnia, modify the mechanical action of taboo; their touch or glance is as fatal to friend as foe, to plant life as to human. Still less does the morality of the taboo-breaker matter; the penalty descends like rain alike upon the unjust and the just. In a word, there is no rational principle of action in the operation of taboo; it is mechanical; arbitrary, because its sole basis is the arbitrary association of ideas; irrational, because its principle is "that causal connection in thought is equivalent to causative connection in fact."[1]

On the other hand, the dominant conception of modern civilisation is that the universe is intelligible, that it is constructed on rational principles, and that the reasons of things may be discovered. This is the avowed axiom of metaphysics, which aims at proving the truth of its axiom by presenting an orderly and rational system of the universe. It is the tacit assumption, or the faith, of science, as is shown by the fact that, if a hypothesis, such as that of evolution, fails to account for all the facts which it professes to explain, the man of science infers, not that the facts themselves are unintelligible and not to be accounted for on rational principles, but that his hypothesis is at fault. The

[1] A. Lang, *Myth, Ritual, and Religion*, i. 95.

same assumption is made by the religious sentiment, which, even when most distressed, for example by the apparent triumph of injustice or by problems such as that of the origin of evil, still holds that the facts are capable ultimately of a satisfactory explanation.

The advance, then, which civilisation has made on savagery consists, partially at least, in shaking off the bonds imposed upon the mind by the association of ideas, in seeking a rational instead of a mechanical explanation of things; in fine, to return to the subject of this chapter, in the rationalisation of taboo. Now, wherever the operation of taboo is accepted as an ultimate fact which requires no explanation, there no advance towards its rationalisation can be made, and progress is impossible. But as soon as a taboo is taken up into religion, its character is changed; it is no longer an arbitrary fact, it becomes the command of a divine being, who has reasons for requiring obedience to his ordinances. Not all taboos, however, are taken up into religion; there is a process of selection and rejection. To the consideration of this process we shall return shortly; here all we are concerned with is to point out that when the taboos which receive the sanction of religion are regarded as reasonable, as being the commands of a being possessing reason, then the other taboos also may be brought to the test of reason, and man may gradually learn to disregard those which are manifestly unreasonable. The conviction begins to gain strength that God does not forbid things without a reason; at the same time, religion, by selecting certain taboos to receive its sanction, strengthens them and thereby relatively weakens the force of those which it rejects. The fact that the latter have not received the religious sanction creates a presumption that they are less binding, and makes it easier for man to discard them if they have no reason and no utility. Hence, all the elaborate precautions which are taken by the savage to prevent his food from becoming tabooed, dwindle down to the etiquette of the dining-table; the removal of a garment, lest it should be tabooed by the glance of a superior, is etiolated into civilised man's form of salutation; and the interdict from fire and water as a social penalty survives only in the cut direct. But though restrictions which are manifestly unreasonable and useless have to a large extent been broken down, there are many which nevertheless continue to exist, because they are associated with occasions and feelings, not religious indeed, but still sacred, for instance, the wearing of mourning. This reflection may serve to remind us that pure reason has no great motor power, and is only one of the factors in progress. Taboo has indeed been rationalised, but not in all cases by reason. To understand this we must return to the taboos taken up into religion.

These taboos, as we have said, when they receive the sanction of religion receive a different character; they are no longer arbitrary facts, they are rules of conduct enjoined by a divine being. In the lower forms of religion they are scarcely more rational than other savage taboos, "but the restrictions on individual licence which are due to respect for a known and friendly power allied to man, however trivial and absurd they may appear to us in their details, contain within them germinant principles of social progress and moral order . . . to restrain one's individual licence, not out of slavish fear, but from respect for a higher and beneficent power, is a moral discipline of which the value does not altogether depend on the reasonableness of the sacred restrictions; an English schoolboy is subject to many unreasonable taboos, which are not without their value in the formation of character."[1] In the higher forms of religion, however, the trivial and absurd restrictions are cast off, and those alone retained and emphasised which are essential to morality and religion. The higher forms of religion, however, are the fewer; the lower include the vast majority of mankind, and this fact suffices to show that there is nothing, even in "the respect for a known and friendly power allied to man," which makes it inevitable that religion should automatically rise from lower forms to higher and the highest, nor—to confine ourselves to the matter in hand—is there anything automatic in the growing reasonableness of the sacred restrictions of the higher religions. If one religion differs from another in the reasonableness and moral value of its restrictions, the difference is due to some

[1] Robertson Smith, *Religion of the Semites*, 154.

difference in their conditions. If the religion of one nation differs from that of another in this way, it must be due to some difference in the two nations; the one nation is more capable than the other of distinguishing between the restrictions which are trivial and the restrictions which are of paramount importance for the progress of civilisation. But on examination it becomes apparent that it is not the mass of a nation which initiates any reform in religion, any discovery in science, any new form of art, any new teaching in morals. It is the individual reformer, artist or moral teacher, who starts the new idea, though it rests with the mass to accept his teaching. We have then two factors to take into account: the individual and the community. As regards the former, no one pretends to have discovered the law of the distribution of genius, or to explain why one age or nation should be rich in men of genius and another barren. We can only accept the fact that Greece produced more geniuses in literature and art than any other country, and that there was a remarkable series of religious teachers in Israel. There is no law to account for the one fact or the other; nor can the manifestations of genius be exhibited as the natural consequence of any general conditions. On the other hand, the behaviour of the mass or generality of the nation in face of the new teaching may be traced to the general conditions at work upon them, and the law of the direction which the new teaching took among them may perhaps be ascertained; "and after all it is for the most part the conditions only, and not the originating causes of great spiritual movements, which admit of analysis at the hands of the historian."[1]

It seems, then, that it is individual religious reformers who have carried out the selective process by which the innumerable taboos of savage life have been reduced to the reasonable restrictions which are essential to the well-being of mankind. And the prophets and religious teachers who have selected this and rejected that restriction have usually considered themselves in so doing to be speaking, not their own words or thoughts, but those of their God. This belief has been shared by the community they addressed, otherwise

[1] Rashdall, *Universities of Europe*, i. 32.

the common man would not have gained the courage to break an ancient taboo. Certainly no mere appeal to reason would counterbalance that inveterate terror, just as it was no mere consideration of utility or of purely human interests which supplied the religious reformer with his zeal, or that prompted the denunciations of the prophets. Their message was a supernatural message; and in the same way the process by which mischievous taboos were weeded out may be termed a process not of Natural but of Supernatural Selection.

CHAPTER IX

TOTEMISM

THE last three chapters, though absolutely necessary for our purpose, have been somewhat of a digression from the direct line of the argument. The occasion of the digression was the necessity of examining the subject of taboo generally, in order to acertain whether the corpse-taboo necessarily implied hostility on the part of the spirit of the dead man and consequent fear on the part of the living. Various reasons have been suggested in the course of the digression[1] for answering this question in the negative; and if these reasons be accepted, we are free to believe that the feasts in which the dead were invited to partake were the spontaneous expressions of natural affection; and that the possibility of dealings between man and spiritual beings may thus have been suggested in the first instance. That the desire existed in man to approach the supernatural beings by which he was surrounded, will hardly be doubted, for the importance of conciliating beings with irresistible power for good and for evil was of the highest. It is clear also that the friendship or alliance which man sought to establish between himself and the spirits that he conceived to be supernatural, would be modelled on that which bound together human friends or allies, for there was no other form of alliance or friendship known to him. We have therefore to ask what was the earliest tie which bound man to man; in other words, what was the earliest form of society?

That the nations of the world, before they settled in the countries now occupied by them, were wanderers on the face of the earth, nomads, is a matter which in the case of some

[1] See above, pp. 80, 81.

peoples admits of historic proof, and is not doubted in the case of the rest. The form which society takes amongst nomads is that of tribes or clans, the members of which are akin (however they count kinship) to one another. The normal attitude of these clans to one another is that of hostility; consequently the very existence of a clan depends upon the promptitude and success with which the whole of the small community comes to the rescue of any one of its members when threatened with danger, or, if too late to save his life, inflicts punishment on the hostile clan. On the other hand, not merely the slayer but all his kin are responsible for his deed: if their clan is to exist, they must protect him as any other member with their united strength; and hence, as the kinsmen of the slain man have the whole of the slayer's clan arrayed against them, it is immaterial to them whether they avenge themselves upon the actual slayer or not, as long as they kill some one of his clan. Thus the individual's only safety was in the help and protection of the clan to which he belonged: outside that circle he was helpless and alone. In fine, the only type of friendship known to man, in this stage of society, is that of clansmen one to another, each of whom is ready to lay down his life to protect or avenge his kinsman.[1] But if a man—or any other being, for the matter of that—is not by birth one of your kin, how then is it possible to form any friendly relation, to enter into any engagement or compact with him? There is only one way: if he is not by birth one of your clan, he must become one; if the same blood does not circulate in your veins, it must be introduced into them; in a word, a blood-covenant must be made between you, and then the fellowship between you becomes sacred and inviolable, for you are now kinsmen, one flesh and one blood. Examples of this proceeding are to be found all over the world; one or two may be given here. "The exchange of blood is often practised amongst the blacks of Africa, as a token of alliance

[1] That the blood-feud is a world-wide and universal institution is so well known that illustrations of it are unnecessary. A good collection will be found in Post, *Die Geschlechtsgenossenschaft der Urzeit*, 155–174. Other instances: Dobrizhoffer, *Abipones*, ii. 280; Im Thurn, *Indians of Guiana*, 329; *Journ. of Anth. Inst.* xxiv. 171 ff.; Bastian, *Der Mensch*, iii. 25, 26.

and friendship. The Mambettu people, after having inflicted small wounds upon each other's arms, reciprocally suck the blood which flows from the incision. In the Unyora country the parties dip two coffee-berries into the blood and eat them. Amongst the Sandeh the proceedings are not so repulsive; the operator, armed with two sharp knives, inoculates the blood of one person into the wound of the other."[1] The exact manner in which this last operation is performed is described by Mr. Ward, who himself submitted to it. After noting that blood-brotherhood is "a form of cementing friendship and a guarantee of good faith, popular with all Upper Congo tribes," he proceeds: "An incision was made in both our right arms, in the outer muscular swelling just below the elbow, and as the blood flowed in a tiny stream, the charm doctor sprinkled powdered chalk and potash on the wounds, delivering the while, in rapid tones, an appeal to us to maintain unbroken the sanctity of the contract; and then our arms being rubbed together, so that the flowing blood intermingled, we were declared to be brothers of one blood, whose interests henceforth should be united as our blood now was."[2] In Surinam, when natives make a compact, the Godoman (priest) draws blood from the contracting parties, pours some on the ground, and gives them the rest to drink.[3] The ancient Scyths preferred to drink the blood. Herodotus[4] says they poured into a great bowl wine mixed with the blood of the contracting parties; then they dipped into the bowl a dagger, some arrows, an axe, and a javelin, and when they had done that, they made many imprecations and drank of the bowl, both they and the most distinguished of their followers. Again, "the drinking of blood on the occasion of an alliance, compact, or oath, was common among the ancient Magyars. The anonymous Notarius of King Béla (c. 5. 6) says, *more paganismo fusis propriis sanguinibus in unum vas ratum fecerunt iuramentum*."[5] Among the Southern Slavs to this day blood-feuds are common, and may be terminated by the parties to the feud becoming blood-brothers. This is effected

[1] Casati, *Ten Years in Equatoria*, i. 177.
[2] Ward, *Five Years with the Congo Cannibals*, 131.
[3] Bastian, *Der Mensch*, ii. 290. [4] *Hdt.* iv. 70.
[5] *Am Urquell*, iii. 270.

by a representative of one *bratstva* sucking blood from the vein of the right wrist of a representative of the other *bratstva*, whereby all the members of the one clan become blood-brothers to all the members of the other. Mohammedan women do not veil themselves in the presence of such blood-brothers, even if Christians, any more than they would before their other blood-relations.[1] This last instance is important, because it faithfully preserves the primitive view that the blood-brotherhood thus established is not a relationship personal to the two parties alone, but extends to the whole of each clan: my brother is, or becomes, the brother of all my brethren; the blood which flows in the veins of either party to the blood-covenant flows in the veins of all his kin.

Thus in this the most primitive form of society, men were divided into clans or tribes; these tribes were usually hostile to one another, but might by means of the blood-covenant make alliance with one another. The individual only existed as long as he was protected by his clan; he can scarcely be said to have had an individual existence, so crushing was the solidarity which bound kinsmen together under the pressure of the clan's struggle for existence with other clans. If the individual kinsman slew a stranger, the whole kin were responsible; if he was slain by a stranger, they all required satisfaction. If the individual kinsman made a blood-covenant with a stranger, the whole of each tribe was bound thereby.

It was inevitable, therefore, that man, who imagined all things, animate or inanimate, to think and act and feel like himself, should imagine that the societies of these other spirits was organised like the only society of which he had any knowledge, namely, that form of human society into which he himself was born. In so doing, primitive man was but anticipating the Homeric Greek who modelled the society of Olympus on an earthly pattern. Now, the things by which man is surrounded are as a matter of fact divided into natural kinds, genera and species; and it is small wonder if man detected a resemblance between the natural kinds of animals, plants, etc., and the kins or clans into which human society

[1] *Am Urquell*, i. 196.

was divided. That he actually did consider these classes of objects as organisations of the same kind as human clans, is shown by the fact that savages have blood-feuds with these natural kinds as they would with clans of human beings. Amongst the Kookies, a man's whole tribe takes vengeance if one of them is killed by an animal or any wild beast; and if a tree has fallen on him and killed him, it is cut up by them into the finest splinters, which are scattered to the winds:[1] it is not essential that the very animal should be killed, but only that it should be one of the same species.[2] On the other hand, it is believed that the whole of the animal's clan will take up the blood-feud on behalf of any one of them against men. The Lapps and Ostiaks dread a blood-feud with the Bear clan, and accordingly, before killing a bear, they try to persuade him to fall a willing sacrifice, by explaining to him at length the exalted and flattering uses to which his flesh, fat, and pelt will be put.[3] The Arabs in the same way must apologise to an animal before killing it.[4] "It is generally believed by the natives of Madagascar, that the crocodile never, except to avenge an injury, destroys innocent persons";[5] an aged native about to cross a river "addressed himself to the crocodile, urging him to do him no injury, because he had never done him (the crocodile) any; and assuring him that he had never engaged in war against any of his species . . . at the same time adding, that if he came to attack him, vengeance, sooner or later, would follow; and that if he devoured him, all his relatives and all his race would declare war against him."[6] The Indians of Guiana endeavour also to avert blood-feuds with animals. "Before leaving a temporary camp in the forest, where they have killed a tapir and dried the meat on a babracot, Indians invariably destroy this babracot, saying that should a tapir, passing that way, find traces of the slaughter of one of his kind, he would come by night on the next occasion when Indians slept at that place, and, taking a man, would

[1] Bastian, *Der Mensch*, iii. 25.

[2] Tylor, *Primitive Culture*, i. 286, referring to *As. Res.* vii. 189.

[3] Bastian, *Der Mensch*, iii. 5.

[4] *Ibid.* 6.

[5] Ellis, *History of Madagascar*, i. 53.

[6] *Ibid*, 57, quoting "Monsieur de V., whose voyage to Madagascar was published in 1722."

babracot him in revenge."[1] It is not, therefore, surprising if man can have blood-feuds with animal clans as he has with human, that he should seek to establish an alliance with one of these kinds of beings, in the same way and on the same principle as with one of the various human kins with which he came in contact. It is to be presumed that in the choice of an ally he would prefer the kind which he believed to possess supernatural powers, or if several possessed such powers, then the kind or species which possessed the greatest power. In any case, however, it was not, and from the nature of the circumstances could not be, an individual supernatural being with which he sought alliance, but a class or kind of beings with supernatural powers. But this is precisely a totem. "A totem is never an isolated individual, but always a class of objects, generally a species of animals or of plants, more rarely a class of inanimate natural objects, very rarely a class of artificial objects."[2] "It is not merely an individual, but the species that is reverenced."[3] Thus, if the owl be a totem, as in Samoa, and an owl was found dead, "this was not the death of the god: he was supposed to be yet alive and incarnate in all the owls in existence."[4] But just as it was impossible in the then stage of society to make an alliance with a single member of another kin or kind, and therefore it was always the species and never an individual merely that became a totem, so it was impossible for the compact to be made between the totem species and one individual man—it was also and necessarily a covenant between the clan and the class of objects chosen as a totem. In other words, from the beginning religion was not an affair which concerned the individual only, but one which demanded the co-operation of the whole community; and a religious community was the earliest form of society.

As a clan consists of those in whose veins the same blood runs, and who are therefore one flesh, the totem animal is spoken of, by the Mount Gambier tribe for instance, as being their *tumanang*, *i.e.* their flesh, and is treated in all respects as a clansman. Now, in the primitive, nomad stage, the most sacred and inviolable duty is to respect the blood of the kin:

[1] Im Thurn, *Indians of Guiana*, 352.
[2] Frazer, *Totemism*, 2.
[3] *Ibid.* 15.
[4] Turner, *Samoa*, 21.

a clan in which the kinsmen should shed each other's blood would speedily perish; only those clans could survive in the struggle for existence which rigorously observed this fundamental duty. All blood, even of animals, was, as we have seen, taboo, but the blood of a kinsman was even more, it was sacred: the restriction, by this change in its content, is raised from the taboo-level to the plane of morality. In times when it became possible or customary to accept compensation, wer-geld, for the slaying of a clansman, in lieu of the blood which could alone originally atone for his death, no compensation could be accepted for the killing of a clansman by a clansman. It was the unpardonable offence; the Erinyes of a dead kinsman were implacable. In this case, and this case alone, killing was murder. Now the totem animal is a clansman, and its life therefore is sacred: a man never kills his totem; to do so would be murder. Thus the Osages "abstained from hunting the beaver, 'because in killing that animal they killed a brother of the Osages.'"[1] Abstaining from killing his totem, he also endeavours to protect it from being killed by others; and if he fails to do so, then, amongst the Indians of Columbia, "he will demand compensation,"[2] as he would for the death of any other kinsman. The dead totem animal is mourned for and buried with the same ceremonies as a clansman. In Samoa, "if a man found a dead owl by the roadside, and if that happened to be the incarnation of his village god, he would sit down and weep over it and beat his forehead with stones till the blood flowed."[3] Of all food, the totem is most taboo; death and sicknesses of various kinds are believed to be the consequence, if a man eats, even unwittingly, of his totem animal or plant. Like other things taboo, the totem as food is dangerous even to see; and it is well generally to avoid mentioning its name.

As the totem animal becomes a member of the human clan, so the human clansman becomes a member of the animal's clan. This he indicates "by dressing in the skin or other part of the totem animal, arranging his hair and mutilating his body so as to resemble the totem."[4] Thus, among the Thlinkets, at a funeral feast a relative of the

[1] Frazer, 8, quoting Lewis and Clark, i. 12.
[2] Frazer, 8.
[3] Turner, *Nineteen Years in Polynesia*, 242.
[4] Frazer, 26.

deceased appears clad in the dress that represents the totem, and is welcomed by the assembly with the cry of the animal.[1] Amongst the Iowas, "the Buffalo clan wear two locks of hair in imitation of horns." [2] Various peoples chip their teeth so that they resemble the teeth of cats, crocodiles, or other animals.

It is at the great crises of life that the totem dress is especially worn, for thus the wearer is placed under the close protection of the totem. The child, which at birth is taboo, and as such is outside the community just as much as a person who has been tabooed or outlawed, is received into "the savage church," [3] by being dressed or painted to resemble the tribal totem. The skin of the sheep, on which, at a Roman marriage, the bride and bridegroom were made to sit, may be a relic of totemism.[4]

At death, the clansman was supposed to join his totem and to assume the totem animal's form—this was intimated sometimes by a ceremony such as that of the Thlinkets described above, and sometimes by the grave-post or tombstone. "In Armenia proper the oldest grave-stones are cut into the shape of a crouching ram with the inscription on the side of the body." [5] In Luzon a deceased chieftain is laid in a monument shaped like a buffalo or a pig; [6] and the Negritos bury in a tomb roughly shaped to resemble an ox or a boar.[7] Again, the ceremonies which amongst savage races generally accompany "the introduction of the young to complete manhood or womanhood, and to full participation in the savage church," which ceremonies "correspond, in short, to confirmation," [8] are a part of totemism. Their design, or the leading part of their design, is to communicate to him the blood of the totem and the clan, and thus to unite him a second time and more closely to the community in its religious aspect. In the Dicyerie tribe of Australians the ceremony is thus described: the boy is taken and his arm bound to the arm of an old man; the latter's vein is opened above the elbow

[1] Bastian, *Rechtsverhältnisse*, 295.
[2] Frazer, 27.
[3] The phrase is Mr. A. Lang's, *Myth, Ritual, and Religion*, i. 281.
[4] Frazer, 34.
[5] Bastian, *Rechtsverhältnisse*, 293.
[6] Bastian, *Oest. Asien*, v. 272.
[7] Bastian, *Der Mensch*, ii. 231.
[8] Lang, *Myth, Ritual, and Religion*, i. 281.

and his blood allowed to flow over the boy. Another and another man is substituted, until the boy is completely covered with blood,[1] and thus is made effectually one blood with the tribe. The blood is the life; and that the ceremony is intended to give a new life to the youth, and to be a new birth for him, is proved by the fact that in some tribes the youth is supposed first to be killed and then after initiation has to pretend to forget all that ever he did or was before the ceremony; whilst in others a mimetic representation of the resurrection of a clansman accompanies the ceremony.

As the totem animal is a member of his human clansmen's tribe and the clansmen are members of the animal's clan, it follows that men and totem animals are descended from a common ancestor, which common ancestor is universally conceived by primitive totem clans to have been animal and not human; and myths are accordingly invented to account for the fact that some of his descendants have assumed human form, "thus the Turtle clan of the Iroquois are descended from a fat turtle, which, burdened by the weight of its shell in walking, contrived by great exertions to throw it off, and thereafter gradually developed into a man."[2] When totemism is decaying, myths are invented with precisely the opposite purpose, namely, to explain how it was that the ancestor ever assumed animal form. The "metamorphoses" of the gods in Greek mythology are probably thus to be accounted for, as Mr. Lang has argued in his *Myth, Ritual, and Religion*.

Let us now see how this alliance between a human kin and a species of natural objects, conceived as superhuman, affected the parties to it. Man's attitude to the world around him was at once changed: he had gained the supernatural ally he sought, and thus was enabled to make that free use of nature which was the condition of material progress, but which was debarred him by the restrictions imposed upon his action by fear of supernatural terrors. But his ally's place in nature was also changed by the alliance: this supernatural power was distinguished from all others by the fact that it was in alliance with him. It became a permanently friendly power; in a word, it became a god, whereas all other spirits remained evil, or at anyrate hostile powers, by whom a man

[1] Bastian, *Allerlei*, i. 171. [2] Frazer, 3.

could only expect to be treated as he was treated by—and as indeed he himself treated—members of a strange clan. Other tribes might and did have their supernatural allies, as my clan had, and those allies were gods, because they had a definite circle of worshippers whom they permanently assisted, but they were no gods of mine. But these two classes of supernatural powers did not exhaust the world of superhuman spirits: there were spirits not attached to any human clan, having no circle of worshippers to whom they were friendly; that is to say, they were hostile to all men, implacable.

In a previous chapter[1] we have examined and combated the view that man begins by endeavouring to constrain and coerce the supernatural powers by which he conceives himself to be surrounded; and that he is encouraged to use such compulsion either because he has not yet learnt to distinguish between the natural and the supernatural, and therefore believes himself to be as strong as these spirits, or because he thinks himself to possess magical powers and so to be stronger than they. Now, this view, that man feels himself a match or more than a match for the non-human powers by which he is surrounded, is absolutely opposed to the abject terror in which savages stand towards these spirits. What Mr. Im Thurn says of the Indians of Guiana is true of all savages: "It is almost impossible to overestimate the dreadful sense of constant and unavoidable danger in which the Indian would live, were it not for his trust in the protecting power of his peaiman."[2] There is, however, an argument in support of this view, which we did not mention at the time, because the proper reply to it would have required us to anticipate this chapter. The argument is that—the lowest savages having none but material conceptions of the universe—evil spirits originally "are dealt with by mere physical force";[3] and instances may be found of the forcible, physical expulsion of evil spirits.[4] But—to say nothing of the fact that taboo, the most potent influence over the savage mind, is not a material

[1] *Supra*, pp. 24 ff., 35 ff.

[2] Im Thurn, *Indians of Guiana*, 333. The peaiman "is not simply the doctor, but also in some sense the priest," p. 328.

[3] Payne, *New World*, i. 390.

[4] Payne, *loc. cit.*, and Frazer, *Golden Bough*, ii. 158-182.

conception[1]—forcible expulsion of evil spirits is in the majority of cases one part of an annual ceremony, of which an essential feature is some rite or other for gaining the protection of the friendly god as a preliminary to this combat with the evil spirits. Probably more accurate observation would show that the assistance of a supernatural ally is a *sine quâ non* of all such demonstrations. At anyrate, if totemism may be taken to be a stage of development through which all peoples have passed, we may fairly argue that it was the consciousness of possessing a supernatural ally which first nerved the savage to attack a supernatural power.

Other writers, again, rightly recognising that the ruling desire of the savage is to avoid giving offence to the many evil spirits, have not only jumped to the conclusion that religion was born of fear—*primus in orbe timor fecit deos*—but have been led by the prejudice to mal-observation of the facts of savage life. For instance, it was in North America that totemism flourished to a degree unequalled elsewhere save in Australia; and yet "amongst all of the American tribes the worship of spirits that are malicious and not of those that are good, is a characteristic that has been noticed with much astonishment, and commented upon by travellers and other writers"[2]—the fact being simply that the totem-god is left out of account by these writers. "Pure unmixed devil-worship prevails through the length and breadth of the land," says another writer,[3] who perhaps, however, only means by "devil-worship" the worship of false gods, just as so many travellers apply the term "sorcerer" to men whose function in the community is actually to counteract magic and sorcery, and who are then quoted to show that the priest is evolved out of the sorcerer and religion out of magic. "But however true it is that savage man feels himself to be environed by innumerable dangers which he does not understand, and so personifies as invisible or mysterious enemies of more than human power, it is not true that the attempt to appease these powers is the foundation of religion. From the earliest times, religion, as distinct from magic or sorcery, addresses itself to kindred and friendly beings, who may indeed be angry with

[1] *Supra*, p. 68.
[2] Dorman, *Primitive Superstitions*, 30.
[3] Shea, *Catholic Missions*, 25.

their people for a time, but are always placable except to the enemies of their worshippers or to renegade members of the community. It is not with a vague fear of unknown powers, but with a loving reverence for known gods who are knit to their worshippers by strong bonds of kinship, that religion in the only true sense of the word begins."[1] "When the Spanish missionaries questioned the Indians as to the origin of their gods, the usual reply was that they had come from the air or heaven to dwell among them and do them good."[2] The last words, which are not quite reconcilable with the view that religion sprang from fear, express the native view.

In virtue of the kinship between the god and his worshippers, the killing of a fellow-clansman comes to be regarded in a totem-clan as the same thing as killing the god. In Mangaia "such a blow was regarded as falling upon the god [totem] himself; the literal sense of *ta atua* [to kill a member of the same totem-clan] being god-striking or god-killing."[3] Thus the blood-taboo, which became an element of morality when it lent its force to the respect for kindred blood, is now taken up into religion, and murder becomes not only a moral but a religious offence. That the taboo on new-born children and immature youths was made to yield a higher significance when taken up by totemism, we have already noted.[4] Here we need only add that the initiation to which the youth was subjected is not merely ceremonial, but is generally accompanied by such moral teaching as the savage is capable of. Amongst the Koranas the boy is taught not to steal, not to jeer at the weak or unfortunate, not to drink the milk of goat or sheep, and not to eat the flesh of jackal or hare.[5]

Thus loyalty to the clan-god is loyalty not merely to the totem, but to the morality which, though elementary, is the highest the savage knows; and fidelity to the clan-god involved hostility to false gods, for as the clans of men were

[1] Robertson Smith, *Religion of the Semites*, 55.
[2] Payne, *New World*, i. 397.
[3] Gill, *Myths and Songs of the South Pacific*, 38, and Frazer, 58.
[4] *Supra*, p. 103. Children are often considered taboo, and therefore outside the community, until they grow up and are initiated.
[5] Bastian, *Oest. Asien*, v. 291.

hostile one to another, so were their gods. Hence the god of each tribe protected his own men, and went in person with them to war—an idea which totemism bequeathed to more advanced stages in religion, for instance to Peruvian polytheism. "During the revolt of the Collao . . . the Colla warriors . . . carried an idol of the Sun during the campaign";[1] and to the polytheistic negroes of the Gold Coast, where "in time of war the struggle is not carried on by the opposing tribes alone, for the protecting deities of each side are believed also to be contending together, each striving to achieve success for his own people; and they are believed to be as much interested in the result of the war as the people engaged."[2] As loyalty to the god of the community is a sentiment without which monotheism could never have triumphed over lower forms of belief, so the recognition that there could be other (hostile) gods as well as the god of a man's own clan was the germ of polytheism. It is only by the fusion of several tribes that a nation can be created, and this fusion carries with it—or is caused by—the amalgamation of their respective cults. But this only takes place after totem times, when the nomad clan has become the village community.

The relation between the human kin and the totem species, which at first is one of alliance, and therefore, in consequence of the blood-covenant, one of blood-relationship, eventually changes its character somewhat, for the kinship between men and animals comes to require explanation. The requisite explanation is afforded by a myth which makes the original ancestor of the two kins an animal. Hence the members of the human community become the god's children, and the god their father—not the actual, human father who begat them, for he is alive (and when he dies, his death makes no difference), but a hypothetical father, so to speak, *i.e.* one that reason led them to assume, as the only way of accounting for the actual facts (namely, their kinship with their totem); and the verification of this primitive hypothesis was found by them in their inner experience, *i.e.* in the filial reverence and affection which they felt towards him. Doubtless it was not all or most men who had this experience, or

[1] Payne, *New World*, i. 515.

[2] Ellis, *Tshi-speaking Peoples*, 77.

rather it was but few who attended to the feeling, but the best must have paid heed to it and have found satisfaction in dwelling on it, else the conception of the deity would never have followed the line on which as a matter of fact it developed. The result was that the god tended to be conceived—and, when the time for art came, to be represented—no longer in animal but in human form.

The compact between the clan and its supernatural ally not only altered the relation of each to the rest of the universe, but it also changed the relation of the clansmen to one another. Henceforth they were united not only by blood but by religion: they were not merely a society but a religious community. The aid rendered by the god to the clan in its conflicts with its enemies, human or superhuman, and his habitual affection for his own people, constituted a claim both upon each member of the community and upon the community as a whole. Hence, if any man offended the clan-god, the god's quarrel was taken up by the whole of the rest of the community, and by them, if necessary, the offender was punished and the god avenged. The acts which offended him were, roughly speaking, things which, according to the savage's *à priori* feeling, "must not be done," *i.e.* are taboo, such as intruding upon the god's privacy, or having to do with persons outside the community, namely, new-born children, strangers, and outlaws, or coming into contact with blood, and so on. Some of these acts, *e.g.* the shedding of kindred blood, are condemned by us as immoral and sinful; we can therefore hardly blame the savage, to whom they were all equally repugnant, for treating them all as offences both against the community and against the god, and punishing them as such. In this joint action of the community as a collective whole, prompted by religion, we have the first appearance of what was hereafter to be the state—the first, because here the authority of the community is not delegated, as it is when a war-leader is elected: the method of executing the criminal is stoning, in which the whole community joins.

If it is in love and not in fear that religion in any true sense of the word has its origin, it is none the less true that fear—not of irrational dangers, but of deserved punishment—

is essential to the moral and religious education of man: it is "the fear of the Lord" that is "the beginning of wisdom." That the lowest savages are a perpetual prey to irrational terror, and believe sickness and death to be unnatural and to be the work in all cases of evil spirits, is matter of common knowledge. It was inevitable, therefore, that the supernatural ally of a human kin should continue to exercise this power of causing disease and death. But whereas the belief that disease is due to evil spirits is fatal not only to a right understanding of the action of natural causes and to all intellectual progress, but also prevents fear from becoming an instrument in the moral education of man, the ascription of sickness to the agency of a friendly power has a different result. This action on his part, his departure from the usually benevolent behaviour shown by him to his own people, can only be explained by the assumption that he has been in some way offended by them. The possible modes of offence are known; they are such as have been mentioned in the last paragraph, and though they at first include many which religion, as it advances, sets aside by a process of "supernatural selection," they include offences which we recognise to be immoral, and on the checking of which the further progress of morality depended. But in that the earliest stage of society, unless the restrictions which we see to be irrational, and stigmatise as taboos, had been enforced, neither could those have been enforced which really contained the germs of morality.

We have seen, at the beginning of this chapter, that there was one such restriction (against shedding kindred blood) on which not merely the morality but the very existence of the clan depended, and that the mere fact of a clan's survival in the struggle for existence is proof conclusive that the restriction was obeyed. But though a clan's survival proves that the restriction must have been obeyed, it does not show what it was that made the clansmen obey it. In some clans it was not obeyed, and those clans perished. That a dim perception of the utility, perhaps of the necessity, of curbing personal animosity may have existed, we will admit. But that a savage, smarting under personal resentment, would stay his hand, out of consideration for such a remote and uncertain contingency as the possibility of eventual injury to a future generation, is a supposition opposed to all we know of savages. There must have been some other motive, and that a strong one, appealing to personal fear. That motive was doubtless in part supplied by fear of punishment at the hands of the collective community. But such punishment was only meted out when the offence was against the god of the community; and what stimulated the community to its duty in this regard was the manifestation from time to time of the god's wrath, in the shape of pestilence, etc., betokening that an offence had been committed against him. Thus in Peru, in the time of the Incas, "when any general calamity occurred, the members of the community were rigorously examined, until the sinner was discovered and compelled to make reparation";[1] and the same interpretation was put upon private calamity, *e.g.* amongst the Abipones, "at his first coming the physician overwhelms the sick man with an hundred questions: 'Where were you yesterday?' says he. 'What roads did you tread? Did you overturn the jug and spill the drink prepared from the maize? What? have you imprudently given the flesh of a tortoise, stag, or boar [totem-gods] to be devoured by dogs?' Should the sick man confess to having done any of these things, 'It is well,' replies the physician, 'we have discovered the cause of your disorder.'"[2] The same thing is reported from Mexico, Peru, Honduras, Yucatan, Salvador,[3] and was common enough in other quarters of the globe. Nor must it be supposed that it was only offences against ritual that provoked the god to manifest his displeasure. "In Tahiti, sickness was the occasion for making reparation for past sins, *e.g.* by restoring stolen property."[4] But sickness and public calamities are not perpetual, and as "sanctions" they are external at the best: they are too intermittent and accidental to exert the uniform pressure necessary if any permanent moral advance is to be made, and they rather punish than prevent transgression. It is not only external and physical

[1] Payne, *New World*, i. 443.
[2] Dobrizhoffer, *History of the Abipones*, ii. 18.
[3] Dorman, *Primitive Superstitions*, 57.
[4] Waitz, *Anthropologie*, vi. 396.

punishment which enforces the restrictions essential to the tribe's existence, but also the internal consciousness of having disregarded the claim which the affection of the protecting clan-god for his people establishes on one and all of the community. In a word, from the beginning, offences against the community are felt not only as immoral but also as sins. To the external sequence of calamity consequent upon transgression there corresponds the internal sense of lesion in the bond of mutual goodwill which marks the alliance between the clansmen and their god.

We have now examined the way in which men and gods were affected respectively by the alliance formed between them. But what shall we say of the third member to the alliance, the totem species of plant or animal? did it remain unaffected by the alliance? Mr. Frazer concludes his *Totemism* with the following pregnant passage: "Considering the far-reaching effects produced on the fauna and flora of a district by the preservation or extinction of a single species of animals or plants, it appears probable that the tendency of totemism to preserve certain species of plants and animals must have largely influenced the organic life of the countries where it has prevailed. But this question, with the kindred question of the bearing of totemism on the original domestication of animals and plants, is beyond the scope of the present article."[1] Neither has a history of religion anything apparently to do with the domestication of plants and animals. Yet it is only by taking it as our starting-point that we can solve the difficult and important problem, why so few traces of totemism are to be found in the great civilisations of the world.

[1] Frazer, *Totemism*, 95, 96.

CHAPTER X

SURVIVALS OF TOTEMISM

IMPORTANT as totemism is as a stage of religious development, it is almost more important in the history of material civilisation, for totemism was the prime motor of all material progress. Material progress means the accumulation of wealth. Of the various forms which wealth can take, the most important is food, for until food is provided it is impossible to proceed to the production of any other kind of wealth. If the whole time and energies of a community are exhausted in scraping together just enough food to carry on with, there is no leisure or strength left for the production of any other kind of wealth. Now, that is the case in which those nomad clans find themselves who depend for their food upon hunting, fishing, and the gathering of fruits and roots—the "natural basis of subsistence."[1] But with those wandering clans which succeed in domesticating the cow, sheep, goat, and other animals, the case is very different. The labour of obtaining food is greatly economised, and the labour thus set free can be employed in the production of those other kinds of wealth which constitute the riches of a pastoral people. When cereals and other food-plants come to be cultivated, and agriculture makes a wandering life no longer possible, food-production is still further quickened, and "the substitution of an artificial for a natural basis of subsistence"[2] is completed. Until this substitution takes place, civilisation is impossible; and whatever started this substitution, *i.e.* led to the domestication of plants and animals, started the movement of material progress.

Now, of the innumerable species of plants and animals

[1] Payne, *New World*, i. 276. [2] *Ibid.*

which exist or have existed on the face of the earth, only a relatively very small number are capable of domestication; and before they were brought under cultivation there was nothing whatever in their appearance or in man's scanty experience to indicate that they, and they alone, could be domesticated. How, then, did he light upon exactly those kinds which were capable of cultivation? Simply by trying all. Those kinds which were incapable of domestication remained wild; the few that could be cultivated became our domestic animals and plants. But though man "tried" all kinds, he was not aware that he was making experiments, still less that the consequence of his attempts would be the "domestication" of certain species. How could he be, when the very idea of "domestic animals" had not yet dawned upon man's mind? It could, then, have been no consideration of utility, no prospective personal benefit, no foresight of the consequences, that made man all over the globe attempt to domesticate every species of animal that he came across—indeed, he did not know that he was "domesticating" it.[1] The suggestion that his motive was amusement[2] does not supply an adequate cause; granted that amusement might lead a man here and there to capture an animal and try to tame it, we cannot suppose the whole human race in every latitude and on every continent giving itself up to this kind of "amusement," as we must suppose, if we are thus to account for the domestication of animals—to say nothing of plants. And when we bear in mind that the savage is usually incapable of steady, continuous, persistent effort, we shall require a more potent cause than amusement as a motive for the long labour of domestication. But in totemism we have a cause persistent, world-wide, and adequate to account for the facts. The totem animal, not merely an individual but the whole species, is reverenced, protected, and allowed, or rather encouraged to increase and multiply over the whole area traversed by the tribe—and the area

[1] The above argument is borrowed from Galton, *Inquiries into Human Faculty*, 243–270. He also recognises the sanctity of certain animals as one of the causes leading to the domestication of animals, but does not mention totemism, and thinks that the savage's habit of making pets is the chief cause.

[2] Lord Kames, *Sketches*, bk. i. sk. 1 (Payne, 282).

required for the support of a nomad family is considerable. This treatment is continued for generations, for it is the religion of the tribe. The appearance of the animal is welcomed with rejoicing as the manifestation of the tribal deity, offerings are made to it, and, being free from molestation, it discovers the fact, acquires confidence, and if it has the instinct of domestication, ceases to be wild. In a word, the animal becomes tame—which is a different thing from being tamed.

It may perhaps seem inconsistent with this theory of the origin of an artificial food-supply, that the totem is never consumed as food. But it is not by eating their cattle that a pastoral people become rich, but by abstaining from eating them. The cattle are their capital; the interest thereof, on which they live, consists of the milk and its products. It is not until nomad life is given up and agriculture has provided another and even more abundant source of food, that the community becomes rich enough to afford to eat the flesh of their cattle; and by that time the clan, of which the totem was an honoured member, and to which its flesh was taboo, has itself dissolved and made way for those local organisations which hold a nation together. In the same way, it is not by consuming corn that wheat is grown, but by abstaining from its consumption. To make it an extinct species, all that is required is to consume every ear of corn existing. The savage required no teaching in the art of consumption; it is the lesson of abstinence which it is hard for him to learn. That lesson he was incapable of teaching himself, but totemism taught him. The fact that the agricultural is universally a later stage in the development of civilisation than the pastoral, is, we may conjecture, because animal preceded plant totems: animals have the blood which is necessary for the blood-covenant between the human kin and the totem kind; and it was only later that plants possessing a sap or juice which may act as blood, especially if it is reddish in colour, came to be adopted as totems.

The domestication of plants is a question to which we shall recur in a subsequent chapter, and the reader is requested, therefore, to suspend judgment on this point. But, as it may appear a paradox to assert that men learnt to eat cattle by abstaining from eating them, perhaps a few more words in elucidation should be given. The ordinary theory of the beginnings of domestication is presumably that the hunter, having learnt by experience that beef was good, or that "mountain sheep are sweet," resolved to spare the young animals and breed from them. To this there are two objections. First, the savage, having practically no thought for the morrow, is habitually reckless and wasteful in consumption, eats all he can, and only goes hunting again when there is absolutely nothing left to eat. Next, as a matter of fact, their cattle are precisely the animals which pastoral peoples do not eat. "The common food of these races is milk or game; cattle are seldom killed for food, and only on exceptional occasions, such as the proclamation of a war,"[1] etc. Amongst the Zulus the killing of a cow "is seldom and reluctantly done."[2] "A Kaffir does not often slaughter his cattle, except for sacrifice or to celebrate a marriage."[3] "Every idea and thought of the Dinka is how to acquire and maintain cattle; a kind of reverence would seem to be paid to them . . . a cow is never slaughtered, but when sick it is segregated from the rest and carefully tended in the large huts built for the purpose . . . indescribable is the grief when either death or rapine has robbed a Dinka of his cattle. He is prepared to redeem their loss by the heaviest sacrifices, for they are dearer to him than wife or child."[4] "Though the Indian women breed fowl and other domestic animals in their cottages, they never eat them . . . much less kill them."[5] The Battas of Sumatra (who are totemists) have domesticated "the buffalo, dog, pig, goat, fowl, and horse; buffaloes and goats, dogs and horses (which latter are carefully fattened), as a rule never serve for food except at festivals."[6]

It is therefore the ordinary theory of domestication that is paradoxical, for it assumes that man domesticates animals

[1] Robertson Smith, *Religion of the Semites*, 297.
[2] *Ibid.* quoting Shaw, *Memorials of South Africa*, 59.
[3] Shooter, *Kafirs of Natal*, 28.
[4] Schweinfurth, *Heart of Africa*, i. 163.
[5] Ulloa, quoted in Galton, *Inquiries into Human Faculty*, 247.
[6] Waitz, *Anthropologie*, v. 1. 183.

for no other purpose than to eat them, and then does not eat them. On the other hand, the view here advanced is that totemism is or has been world-wide—it can be traced in Australia, North America, Central America, South America, Africa, Asia, Polynesia[1]—that probably every species of animal has been worshipped as a totem somewhere or other, at some time or other; that, in consequence of the respect paid to them, those animals which were capable of domestication became gradually tame of themselves; and finally, in consequence of changing circumstances—religious, social, and economic—as totemism and the taboo on the flesh of the totem faded away, the habit of eating those domesticated animals which are good for food grew slowly up. The growth of this habit will be traced in the chapter on the Sacrificial Meal. Here, however, one or two points may be noted. If our theory be true, we should expect to find, even amongst those peoples who have taken to eating domesticated animals, traces of reluctance to kill or consume animals which once were forbidden food. Such traces are found. To kill an ox was once a capital offence in Greece,[2] and the word *βουφόνια* implies that such slaughter was murder.[3] In England, it was in Cæsar's time a religious offence to eat fowl (as it was amongst the South American Indians mentioned above in the quotation from Ulloa), goose, or hare;[4] and yet they were bred, he says. Cæsar feels that there is something strange in this, but (anticipating Lord Kames) he conjectures that the creatures were bred for amusement, "animi voluptatisque causa." But there are two obvious objections to this: first, if they were bred merely for amusement, there could have been no religious offence in eating them; next, if there was a taboo on eating them, they were not domesticated merely for amusement. Wild animals are undoubtedly commonly kept as pets by savages,[5] but savages have no scruples about killing pets. Thus Captain Speke says, "I was told Suna kept buffaloes, antelopes, and animals of all sorts . . . M'tese,

[1] Frazer, *Totemism*, 91-9. [2] Varro, *R. R.* ii. 5.
[3] Robertson Smith, *Religion of the Semites*, 306.
[4] Cæs. *B. G.* v. 12: "gustare fas non putant; haec tamen alunt."
[5] Galton, *Human Faculty*, 243 ff., gives instances.

his son, no sooner came to the throne than he indulged in shooting them down before his admiring wives, and now he has only one buffalo and a few parrots left."[1] If the fowl and other domestic animals bred by the South American Indians were merely pets, we should not find that "if a stranger offers ever so much money for a fowl they refuse to part with it,' or that, on seeing it killed, the Indian woman "shrieks, dissolves into tears, and wrings her hands as if it had been an only son."[2]

Other animals which civilised man is reluctant to feed on are swine,[3] dogs, and horses. The two latter animals are of importance for our argument, not merely because they show how long the loathing set up by the original taboo can survive its cause, but also because they remind us that domestic animals serve other purposes than that of providing an artificial food-supply. According to our theory, animals that were capable of domestication became tame of themselves, in consequence of the respect and protection afforded to them as to other totem animals; and it was only in the course of time that it gradually dawned on the mind of man that he might make economic use of them. On the other hand, the ordinary view is that man first saw how useful

[1] Galton, *op. cit.* 249. [2] Ulloa, *ap.* Galton, 247.

[3] The swine, like the hare, was forbidden food to the Hebrews. With regard to the former animal, the facts seem to be as follows: The swine as a domesticated animal was not known to the undispersed Semites or to the Sumerian population of Babylon (Schrader, *Prehistoric Antiquities*, 261); on the other hand, its flesh was forbidden food to all the Semites (*Religion of the Semites*, 218). The inference, therefore, is that (1) it was after their dispersion that the Semites became acquainted with the swine as a domestic animal, (2) it was forbidden food from the time of its first introduction and spread amongst them. In the next place, (1) the pig can only be housed and reared amongst a settled, *i.e. agricultural*, population, (2) the pig is associated especially with the worship of agricultural deities, *e.g.* Demeter, Adonis, and Aphrodite. The inference again is that, as agriculture and the religious rites associated with it spread together, it was in connection with some form of agricultural worship that the domestication of the pig found its way amongst the various branches of the Semitic race. Finally, the swine (1) was esteemed sacrosanct by some Semites, (2) is condemned in Isaiah (lxv. 4, lxvi. 3, 16; cf. *Religion of Semites*, 291) as a heathen abomination. The inference, then, is that the worship with which the swine was associated did not find equal acceptance amongst all the Semites. Where it did find acceptance, the flesh was forbidden because it was sacred; where it did not, it was prohibited because of its association with the worship of false gods.

the dog would be in hunting, and how pleasant, I suppose, the horse would be to ride; and then, without more ado, deliberately set to work to domesticate the animals. The early history of man's first faithful comrade, the dog, escapes our ken; but not so with the horse. It is as certain as things of this kind can be, that the primitive Indo-European reared droves of tame or half-tame horses for generations, if not centuries, before it ever occurred to him to ride or drive them,[1] and this fact, inexplicable on the ordinary theory, confirms our hypothesis. To sum up, the cause which our hypothesis postulates, namely, that man spared and protected certain animals without any thought of making economic use of them, is a *vera causa*, for men do so treat their totem animals. That animals worshipped as totems do become tame, is also matter of fact. In Shark's Bay "the natives there never kill them [kites], and they are so tame that they will perch on the shoulders of the women and eat from their hands."[2] Further, our hypothesis accounts for all the facts, especially for such survivals as the lingering reluctance of civilised man to eat the flesh of certain animals. It also accounts for savages making pets. It is the tameness of the totem animal which suggests the idea of taming other creatures. Again, it alone supplies a motive strong enough to restrain the savage from recklessly devouring or destroying (instead of breeding from) the animals he caught or tamed. Finally, it admits of verification; for if it can be shown that not merely is the treatment of totem animals such as would naturally result in the taming of those that were domesticable, but that some domestic animals were actually totems, all the verification that can be required will be forthcoming. This will be seen to be the case with cattle in Egypt, and probably elsewhere also.

It seems, then, if the above argument commends itself to the reader, that totemism, and totemism alone, could have led to that "substitution of an artificial for a natural basis of subsistence" which consisted in the domestication of plants and animals, and which constituted the advance from savagery

[1] Schrader, *Prehistoric Antiquities*, 263; and Hehn, *Kulturpflanzen und Hausthiere*,[6] 19 ff.

[2] Woodfield, *ap.* Galton, *op. cit.* 251.

to civilisation. But totemism did not universally lead to civilisation, or invariably develop into a higher form of religion. On the contrary, the civilised and civilising peoples are in the minority, and totemism still exists.

Now, if we consider the geographical distribution of totemism, we find that the two countries in which it is (or was at the time of the discovery of those countries) most marked are Australia and North America; while the peoples in which its traces are hardest to find are the Semitic and the Indo-European. If, again, we consider the geographical distribution of those species of animals which are capable of domestication and on the domestication of which the possibility of civilisation depended, we shall find that "the greatest number belonged to the Old World, those of America were fewer, and Australia had none at all"[1]; indeed, of the three species occurring in America (reindeer, llama, and paco), none come into account in this argument, for they are outside the totem-area of North America. It will scarcely be considered a merely fortuitous coincidence—however we may explain it—that the two areas in which totemism lasted longest and flourished most are precisely those in which there are no domesticable animals. Nor is it a merely accidental occurrence that the peoples who have most completely thrown off totemism, are precisely those which have by the domestication of plants and animals attained to civilisation. The inference is that the domestication to which totemism inevitably leads (when there are any animals capable of domestication) is fatal to totemism.

The fundamental principle of totemism is the alliance of a clan with an animal species, and when the clan ceases to exist as a social organisation the alliance is dissolved also. But with the transition from a nomad to a settled form of life, which the domestication of plants and animals entails, the tie of blood-relationship, indispensable to the existence of a wandering tribe, is no longer necessary to the existence of the community: local association and the bond of neighbourhood take its place, for the restriction of civic and political rights to the actual descendants of the original clan is inconsistent with the expansion of the community. By

[1] Payne, 283.

this expansion of society beyond the narrow bounds of blood-relationship, the germ of higher religious belief which totemism envelops is enabled also to burst its sheath, and man's conception of the deity sloughs off the totem-god. But though totemism perished in the very process of producing the advance from savagery to civilisation, still even in the civilisation of the Old World survivals of the system may be traced.

"For the Egyptians totemism may be regarded as certain."[1] Egypt was divided into nomes or districts, in each of which a different animal was revered by the inhabitants. It was not an individual animal, but the whole species which was thus reverenced, and it was by all the inhabitants of the nome that it was revered. The lives of such animals were sacred, each in its own nome, and their flesh might not be consumed as food by the inhabitants of that nome. The god of the district manifested himself in the species sacred to that district. But this is not a survival of totemism. It is totemism, the thing itself.

No one, however, alleges that the religion of Egypt never got beyond totemism. On the contrary, we can see side by side with it in Egypt many of the stages and processes by which religion gradually divested itself of this its first protecting envelope, just as we may see sedimentary rocks by the side of the igneous rocks from which they are derived. Indeed, even in the lowest stratum of Egyptian totemism we may detect signs if not evidence of the disintegrating process: the bond of kinship, the tie of blood is relaxed. It is to be presumed that the inhabitants of a nome did not for ever continue to be blood-relations of one another, as they probably were when first they settled in the district; and the belief that the sacred species of animal was one blood and one flesh with the human tribe also faded. But though the blood-tie which held the human clansmen together, and which also bound the human clansmen to the animal, was relaxed and faded away from memory, the effects which it produced continued to exist. Thus, the sacred animal, whether it was still believed to be a blood-relation or not, received the same obsequies and was mummified in the

[1] Frazer, 94.

same way as man; and the killing by one nome of an animal sacred to another was avenged in effect, if not consciously, in the spirit with which the blood-feud was exacted on behalf of a slaughtered kinsman.

Another and a further stage of development is reached, when one particular specimen of the species is selected as being the one which the deity has chosen to abide in, as, for instance, the calf marked by twenty-nine particular signs which showed that the Calf-god Apis was present in him. On the one hand, the concentration of veneration on an individual would tend to withdraw sanctity from the rest of the species, and the result might easily be a final separation of the animal-god from the animal species. On the other hand, that in Egypt at anyrate the worship of an individual animal, such as the Apis-calf, is the outcome of totemism, is plain from two things: first, the rest of the species did continue to be sacred—eating cow's flesh was as abhorrent to the Egyptians as cannibalism—and, next, "when the sacred animal died, the god as such did not die with him, but at once became incorporated in another animal resembling the first,"[1] evidently, as in Samoa, when an owl died, "this was not the death of the god; he was supposed to be yet alive and incarnate in all the owls in existence."[2]

That, in spite of the ties which bound him to the rest of his species, the animal-god did shake off his humbler relations, and came to be worshipped in his higher aspect exclusively, is certain; and the process was facilitated by the dissolution of the bonds which tied down his worship to one particular nome. Apis, *e.g.*, came to be worshipped all over Egypt. But the fact that his cult was originally local, not universal, is shown by the circumstance that his calf, wherever in Egypt it appeared, was taken to Memphis and kept there. Thus not only was the individual animal exalted above the rest of his species, but the god that dwelt in him was far removed from all his worshippers, except those who dwelt in the immediate neighbourhood of his animal manifestation. Thus he gained in magnificence both ways, and in both ways the associations which bound him to his animal form and

[1] Wiedemann, *Die Religion der alten Aegypter*, 96.

[2] Turner, *Samoa*, 21, see above, p. 101.

origin were weakened. The universalising of a cult is due to political causes: the political ascendancy of the nome from which the reigning dynasty derived would be marked by the extension of the local worship. The *synoikismos* which makes a nation also makes a pantheon.

But these causes are external, social, and political, not religious. They may and did loosen bonds which checked the progress of religion, but they were not themselves the force which was struggling to get free. But it is to the action of that force that we must attribute the dissociation of the god from his animal form, and his gradual appearance in human shape, which took place in Egypt. Here, however, our immediate concern is not to explain how this force operated, but to point out that the totemism which, as we have seen, demonstrably existed in Egypt, along with other higher elements of religion, did eventually become refined into a pantheon of anthropomorphic gods. "It is remarkable," says Dr. Wiedemann,[1] "in view of the important part which the sacred animal plays in cultus, how relatively seldom it is portrayed. For a thousand representations of the gods, scarcely one will be found of an animal. The god appears either in human form, or as a man with the head of the animal sacred to him." Now, whether the *mischbild* of an animal-headed man was intended to intimate the idea that the god was of the same flesh with both his human kin and his animal kind, or is due to purely graphic considerations, as Dr. Wiedemann, who does not believe in totemism, is inclined to think, the fact remains that in the nome where a certain species was sacred the god is represented as a man with the head of that animal. In Mendes, *e.g.*, the goat was sacred and the god goat-headed. And as for the great gods universally worshipped in the Egyptian religion, as Mr. Lang says, "it is always in a town where a certain animal is locally revered that the human-shaped god wearing the head of the same animal finds the centre and chief holy place of his worship."[2] The last stage is reached when the god casts aside his animal garb altogether, and the animal is thought and spoken of as being sacred to him, but has no other or more intimate relation with him.

[1] *Op. cit.* p. 97.

[2] Lang, *Myth, Ritual, and Religion*, ii. 104.

The question now arises, whether, supposing that in Egypt or elsewhere we find a purely anthropomorphic god having an animal associated with him in art and sacred to him in ritual, but having none of those further relations to a sacred species of animals and a particular human kin which are of the essence of totemism, we are justified in assuming that the worship (or part of the worship) of that god is a survival of totemism? Plainly the answer to this question depends on whether there is any other way in which gods become associated in ritual and art with animals. If there is, we shall have to consider in each particular case which is the more probable genesis of the given association. If not, we may provisionally, and until further cause be shown, assume the association to have been totemistic. Now, there is only one other way which has been suggested to account for the association, and which is also a method applicable to other countries in which gods are associated with animals as well as to Egypt.[1] It is that the animals were chosen as symbols to express some attribute, some aspect of the might and majesty, of the gods.

We will begin by admitting the beauty and the value of symbolism. Nay! we will insist that there are truths which can only be shadowed forth by means of symbols. At the same time, as it is possible to detect a symbolism where it was never meant, we must be on our guard against "ridiculous excess." The fact to be explained is that certain animals are considered sacred. The suggestion is that the animals were chosen to typify certain divine attributes, and as the symbols of certain excellences. But "if one surveys the list of sacred beasts, it is found to include all the more important representatives of the fauna of Egypt, mammals, birds, fishes, amphibia, insects."[2] Surely this should give us pause. Innocence may be typified by the dove, and cunning have the serpent for its symbol; and as regards insects, for the ant and the bee—let them pass. But *all* insects? The symbol theory is getting strained. How-

[1] The suggestions that the hieroglyphs reacted on worship, and that the ambiguity of some Egyptian names of gods led to animal-worship, apply only to Egypt, and are inadequate to account for all even of the Egyptian facts.

[2] Wiedemann, *Rel. d. alten Aegypter*, 94.

ever, even if "the lord of flies" derived his title from some quality unstated, but typified by those insects, was it not, from the symbolic point of view, superfluous to offer them a sacrifice, a whole ox, as was done in Leucas?[1] Again, the sacred animal or plant may not be eaten, which is hard to explain on the symbolic theory. The Ioxidæ may have abstained from eating asparagus,[2] but does anyone believe that it was for its symbolism? There is no evidence to show or reason to believe that the asparagus symbolised anything whatever. And why should this devotion to a symbol, wholly inexplicable on the symbolist theory, be limited in each case to one clan or neighbourhood? That nobody but the Ioxidæ—if they—saw anything symbolical in the asparagus, can be understood; but when the symbol was one that could be appreciated by "the meanest understanding," why was it appropriated exclusively by one clan?

The symbol theory simply does not account for the facts which it is framed to explain; and totemism at present is the only satisfactory answer to the question why certain plants and animals are sacred. When, then, we turn to Greece, and find that every god and goddess has his or her sacred animal, we may consider that mere fact as constituting a reasonable presumption that part of the deity's ritual has its roots in totemism. It is also, however, not unreasonable to demand other confirmatory evidence. Now, in Greece we do not find totemism anywhere as a living, organic system, as in Ancient Egypt. This may be due to our ignorance of Greek peasant life. But we do find fragments of the system, one here and another there, which, if only they had not been scattered but had been found together, would have made a living whole. Thus we have families whose names indicate that they were originally totem clans, *e.g.* there were Cynadæ at Athens, as there was a Dog clan amongst the Mohicans; but we have no evidence to show that the dog was sacred to the Cynadæ in historic times. On the other hand, storks were revered by the Thessalians, but there is nothing to show that there was a

[1] Aelian, xi. 8 (Lang, *op. cit.* 278).
[2] Plutarch, *Theseus*, 14 (Lang, *ibid.*).

Stork clan in Thessaly. And though "the Myrmidons claimed descent from the ants and revered ants,"[1] even this is not quite enough to establish totemism as "a going concern"; we should like to know a little more about the "reverence" paid them. Were they, when found dead, buried like clansmen? It is said that at Athens "whosoever slays a wolf, collects what is needful for its burial."[2] Elsewhere in Greece there was a Wolf clan, and in Athens itself a Wolf-hero, *i.e.* a totem which had cast off its animal form and emerged human. The wolf was also a sacred animal, but its worshippers were not a Wolf clan. Again, "the lobster was generally considered sacred by the Greeks, and not eaten; if the people of Seriphos . . . found a dead one, they buried it and mourned over it as over one of themselves."[3] But there is no Lobster clan on record. Thus, in Greece, though we have all the parts of the system, we do not find them combined in a living whole. Still, no fair-minded man will deny that for the Greeks totemism is "highly probable."[4] The wonder is not that there are so few, but that there are so many traces left. Even in the Mycenæan period there are indications, slight and conjectural of course, that animal-worship, which undoubtedly existed then, had passed beyond the purely totemistic stage.[5] Agriculture, and with it those agricultural rites and myths which overlaid and undermined totemism, had been known not only to the Greeks before they entered Greece, but to all the European members of the Aryan race before they scattered and settled in their historic habitations.[6] Pastoral life, which is itself the result of totemism, and in its turn reacts upon and modifies the totemistic system, was a stage of development which had been reached by the Aryan race even before the European branch had separated from the Hindo-Persian. How remote, then, must be the period when the undivided Aryans were hunters, living on the "natural basis of subsistence," and making those blind

[1] Lang, *op. cit.* 277.

[2] Schol. *ad* Apoll. Rhod. ii. 124 (Lang, *loc. cit.*).

[3] Frazer, 15, and Aelian, *N. A.* xiii. 26.

[4] Frazer, 94.

[5] *Journal of Hellenic Studies*, xiv. 81, 270.

[6] Schrader, *Prehistoric Antiquities of the Aryan Peoples*, 284 ff (English translation).

attempts to domesticate their totem-animals without which there were no civilisation now.

We have seen it to be, as the late Professor Robertson Smith showed, "a universal rule, that even the most primitive savages have not only enemies, but permanent allies (which at so early a stage in society necessarily means kinsfolk) among the non-human or superhuman animate kinds by which the universe is peopled,"[1] and those allies are animals, plants, etc., conceived as having supernatural powers, that is to say, are totems. All peoples in a state of savagery, on a "natural basis of subsistence," in the hunter stage, are totemists. Further, it is totemism alone which could have produced that transition from the natural to an artificial basis of subsistence, which is effected by the domestication of plants and animals, and which results in civilisation. In other words, the mere fact that a people possesses material civilisation requires us to believe that in a state of savagery it was totemist. Again, the association of an animal with a god in art and ritual has as yet found no other, even plausible, explanation than that the worship of the god contains in it, as one of its elements, a survival of totemism. Finally—and this is a new point—"unclean" animals are animals which may neither be eaten nor be touched even, that is to say, they are totem animals (they are always species, not mere individuals), which have become detached both from the human clan by which originally they were revered, and from the god to whom in course of time they came to be sacred.

Amongst the Semites, as amongst the Aryans, we nowhere find totemism a living organism, though we find all the *disjecti membra*. Or, to change the metaphor, we may represent to ourselves totemism as a triangle, of which the three sides are, (1) a clan, (2) a species of animals, and (3) a god, varyingly conceived as animal or human; while the angles of the triangle are the relations in which the gods, men, and animals stand to each other. There are many relations in which animals and men may stand to each other, as there are many angles at which one straight line can stand to another; but as there is only one angle at which the

[1] Robertson Smith, *Religion of the Semites*, 137.

two sides of a triangle can stand to each other, namely, that determined by the side which the angle subtends, so there is only one relation in which men can stand to animals in totemism, namely, that determined by the system. Now, amongst the Semites we never find the complete triangle of totemism: sometimes one side is missing, sometimes another, sometimes the third, but in every case the angle of the two remaining sides, *i.e.* the relation between men and god, god and animal, animal and men, shows what the missing side must have been. To begin with the first side of the triangle: we find deities in animal or semi-animal form, such as Dagon. Then we have deities associated—at the totemistic angle, so to speak—with particular species of animals, *e.g.* Astarte with swine, the Syrian Atargatis with fish, the Sun-god with horses.[1] The animal side of the triangle, again, is connected with the third side, men, at the totemistic angle, that is to say, we have a human clan treating a species of animal as they do their clansmen, *e.g.* "when the B. Hārith, a tribe of South Arabia, find a dead gazelle, they wash it, wrap it in cerecloths, and bury it, and the whole tribe mourns for it seven days."[2] When, then, we find the animal side of the triangle by itself, and apart from the other two sides, we still can infer the triangle to which it belonged; or, to drop metaphor, when we find that vermin were "sacred"[3] and mice "unclean,"[4] we remember that mice were totem animals in Greece,[5] and insects among the sacred beasts of Egypt. Finally, to complete our round of the totemist triangle, we find men in the totemist relation to the animal god in Baalbek, where the god-ancestor of the inhabitants was worshipped in the form of a lion.[6]

Thus the *à priori* argument that the prehistoric Semites, while they were yet an undivided people, and before they had settled down in those territories in which history knows them, were (like all other peoples in a state of savagery) acquainted with totemism, is confirmed not only by the

[1] 2 Kings xxiii. 11 (Robertson Smith, *Semites*, 293).
[2] Robertson Smith, *Semites*, 444.
[3] Ezek. viii. 10 (*Semites*, 293).
[4] Isa. lxvi. 17 (*ibid.*).
[5] Lang, *op. cit.* i. 277.
[6] Robertson Smith, *op. cit.* 444.

reflection that but for totemism their material civilisation, their transition to pastoral and agricultural life, is not to be accounted for, but also by the survivals to be found amongst them even in historic times.

And yet the most remarkable argument in support of the theory remains to be set forth.

CHAPTER XI

ANIMAL SACRIFICE: THE ALTAR

In the last chapter we saw[1] that the practice of selecting one individual of the totem species, *e.g.* the calf in which Apis was supposed to manifest himself, and concentrating on it the reverence which was due to the whole species, was a relatively late development of totemism. It is also, in its ultimate consequences, inconsistent with the principle of totemism, according to which the owl totem god, for instance, was not incorporate in any one bird more than in any other, but was "incarnate in all the owls in existence."[2] We have also seen that it is the belief of societies which are held together by the bond of blood-relationship, that it is the same blood which runs in the veins of all blood-relations—it is the blood of their common ancestor. Hence the blood-covenant between two individuals is a covenant between their respective kins: it is not merely the blood of the two persons that has been mingled and made one, but the blood of the two clans. It follows, therefore, that the blood of any one animal of the totem species is not the blood of that individual merely, but of the whole species. In the same way, therefore, that the blood of the tribe as a whole is communicated in initiation ceremonies to the youth, by allowing the blood of older members to flow over him,[3] so it is obvious the blood of the totem species as a whole might be communicated to the person or thing over which the blood of any individual of the species was allowed to flow. But the blood is the life: it is—like breath, heart, etc.—one of the things identified by savages with the spirit or soul. The blood of any individual totem animal, therefore, is the spirit, not of that particular

[1] *Supra*, p. 122. [2] Turner, *Samoa*, 21. [3] *Supra*, p. 103.

animal, but of the totem species: it is, if not the totem god, at anyrate that in which he, as the spirit or soul of the species, resides, and by which his presence may be conveyed into any person or thing.

When, therefore, a totem clan required the presence of its supernatural ally, the procedure, we may say the ritual, to be adopted was obvious: the blood of a totem animal must be shed. It must not, however, be spilt upon the ground—that, as we have seen,[1] was taboo, a thing not to be done, for the ground on which it was spilt would thereby become charged with all the sanctity of the sacred blood; and any person who thereafter, when there was nothing to distinguish that dangerous spot from the surrounding soil, in unavoidable ignorance set foot upon it, would become taboo. Approaching the subject from this point of view, we shall not be surprised to find it a widespread and ancient custom to apply the blood of the sacred animal either to a pile of stones, heaped together for the purpose, or to a monolith erected for this end. We may not be able to say why races in the most opposite quarters of the globe and in all ages, races which have attained to civilisation, those which have remained in savagery, those which have produced the semi-civilisations of the New World, should all adopt this particular mode of avoiding spilling the sacred blood of the divine animal on the earth, or at anyrate of thus notifying that such blood had so been spilled on the spot, but the fact itself is certain. The reason can hardly be that there was no other ready and convenient way of attaining the same object, for an upright pole would serve the same end, and, as a matter of fact, is used for the same purposes both in the Old World and the New. But as it takes more labour to dress and set up a pole, or to erect a monolithic pillar, than to heap together a pile of stones, we may regard the heap of stones as the earliest object to which the blood was applied.

Now, that the altars of the Old World religions, though used for other purposes as well, and for the expression of far higher religious conceptions, were also used to receive the blood of sacrifice, is too well known to need illustration. In the words of the late Professor Robertson Smith, whose line

[1] *Supra*, p. 73.

of argument we shall now follow, with some illustrations of our own, "whatever else was done in connection with a sacrifice, the primitive rite of sprinkling or dashing the blood against the altar, or allowing it to flow down on the ground at its base, was hardly ever omitted; and this practice was not peculiar to the Semites, but was equally the rule with the Greeks and Romans, and indeed with the ancient nations generally."[1] The altar of the more civilised members of these races was, of course, not a mere heap of stones: it was a much more elaborate and artistic structure of stone than a mere cairn or rough monolithic pillar. But when we find that amongst the more backward members of these races piles of stones or rough single stones were used for the same purposes as the more finished structure, we can hardly draw a line between them. Thus, in the sacred enclosure of the Dioscuri at Pharæ there was a primitive structure of this kind which was both used as an altar and called an altar, *βωμὸς λίθων λογάδων*;[2] and in Arabia "we find no proper altar, but in its place a rude pillar or heap of stones, beside which the victim is slain, the blood being poured out over the stone or at its base."[3] Even amongst the northern Semites, in their earlier days, the ancient law of Ex. xx. 24, 25 "prescribed that the altar must be of earth or unhewn stone; and that a single stone sufficed appears from 1 Sam. xiv. 32 *sqq.*"[4] In the semi-civilisations of the New World, as well as in the greater civilisations of the Old, the primitive cairn came to assume the shape first of a dresser on which the victim was cut up, and then of a table on which offerings were laid; but the transition is even clearer in the New World than the Old, for in the former the primitive pile of stones was not discarded, but a table-stone was placed upon it: "the flat stones on which the flesh and blood-offerings were left for the spirits, raised on a pile of smaller stones, became the altar. In the most advanced times, in Mexico and Central America, the human sacrifice was slain with a stone knife on a stone slab, slightly elevated in the middle."[5] We find the same connecting link between

[1] *Religion of the Semites*, 202.
[2] Pausanias, viii. c. 22.
[3] *Religion of the Semites*, 201.
[4] *Ibid.* 202.
[5] Payne, *New World*, i. 410.

the primitive heap of stones and the perfect altar in a quarter of the globe far removed alike from the Old World and the New. In Samoa, Fonge, and Toafa "were the names of two oblong smooth stones on a raised platform of loose stones . . . offerings of cooked taro and fish were laid on the stones, accompanied by prayers for fine weather."[1] This instance is the more valuable, because it comes from a community which was still totemistic at the time. Finally, in a latitude and amongst a race of men widely different from any yet mentioned, we have the so-called "sacrificial piles" of the Samoyeds (a Mongoloid and probably Finnic race), which occur in the Island of Waigatz and along the coast between the Pechora and the Yenesei; a slight natural eminence is chosen for the site, and on it "a rough layer or platform of stones and driftwood" is constructed, and masses of bones of bear and deer that have been sacrificed mark the use to which this, the most primitive form of altar, has been put.[2]

But whereas the primitive heap of stones ultimately developed into a dresser or table and became an altar in the specific sense of the word, the primitive unhewn stone or pillar continued, where it remained in use, to be a baetylion, a beth-el, the object in which the god manifested himself when the blood was sprinkled or dashed upon it. Such a primitive rude stone pillar was the *maṣṣēba* of which Hosea speaks[3] "as an indispensable feature in the sanctuaries of northern Israel in his time,"[4] and the Arabian *noṣb* with its *ghabghab* (trench or pit) in front of it, into which the blood collected. Such, too, was the monolith mentioned in the *Popol Vuh*, a collection of the sacred traditions of the Quichés (Central America), put together and committed to writing by a native shortly after the conquest. It, too, had a *ghabghab* or trench before it, which was filled with the blood of sacrifice;[5] and that the deity entered the stone when the blood was dashed on it, is clear from such passages as these—"but in truth it was no stone then: like young men came

[1] Turner, *Samoa*, 24.

[2] *Journal of the Anthropological Institute*, xxiv. 400.

[3] iii. 4; cf. Isa. xix. 19.

[4] *Religion of the Semites*, 203.

[5] Brasseur de Bourbourg, *Popol Vuh*, 259.

each of them [the gods] then,"[1] or "the blood of birds and deer was poured by the hunters on the stone of Tohil and Avilix [gods]; and when the gods had drunk the blood, the stone spake."[2] So, too, the offering of blood gave the stones worshipped by the Scandinavians the power of prophecy.[3]

The consequence of this differentiation of the altar and the pillar was that, though originally they were identical in use and purpose, in Hebrew and Canaanite sanctuaries "the two are found side by side at the same sanctuary, the altar as a piece of sacrificial apparatus, and the pillar as a visible symbol or embodiment of the presence of the deity."[4] Similar causes produce similar results, and we shall therefore not be surprised to find that in Polynesia the same evolution took place. In Ellice Island, "Foilape was the principal god, and they had a stone at his temple," that is the unhewn monolith, but "there was an altar also on which offerings of food were laid."[5] The "sacrificial piles" of the Samoyeds exhibit the same association: "from the midst of all this [mass of bones] there rise a number of sticks and poles—some being less than a foot and others as long as 6 feet,"[6] only here the altar is associated, not with the stone pillar, but with the wooden post which serves the same purpose; in the same way as in "the local sanctuaries of the Hebrews, which the prophets regard as purely heathenish . . . the altar was incomplete unless an *ashera* stood beside it."[7] This *ashera* appears again amongst peoples which differ as widely as possible from one another in race and place and time: it is presupposed by the *ξόανα* of the Greeks; it is found amongst the Ainos;[8] the gods of the Brazilian tribes were represented by poles stuck upright in the ground, at the foot of which offerings were laid; the Hurd Islanders "in their houses had several stocks or small pillars of wood, 4 or 5 feet high, as the representatives of household gods, and on these they poured oil [which takes the place of fat

[1] Brasseur de Bourbourg, *Popol Vuh*, 259.

[2] *Op. cit.* 253.

[3] Bastian, *Der Mensch*, ii. 269.

[4] *Religion of the Semites*, 204.

[5] Turner, *Samoa*, 281.

[6] *Journal of the Anthropological Institute*, xxiv. 400.

[7] *Religion of the Semites*, 187.

[8] Howard, *Trans-Siberian Savages*, 45, 84, 198.

or blood], and laid before them offerings of cocoa-nuts and fish";[1] the Kureks at irregular times slaughter a reindeer or a dog, put its head on a pole facing east, and, mentioning no name, say, "This for Thee: grant me a blessing."[2]

It is evident that we have already passed the dividing line between the primitive unhewn monolith and the idol; indeed, the Samoyed poles "at and near their summits are roughly cut to resemble the features of the human face."[3] Thus the *ashera* becomes the wooden idol, the monolith the marble statue of the god, with which the altar still continues to be associated. In confirmation of this, we may note that in many cases, of which illustrations will be given shortly, the idol is smeared with blood in the same way as the stone pillar or wooden post originally was. But, as the idol grows more artistic, this practice is discontinued, and it is the altar alone on which the blood is dashed or sprinkled. Then a house is built for the god, in which his treasures may be stored; the idol, which from the value of its materials and workmanship is the most precious of the god's own treasures, is removed into this temple, and altar and idol are dissociated, for the altar remains where it was originally, and the slaughter of the victim and the sprinkling of the altar with blood are therefore done outside the temple. In Peru, as in the Old World, even when the god had come to dwell in the house which men provided for him when they took to dwelling in houses themselves, his ritual continued to be celebrated outside the temple, in the open air, as it had been celebrated before any building was erected in his sanctuary.[4] It was not the altar that was set up near the temple, but the temple which was erected there, because there was an altar near. And it was not in any and every place that an altar could be set up—not even the primitive heap of stones or wooden post. Nor would every stone or any piece of wood serve. To understand this we must return once more to the subject of taboo.

The principle of the transmissibility of taboo is the

[1] Turner, *Samoa*, 294. [2] Bastian, *Der Mensch*, ii. 109.

[3] *Journal of the Anthropological Institute*, xxiv. 400.

[4] For Peru, see Payne, *New World*, i. 460; for the Semites, Robertson Smith, *Religion of the Semites*, 197.

arbitrary and irrational association of ideas: blood, for instance, is inherently taboo and to be shunned; anything, therefore, that reminds the savage of it, either by its fluid consistency or merely by its colour, awakens the same terror, and is equally to be avoided. Hence certain localities, whether because of their blood-red soil, or of their trees with trunks of ghastly white (for white also is a taboo colour, possibly from the pallor of the corpse—even negro corpses are said to be pallid), or from some other accidental association of ideas, arouse the taboo terror in the savage and are shunned by him. Of the law of the association of ideas he knows nothing: he only knows that on approaching certain places he is filled with the same sort of terror as he experiences on seeing blood or a corpse. If and when he reasons on the matter, the explanation he gives to himself and others is that the spot is the haunt of a supernatural power, and that is why he feels as he does feel. For the savage the world is full of such haunted spots. On the Gold Coast every spot where the earth is of a red colour is the abode of a Sasabonsum, a malignant spirit.[1] When, however, the savage has gained an ally amongst the supernatural powers surrounding him, if in one of these haunted places he sees his totem, animal or plant, the character of the locality is thereby somewhat changed to his apprehension: it is still the haunt of a spirit, but of a friendly one; it still is to be avoided, but not from slavish fear, rather from a respectful desire not to intrude on the privacy of the god—so he now interprets his feeling, which is indeed really changed by the new association of ideas. Above all, it is now a place which, under due restrictions and with proper precautions, may be approached by him, when he wishes to seek the presence of his powerful protector for a legitimate end, *e.g.* to renew the blood-covenant with him. Again, everything in this holy place—earth, stones, trees, and, excepting animal life, there can hardly be anything else in it—everything in it partakes of its sanctity. As we have seen,[2] both in West Africa and in ancient Mexico, the soil was holy. And according to the prescription in the ancient law of Exodus, already referred

[1] Ellis, *Tshi-speaking Peoples*, 35.

[2] *Supra*, p. 64; cf. also the chapter on Fetishism.

to, the altar must be made of earth or unhewn stone. It was the earth, stones, or wood of such a holy place which alone could have possessed the sanctity desirable in a structure which the god was to be invited to enter in order that his worshippers might have communion with him. The sentiment of the supernatural which filled the hearts and minds of the worshippers during the rite seems to be different, however, from the awe which prevents transgression on holy places. The latter is—except when mingled with the former—purely negative, restrictive, prohibitory. The former is a feeling psychologically as distinct from the feelings of awe or terror, as, say, the feeling of beauty from other pleasurable feelings; its earliest manifestation appears to be on occasions when the natural order of things is suspended, and it is thereafter revived when man is conscious of the presence of the cause of that suspension.

In the earliest times, then, there were holy places; it was out of the materials spontaneously offered by them that the primitive altar was made, the idol elaborated, and within their bounds that the temple eventually was built.

The theory, on the other hand, that the idol was an "elaborated fetish," is one against which some arguments will be offered in a subsequent chapter on Fetishism. Here, however, we must make some remarks on a slightly different view, namely, that which would confound the primitive altar with rocks which form a conspicuous feature in many landscapes, and which are often believed by savages to possess supernatural powers, like waterfalls and other striking natural features. Now, in the first place, these rocks are natural features of the landscape, whereas the primitive altar is always an artificial structure; and, next, they possess their supernatural powers inherently, *i.e.* quite independently of anything man does, whereas the altar requires the application of the blood of sacrifice, if the deity is to enter it. In fine, these natural objects and the dread of them are survivals from the pre-totemistic stage, when everything which was supposed by the savage to possess activity, or was associated by him with events affecting his fortunes, was also supposed to possess a life and powers like his own.[1] The primitive

[1] *Supra*, p. 21.

altar, on the other hand, is the creation and the outcome of the needs of totemism.[1] Further, as long as it remains an altar pure and simple, it never becomes the embodiment of the god, nor, though highly sacred, does it acquire supernatural power. As long as totemism was a living force, it would be difficult or impossible to confuse the sacrificial pile, at which the deity manifested himself, with the god himself, or even to imagine that he was permanently present in the altar, for the totem animals were seen by the savage daily, and it was with their species that his clan made the blood-covenant, and in each and every member of the species that the god dwelt. Mr. Williams has accurately observed and precisely stated the totemist's attitude towards his sacrificial piles, when, after noting that "idolatry—in the strict sense of the term—the Fijian seems never to have known; for he makes no attempt to fashion material representations of his gods,"[2] he goes on to say, "stones are used to denote the locality of some gods and the occasional resting-places of others."[3] The same observation has been made with regard to savages generally by Mr. Howard: "My personal inquiries amongst almost every variety of heathen worshippers, including the most degraded types in India, in China, and also the devil-worshippers in Ceylon, have never yet secured from any of them the admission which would justify me in thinking that the red-bedaubed stone or tree, or any image in front of which they worshipped, was supposed to contain *in esse* the god to which that worship was addressed."[4]

In the course of time, however, three changes do undoubtedly take place: the rite of sacrifice tends to become formal; the god comes to be conceived as the ancestor of the race; the clan expands into a tribe, of which the majority of members dwell remote from the original monolithic altar. Consequently, when, at stated intervals, the tribe does gather together at the old altar-stone of their forefathers to do sacrifice, the stone itself, in which the god is to manifest himself, easily becomes identified with the god—the majority of the tribe know it only in this aspect—and with the god as their common ancestor. Thus amongst the Red Indians,

[1] *Supra*, p. 131.
[2] Williams, *Fiji and the Fijians*, 216.
[3] *Ibid.* 221.
[4] Howard, *Trans-Siberian Savages*, 202.

totemists, the place of national worship for the Oneidas was the famous Oneida stone from which they claim descent. The Dacotahs also claimed descent from a stone, and offered sacrifices to it, calling it grandfather. "They thought the spirit of their ancestor was present in this stone, which is their altar for national sacrifices. The Ojibways had such stones, which they called grandfather."[1] That, in such circumstances, a rough likeness to the human face should be given to the monolith or pole, and the transition from the altar to the idol made, is easily comprehensible. But this did not always take place: the idol of Astarte at Paphos was never anthropomorphised, but remained a mere conical stone to the last; and countless other monolithic altars, which never attained to such dignity as to have a temple erected behind them, have survived all over the world. It is the fortunes of these unhewn stones—the posts and the cairns would soon perish and be forgotten when not renewed—that we have now to follow.

It seems to be a law that a people must either advance in religion or recede. The choice is always before it; and evolution—which is not the same thing as progress—takes place, whichever course be chosen. Where no higher form of religion was evolved out of totemism, therefore, retrogression took place; and it is this retrogression, so far as it is exhibited in the fate of the monolithic altar, which now will be traced. The beginning of the process has been indicated in the last paragraph in the case of the Oneidas and other Red Indians: in the identification of the god with the father of the race was implicit the idea of the divine fatherhood of man; but this germ, which in the Old World bore its fruit, thanks to certain select minds who dwelt upon what was thus disclosed to them, amongst the Indians mentioned was sterilised by the further identification of the god with the monolith. This was in part, as we said in the last paragraph, directly due to the expansion of the community; the framework of totemism is a narrow circle of blood-relations; and when that circle expands the framework cracks, and the disintegration of the system begins.

When the stone has in this way become, not the

[1] Dorman, *Primitive Superstitions*, 133.

occasional, but the permanent dwelling-place of the god, the rite of sacrifice is in danger of becoming a meaningless and superfluous ceremony, for its object is to procure the presence of the god, and the god now is already present, or rather the stone is the god. Hence the rite dwindles until the only trace left of it is that the stone is painted red, as amongst the Waralis of Konkan.[1] By this time the totem-alliance is so completely dissolved that the totem animal, which has hitherto been required to provide the blood for smearing the stone, now is completely dissociated from the worship, and drops altogether out of view. But when the totem animal is no longer sacrificed, when the stone has itself become the god, and its history has been forgotten, there is little left by which to distinguish it from the other class of stones, notable natural features of the landscape, to which supernatural powers were ascribed in the pre-totemistic period. There are, however, still some distinguishing marks. The natural stones still are what all supernatural powers were until man learnt to make allies amongst them, hostile; but the quondam altar stones are still, traditionally, friendly powers, who will, like the stone of the Monitarris, if a sacrifice is offered, cause an expedition to be successful,[2] and not merely abstain from doing injury. The friendly relation of the primitive altar or rather god to its original circle of worshippers is clear in a case such as that mentioned by Caillié, of a stone which travelled of its own accord thrice round an African village whenever danger threatened the inhabitants. And the rock in Fougna, near Gouam, in the Marian Islands, which is regarded as the ancestor of men, ranks itself at once with the Oneida stone. In many cases, however, the quondam altar has lost even these traces of its once higher estate; natural stones have attracted to themselves, or have come to share in, the few remnants of the full rite of worship once accorded to the artificial structure; and all distinction between the two classes is obliterated. Thus the retrograde totemist

[1] Bastian, *Oest. Asien*, v. 139.

[2] This and the other examples of stone-worship in this chapter are taken, unless other references are given, from Girard de Rialle, *Mythologie Comparée*, 12–32, who, however, draws no distinctions between the various kinds of stone-worship.

apparently relapses into precisely the same stage as that which his pre-totemist forefather occupied. But as this is a matter which raises the important question, how far we can take the savage to represent "primitive" man, it is necessary to note that the post-totemistic stage, though in much it resembles the pre-totemistic, also differs much from it. In both stages, any and every rock that impresses the imagination of the savage may by him be credited with life and even with supernatural powers; he simply returns in the later period to the animism of the earlier, or rather he has never abandoned it. But he returns to it with an idea which was wholly unknown to him in the first period, namely, the conception of "worship," the idea, not merely of sacrifice, but of offering sacrifice "to" someone. Now, this conception, or rather these conceptions, as should be by this time clear, have their origin in totemism: "worship," as an act in its rudimentary stage, means only the sprinkling of blood upon the altar; the blood sprinkled is that of the totem animal, and the only object of the rite is to renew the blood-covenant between the totem clan and the totem species and to procure the presence of the totem god. The idea of offering a sacrifice "to" a god is a notion which can only be developed in a later stage of totemism, when, on the one hand, the monolith has come to be identified with the god, and, on the other, the god is no longer in the animal. Above all, "worship," on its inner side and in the ideas and emotions correlated with the rite and the external act, implies the existence, for the worshipper, of a god, *i.e.* not merely of a supernatural being as such, but of a supernatural being who has "stated relations with a community."[1] The ex-totemist, therefore, who retains nothing of his forefathers' beliefs and rites but the idea that it is possible to appease a supernatural being by offering sacrifices "to" him, may gravely mislead the historian of "primitive" religion. Indeed, he has led some students to imagine that his inherited habit of offering sacrifices to stones and rocks is a primitive practice out of which religioñ has sprung, while the truth is that the worship of stones is a degradation of a higher form of worship. The mere existence of sacrifice is an indication of the former

[1] Robertson Smith, *Religion of the Semites*, 119.

existence of totemism. The very idea of a temporary compact between an individual man and a supernatural power is derived from the original form of alliance, which was always and necessarily between clans, not between individuals.

A more varied and interesting chapter in the history of the monolithic altar is that of its fortunes when a higher form of religion invades the land. If the cult of any given altar and the local sanctuary in which it stands is too vigorous to be extinguished, it may be adopted by the invading and dominant race, and incorporated into their religion. This amalgamation of cults bears the technical name of "syncretism." Thus, in the New World, the Incas, when they invaded Peru, bringing with them their worship of the Sun, built temples of the Sun in some of the local sanctuaries; and, in the Old World, the totem animals whose blood from of old had been dashed on the primitive monolith, continued to be offered at the same altar even when it had been appropriated to the service of the Sun-god or Sky-spirit, Zeus or Apollo. If, on the other hand, the local cult had already decayed, if sacrifice was rarely offered, and the monolith was but the object of traditional veneration, then the respect or the sanctity attaching to it came in course of time to require explanation, and an explanation spontaneously sprang up which commended itself to the now dominant beliefs and traditions of the new religion. Thus, in Mexico, the sanctity of the monolith of Tlalnepautla was accounted for by the belief that the great culture-god Quetzalcoatl had left on it the imprint of his hand; and, in the Old World, "monolithic pillars or cairns of stone are frequently mentioned in the more ancient parts of the Old Testament as standing at sanctuaries, generally in connection with a sacred legend about the occasion on which they were set up by some famous patriarch or hero." [1] But matters did not always progress so peaceably. Frequently, both in its own interests, and, we may add, to the ultimate benefit of mankind, the higher religion found it necessary to undertake the suppression of the older cults. Thus Inca Roca threw down the monolith worshipped by the inhabitants of a certain village; the Councils of Tours (567) and Nantes (895) ordered the

[1] Robertson Smith, *op. cit.* 203.

destruction of such stones and the excommunication of their worshippers; in the seventh century, Archbishop Theodore, and in the eighth, King Edgar, found it necessary to denounce the worship of stones in England. In most cases the new religion eventually triumphed, but in none without a long struggle. The superstitious man of Theophrastus' time still anointed the stones at the cross-ways. Arnobius tells us that, when he was yet a pagan and came across a sacred stone anointed with oil, he spoke low and prayed to it; in many parts of France, at this day, *pierres fites* are the objects of superstitious veneration, and are believed to influence the crops; and finally, in Norway certain stones are still anointed, and supposed to bring good luck to the house.

Now, that the practice of anointing these stones has been handed down to the modern peasant from the time when they were altars on which the blood of sacrifice was smeared, will not be doubted. But if that be admitted, then the case for the view, advanced above, that the sacrifices offered to stones by the ex-totemist are also survivals of worship at an altar, is strengthened. The only difference, from this point of view, between the peasant and the savage is that the ancestral totemism of the savage died a natural death, so to speak, while that of the peasant was killed by an invading religion. Both return to their original animism, or rather have never got, in this respect, beyond it; and both retain practices which are manifestly survivals of that "primitive rite of sprinkling or dashing the blood against the altar, or allowing it to flow down on the ground at its base," which, "whatever else was done in connection with a sacrifice, was hardly ever omitted."

What else was done in connection with a sacrifice we have now to state.

CHAPTER XII

ANIMAL SACRIFICE: THE SACRIFICIAL MEAL

THAT, amongst the Semitic and Aryan peoples, the eating of the victim was part of the sacrificial rite, is too well known to need illustration. We shall therefore confine ourselves to quoting the late Professor Robertson Smith's account of the most primitive form of the Semitic ceremony, as practised by certain heathen Arabs (Saracens), and described by Nilus: "The camel chosen as the victim is bound upon a rude altar of stones piled together, and when the leader of the band has thrice led the worshippers round the altar in a solemn procession accompanied with chants, he inflicts the first wound, while the last words of the hymn are still upon the lips of the congregation, and in all haste drinks of the blood that gushes forth. Forthwith the whole company fall on the victim with their swords, hacking off pieces of the quivering flesh and devouring them raw, with such wild haste that in the short interval between the rise of the day-star, which marked the hour for the service to begin, and the disappearance of its rays before the rising sun, the entire camel, body and bones, skin, blood, and entrails, is wholly devoured." [1]

As for the Aryan peoples, we have nothing so primitive as the Semitic ceremonial described in this extract, but the ancient Prussians retained some ancient features of the original rite in one of their festivals, though with later accretions. The community met together in a barn, and a ram was brought in. The high priest laid his hands upon this victim, and invoked all the gods in order, mentioning each by name.

[1] Robertson Smith, *Religion of the Semites*, 338. In this chapter, again, I follow his line of argument to the best of my ability, and add one or two illustrations from the rites of non-Semitic peoples.

Then all who were present lifted up the victim and held it aloft whilst a hymn was sung. When the hymn was finished, the ram was laid upon the ground, and the priest addressed the people, exhorting them to celebrate solemnly this feast transmitted to them from their forefathers, and to hand on in their turn the tradition of it to their children. The animal was then slain, its blood was caught in a bowl, and the priest sprinkled with it those present. The flesh was given to the women to cook in the barn. The feast lasted all night, and the remnants were buried early in the morning outside the village, in order that birds or beasts might not get them.[1]

The more revolting details of the Semitic rite, "the scramble described by Nilus, the wild rush to cut gobbets of flesh from the still quivering victim,"[2] are not of the essence of the ceremony, but incidental, and due merely to the uncivilised condition of the worshippers. As such they give way among the later Arabs to a more orderly partition of the sacrificial flesh amongst those present. It was, however, necessary to mention them here for two reasons: first, they show, by their very want of civilisation, that the Arabians retained the primitive form of the rite; and next, they find their parallel not merely amongst other uncivilised peoples, but also in the strange reversions practised in the "mysteries" of the ancient world. These will be discussed in a later chapter, and so all we need say of them here is that different local sanctuaries differed in the degree of tenacity with which they adhered to primitive "uses": some gave them up soon, others retained them long and late. We may conjecture, therefore, that when a reversion to a lower or more barbarous ritual suddenly spreads in a civilised community, it is one of these more conservative and out-of-the-way sanctuaries which is the centre of diffusion.

Turning, however, from these barbarous and accidental adjuncts to the more important features of the rite, we may notice how the sacrificial meal differs from ordinary eating. In the first place, the victim must be consumed there and then, *αὐτόθι*, on the spot where the sacrifice takes place, "there before the Lord," in the sanctuary wherein the altar

[1] Bastian, *Der Mensch*, iii. 154.   [2] *Religion of the Semites*, 341.

is erected. The Rev. G. Turner noted this feature in the Polynesian ritual. At the annual feast in May, he says, "the food brought as an offering was divided and eaten, 'there before the Lord,'"[1] and, at their annual festival, "they feasted with and before their god."[2] Far away from Polynesia, the Tehuelche Patagonians celebrate births, marriages, and deaths by the sacrifice of mares, and the animals are eaten on the spot.[3] In a similar clime, but at the opposite end of the earth's pole, the same rule is observed; amongst the Jakuts, when a sacrifice is offered for a sick man's recovery, "tongue, heart, and liver are cooked and placed on a specially prepared one-legged table, the top of which has a round hole in the centre. The rest of the meat is consumed by the Jakuts."[4] The Mongols regard it as sacrilege to leave any of the sacred victim unconsumed;[5] and in certain feasts of the Red Indians the meat must be wholly consumed.[6] Returning to the Old World, we find that in Arcadia, the home of lingering cults, the sacrifice to Apollo Parrhasios must be consumed in the sanctuary: *ἀναλίσκουσιν αὐτόθι τοῦ ἱερείου τὰ κρέα.*[7] Even more interesting is the case of the Meilichioi. The festival at which the Athenians made sacrifice to Zeus Meilichios, the Diasia, was one of the most ancient of their institutions; but though they adhered closely to the ancient and primitive use, the Locrians of Myonia were still more faithful to the ritual which they had received from the common ancestors of Locrians and Athenians alike, for, like the Saracens and the Prussians, they offered the sacrifice by night, and consumed the victim before the rising of the sun: *νυκτεριναὶ δὲ αἱ θυσίαι θεοῖς τοῖς Μειλιχίοις εἰσὶ καὶ ἀναλῶσαι τὰ κρέα αὐτόθι πρὶν ἢ ἥλιον ἐπισχεῖν νομίζουσι.*[8] It is therefore interesting to note the recurrence of this feature in another branch of the Aryan race, the Hindoos. According to the Grihya Sútra, "the time" for the Súlagava sacrifice "was after midnight, but some authorities preferred the dawn."[9]

In the next place, it was of the essence of the rite that

[1] Turner, *Polynesia*, 241.
[2] Turner, *Samoa*, 26.
[3] *Journal of the Anthropological Institute*, i. 200.
[4] Bastian, *Allerlei*, i. 208.
[5] Bastian, *Der Mensch*, iii. 151.
[6] Müller, *Geschichte der Amerikanischen Urreligionen*, 86.
[7] Pausanias, viii. 38.
[8] *Ibid.* x. 8.
[9] Rajendralála Mitra, *Indo-Aryans*, i. 364.

all, without exception, who were present should partake of the victim; and as the rite originally was a blood-covenant, or the renewal thereof between the totem clan and its supernatural ally, the primitive usage required the presence of every clansman. But even in later times, when private sacrifice had come to be common, custom required that the whole of the household, or whatever the society making the sacrifice was, should partake of the victim. In some cases it is the individual members of the community who, like the Saracens, are eager to obtain their share of the sacred flesh; while elsewhere it is the community as a whole which is impressed with the necessity of compelling its members to partake. In the West Indies, the former was the case. The priest, says Hakluyt, "cutteth him (the victim) into smal peeces, and being cutte diuideth him in this manner to be eaten . . . and whosoeuer should haue no parte nor portion of the sacrificed enemie woulde thinke he shoulde bee ill accepted that yeere."[1] In Peru, also, the same alacrity was shown. "The bodies of the sheep were divided and distributed as very sacred things, a very small piece to each person."[2] The Red Indians represent probably a stage through which the ancestors of the Incas passed, and with them the whole community partook of the victim.[3] In Hawaii, there may not have been less alacrity, but there was more compulsion. On the eighth day of the temple feast, the whole of the sacred offering (a pig) had to be eaten; any man who refused to eat would be put to death, and if the whole offering were not consumed, a terrible visitation would descend upon all the inhabitants.[4] Amongst the Kaffirs, when an ox is offered to the Amachlosi, "the flesh is distributed and eaten."[5] As regards societies smaller or other than that of the clan or village community; at the Yagna sacrifice to the sun, each of the company of Brahmins ate a piece of the liver of the sacrificial ram, and thereby entered into communion with the deity.

As the development of religion in China has many

[1] Hakluyt, *Historie of the West Indies*, Decade vi. ch. vi.

[2] Markham, *Rites and Laws of the Yncas*, 28.

[3] Müller, *Amerik. Urreligionen*, 86.

[4] Bastian, *Der Mensch*, iii. 152.

[5] Hartmann, *Die Völker Afrikas*, 224.

peculiar features, it is the more necessary to call attention to the important points in which it follows the same laws and lines as other countries; and if, as we have sought to show, totemism has at one time or other been universal throughout the world, then its outcome, namely, animal sacrifice, should be found in China as well as elsewhere. It is so found; it is the subject of one of the Confucian books, the Li Ki; and it is a large part of the state religion. The greatest of the sacrifices was, like several which we have already mentioned, annual (at the winter solstice).[1]

The victim was not only killed, but eaten: "the viands of the feast were composed of a calf."[2] The practice of eating the flesh raw, as in the Saracen rite, seems once to have been known. "At the sacrifices in the time of the Lord of Yu . . . there were the offerings of blood, of raw flesh, and of sodden flesh."[3] Even the reversion to this savage practice, which is seen in some of the "mysteries" of ancient Greece, appears also in China, for in times of public calamity animals are torn in pieces,[4] as by the Bacchæ. And, to come back to the matter in hand, namely, the primitive custom which demanded that the whole clan should partake of the victim, "when there was a sacrifice at the Shê altar of a village, some one went to it from every house."[5] Again, by a post-Confucian custom, the Chinese pour wine (a very general substitute for blood) from a beaker on the straw image of Confucius, and then all present drink of it and taste the sacrificial victim in order to participate in the grace of Confucius.[6]

In Thibet, in the time of Marco Polo, when a wether was offered on behalf of a child, the flesh was divided amongst the relatives.[7] Finally, to conclude these illustrations of the primitive custom requiring all present to partake of the victim, in the Pelew Islands sickness is attributed to the wrath of a god, who is appeased by the sacrifice of a pig, goat, or turtle, which must be consumed by the invalid's relatives and by the god.[8]

In the last quotation, it will be noted that the victim is

[1] Legge, *The Li Ki*, i. 416 (*Sacred Books of the East*). [2] *Ibid.* 417.
[3] *Ibid.* 443. [4] *Ibid.* 307. [5] *Ibid.* 425. [6] Bastian, *Der Mensch*, iii. 154.
[7] *Ibid.* 157. [8] Bastian, *Allerlei*, i. 43.

to be consumed by the god as well as by his worshippers, just as in Samoa the people feasted, as the Rev. G. Turner says, "with" as well as "before their god."[1] But in the Yagna sacrifice the victim is eaten sacramentally, as a means of entering into communion with the god; and the Chinese view of sacrifice is the same. According to Professor Legge, "the general idea symbolised by the character Ki is an offering whereby communication and communion with spiritual beings is effected."[2] These are two different, though not necessarily inconsistent aspects of the sacrificial rite: one is the eating with the god, the other the eating of the god. Both require examination and illustration. We will begin with the latter.

In the Saracen rite, with a description of which this chapter began, the whole of the victim, "body and bones, skin, blood, and entrails," was consumed by the worshippers. The same thing is perhaps implied by the words of Pausanias in what he says about the offerings to Apollo Parrhasios and to the Meilichioi. The Mongols also regarded it as sacrilege to leave any of the sacred victim unconsumed; and in Hawaii a terrible visitation was the penalty for not consuming the whole of the offering. The consumption of the bones, blood, skin, and entrails is evidently a practice which advancing civilisation could not but discard; and we find that the ancient Prussians had left it behind, but what they did not eat had to be disposed of somehow, and it was buried. In Samoa the custom was the same as in ancient Prussia: "whatever was over after the meal was buried at the beach";[3] and so elsewhere in Polynesia: "they were careful to bury or throw into the sea whatever food was over after the festival."[4] In Thibet, at the end of the rite already described, the bones of the animal were carried away in a coffer. Amongst the Jakuts, "the bones and other offal are burnt, and the sacrifice is complete."[5] The Tartars, who make their gods of a sheep-skin, eat the body of the sheep and burn the bones.[6] In the Hindoo Súlagava sacrifice, "the tail, hide, tendons, and hoof of the victim are to be thrown

[1] *Samoa*, 26.
[2] Legge, *op. cit.* 201 (note).
[3] Turner, *Samoa*, 57.
[4] Turner, *Polynesia*, 241.
[5] Bastian, *Allerlei*, i. 208.
[6] Bastian, *Der Mensch*, ii. 257.

into the fire."[1] Amongst the Kaffirs, on occasion of the sacrifice of an ox to the Amachlosi, when the flesh has been eaten, "many tribes burn the bones of the victim."[2] The Tscheremiss at the annual feast to their supreme god Juma, poured the blood of the victim in the fire: head, lungs, and heart were offered, the rest eaten, and the remnants, if any, were thrown into the fire.[3] Our English word "bon-fire" = bone-fire points in the same direction. Finally, burning was the mode adopted by the Hebrews.[4]

Now this custom (of eating the whole of the victim) requires explanation, not the custom of burning or burying what was not eaten, that is plainly the mode adopted by advancing civilisation for effecting the same end—whatever it was—that the primitive worshipper accomplished by consuming the whole of the victim. But the custom of consuming everything, even bones, entrails, tendons, etc., could only have originated in a barbarous stage of society. Evidently, therefore, the belief also which led to the custom could only have originated in savagery. Therefore, again, it is to savage ideas that we must look for an explanation, not to conceptions which could only have been formed long after the custom. Of such savage ideas there are several which might well have given rise to the practice in question. It is, for instance, a belief amongst various savage hunters that if the bones of an animal are put together and carefully buried, the animal itself will hereafter revive. They accordingly take this precaution, partly in order to secure a supply of game in the future, and partly because they think that, if the animal is not thus buried, the surviving animals of the species resent the indignity, and desert the country or decline to be captured.[5] But this custom and belief do not help us: they might account for the burying of the bones, but they do not account for burning the bones or for what really requires explanation, namely, the custom of consuming the bones, etc. Indeed, the two customs are, as we now see, fundamentally

[1] Rajendralála Mitra, *Indo-Aryans*, i. 365.

[2] Hartmann, *Die Völker Afrikas*, 224. [3] Bastian, *Der Mensch*, iii. 157.

[4] Robertson Smith, *Religion of the Semites*, 239, referring to Lev. vii. 15 ff., xix. 6, xxii. 30.

[5] For instances, see Frazer, *Golden Bough*, ch. iii. § 12.

inconsistent with one another: the one aims at destroying the bones, and is observed in the case of sacred animals; the other at preserving them, and is observed in the case of game.

Another savage parallel may be found in a belief already illustrated,[1] namely, that the food of a divine king, such as the Mikado, or a superior chief, is fatal to his subjects or slaves. Much more, therefore, would the sacrificial animal of which a god had partaken be fatal, and great would be the need to save incautious, heedless persons from the danger of eating the remains which they might find lying about. Here we are approaching the true explanation; but, since we hope to show before the end of this chapter that the conception of the god's eating the victim only came relatively late, we cannot see in it the origin of the primitive custom in question, though we do see in it a powerful reinforcement thereof.

Again, it is a savage belief that you can injure a man not merely by means of his nail-parings, hair-clippings, and other things associated with him, but also by the refuse of his food. In Victoria, the natives believe that "if an enemy gets possession of anything that has belonged to them, even such things as bones of animals they have eaten, broken weapons, feathers, portions of dress, pieces of skin, or refuse of any kind, he can employ it as a charm to produce illness in the person to whom they belonged. They are therefore very careful to burn up all rubbish or uncleanness before leaving a camping-place";[2] and "the practice of using a man's food to injure him is found in Polynesia generally, Tahiti, the Washington Islands, Fiji, Queensland, and amongst the Zulus and Kaffirs."[3] Now, this belief, coexisting as it does in Polynesia with the custom of burying the remnants of the sacrificial meal, cannot but strengthen the observance of that custom. But it is to be doubted whether it was the origin of the practice. The eagerness displayed by the Saracen worshippers to obtain a portion of the victim, and the dismay of Hakluyt's West Indians if they failed to get a piece, both show that originally, as in Peru, the victim was accounted

[1] *Supra*, pp. 83, 84.
[2] Dawson, *Australian Aborigines*, 54.
[3] *Folk-Lore*, vi. 134, note 2.

"very sacred indeed"; and that the emotion which swayed the worshippers, and their motive for devouring the whole of the victim, was not fear lest the remnants should be used against them, still less anxiety about what might happen to incautious strangers, but desire on the part of each to obtain for himself as much as possible of something that was in the highest degree desirable. Now, that the sacrificial animal should be accounted "very sacred indeed" is intelligible enough, if it was (in the savage times when the whole victim was consumed) the totem animal and god of the clan making the sacrifice. As for the eagerness of the worshippers, it need not be doubted; but of the savage's motives for that eagerness we ought to try and form for ourselves some clear idea.

In the sacrificial rite itself, as an external act of worship, the essential feature is that the worshipper should partake of the offering; but it is only after a time that this central feature disengages itself from the repulsive accessories which were indeed inevitable concomitants of a savage feast, but were no part of the essence of the rite. We may therefore reasonably expect to find the rite on its inward side, *i.e.* as it presented itself to the worshipper, following a parallel line of development. That the idea of "communication and communion with spiritual beings," which, as we have seen, is the Chinese conception of sacrifice, is the aspect of the rite which has persisted longest, we will take for granted. Whether it was present dimly, and obscured or overlaid by other associations, but still implicitly present to the consciousness of savage man, is a question which depends for its answer on what view we take of that identity in difference which exists between civilised and uncivilised man, and makes the whole world kin. We may regard selfishness and the baser desires as alone "natural" and as constituting the sole identity; or, by the same question-begging epithet, we may credit the savage with the "natural" affections as well. The question has always divided philosophers, not merely in Europe, but in China, where Seun sides with Hobbes, and Han-yu anticipated the view of Butler that good instincts as well as bad are natural. If, therefore, here we take our stand, without hesitation, but without argument, on the side of the latter, it is not that we wish to ignore the other view, but because this is not the place to discuss it. We shall therefore, with the reader's leave, assume that the mere existence of the family and of the clan implies the existence of some measure of affection between parents and children and between blood-relations.[1] But if this be granted, the rest follows: where affection exists in one direction it may come to exist in others; and communion is sought only with those towards whom we have affection. Here, then, lay the germ: in the conception of the clan-god as a permanently friendly power. As the leader of the clan in war, he claimed and received the affectionate loyalty of those on whom he conferred protection and victory; as the father of his worshippers, the filial affection of his children. It was not always or everywhere that the seed bore fruit: in the case of many savages still existing, *e.g.* most or all of the Australian aborigines, the conception of the totem-god as a protecting power has been lost, and they have lapsed almost into their original animism. But where it did germinate, its growth was accompanied by the intellectual and material development, by the movement towards civilisation, of the peoples amongst whom it flourished.

But the desire for union with the spiritual being with whom the fate and fortunes of the tribe were identified, was necessarily in savage times enveloped and conditioned by savage modes of thought and savage views of nature and her processes. One of these views has been called in by some writers to explain in part the motive with which the sacrificial victim was originally eaten: it is that with the flesh the qualities of the animal are absorbed and assimilated; and as a matter of fact some savages do eat tiger to give them courage, or deer to give them fleetness. But, it is important to note, it is not the characteristic quality of the totem animal that the savage, in his sacrificial meal, desires to appropriate: many or most totems—turtle, snail, cockle, etc. —have, as mere animals, no obviously desirable qualities to recommend them. It is not the natural but the supernatural

[1] Professor Tylor (*Academy*, No. 1237, N.S. p. 49) regards it as a "fact that savage families, with all their rough ways, are held together by a bond of unselfish kindness, which is one of the wonders of human nature."

qualities of the totem that the savage wishes to assimilate. It is as god, not as animal, that the totem furnishes the sacrificial meal. The savage seeks against the supernatural powers by which he is surrounded a supernatural ally; and it is in the confidence which the sacrificial rite affords him that he undertakes that forcible, physical expulsion of evil spirits which has already been mentioned.[1] Hence, then, his eagerness to partake of the victim—an eagerness so great that none of the animal was left uneaten. It was the desire to fortify himself as completely as possible for the dangerous encounter for which it was the preparation.

When, however, advancing civilisation made the complete consumption of the animal impossible, the remnants of the sacrificial feast were naturally treated with every precaution known to the savage, both to protect himself against his enemies, and to protect his friends against the danger of inadvertently eating food so highly taboo as was the flesh of a totem animal. Here, perhaps, the reader may feel it a difficulty that the totem animal should be tabooed food and yet should be eaten by his worshippers. The difficulty and its solution are exactly the same here as in connection with intruding on holy places. Such places are indeed forbidden ground, yet those who would seek the god must enter them, and so may enter them for that purpose and with due precautions. On the Loango Coast, the sanctuary of a certain god may be entered by those who seek his aid, but all others become his slaves for ever if they trespass on his precincts.[2] Now, what is characteristic of the sacrificial meal all over the world is precisely the fact that it is distinguished from ordinary eating by restrictions and precautions which are the same everywhere and amongst all races: the meal must be eaten in a certain place, at a certain time, by certain persons, in a certain way, for a certain purpose. As we have seen, only clansmen may eat of it, and everyone of them must partake of it. They must consume it, wholly, in the sanctuary, there and then. It is not at all times that the rite is celebrated, but once a year that the feast is held and the conflict with evil spirits undertaken—and then only after due preparation by fasting, etc.; for, as those who have come into contact with

[1] *Supra*, p. 105.

[2] *Supra*, p. 63; Bastian, *Loango Küste*, 218.

things taboo, *e.g.* mourners, have to fast, etc.,[1] so those who are about to enter into such contact have to observe the same rule. The "unclean" must not communicate their uncleanness to the community; much more, therefore, must those who are about to enter into relation with sacred things avoid carrying with them any uncleanness; and in both cases they are tabooed, *i.e.* isolated, for a time, that they may not, in the one instance, contract, or in the other, communicate, "uncleanness." From this point of view it is possible to explain another restriction, or rather precaution, namely, that which requires the sacrifice to be nocturnal. The fasting which is obligatory on mourners is only compulsory during the daylight; and the same remark applies to the fasting of those who are under a vow.[2]

The annual sacrifice and eating of the god could not, however, continue to be the only sacrifice: pestilence, which proved the presence of evil spirits and the necessity of expelling them; war, which involved an encounter not merely with the human foe but with his supernatural ally,[3] came at irregular periods, and consequently the annual rite came to be supplemented by other sacrifices. Not only did the number of these supplementary sacrifices come to be increased, but the character of the rite was greatly changed in pastoral times.

But, before going on to pastoral times, it will be well to ask how our argument stands exactly with regard to the pre-pastoral period, when man lived by hunting and fishing, and, in a word, was on the natural basis of subsistence. It stands thus: on the one hand, we find savages, who are still on the natural basis, treating their totem animals as gods, sometimes—not always, for we know totemism only in various stages of decay. On the other hand, we find in pastoral times, or later, animals sacrificed which once had been, and in Egypt even still were, totems. For instance, on the Gold Coast there is a god Brahfo, "antelopes are sacred to him, and no worshipper of Brahfo may molest one or eat of its flesh,"[4] yet once a year an antelope is killed and "the

[1] *Supra*, pp. 77, 78. [2] *Ibid.*

[3] Hence it is that war is regarded by so many savages as a religious function, for which preparation must be made by various forms of abstinence and purification and other religious rites and ceremonies, *e.g.* those of the *fetiales*.

[4] Ellis, *Tshi-speaking Peoples*, 64.

flesh is cut up and divided between the chiefs, head-men, and priests."[1] But we have as yet no instance of a totem animal sacrificed by a totem clan in the hunting stage. It is therefore conceivable, though improbable, that the sacrifice of totem animals dates from pastoral times, *i.e.* the period of domesticated animals, and does not go back to the hunter stage. This is improbable for two main reasons : first, if sacrifice originated with the slaughter of domesticated animals, we should expect only domesticated animals to be sacrificed, whereas wild animals also are sacrificed, as we have just seen ; next, the sacrificial rite, altar stones, the idols which grew out of them, the partition of the victim amongst all the worshippers, are known to the Red Indians, who cannot have first learnt the rite in connection with domesticated animals and then extended it by analogy to wild animals, because they have not any domesticated animals. Indeed, the horrible human sacrifices of the semi-civilised peoples of Central America are due, I conjecture, to the fact that in their nomad period they sacrificed wild animals; and in their settled, city life they could get little game, and had no domesticated animals to provide the blood which was essential for the sacrificial rite. Still, though in North America the circle of worshippers was a totem clan, which offered animal sacrifice, and though there are traces of the annual killing, by the clan, of its totem animal,[2] still, in the absence of an actual instance of the eating as well as the killing of the totem, we must regard it merely as a working hypothesis that in pre-pastoral times the animal sacrificed and eaten by the totem clan was the totem animal. The point, however, is of less importance, if we were right in contending[3] that domesticated animals were totems before they were domesticated, and owed their domestication to the fact that they were totems. For we have instances in which they are sacrificed by the clan to which they are sacred. Once a year the Todas, by whom the buffalo is held sacred, and treated "even with a degree of adoration," kill and eat a young male calf, and "this is the only occasion on which the Todas eat buffalo flesh."[4] The Abchases once a year sacrifice an ox: "any man who did not

[1] Ellis, *Tshi-speaking Peoples*, 225.
[2] Frazer, *Golden Bough*, ii. 90.
[3] *Supra*, p. 114 ff.
[4] Frazer, *op. cit.* 136.

get at least a scrap of the sacred flesh would deem himself most unfortunate. The bones are carefully collected, burned in a great hole, and the ashes buried there."[1]

We have already had occasion to note that in the beginning pastoral peoples do not kill their cattle.[2] In East Africa, "the nomad values his cow above all things, and weeps for its death as for that of a child."[3] He cannot afford to kill his cattle, for one thing; and, for another, they are his totem animal. Hence, in the beginning of the pastoral period, sacrifice is a rare and solemn rite. The cattle are the property of the clan, and are only slaughtered for the annual clan sacrifice. But if the clan prospers, things alter. The taste for flesh-meat develops, and with the increase of wealth in the shape of flocks and herds, the means for the more frequent gratification of the taste are afforded. Excuses for killing meat, under the pretext of sacrifice, become common; thus a Zulu said to Bishop Callaway, "Among black-men slaughtering cattle has become much more common than formerly . . . O, people are now very fond of meat, and a man says he has dreamed of the Idhlozi, and forsooth he says so because he would eat meat."[4] Hence, sacrifice tends to become less awful and more frequent. The Madi or Moru tribe sacrifice a sheep annually, for religious purposes; but "this ceremony is observed on a small scale at other times, if a family is in any great trouble, through illness or bereavement . . . the same custom prevails at the grave of departed friends, and also on joyous occasions, such as the return of a son home after a very prolonged absence."[5] Thus the sacrificial feast becomes a festival of rejoicing; and private generosity manifests itself in an invitation to the whole of the community to make glad in the name of religion. Nor is the god excluded from the invitation, for he too is a member of the clan. In Samoa, "the people feasted with and before their god."[6] In a different zone, "when a Jakut is about to start on a long journey to get skins, he carves an

[1] Frazer, *Golden Bough*, ii. 135 (note). [2] *Supra*, p. 116.

[3] *Religion of Semites*, 297, quoting Munzinger, *Ostafr. Studien*,[2] 547.

[4] Callaway, *Religious System of the Amazulu*, 172.

[5] Felkin, *Notes on the Madi or Moru Tribe of Central Africa*, quoted by Frazer, *Golden Bough*, ii. 138.

[6] Turner, *Samoa*, 26.

idol of wood and smears it with the blood of an animal which he sacrifices in its honour. With the flesh he entertains the shaman and guests, the idol occupying the seat of honour."[1] The Tartars do not begin a meal until they have first smeared the mouth of their god Nacygai with fat.[2] On the Slave Coast, every god has his festival or sacred day, when sacrifice is offered, and the blood of the sacrifice is always smeared on his image, as it is the blood which "especially belongs to or is particularly acceptable to the god," whilst the body is eaten (unless it is a human body) by the worshippers.[3] The Quichés rubbed the mouths of their idols with blood,[4] evidently that they might drink it. The ancient Peruvians, according to a contemporary, "every month sacrifice their own children and paint the mouths of their idols with the blood of their victims,"[5] or, as it is put more generally, "they anointed the *huaca* with the blood from ear to ear."[6] In Mexico, the blood of the captives offered to any god was smeared on the idol's mouth.[7] When the Samoyedes offer sacrifice, at their "sacrificial piles," "the blood of the sacrifice is smeared on the slits which represent the mouths of the gods."[8] Whether the blood which was dashed on the altar stone, before it had come to be shaped into an idol, was supposed to be consumed by the god, there is nothing to show; and it would be hazardous to affirm it.

This state of things, the period when all slaughter of cattle was sacrificial, and every member of the clan was entitled to his share of the victim, has left its traces behind it in various parts of the world. Among the Zulus, "when a man kills a cow—which, however, is seldom and reluctantly done, unless it happens to be stolen property—the whole population of the hamlet assemble to eat it without invitation."[9] Among the Damaras "another superstition [*i.e.* in addition to that which forbids clans from eating their totem animals] is that meat is common property. Every slaughter is looked upon as a kind of sacrifice or festal occasion. Damaras cannot conceive that

[1] Bastian, *Allerlei*, i. 213.
[2] Bastian, *Der Mensch*, iii. 154.
[3] Ellis, *Ewe-speaking Peoples*, 79.
[4] Bastian, *Der Mensch*, ii. 269.
[5] Xérès, *La Conquête du Pérou* (Ternaux-Compans, iv. 53).
[6] Markham, *Rites and Laws of the Yncas*, 55.
[7] Sahagun, Appendix.
[8] *Journ. Anth. Inst.* xxiv. 400.
[9] Shaw, *Memorials of South Africa*, 59, quoted in *Religion of Semites*, 284.

people should eat meat as their daily food. Their chiefs kill an ox when a stranger comes, or half a dozen oxen on a birth or circumcision feast, or any great event, and then everybody present shares the meat. . . . Damaras have a great respect, almost reverence, for oxen."[1] The same notion that sacrifice is the only excuse or reason for killing meat, reappears far from South Africa, in Polynesia. In Hudson's Island, "even the killing of a pig had to be done in a temple, and the blessing of the god asked before it could be cooked or eaten."[2] So in New Guinea, all "their great festivals are connected with the worship of the gods. Many pigs are killed on these occasions."[3] The idea that all the clan have a right to partake, shows itself amongst the Tehuelche Patagonians, who celebrate births, marriages, and deaths by the sacrifice of mares, to the feast on which all may come.[4] In the Old World, the idea that all slaughter is sacrifice is found amongst the Aryan peoples: it is Indian and Persian;[5] and at Athens the *hestiaseis* or feasts at which the *hestiator* entertained his tribe[6] or his phratry or his deme[7] are a survival of the same feeling. Finally, amongst the Hebrews, "a sacrifice was a public ceremony of a township or of a clan (1 Sam. ix. 12, xx. 6) . . . the crowds streamed into the sanctuary from all sides, dressed in their gayest attire (Hos. ii. 15, E. v. 13), marching joyfully to the sound of music (Isa. xxx. 29), and bearing with them not only the victims appointed for sacrifice, but store of bread and wine to set forth the feast (1 Sam. x. 3). The law of the feast was open-handed hospitality; no sacrifice was complete without guests, and portions were freely distributed to rich and poor within the circle of a man's acquaintance (1 Sam. ix. 13; 2 Sam. vi. 19, xv. 11; Neh. viii. 10). Universal hilarity prevailed; men ate, drank, and were merry together, rejoicing before their god."[8] The ideal here implied was earthly, but it was not selfish. The interests prayed for were those of the community, not of the individual. The festival was a renewal of the bond between the worshippers

[1] Galton, *South Africa*, 138.
[2] Turner, *Samoa*, 290.
[3] *Ibid.* 349.
[4] *Journ. of Anth. Inst.* i. 200.
[5] *Religion of Semites*, 255; Manu, v. 31; Hdt. i. 132; Strabo, xv. iii. 13.
[6] Poll. iii. 67.
[7] *Corpus Inscr. Atticarum*, ii. 163, 578, 582, 602, 603, 631.
[8] *Religion of the Semites*, 254.

and his god, but it also strengthened the bonds of family, national, social, and moral obligations. The joint eating and drinking was a bond of fellowship. By it the god and his worshippers were united. But it was only as a member of the clan, not on his private merits, that the individual was admitted to this meal. All worship of this kind was public, and taught that a man lived not to himself but also for his fellows.[1] Again, when all feasts are religious, and the gods are invited to all rejoicings, there is and can be "no habitual sense of human guilt."[2] Nor, as the god is the god of the community[3] rather than of the individual, could any such feeling be awakened as long as the community prospered. But when public disaster or national calamity supervened, one or both of two things happened: the individual sought supernatural protection by means not included in or recognised by the public worship of the community; and the older, gloomier rite of worship,[4] which still continued, regained its former and more than its former importance.

Public disaster, as we have seen,[5] was interpreted as the sign of individual sin. At the same time, the older annual sacrificial rite, so different from the common joyous festivals, was felt, in consequence of its difference, to require some explanation. That explanation was found in the view that it was an atonement for the sins of the people; that it was piacular: hence its gloomy nature. The feasting with the god, which was characteristic of the ordinary festival, was here out of place; and the worshipper left the whole of the victim for the offended god. Thus doubly consecrated to the service of the god, the victim was sacrosanct, and contact with it proportionately dangerous. The whole of the victim therefore was treated as the uneaten remains alone had been treated before—burnt. Doubtless also a motive for burnt-offerings was the feeling that the offering was etherealised, and thus made a more fitting form of food for a spiritual being. But it was the sacrosanct nature of the piacular

[1] *Religion of the Semites*, 263, 264.

[2] *Ibid.* 255.

[3] "The natives worship not so much individually as in villages or communities. Their religion is more a public than a private matter."—The Rev. Duff Macdonald, *Africana*, i. 64.

[4] *Supra*, p. 155.

[5] *Supra*, p. 111.

victim which first made burning necessary; and then sacrifice by fire was extended to the god's portions of the victim, even in ordinary sacrifices.

But the revival of the gloomy annual rite, in the new shape of piacular sacrifice, reacted not only on the mode of sacrifice, but on the nature of the victim. The piacular sacrifice was conceived as the atonement for the sin of a member of the community; it was a member of the community, therefore, that ought to suffer, or, if he could not be discovered, then at least a life of the same kind, *i.e.* human, must be offered. This was probably the origin of the sacrifice of human beings to the gods amongst the Mediterranean peoples. Amongst the Americans it was, as we have said, due to the lack of domesticated animals—an explanation which also covers the case of Polynesia, where the pig and the rat were the only quadrupeds that were known. The slaughter of human beings to accompany a dead chief to the next world is not sacrifice in the sense in which the word has been used in this chapter. Such slaughter was in all probability known in early Indo-European times,[1] and is widespread in Africa, where the sacrifice of human beings in the worship of the gods may have been simply borrowed from the ritual at the grave.

If, however, at the piacular sacrifice, an animal continues to be sacrificed, as it originally was, then an explanation has to be found to account for the victim's being animal and not human. The explanation forthcoming is that the animal is a "scape-goat" and a substitute for the human being who ought to be slain. Thus in Cochin-China the king makes a yearly offering in February to the heaven and the earth for benefits received. In ancient times this offering consisted in a slaughtered animal, placed on an altar, over which wine was poured. The offering is now conceived as a piaculum for the sins which every man is conscious of having committed, and which could only be expiated by death: the animal is regarded as being slain instead of a man.[2] If,

[1] Tylor, *Primitive Culture*, i. 464.

[2] Bastian, *Oest. Asien*, iv. 411. For the scape-goat amongst the Hebrews, see Robertson Smith, *Religion of the Semites*, 397, 422; in classical antiquity and amongst other peoples, Frazer, *Golden Bough*, ii. 182–217.

again, the god insists on human life, an alien is offered, as, *e.g.*, on the Gold Coast,[1] amongst the ancient Greeks, and universally amongst the ancient Mexicans.

The primitive, annual, nocturnal rite was also revived in the "mysteries" of the ancient world, but with them we shall deal hereafter. It remains for us now to discuss the devices to which the individual resorted, when the god of the community failed to render him efficient protection, or when the services required were not such as a god of the community ought to afford. This will require a fresh chapter.

[1] Ellis, *Tshi-speaking Peoples*, 169.

CHAPTER XIII

FETISHISM

Fetishism is often supposed to have its home and place of origin amongst the negroes of West Africa. It is certainly amongst the inhabitants of the Gold Coast and Slave Coast that the subject can best be studied; but if our conclusions are to be of any value, they should not be based on the hasty reports of passing visitors or the statements of semi-civilised natives, and "fetishism" should not be detached from the general religious beliefs of those who practise it. Fortunately, within the last few years trustworthy information has been placed at the command of the student, and a signal service to the science of religion has been rendered by Lieutenant-Colonel Ellis, First Battalion, West India Regiment, from whose valuable works (*The Tshi-speaking Peoples*, *The Ewe-speaking Peoples*, and *The Yoruba-speaking Peoples*) the following account is taken.

The Gold Coast is inhabited by various Tshi-speaking tribes (of whom the best known are the Fantis and the Ashantis), who are all of the true negro type, as distinguished from the Negroids in the Mohammedan States to the north and the Congoese in the regions to the south. There are four classes of deities worshipped by them: (1) General Deities, few in number; (2) Local Deities, very numerous; (3) Tutelary Deities of sections of the community; (4) Tutelary Deities of individuals. General deities are those generally worshipped by all or most of the different tribes, such as Bobowissi ("blower of clouds") or Nana-Nyankupon ("lord of the sky"). Local deities are confined to one locality and one particular natural object, such as Tahbi, who resides in or under the rock on which Cape Coast Castle is built; Cudjo, the god of a shoal or reef between Cape Coast Castle and Acquon Point; Kottor-krabah, who resided at the wells now known by that name; Behnya, the god of the river Behnya, and so on. To which of these two classes Srahmantin and Sasabonsum are to be assigned, it is difficult to say. "In one sense they are local, since every district has one or more; and in another sense they are general, since they are known all over the coast by these names. Properly speaking, it seems as if Srahmantin and Sasabonsum were each a name of a genus of deities, every member of which possesses identical characteristics; though these names are in each locality used to designate individual deities." Sasabonsum is implacable; once angered he can never be mollified or propitiated. Wherever the earth is of a red colour, there is, or has been, a Sasabonsum: the redness is caused by the blood of the wayfarers he has devoured. The third class of deities are the tutelary deities of particular sections of the community, such as towns, families, the inhabitants of any division of the town (a town-company), the frequenters of any market, etc. These tutelary deities differ from the local deities in this respect: the latter usually dwell each in his own locality (hill, river, rock, lagoon, etc.), and enter the images which are made of them to receive their worshippers' sacrifices and prayers; but the tutelary deity, though it is not absolutely and irrevocably confined to the material object (wooden figure, stone, calabash, etc.), which is its usual abode, for it can leave that abode and enter into and "possess" a priest, does usually and at ordinary times dwell in that material object. When a family grows so large that it must divide, and the branch in whose keeping the tutelary deity does not continue consequently requires a new one, or when a new "town-company" is formed, application is made to the priest of some local deity, who goes to the hill, rock, or river, etc., where the local deity resides, and communicates with him; subsequently the priest becomes "possessed," and, being inspired by the local deity, whose priest he is, says he is directed to go to the abode of the local deity, "and take therefrom a stone or some of the earth; or to make a wooden figure out of the wood of a tree growing there, or something of that kind." This he does, pouring some rum on the ground as an offering, "and then, dancing before them, and, bearing the object which is now believed to be the receptacle or ordinary abode of an in-dwelling god," he proceeds to install it in the place where it is henceforth to be and continue as a tutelary deity; as such it, like local and general deities, has a sacred day of its own, on which its worshippers do no work, shave their heads, paint themselves with white clay, and wear white clothes. Sacrifices are offered to the tutelary as to the general and local deities. The tutelary deity of a family protects the members from sickness and misfortune generally. The tutelary deities of a "town-company" have each a special function: the principal one protects the fighting men of the company in war; another "perhaps watches that no quarrel or division takes place between the members of the company; another may watch over them when dancing or holding a festival; and a third may take care of the drums." We now come to the fourth and last class, termed by Colonel Ellis "the Tutelary Deities of individuals." These "deities" resemble those of the third class, inasmuch as they dwell in exactly the same sort of objects—wooden figures, stones, or a pot containing a mixture of earth and blood—but they differ from them in several important points. First, the spot from which the wood or stone or earth is taken is not a spot frequented by a local deity, but one haunted by a Sasabonsum. Next, no priest is employed or consulted by the man who wants such a *suhman*, as its name is. Third, though offerings are made to the *suhman* by its owner, they are made in private—public opinion does not approve of them. Fourth, whereas the function of the tutelary deity of a family or town-company, etc., is to protect the members of that section, "one of the special attributes of a *suhman* is to procure the death of any person whom its worshipper may wish to have removed"—indeed, "the most important function of the *suhman* appears to be to work evil against those who have injured or offended its worshipper; its influence in other matters is very secondary." Fifth, a *suhman* can communicate its own powers to other objects, and the owner of a *suhman* sells such charms. Finally, if a *suhman* does not prove efficacious, the man concludes that either a spirit does not dwell in the object, or that, if it does, it is indisposed to serve him: "in either case he throws away the receptacle he had prepared for the spirit, and recommences *de novo.* But, so great is the fear of giving possible offence to any superhuman agent, that before discarding it he invariably makes some offering to it to avert its anger."

Here I interrupt the summary of Colonel Ellis's account to make some remarks. As we have seen, Colonel Ellis finds a difficulty in saying what class of god Sasabonsum belongs to. I would suggest that the source of the difficulty is that Sasabonsum is not a god at all; and I would point to several differences between Sasabonsum on the one hand, and general deities, local deities, and tutelary deities of sections of the community on the other hand. The latter have each a definite circle of worshippers; Sasabonsum, none. They have priests of their own; Sasabonsum has not. Further, their worship is public and approved; Sasabonsum's is secret and illicit. They do good, more or less, to their worshippers; Sasabonsum ("malignant") is implacable and does good to nobody. In fine, Sasabonsum is a spirit with whom no body of worshippers has established permanent friendly relations, and is not, therefore, a god at all. The worship of the general deities, the local deities, and the tutelary deities of particular sections of the community is religious worship, for they are gods of the or a community; but dealings with Sasabonsum and the manufacture of *suhmans* are in the nature of "black art," as Sasabonsum is not one of the community's gods.

Now, let us listen to Colonel Ellis again. The Portuguese discoverers of West Africa (1441–1500) were familiar in Europe with relics of saints, charmed rosaries, amulets, and charms generally, for which the Portuguese term was *feitiços.* When, then, they found the Tshi-speaking negroes worshipping pieces of stone and other tangible, inanimate objects such as the tutelary deities (whether of individuals or of sections of the community) dwelt in, they naturally regarded these small objects as charms, and called them *feitiços.* They could not have applied the term to a natural feature of the landscape, such as a river, valley, rock, etc., in which a general or local deity dwelt and where he was worshipped. Now the term *feitiço* or fetish is not strictly applicable even to a *suhman*, much less to the tutelary deity of a family or town-company, because the *feitiços* of Europe at the end of the fifteenth century were genuine charms, *i.e.* tangible and inanimate objects believed to possess inherent supernatural powers of their own; whereas even the *suhman* was, and is, conceived to be a spirit dwelling in the inanimate object. This error, sufficiently misleading if it had only involved a false conception of the nature of tutelary deities of individuals and sections of the community, unfortunately has grown still further, for the term fetish has come to be applied to all the objects of negro-worship, even to local and general deities. For this error we have principally to thank De Brosses, who thought he had discovered in fetishism the origin of religion, and was led to define a fetish (in his *Du Culte des Dieux Fétiches*, 1760) in this misleading manner: "Anything which people like to select for adoration," for examples, "a tree, a mountain, the sea, a piece of wood, the tail of a lion, a pebble, a shell, salt, a fish, a plant, a flower, certain animals, such as cows, goats, elephants, sheep, or anything like these." Hence the mistaken belief, widespread once in the learned world, that the negro worships an inanimate object, a stock or a stone, knowing it to be inanimate. For another, if possible, more misleading error Bosman (through De Brosses) is ultimately responsible. He gives the following as a statement made to him by a native: "If any of us is resolved to undertake anything of importance, we first of all search out a god to prosper us in our designed undertaking; and, going out of doors with this design, take the first creature that presents itself to our eyes, whether dog, cat, or the most contemptible animal in the world, for our god, or, perhaps, instead of that, any inanimate object that falls in our way, whether a stone, a piece of wood, or anything else of the same nature. This new-chosen god is immediately presented with an offering, which is accompanied by a solemn vow, that if he pleaseth to prosper our undertakings, for the future we will always worship and esteem him as a god. If our design prove successful, we have discovered a new and assisting god, which is daily presented with fresh offerings; but if the contrary happen, the new god is rejected as a useless tool, and consequently returns to his primitive estate. We make and break our gods daily, and consequently are the masters and inventors of what we sacrifice to." The contemptuous tone of this description must strike the reader. The explanation is that the native informant of Bosman "in his youth lived among the French, whose language he perfectly understood and spoke," and as a consequence he "ridiculed his own country gods." Doubtless he was, as Colonel Ellis suggests, "anxious to appear superior to his more superstitious fellow-countrymen, and to greater advantage to his European acquaintance," and so he stated the native practices, but suppressed everything that would make them intelligible and rational. The idea of coercion, as applied to a deity, appears to Colonel Ellis, after making inquiries in all directions, and after an experience of the Gold Coast extending over thirteen years, "to be quite foreign to the mind of the negro . . . the negroes so implicitly believe in the superhuman power of the gods, and hold them generally in such awe, that I am convinced no coercion is ever there attempted or even thought of. The testimony of all the natives I have consulted on this point seems to me conclusive."

The best proof of the accuracy of Colonel Ellis's observations is that they are, as we shall shortly see, confirmed, unintentionally, by the parallels afforded by observers of other widely remote races and religions. As a preliminary to resuming our argument where we dropped it at the end of the last chapter, however, let us ask, What now is the meaning of "fetishism"? Colonel Ellis has classified for us the general, local, and sectional deities of the Gold and Slave Coasts, together with the guardian spirits of individuals and the charms to which a guardian spirit or *suhman* has communicated its own powers. We may, if we like, call all these things fetishes, as De Brosses and Comte did and Bastian does. The only objection to this is that then the word has no meaning, or a meaning so nebulous as to be useless for scientific purposes. Thus, if we included under the term all the objects enumerated except the *suhman* charms, we might put a meaning on the word, for then all the things designated by it would be things worshipped. But the *suhman* charms are not worshipped. Nor can we, if we apply the name to all the objects enumerated above, define a fetish as everything connected with religion; for the feeling with which the *suhman* charm is viewed by its owner is not religious. But, without pressing these objections, we may observe that the very business of a history of religion is to ascertain in what relation the classes of things enumerated above stand to one another; and to lump them all together as fetishes does not help forward the work of distinction and arrangement, but rather retards and confounds it; for what does it help us to be told that all religion originates in fetishism, if fetishism means everything that has to do with religion? or that Zeus was a fetish, if a fetish only means anything that is worshipped?

On the other hand, we may, if we like, consider that fetishism must be something very low and degraded, and that therefore the term had better be confined to the *suhman* and the charms derived from it, the lowest of Colonel Ellis's classes. But in that case, so far from the idol's being "an elaborated fetish,"[1] the *suhman* or fetish is itself but an imitation idol, made after the fashion and on the pattern of the genuine idol of a local or general deity. And if we confine the term fetish to the charm made from the *suhman*, then it is not the idol that is an elaborated fetish, but the fetish that is the remnant or survival of an imitation idol.

Finally, whatever the meaning we choose to put upon the term "fetish," no harm can be done, if when we mean "local deity" or "guardian spirit," etc.—terms fairly plain—we say "local deity" or "guardian spirit," etc., as the case may be, instead of calling them "fetishes," which may mean one thing to one person and another to another, because it has no generally accepted scientific definition. Let us now pick up the thread of our argument from the end of the last chapter.

A god, we will repeat, is not a supernatural being as such, but one having stated, friendly relations with a definite circle of worshippers, originally blood-relations of one another. It is with the clan that his alliance is made, and it is the fortunes of the clan, rather than of any individual member thereof, that are under his protection. Consequently, if

[1] *Supra*, p. 137.

things go ill with the individual clansman, he must do one of two things: he must either commend himself specially to the protection of the god of the community, or he must seek the aid of some other supernatural power. The latter course, however, is disloyal to the community, and if the community is vigorous and strong enough to suppress disloyalty, such infidelity is punished by outlawry. It was therefore the former course which was first attempted, and we will begin with it accordingly.

The answer to the question, how to commend oneself to the protection of the deity, could not have been difficult to find, it was hit on by so many different races in exactly the same form. The alliance between the community and the god took the shape of a blood-covenant. Even private individuals can, as we have already seen,[1] at a certain stage in the development of society, form a blood-covenant between themselves, which only binds themselves, and does not include their clansmen in the benefits to be derived from it. Obviously, therefore, a covenant between the god and the individual worshipper could be sealed in the same way; and the individual accordingly offers his own blood on the altar or to the idol. The occasions on which the worshipper requires the god's special favour are various. It may be that the god's favour has been lost and must be regained; thus amongst the Quissamas an offering of the worshipper's own blood appeases the offended "fetish."[2] Sickness may be the mark of his anger, so on the Loango Coast whoever wishes to be healed by the "fetish" Bingu, must shave his head and paint himself red,[3] which is equivalent to covering himself with his own blood. In the Tonga Islands equivalents are not accepted; a finger joint must be cut off to procure the recovery of a sick relation.[4] The Australian aborigines and the Tscherkess also cut off a finger in sickness. Wealthy women of the Sudra caste offer a golden finger in place of the real flesh and blood. The Abipones substituted an offering

[1] *Supra*, p. 101.

[2] As he is called in the *Journal of the Anthropological Institute*, i. 192. What kind of god he really was, I cannot make out.

[3] Bastian, *Loango Küste*, i. 270. Here, too, I cannot make out whether this "fetish" is a general or a local god, or even whether he is a god at all.

[4] Mariner, *Tonga Islands*, ii. 210.

of hair for an offering of blood.[1] This last is a common practice: it is probably what is meant by the shaving of the head on the part of the worshipper of Bingu just mentioned; it was frequent amongst the Semites and the Greeks, and even survives in modern times.[2] To return to the blood-offering: evil dreams are due to evil spirits, so in the New World, "among the Ahts, when a person starts in a dream with a scream, a relative will cut his arms and legs and sprinkle the blood around the house."[3] In Greece, the χαλαζοφύλακες, if they had no victim to offer to avert the threatening hail-storm, fell back on the ancient ways, and drew blood from their own fingers to appease the storm.[4] The transition from boyhood to manhood was a time when the youth required specially to be placed under the protection of the god, and this was effected by scourging him till his blood ran on the altar, amongst the Spartans; by cutting off a finger, amongst the Mandans;[5] amongst the Dieyeric tribe of the Australians, by making down his back ten or twelve long cuts, the scars of which he carries to his grave.[6]

Other special occasions on which the worshipper offers his blood are great festivals. Thus, in Samoa, at the feast in June in honour of Taisumalie, after the meal "followed club exercise, and in terrible earnestness they battered each other's scalps till the blood streamed down and over their faces and bodies; and this as an offering to the deity. Old and young, men, women, and children, all took part in this general mêlée and blood-letting, in the belief that Taisumalie would thereby be all the more pleased with their devotedness, and answer prayer for health, good crops, and success in battle."[7] Amongst the Semites, a familiar instance of the blood-offering in distress is that of the priests of Baal.[8] On joyful occasions, also, the rite is observed, as, for instance, at marriages. In Samoa, the bride "was received with shouts of applause, and as a further expression of respect" (?), "her immediate friends, young and old, took up stones and beat themselves until their

[1] Bastian, *Der Mensch*, iii. 4.
[2] *Religion of the Semites*, 335.
[3] Dorman, *Primitive Superstitions*, 61.
[4] Plutarch, ed. Wyttenbach, ii. 700 E.; Seneca, *Quæst. Nat.* 4. 6.
[5] Bastian, *Der Mensch*, iii. 4.
[6] Bastian, *Allerlei*, i. 171.
[7] Turner, *Samoa*, 57.
[8] 1 Kings xviii. 28.

heads were bruised and bleeding."[1] In Equatoria, part of the Donagla wedding ceremony is a survival of the blood-letting rite. "The husband scratches the sides and shoulders of the bride (with nails prepared a long time before) till the blood starts, as is required by custom."[2] To commend themselves and their prayers, the Quichés pierced their ears and gashed their arms, and offered the sacrifice of their blood to their gods.[3] The Mexicans bled their ears or tongues in honour of Macuilxochitl[4] and many other gods. The practice of drawing blood from the ears is said by Bastian[5] to be common in the Orient; and Lippert[6] conjectures that the marks left in the ears were valued as visible and permanent indications that the person possessing them was under the protection of the god with whom the worshipper had united himself by his blood-offering. In that case, earrings were originally designed not for ornament, but to keep open and therefore permanently visible the mark of former worship. The marks or scars left on legs or arms from which blood had been drawn were probably the origin of tattooing, as has occurred to various anthropologists. Like most other ideas, we may add, that of tattooing must have been forced on man; it was not his own invention, and, being a decorative idea, it must have followed the laws which regulate the development of all decorative art. A stick or bone is prized because of itself it suggests, or bears somewhat of a likeness to, some object, *e.g.* the head of an animal; and the primitive artist completes the likeness suggested. So the scars from ceremonial blood-letting may have suggested a figure; the resemblance was deliberately completed; and next time the scars were from the beginning designedly arranged to form a pattern. That the pattern then chosen should be a picture of the totem animal or the god to whom the blood was offered, would be suggested by a natural and almost inevitable association of ideas. That the occasion selected for the operation should be early in life, and should be one of which it was desirable that the worshippers should carry a visible and permanent record, *e.g.* initiation, whether into manhood

[1] Turner, *Polynesia*, 187.
[2] Casati, *Ten Years in Equatoria*, i. 69.
[3] Brasseur de Bourbourg, *Popol Vuh*, 229, 259.
[4] Sahagun, i. xiv.
[5] *Der Mensch*, iii. 4.
[6] *Culturgeschichte der Menschheit*, ii. 328.

or, as amongst the Battas,[1] priesthood, is also comprehensible;[2] and when we recollect that in death the clansman is often supposed to be reunited to his totem,[3] we can understand the belief of the Esquimaux and Fiji Islanders, that none but the tattooed can enter their respective paradises.[4]

By the time that the blood-letting rite has come to be stereotyped and obligatory on all in the form of tattooing, or in its original form has come to be too usual to secure the undivided attention which a man's own fortunes seem to him to require, there will be a tendency—unless the community exhibits that loyalty to its own gods which is essential both to the existence and to the moral and religious development of the tribe—to seek the aid of supernatural spirits other than the tribal god. Now, for the savage, supernatural beings are divided into three classes—the gods of his own tribe, those of other tribes, and spirits which, unlike the first two classes, have never obtained a definite circle of worshippers to offer sacrifice to them and in return receive protection from them. This last class, never having been taken into alliance by any clan, have never been elevated into gods. There is, in the case we are now considering, no question of seeking the aid of strange gods—they are presumably already too much engaged in looking after their own worshippers to meet the exorbitant demands of the man who is dissatisfied with his own proper gods. Thus in Peru, "each province, each nation, each house, had its own gods, different from one another; for they thought that a stranger's god, occupied with someone else, could not attend to them, but only their own."[5] It is therefore to the third class of spirits that he must turn. He has not far to go to find them: he can scarcely set out from the camp or village in any direction without passing some spot, a conspicuous rock, a gloomy

[1] Bastian, *Oest. Asien*, v. 45.

[2] The rite of circumcision has probably been diffused from one single centre. Whether the practice belongs in its origin to the class of ceremonies described in the text, is matter of conjecture. The existence, in the New World, of a rite similar, except that it is confined to an offering of blood, seems to favour the conjecture.

[3] *Supra*, p. 103.

[4] Bastian, *op. cit.* vi. 151.

[5] Garcilasso de la Vega, *Royal Commentaries of the Yncas* (Hakluyt Soc.), i. 47.

glade, which tradition or the taboo-fear[1] has marked as the abode of one of these spirits. In the Pelew Islands, for instance, a most trustworthy observer[2] says that, besides the tribal and family gods, there are countless other spirits of earth, mountain, woods, and streams, all of which are mischievous and of all of which the islanders are in daily fear. So, too, on the Slave and Gold Coasts, the malignant spirits Srahmantin and Sasabonsum haunt places easily recognisable —where the earth is red, or silk cotton trees grow. If the savage has little difficulty in finding the abode of him whom he seeks, he has also little doubt as to the manner of approaching him: he will treat him as he would his tribal god —he knows no other way of opening communication with supernatural beings. He adapts, therefore, the tribal ritual. Bishop Caldwell's very careful observations in Tinnevelly are so instructive in this respect, that we will summarise them here, inserting in brackets what is necessary to bring out the parallel between the religious and the sacrilegious rites. In Tinnevelly evil spirits have no regular priests; but when it becomes necessary, in consequence of some pressing need, to resort to the aid of these spirits, some one is chosen or offers himself to be the priest for the occasion, and is dressed up in the insignia of the spirit. [As blood is the sacrifice to a god, so] in the dance with which the evil spirits [like the tribal god[3]] are worshipped, the dancer in an ecstasy draws his own blood and drinks that of the victim,[4] a goat, say, and thus the spirit passes into him and he has the power of prophecy. [As the sacrifice of the sacred victims was a solemn mystery to be celebrated by night and terminated before sunrise, so] the worship of the evil spirits must be performed by night, and the general opinion is that night is the appropriate time for their worship. [As the god was supposed to be in or to enter the victim, and the entrance of a god into possession of a human being is universally manifested by the shivering, convulsive movements of the possessed person, it was a common custom to pour water on

[1] *Supra*, p. 136.

[2] Kubary (long a resident in the islands) in Bastian, *Allerlei*, i. 46.

[3] *Religion of the Semites*, 432.

[4] See, below, the chapter on the Priesthood.

the animal victims, which naturally shivered, and by their shivering showed that the god had entered the victim. So in Tinnevelly] water was poured on the animal, which, when it shivered, was pronounced an acceptable sacrifice. [As the god was sacramentally consumed, so] "the decapitated victim is held so that all its blood flows over the altar of the evil spirit. When the sacrifice is completed, the animal is cut up on the spot and stripped of its skin. It is stuffed with rice and fruit and offered to the spirit, and forms a holy meal in which all present at the sacrifice partake."[1]

Bishop Caldwell's account shows that in Tinnevelly the mode of approaching the spirits who are as yet unattached to any body of regular worshippers, is modelled on the sacrificial rite of the established gods. In the Tinnevelly proceedings, indeed, it is not an individual who is seeking the assistance of one of these unattached spirits, but a reference to the early part of this chapter will show that the method by which the negro of Western Africa obtains a *suhman* is an exact copy of the legitimate ritual by which a family obtains a family god; and in the next chapter we shall see that all over the world these private cults are modelled on, derived from and later than the established worship of the gods of the community. The difference between the private cult of one of these outlying, unattached spirits and the public worship of the community's gods does not lie in the external acts and rites, for these are the same in both cases, or as nearly the same as the imitator can make them. Nor does the difference lie in the nature of the spirits whose aid is invoked; for, on the one hand, the community originally drew its god from the ranks of the innumerable spiritual beings by which primitive man was surrounded; and, on the other hand, the outlying, unattached spirits, who were not at first taken into alliance, and so raised to the status of gods, may ultimately be domesticated, so to speak, and made regular members of a pantheon. The difference lies first in the division which this species of individual enterprise implies and encourages between the interests of the individual and of the community, at a time when identity of interest is

[1] Bishop Caldwell in *Allerlei*, i. 164-8.

essential to the existence of society, and when the unstable equilibrium of the small community requires the devotion of every member to prevent it from falling. From this point of view the proceedings in Tinnevelly, being the act of the community, are quite different from those of a private individual: they may, if great benefit to the community is derived from them (*e.g.* if a pestilence is stayed in consequence thereof), result in the community's acquiring a new god, and one who takes an active interest in the welfare of his new worshippers collectively. In the Pelew Islands at the present day, unattached spirits not unfrequently become gods in the proper sense of the word [1] in some such way; and in ancient Greece friendly relations were similarly established with all the local spirits. But in these cases it is the public good which is sought and promoted by the joint act of the community, and under the directions of a priest acting in the name of the community's gods. Thus, the negro, according to Colonel Ellis,[2] who requires a tutelary deity for his family, applies to the priest. In the New World, also, the natives of Hispaniola did not make and break their gods at will. It was not enough, for instance, that a tree should move in a mysterious way for it to be straightway worshipped by the individual who was awestruck. Before it could become an object of worship, it must be recognised as the residence of a god by a priest, and a due ritual must be provided for it, as appears from the account given by Father Roman, a companion of Columbus: "A person travelling sees some tree that seems to move or shake its roots, on which, in great alarm, he asks who is there? To this the tree answers that such and such a Buhuitihu knows and will inform"; the Buhuitihu is fetched, and "then standing up addresses the tree with many titles as if some great lord, then asks who it is, what he does there, why he sent for him, and what he would have him do; whether he desires to be out, whether he will accompany him, where he will be carried, and if a house is to be built and endowed for his reception? Having received satisfactory answers, the tree is cut down and formed into a cemi [idol], for which a house is built and endowed, and cogiaba or religious ceremonies performed there at certain

[1] Kubary in *Allerlei*, i. 46. [2] *Supra*, p. 164.

stated times."[1] Very different is it when an individual privately resorts to one of these spirits, because the request which he has to prefer is such that he dare not make it publicly to the clan-god, who is the guardian of the community's interest and the tribal morality. There is all the difference in the world between applying to the clan-god and to a spirit who has no reason to look with friendly eyes on your fellow-clansmen, but rather, presumably, takes a pleasure in injuring them. Naturally, such a suspicious proceeding is resented by the community, and, should disastrous consequences ensue to any of its members, is punished by death. Certainly it implies malignity in the person dealing with such spirits, and a conscious, deliberate opposition to the public interest and the recognised morality of the tribe. In fine, the witch, whether of present-day Africa or mediæval Europe, is a person who, believing him or herself to possess the power, by means of magic, to cause loss, bodily torture, and death to his or her neighbours, uses that power, and is therefore morally exactly on a par with a person who, intending to poison by strychnine, should accidentally administer nothing more dangerous than phenacetine. If amongst the persons thus attacked some by a coincidence happen to die, and the poisoner regards their deaths as evidence of his success, the community (being equally unable to tell strychnine from phenacetine) may regard them as reason for his execution. A more accurate knowledge of science, of course, would have enabled the tribunals to distinguish the innocent from the guilty, and the murderer to distinguish poisons from non-poisons.

Magic is, in fact, a direct relapse into the state of things in which man found himself when he was surrounded by supernatural beings, none of which was bound to him by any tie of goodwill, with none of which had he any stated relations, but all were uncertain, capricious, and caused in him unreasoning terror. This reign of terror magic tends to re-establish, and does re-establish wherever the belief in magic prevails. The first step towards man's escape from it was the confidence, given to him by his alliance with the clan-god,

[1] Kerr, *Voyages*, iii. 138–9. A fuller account in Payne, *New World*, i. 396.

that his fortunes and his destiny were no longer at the mercy of capricious powers, but in the hands of a being who was friendly to him and was actuated by intelligible and reasonable motives. Magic, therefore—the dealing with spiritual beings other than the gods of the community—is in two ways the negation of religion, and necessarily incurs its hostility. First, the desertion of a worshipper is offensive ingratitude to the clan-god, who accordingly may withdraw his protection from the community, which is collectively responsible (as in the blood-feud) for the acts of any of its members. Next, the fundamental principle of religion—belief in the wisdom and goodness of God—is violated by the belief in magic, by the idea that a good man can come to harm, or that a bad man is allowed to injure him.

But magic is more than a mere reversion, for in his relapse man carries with him in a perverted form something of his higher estate. In the beginning, if he could not influence the supernatural powers which surrounded him to his own good, neither could he to his fellow-man's harm. But in his relapse he takes with him the only idea which a mind so relapsing can entertain of worship, namely, that it is a sequence of external actions, particularly potent over supernatural beings. The armoury, therefore, on which he relies for working evil to his fellow-man consists in rites which are parodies or perversions of the worship of the community's gods; or "sympathetic magic," which has already been explained in Chapter IV.; and charms, of which a word here. Charms or amulets are material objects, in which no spirit resides either permanently or occasionally, but which are associated with something, be it blood, or babe, or corpse, or good spirit or bad, which is taboo. They therefore catch the taboo-infection and become charged with the properties of the thing taboo. They may serve, therefore, to do injury to others, by communicating the taboo-contagion; or, by their dangerous character and the fear they inspire, they may protect the owner from both human and superhuman foes; or they may, from some association or other of ideas, be lucky.

To sum up: the difference between religion and magic is radical. Psychologically, it is impossible, from the malignity which is the motive of magic, to derive the tie of affection which binds fellow-worshippers to one another, and to the being they worship. And as for the external acts which are common to the two, the sacrificial rite originates with the worship of the gods of the community: wherever else it occurs it is borrowed from their worship—and this brings us again to Family Gods and Guardian Spirits of individuals.

CHAPTER XIV

FAMILY GODS AND GUARDIAN SPIRITS

It is still a much disputed question what was the original form of human marriage, but in any case the family seems to be a later institution than the clan or community, whatever its structure, and family gods consequently are later than the gods of the community. If promiscuity, or if polyandry and the matriarchate, were the original state of things, then the family was admittedly a later development. And so also it was, if the patriarchate with monogamy or polygamy prevailed from the beginning. In the latter case, the gods of the patriarch were necessarily also the gods of his married children and his grandchildren; as long as the patriarch and his children and children's children dwelt together and formed the community, the married children and their respective families could have no separate gods of their own. When, however, circumstances made it possible for the families which formed such a patriarchal community to exist apart from one another, and this was only possible in relatively late times, then it became also possible for them to have gods of their own in addition to those that they worshipped along with their kinsmen. In Western Africa, as appears from the account cited at the beginning of last chapter from Colonel Ellis, families obtain their cults from the sanctuaries of the established gods, by the mediation of the priests. It is from the gods of the community also that individuals in some cases obtain their guardian spirits. Thus in Samoa, "at child-birth the help of several 'gods' was invoked in succession, and the one who happened to be addressed at the moment of the birth was the infant's totem"[1] (this individual totem is quite distinct in Samoa from the clan totem, and is the child's guardian spirit).

But though both guardian spirits and family gods may be obtained from the ranks of the community's gods, it is quite possible for the reverse process to take place. Thus in the Pelew Islands, where the gods are totem-gods, each tribe and each family has its own totem-god, and as a tribe develops into a state, the god of the family or tribe which is the most important politically becomes the highest god.[2] And as a guardian spirit in some cases becomes hereditary and so a family god, the circulation of gods becomes complete; but as the community is prior chronologically to the family, and the emancipation of the individual from the customs which subordinate him and his interests to the community is later even than the segregation of the family, the flow of gods has its source in the gods of the community originally. It is not, however, always that a tribe has sufficient cohesion amongst its members to develop into a state. More often, indeed usually, the clan is unstable and eventually dissolves. Then its members, formerly united in the worship of the god that protected them, scatter; and the god becomes a mere memory, a name. His worship ceases, for now nothing brings his worshippers together. He is remembered vaguely as a good god; and if a white man asks the savage why then he does not worship him, the savage, not knowing, invents, and says it is unnecessary, the god is good and is quite harmless. So the white man falls into one of two errors: either he concludes that fear is the source of the savage's religion, and that he only worships evil spirits, or he sees in it "a monotheistic tendency," or perhaps a trace of primeval monotheism. The first error is due to the fact that, though the savage's conscience reproaches him, when he falls ill, for neglecting his gods, and so far fear plays a part in his education, still he does receive benefits from his gods, assistance in war, etc., and looks on them with friendly eyes. The other error lies in taking a single fact, and explaining it without reference to its context.

When a clan does so dissolve, or when in consequence

[1] Frazer, *Totemism*, 55. [2] Bastian, *Allerlei*, i. 16.

of the clan's expansion the clan-altar becomes remote from the majority of the tribe, the need of a more immediate protector and of more intimate and constant relations with him makes itself felt, with the result that a guardian spirit or family god is chosen, not always and probably not originally from amongst the gods of the community (if there be more than one). But whether the guardian spirit of the individual be drawn from the gods or from other unattached, supernatural spirits, the ritual adopted by the individual is that used by the community in worshipping its own gods. In North America, where totemism is the form of the community's religion, the individual also selects an animal species (not an individual animal) which is to be to him what the clan totem is to the clan. We may call it an individual totem, or a manitoo (an Indian word for spirit, familiar to English readers in the phrase Great Manitoo, *i.e.* the Great Spirit), or a guardian spirit. The period at which such a manitoo is chosen is the time when the boy is to enter on the rights and duties of full manhood—a time of life often chosen by totem peoples for the initiation of the youth into the worship of the clan totem. The blood-offering which forms part of the latter ceremony is found in the former also. The Mosquito Indians in Central America "sealed their compact with it [the individual totem] by drawing blood from various parts of their body."[1] The tattooing which is the outcome of the blood-letting rite accompanies and marks the choice of a guardian spirit. The Indians of Canada "tattooed their individual totems on their bodies."[2] The fasting which is the preparation for contact with things holy, and therefore for participation in the clan sacrifice, is an indispensable preliminary to the selection of a manitoo.[3] The animal of which the youth dreams first during these rites becomes his individual totem. As the community seal their alliance with the totem species by the sacrifice of one of its members, so the individual kills one of the species which is to be his totem, and which henceforth will be sacred to him, and will be neither killed nor eaten by him. From the skin of the one member of the species which he

[1] Frazer, *Totemism*, 55 (Bancroft, *Native Races*, i. 740).

[2] Frazer, *loc. cit.*

[3] Waitz, *Anthropologie*, iii. 118, 191.

kills he makes his "medicine-bag";[1] and though the whole species is sacred to him, it is to this bag that he pays his especial devotion, just as in Egypt, though all cows were sacred, one was chosen and considered to be the special embodiment of Apis. "Feasts were often made, and dogs and horses sacrificed to a man's medicine-bag."[2] So, too, the West African negro, it will be remembered, offers sacrifices to his *suhman*, which is thus to be distinguished from an amulet. What Colonel Ellis says of the respect which the negro shows to his *suhman* is amply corroborated by the reverence the Indian pays to his medicine-bag: so far from abusing it, or punishing it, if it did not act, "days and even weeks of fasting and penance of various kinds were often suffered to appease this fetish, which he imagined he had in some way offended."[3] So far from throwing it away, "if an Indian should sell or give away his medicine-bag, he would be disgraced in his tribe. If it was taken away from him in battle, he was for ever subjected to the degrading epithet of 'a man without medicine.'"[4] Finally, we may notice that throughout the Red Indian ritual no priest appears—a fact which indicates that here we have to do with a fairly primitive state of things.

Going north, we find that amongst the Samoyedes every man must have a protecting spirit: he gives the shaman the skin of any animal he chooses, the shaman makes it into human likeness, and the worshipper makes offerings to it when he wants anything.[5] Here, where totemism as the form of the community's religion has faded, the individual totem has also shrunk somewhat; the skin of the animal evidently corresponds to the medicine-bag of the North American Indians, but the animal species is apparently not held sacred by the individual any longer. The rites of fasting, blood-letting, etc., and the method of choosing an animal, are not mentioned; and the intervention of the priest indicates that we have to do with a comparatively advanced stage of religion. But the human likeness given to the skin, and, above all, the offerings made to it, show that it

[1] This is not a native expression, but the French settlers'.

[2] Dorman, *Primitive Superstitions*, 158 ff.

[3] Dorman, *loc. cit.* [4] *Ibid.* [5] Bastian, *Der Mensch*, ii. 129.

has not dwindled to a mere charm, but is still the abode of a protecting spirit. Amongst the Jakuts—to keep in northern zones—the skin has disappeared, the human likeness is given to a wooden idol, the connection of the idol with a totem animal survives only in the fact that the idol is smeared with blood, and it is not for life but for some special occasion or purpose that a guardian spirit is thus invoked. But the sacrifice to the idol and the feast at which it occupies the seat of honour [1] show that it is still the abode of a spirit, and not a mere mechanical charm. Here, too, the shaman takes part in the proceedings.

In Brazil, the maraca or tammaraca is a calabash or gourd containing stones and various small articles. Every Brazilian Indian has one. It is all-powerful. Its power is communicated to it by a priest, who gets it from a far-off spirit. Sacrifices, especially human, are made to it.[2] Here, the original totem animal has left not even its skin. The bag of animal skin—which amongst the Red Indians also is a receptacle for various small articles that are "great medicine"—has been given up for what we may call a box, supplied by the vegetable world. The Brazilian maraca finds its exact parallel in East Central Africa. When the "diviners give their response they shake a small gourd filled with pebbles, and inspect pieces of sticks, bones, claws, pottery, etc., which are in another gourd."[3] Returning to the New World, it was usual for the priests amongst the northern Indians of Chili to have "some square bags of painted hide in which he keeps the spells, like the maraca or rattle of the Brazilian sorcerers."[4] Elsewhere in the New World, in the Antilles, there were tutelary deities (Chemis) of the individual and of the family which resided in idols, of human or animal form, and the figure of the Chemi was tattooed on the worshipper.[5] In Peru, "conopas" were the tutelary deities of individuals; they received sacrifices, and might be handed down from father to son.[6]

Leaving the New World, we may note in passing that

[1] Bastian, *Allerlei*, i. 213.

[2] Müller, *Amerikan. Urreligion.* 262; cf. Dorman, *op. cit.* 159.

[3] Duff Macdonald, *Africana*, 44.

[4] Kerr, *Voyages*, v. 405.

[5] Müller, *op. cit.* 171.

[6] Dorman, *op. cit.* 160.

"the evidence for the existence of individual totems in Australia, though conclusive, is very scanty."[1] We go on, therefore, to Polynesia, where "tiki" is what "totem" is in North America. To every individual, every family, and every community, there is a tiki or totem animal. The individual totem is chosen from amongst the animals worshipped as totems by the various communities. It is chosen, by a method already described,[2] at the birth of the child. But there are indications that originally the ceremony took place, not at birth, but at the same time of life as amongst the Red Indians.[3] It is therefore interesting to notice that the tendency to antedate the ceremony, which in Polynesia has become fully established, had already begun to manifest itself in America; and further, that the mode of choice is the same in both cases, but that in America, apparently, the field of choice had not yet become limited to animals already totems. "Among the tribes of the Isthmus of Tehuantepec, when a woman was about to be confined, the relations assembled in the hut and drew on the floor figures of different animals, rubbing each one out as soon as it was finished. This went on till the child was born, and the figure that remained sketched on the ground was the child's *tona* or totem."[4] That in Polynesia also the choice was not originally limited to animals or plants already totems and therefore domesticated—if they were species capable of domestication—may be indicated by the fact that amongst the Maoris Tiki is the name of a god—the god of plants that have not been domesticated. Elsewhere Tiki is the god of tattooing—which again points to the connection between tattooing and the totem.

As, then, guardian spirits and family gods are found in Africa, Asia, America, Australia, and Polynesia, we may not unreasonably look for them in the Old World. We shall

[1] Frazer, *op. cit.* 53.

[2] *Supra*, pp. 180, 181.

[3] Waitz, *Anthropologie*, vi. 320.

[4] Frazer, *op. cit.* 55. In Eastern Central Africa, at the "mysteries" which take place at puberty "in the initiation of males, figures of the whale are made on the ground, and in the initiation of females, figures of leopards, hyenas, and such animals as are seen by those that never leave their homes."—Duff Macdonald, *Africana*, i. 131. Perhaps these puberty-mysteries are remnants of the custom of choosing an individual totem at that time of life.

also expect to find that their cult is modelled there as elsewhere on the cult of the great gods. As totemism had been almost completely metamorphosed by subsequent developments of religion, we need not expect to find much of it in the guardian spirits and family gods of the Old World; and if the idols in which the Chemis of the Antilles dwelt had come to be anthropomorphic in some cases, we need not be surprised if they were invariably anthropomorphic in Greece or Rome, nor if the tutelary deities of families or individuals in those countries were drawn from the ranks of the community's gods, as was the case in Polynesia.

Amongst the Semites, the *teraphim*, the worship of which was apparently not considered idolatrous amongst the Hebrews, were family gods. They were figures of wood or metal, with heads shaped into the likeness of a human face; they served as house-oracles, and were worshipped by the Chaldæans and by the inhabitants of Syria.[1]

That at Rome the Genius was the guardian spirit of the individual, and that the Lares and Penates were family gods, no one will question. It is, however, interesting to note that both the Genius and the Lares are associated with animals, the former with the snake and the latter with the dog, and so betray probably their totemistic origin. The life of the individual was in some cases supposed to depend upon the life of the snake in which his genius lived; the man's health depended on his genius,[2] and "when the serpent which was the genius of the father of the Gracchi was killed, Tiberius died."[3] This exactly agrees with the account given of the individual totem amongst the Guatemaltecs: many "are deluded by the Devil to believe that their life depends on the Life of such and such a Beast (which they take to them as their familiar Spirit), and think that when that beast dies they must die; when he is chased, their hearts pant; when he is faint, they are faint; nay, it happens that by the Devil's delusion they appear in the shape of that Beast (which commonly by their choice is a Buck or Doe, a Lion or Tigre, Dog or Eagle), and in that Shape have been shot at and wounded."[4]

[1] *Am Urquell*, v. 92.
[2] Preller, *Römische Mythologie*,[3] ii. 198.
[3] Jevons, *Plutarch's Romane Questions*, xlviii.
[4] Gage, *A New Survey of the West Indies*,[4] 334.

The resemblance between the Guatemaltec belief and the European belief about the wounding of witches is so close as to suggest that the animal in which the familiar spirit of the European witch appeared may have been a last lingering survival—like the serpent of the Gracchi and the Genius of the Romans—of an individual totem. The dog, with which the Lares are associated, appears in European folk-lore as a form in which ghosts manifest themselves,[1] and the Lar is conceived not only as the house-spirit but as the spirit of a deceased ancestor. Probably we here have ancestor-worship amalgamating with the worship of a guardian spirit, who originally appeared in totem shape. In Polynesia, a deceased ancestor, and not a god, is sometimes chosen as a totem,[2] but that is an exception to the general rule, and probably late.

In Greece, the Athenians distinguished between *θεοὶ πάτριοι, ἱερὰ πάτρια* and *θεοὶ πατρῷοι, ἱερὰ πατρῷα*. The former were certainly the national gods. Whether the latter were family gods is less certain. On the one hand, the privilege of worshipping them seems to have been confined to true-born Athenians, and to have been a mark of full citizenship,[3] which would show that they were the gods of the Athenians as distinguished from other Greeks. On the other hand, their worship was carried on in the private houses of those qualified to worship them, which rather points to their being family gods drawn, as in Polynesia, from the ranks of the community's gods. These *θεοὶ πατρῷοι* or *ἑρκεῖοι* or *μύχιοι* were worshipped in the *μυχοί* of the house, and one of them was apparently Hecate,[4] to whom the dog was sacred; and the dog is, as we saw, associated with the household gods of the Romans also. An apparent trace of guardian spirits in Greece is the Hesiodic doctrine of *δαίμονες* and what is obviously implied in the word *εὐδαίμων*, namely, that the man to whom the word is applied has a good *δαίμων*. The *ἀγαθὸς δαίμων*, again, like the genius of the Romans, appears as a snake; and there was a variety of harmless snake, the specific name of which was *ἀγαθοδαίμονες*.[5] We may note that before Hesiod, *i.e.* in the Homeric poems, there is no

[1] Jevons, *op. cit.* xl.-xlii.

[2] Waitz, *Anthropologie*, vi. 317, 321, 324.

[3] Ar. *Ath. Pol.*

[4] Eur. *Med.* 397; Rohde, *Psyche*, 232.

[5] Rohde, *op. cit.* 233.

mention of ancestor-worship, and after him no cult of guardian spirits. Whether we are to connect these two facts, and infer that ancestor-worship, springing up in post-Homeric times, amalgamated with the cult of the guardian spirit (as in Rome with the cult of the Lar), and then overshadowed it altogether, is a point which I will not do more than suggest for consideration. At any rate, it is obviously desirable that we should now go on to consider the question of ancestor-worship in general; and, bearing in mind that it is essentially a private worship and a purely family affair, we may not inappropriately sum up the results of this chapter as affecting cults of this kind. They are as follows. Whenever and wherever cults of this kind are found—and they are found in every quarter of the globe—they are assimilated to the ritual used in the worship of the community's gods; and the tutelary spirits themselves assume the same external form as the public gods. Next, it is more probable that the individual should imitate the community's ritual than the community an individual's; and in some cases it is avowedly the individual that borrows his guardian spirit from the ranks of the community's gods. Finally, the family is an institution which appears relatively late in the history of society. If, therefore, we find points of similarity between the ritual used in ancestor-worship and that used in the worship of the public gods, we shall not fall into the error of treating it as an isolated and unparalleled fact in the history of religion, but shall rather regard it as subject to the same laws and to be explained in the same way as the rest of the class of private cults to which it belongs.

CHAPTER XV

ANCESTOR-WORSHIP

A DESCRIPTION has already been given, in Chapter V., of the spontaneous outbursts of sorrow, "the indescribable scenes of lamentation and wailing," as Mr. Turner calls them, which take place amongst savages on the occasion of a death; and of the uncertainty whether death has really supervened, the reluctance to believe that it has, the endeavours to detain the soul of the dying man by offering him his favourite dishes, displaying his most cherished possessions, praising his noble deeds; the attempts to recall the soul, when the man is dead, to induce it to abide with the survivors; in fine, the desire to dwell on the memory and to seek communion with the spirits of those who have been loved and lost. The object of that chapter was to suggest that the avenue of communication thus opened between the savage and the spirits of his dead may have served to suggest to him a way of approaching other beings, who like the dead were spirits, but unlike them possessed supernatural powers; for the dead do not seem, in any of the ceremonies described, to appear as supernatural beings. The being with whom the savage seeks communion in these rites is "the father whom he knew," not a dæmon of any kind. At death, as in sleep, the spirit deserts the body, but does not in either case necessarily thereby gain supernatural powers. After death, indeed, the ghost's relation to the living is rather one of dependence, for food, comfort, and even continuance of existence. In fine, these spontaneous demonstrations of affection, grief, and desire for reunion with the departed do not amount to worship. We have therefore now to trace the process by which they developed into ancestor-worship.

The first condition of any such development is that the demonstrations, at first spontaneous, should become conventional and harden into custom. This is not the same thing as saying that grief ceases to be genuine when the manner of its expression becomes conventional. On the contrary, in the first place, beneath "the outward trappings and the signs of woe" there may be "that which passes show"; and, in the next place, the existence of a conventional mode of expressing the mourner's woe shows that public opinion considers grief in these circumstances right and proper; such demonstrations, in fact, are not the isolated expression of unusual susceptibility, but an indication of the habitual affection even of a savage for those nearest and dearest to him. When, then, it has become the tribal custom for relatives to perform certain acts, on the occasion of a death, which were originally spontaneous and now are the conventional expressions of grief, it becomes possible for fear to operate in support of this as of other tribal customs, though it was not in fear that either it or they originated. Custom is one of the earliest shapes in which duty presents itself to the consciousness of the savage: it is what is expected of him, both by the community and, in his better moments, by himself as a good member of the community. Now, the savage regards all sickness as the work of spirits — not necessarily of evil spirits, as is commonly and carelessly said. When, therefore, he falls ill, he casts about in his mind for the spirit who may be the cause of his sickness; and if, like the African chief mentioned by Lippert,[1] he has been negligent of the rites which it is customary to perform to a deceased parent, he naturally interprets his headache as a reminder from the neglected ghost. In a word, fear of punishment is an indispensable instrument in the education of man, be he savage or be he civilised; but fear of punishment is not the same thing as fear of evil spirits. The latter is irrational, and is sterile both morally and intellectually, while the former implies a standard of duty (or custom), and opens out the possibility of moral and intellectual progress.

That the ceremonies out of which ancestor-worship was

[1] Lippert, *Kulturgeschichte*, iii. 75.

to develop did not originate in fear, and that the spirit of a deceased kinsman was not a mere evil spirit, is a contention in support of which some arguments have been already adduced in Chapter V.; and which is also supported by the examination of some other customs not mentioned in that chapter—for instance, that of blood-letting at the grave. Thus, in Australia, "members of the tribe stand or kneel over the body in turns, and with a large boomerang they strike each other on the head till a quantity of blood flows over the body"[1] In Central Australia, "they beat their heads until the blood flows, and weep bitterly, if a near relation."[2] In the Northern Territory of South Australia, "the women score their heads and thighs till the blood flows freely . . . the men score their thighs only."[3] Elsewhere in South Australia, "besides weeping and howling, the female relatives make numerous superficial incisions upon the thigh from 6 to 12 inches long."[4] In the New World, at a funeral, the Dacotahs "gash their legs and arms,"[5] and as for the Crows, "blood was streaming from every conceivable part of the bodies of all."[6] In the semi-civilisation of Central America, the Aztecs "mangled their flesh as if it had been insensible, and let their blood run in profusion."[7] In South America, Brazilian aborigines cut off fingers, and the same mutilation appears in Fiji: "his little finger had been cut off in token of affection for his deceased father."[8] The Scyths wounded the lobes of their ears at their king's death.[9] In the New Hebrides, the wounding took a less severe form: "they scratched their faces till they streamed with blood."[10] In Rome, the women scratched their faces till the blood ran.[11] In Tahiti, it sufficed to smear some blood on a rag and drop the rag in the grave.[12] In Tanna, it was enough if the face of the corpse, instead of being smeared with the relatives'

[1] *Journal of Anthropological Institute*, xxiv. 187.
[2] *Ibid.* 183. [3] *Ibid.* 178. [4] *Ibid.* 185.
[5] Dorman, *Primitive Superstitions*, 217. [6] *Ibid.* [7] *Ibid.* 218.
[8] Williams, *Fiji and the Fijians*, i. 177.
[9] Bastian, *Der Mensch*, ii. 328. [10] Turner, *Samoa*, 335.
[11] Cic. *de Leg.* 2, 23, 59; 25, 64; Festus, s.v. *radere*; Plin. *N. H.* 11, 37, 157; Propert. 3. 13*b*. 11; Serv. *ad Aen.* iii. 67, v. 78, xii. 606; Roscher's *Lexikon*, ii. 238.
[12] Bastian, *loc. cit.*

blood, was painted red.[1] In West Africa, it was the relatives (wives) who were painted on this occasion.[2]

To interpret this ceremony as due to fear and as an indication that the spirit of the deceased is regarded as an evil spirit, would be unreasonable on two accounts. First, the ceremony is always associated with demonstrations of grief, and therefore probably adds volume to the flow of that emotion, whereas fear would check it. Next, death is not the only occasion on which the blood of the tribe is applied to the body of a clansman: at birth,[3] at the dawn of manhood,[4] and at marriage,[5] the same ceremony is observed, and it is reasonable, therefore, to suppose that it has the same intention. On those occasions the object is to communicate the blood which is the life of the clan to the clansman when he has especial need of it. I would suggest, therefore, that originally the blood-letting rite at the grave was one of the various devices, described in Chapter V., for retaining or recalling the life which was on the point of leaving, or had left, perhaps not beyond recall, its earthly tenement; and that the blood was intended to strengthen the bond between the clansman and his clan at a time when it was obviously tending to snap.

But as the outward acts which constitute the ceremony tend by a natural process to become less revolting and less cruel until eventually the actual effusion of blood is dispensed with, and some other colouring matter takes its place; so the feeling and the ideas of which the outward act was the expression, tend to change with changing circumstances. When this demonstration of grief and of affection has become conventional, the neglect of it inevitably comes to be regarded as a want of respect to the deceased, and the performance of it is regarded no longer as a crude attempt to give fresh life to the deceased, but as something done to please him. Hence, in the Tonga Islands, they "wound the head and cut the flesh in various parts with knives, shells, clubs, spears, etc., in honour of the deceased";[6] and in Samoa the blood is regarded as an offering to the dead. "Doleful cries are

[1] Turner, *Polynesia*, 93.
[2] Ellis, *Tshi-speaking Peoples*, 268.
[3] *Supra*, p. 76.
[4] *Supra*, p. 103.
[5] *Supra*, p. 171.
[6] Mariner, *Tonga Islands*, ii. 212.

accompanied by the most frantic expressions of grief, such as rending garments, tearing the hair, thumping the face and eyes, burning the body with small piercing firebrands, beating the head with stones till the blood runs; and this they called an 'offering of blood' for the dead. Everyone acquainted with the historical parts of the Bible will here observe remarkable coincidences."[1] But offerings of the worshipper's blood are, as we have seen,[2] made to gods, and the scars which the operation leaves, or the tatooing to which it leads, are interpreted as marks showing that the worshipper is under the protection of the god to whom the offering has been made.[3] When, therefore, as in Australia, "widows as a rule have a number of cuts made on their back as a sign of mourning,"[4] and the blood shed by the relatives comes to be regarded as an offering "to" the deceased, there is an obvious danger of the ceremony coming to be considered as worship of the deceased, by those who practise it as a matter of custom, and explain it by obvious, and incorrect, analogies. Hence it was forbidden to the Hebrews: "Ye shall not make any cuttings in your flesh for the dead, nor print any marks upon you: I am the Lord,"[5] whereas the cuttings and marks would imply that the dead man was the lord of those who made the cuttings in their flesh. Where, however, the tendency was not thus checked, *i.e.* everywhere else, ancestor-worship was free to develop; but its development required the co-operation of other causes, which we shall shortly set forth. But first it is necessary to consider the very interesting question of the hair-offering.

The fact that mourners all over the world do cut off their hair and shave their heads, is well established. The reason for their doing so is disputed. Mr. Frazer[6] regards the proceeding as a means of disinfecting the mourners from the taboo contagion, analogous to the breaking of the vessels used by a taboo person. The late Professor Robertson Smith[7] regarded it as an offering of the hair, in which, as in the blood, the life of the individual is commonly believed to

[1] The Rev. G. Turner, *Polynesia*, i. 227.

[2] *Supra*, p. 170.

[3] *Supra*, p. 172.

[4] *Journal of Anthropological Institute*, xxiv. 195.

[5] Lev. xix. 28.

[6] *Golden Bough*, i. 206–7.

[7] *Religion of the Semites*, 325 ff.

reside. The two views, however, are not irreconcilable, and the analogy of the blood-offering, as explained in our last paragraph, enables us to combine them. Originally, the hair was cut off at once in order that it might not catch and convey the taboo infection: the hair was not an offering to the deceased, any more than the blood of the clan, which was communicated in order to revivify him, was an offering in his honour. Then the custom is continued even when the reason is forgotten; and meanwhile the practice has grown up of commending one's individual prayers and fortunes to the gods by offering one's blood or hair to them. Finally, the mourning custom, the original reason of which has been forgotten, calls for explanation, and is explained on the analogy of the offerings to the gods. That it is so explained by those who practise it, is clear from examples of the custom, in which it is done in honour of or "for" the deceased.[1] That originally it was a measure of disinfection, is clear from the fact that it is observed in cases where the theory of an offering is quite inapplicable.[2]

The history of food-offerings to the dead is, on the theory here suggested, exactly parallel to that of hair and blood-offerings. Originally, the dead were supposed to suffer from hunger and thirst as the living do, and to require food—for which they were dependent on the living. Eventually, the funeral feasts were interpreted on the analogy of those at which the gods feasted with their worshippers—and the dead were now no longer dependent on the living, but on a level with the gods. The food-offering is, however, more interesting in one way than the offerings of blood or hair: it enables us to date ancestor-worship relatively. It was not until agricultural times that the sacrificial rite became the cheerful feast at which the bonds of fellowship were renewed between the god and his worshippers.[3] It could not therefore have been until agricultural times that the funeral feast came to be interpreted on the analogy of the sacrificial feast.

Offerings of food, hair, and blood, then, are elements both of the rites for the dead and of the worship of the gods. But they do not together constitute ancestor-worship: they are its elements—as yet, however, held in suspension and

[1] *Supra*, p. 192. [2] Frazer, *loc. cit.* [3] *Supra*, p. 159.

waiting for something to precipitate them. In other words, worship in any proper sense of the word implies worshippers, united either by the natural bond of blood or by the artificial bond of initiation. In the case of ancestor-worship, the body of worshippers is supplied by the family and united by the natural bond of blood. But the family is a comparatively late institution in the history of society. It does not come into existence until nomad life has been given up. A nomad society, to maintain itself in the struggle for existence at all, must consist of a larger group than that of parents and children, *i.e.* two generations; and in the patriarchal form, the group consists of three or four generations. It is not until the comparative safety of settled life and of village communities has been attained, that it is possible for a son, as soon as he marries, to sever himself from the group into which he was born, and become the founder of a family. In nomad times, he and his wife and children are not a family, but members of the group to which he belongs by birth: they do not form a separate organism or institution, having separate interests from the rest of the community, regulating its own affairs. Thus once more we are brought to the period of settled, agricultural life as the earliest time at which the "worship" of ancestors begins.[1]

When ancestor-worship is established as a private cult, it, like other private cults, is steadily assimilated in form, in its rites and ceremonies, to the public worship of the gods. The animals which provided the food that the deceased originally was supposed to consume, are now sacrificed according to the ritual observed in sacrificing animals to the gods. In West Africa, "water and rum are poured on the grave, and the blood of living sacrifices, who are killed on the spot, is sprinkled on it."[2] In Equatorial Africa, "the son who succeeds the deceased in power immolates an ox on the grave."[3] Amongst the Basutos an ox was slaughtered on the grave as soon as the deceased was

[1] "But the worship of ancestors is not primal. The comparatively late recognition of kinship by savages, among whom some rude form of religion existed, tells against it as the earliest mode of worship."—Clodd, *Myths and Dreams*,[2] 113.

[2] Ellis, *Ewe-speaking Peoples*, 112.

[3] Casati, *Ten Years in Equatoria*, ii. 210.

buried.[1] The Battas pour the blood of a fowl on the corpse.[2] The Tehuelche (Patagonians) sacrifice mares with all the rites previously described.[3] It is not surprising, therefore, that the graves on which these sacrifices were offered should, like the sacrifices themselves, be affected by the tendency to assimilate the private cult of ancestors to the public worship of the gods. The cairns which are frequently erected to mark a grave, and on which the sacrifice was offered, would recall the primitive altar to mind. The single stone or wooden post erected on a grave was converted into a human shape, on the analogy of the idol to which the community's sacrifices were offered. Thus, in De Peyster's Island, "a stone was raised at the head of the grave, and a human head carved on it."[4] Amongst many American tribes "a grave-post is roughly hewn into the image of the person over whose body it is placed."[5] The practice is reported of the Indians of Quebec ("anointing and greasing that man of wood as if living," says Father Salamant), the Ottawas, Algonkins, Alaskans, the Indians of the North-West, the natives of Chili, of the West Indies, Nicaragua, the Isthmus, Peru, and the Mayas and the Aztecs. Where cremation prevailed, the ashes were placed in hollow wooden statues, hollow clay images, or urns having on the outside a representation of the deceased.[6]

When the assimilation of the rites for the dead to the ritual of the gods has proceeded thus far, it naturally happens that in many cases some superhuman powers are ascribed to the spirits of the dead. But it never happens that the spirits of the dead are conceived to be gods. For this there are several obvious reasons. Man is dependent on the gods; but the spirits of his deceased ancestors are dependent on him. The house-father, when he dies, does not cease to be "the father whom they knew"; though dead, and sometimes differing in degree of power from his sons, who in their turn will be "worshipped," he does not—like the gods—differ in kind from mortal men. Above all, the gods of the community, merely from the fact that they have the whole of the community for their worshippers and under their

[1] Casalis, *Les Bassoutos*, 264.
[2] Bastian, *Oest. Asien*, v. 365.
[3] *Supra*, p. 146.
[4] Turner, *Samoa*, 286.
[5] Dorman, *Primitive Superstitions*, 117.
[6] *Ibid.*

protection, must inevitably be regarded as greater powers than a spirit who is only worshipped by the narrow circle of a single family, and cannot do much even for them.

To speak of the gods as "deified ancestors," is to use an expression which covers some ambiguity of thought. If what is implied is that in a community possessing the conception of divine personality, certain ancestors are, by some unexplained process, raised to the rank of gods, the statement may be true, but it does not prove that the gods, to whose rank the spirit is promoted, were themselves originally ghosts—which is the very thing that it is intended to prove. What then of these gods? Either they are believed to be the ancestors of some of their worshippers, or they are not. If they are believed to be the ancestors of their worshippers, then they are not believed to have been human: the worshipper's pride is that *his* ancestor was a god and no mere mortal. Thus certain Greek families believed that they were descended from Zeus, and they worshipped Zeus, not as ancestor but as god. The "deified ancestor" theory, however, would have us believe that there was once a man named Zeus, who had a family, and his descendants thought that he was a god. Which is simplicity itself. If, on the other hand, a god is not believed to be the ancestor of any of his worshippers, then to assert that he was really a "deified ancestor" is to make a statement for which there is no evidence—it is an inference from an assumption, namely, that the only spirits which the savage originally knew were ghosts. This assumption, however, is not true: the savage believes the forces and phenomena of nature to be personalities like himself, he does not believe that they are ghosts or worked by ghosts. In fine, the notion that gods were evolved out of ghosts is based on an unproved assumption and the simple fallacy of confusing ancestors human and ancestors divine. The fact is that ancestors known to be human were not worshipped as gods, and that ancestors worshipped as gods were not believed to have been human.

This last remark leads us to a generalisation which, though obvious, is important: it is that wherever ancestor-worship exists, it exists side by side with the public worship of the gods of the community. The two systems develop on lines which are parallel, indeed, and therefore never meet; whereas, if they had moved on the same line of development, one would have absorbed the other. In other words, if ancestor-worship were the source of religion, if gods were originally ghosts, we may be reasonably sure that ancestor-worship would have died in giving birth to the higher form of religion, or rather that it would have been transformed into it. In the newly-evolved organism we should have traced survivals here and there, rudimentary organs inherited from the previous state of things. We should also have found races who had never got beyond the earlier stage, or had relapsed into it. But we should not everywhere have found the two systems alive together: we might as well expect to find the chrysalis still living by the side of the butterfly which has emerged from it.

The clear demarcation between the two systems, their mutual exclusiveness to the last, is an indication that they start from different presuppositions and are addressed to different objects. At the same time, the parallelism between them shows that they have their respective sources in the same region of feeling. That feeling is piety, filial piety in the one case, piety towards the protecting god of the clan in the other. Here we have displayed the secret of the strength of ancestor-worship, and also of its weakness. Of its strength, because, as Confucius says, "Filial piety and fraternal submission! are they not the root of all benevolent actions?"[1] Of its weakness, because it is inadequate of itself to satisfy the demands of the religious instinct. In China, the people, excluded from participation in the state-worship of Heaven, decline upon the lowest forms of religion, in their desire for communion with a supernatural power. This desire, where it exists, cannot be satisfied by the substitution of a human object of adoration for the supernatural which it craves to feed on; and the present religious condition of China shows how unpractical Confucius was in recommending the average man to regard his human father as a god: "nor in [filial obedience] is there anything so essential as to reverence one's father; and as a mark of reverence there is nothing more important than to place him

[1] Lun-yu, i. 2. 2 (Douglas, *Confucianism*, 119).

on an equality with Heaven. Thus did the noble lord of Chow. Formerly he sacrificed on the round altar to the spirits of his remote ancestors, as equal with Heaven; and in the open hall he sacrificed to Wăn Wang (his father) as equal with Shang-te [the Supreme Being]." [1]

The organised worship of ancestors is bound up with the patriarchate and the patria potestas. The service which it rendered to civilisation consists in the aid it afforded to the development of the family, the nidus of mortality. "Filial piety," said Confucius, "is the beginning of virtue"; and before him E-yin had said, "the commencement is in the family and state; the consummation is in the Empire." [2] But when ancestor-worship has rendered its service to civilisation, there is a reason for its being cast aside. As an institution, it works in support of the patria potestas: the worship can only be carried on by sons, sons therefore are ardently desired; marriage is a means simply to the worship which the man requires for himself after death, and is not a holy estate in and for itself. Woman is in the family but not of it; she is treated as an inferior, and is debarred from co-operating in the cause of civilisation and from rendering to the progress of morality the services which are peculiarly her own. Rooting out ancestor-worship in Europe gave the Christian Church much trouble for many centuries.

There remain certain topics connected with ancestor-worship—human sacrifice and cannibalism—which are not attractive, but cannot be ignored, especially by a writer who argues for the origin of ancestor-worship in the filial piety of the patriarchal family of a comparatively late, *i.e.* the agricultural, period. We will begin with human sacrifice. The first thing to note is that it appears at a much earlier period in the rites for the dead than it does in the ritual of the gods. As regards the latter: in the totemistic period the only sacrifice known is that of animals; in the beginning of the agricultural period also human sacrifice is foreign to the cheerful feast in which the god and his worshippers meet together; it is not until the self-satisfaction of that time has given way to the "habitual sense of human guilt" of a still later period, that human life comes to be regarded as the

[1] Douglas, *op. cit.* 121. [2] *Op. cit.* 123 and 118.

necessary expiation of human sin.[1] But whereas human sacrifice comes thus late in the history of religious ritual, the practice of immolating human beings at a tomb apparently comes fairly early in the development of the rites of the dead; such immolation certainly has a totally different origin and meaning from human sacrifice in religious ritual. The persons butchered at the grave of a savage chieftain are usually his wives and other attendants; and the object of the slaughter evidently is exactly the same as that of providing food for the dead—the deceased follows the same pursuits, enjoys the same rank, and requires the same food and attendance when dead as during life. It is this identity between the purpose of food-offerings and of the slaughter of attendants which shows the latter to be one of the primitive elements out of which systematic ancestor-worship was subsequently organised. Where such slaughter continued to be customary at the time when human sacrifice had come to be part of the ritual of the gods, it came to be interpreted on the analogy of human "sacrifice" in the proper (*i.e.* religious) sense of the word, just as the offerings of blood, hair, and food came to be similarly interpreted, or misinterpreted. But human sacrifice (again in the proper sense of the word) was only offered in seasons of fear and tribulation; and slaughter at the tomb now came to be ascribed to the same emotion of fear. The idea that slaughter at the tomb was from the beginning due to fear of the ghost, seems to me to overlook two important facts: the first is that the ghost is from the beginning dependent on the living—according to many peoples, he cannot even find his way to the place where he would be, without their assistance; the next is, that affection is quite as capable of extravagant excess as fear. Let the reader recall the well-known instance of the Red Indian son who coolly killed a white man, the close friend of his father, because he could not think how his father, just dead, would be able to get on without his old friend to talk to. The fact is that an utter disregard for human life may well exist, does frequently coexist, with devoted attachment to particular persons.[2] So much for that unpleasant topic.

[1] *Supra*, p. 161.

[2] Mr. James Dawson, who is well qualified to speak, says of the Australians

As for cannibalism: it is not sufficiently general or uniform in its manifestations to allow of any general statement with regard to it. Sometimes it is religious in intention, sometimes the alternative to starvation; sometimes it is due to a perverted taste for food, sometimes it is practised medicinally; here it is only clansmen that are eaten, there only aliens. The cases in which it is religious in intention have been discussed in a previous chapter.[1] They are highly exceptional, and need not detain us. Nor need we do more than note that "the negro man-eater certainly takes human flesh as food purely and simply, and not from any religious or superstitious reason."[2] The Caribs bred children as a food-supply of this kind, as they might poultry. That the belief in the possibility of acquiring the courage or other attributes of an animal or man by consuming his or its flesh, does lead to cannibalism in some cases, may be taken as proved;[3] in such cases it is only selected portions of the body that are consumed, and those "medicinally," not as food. That some peoples eat only aliens is undoubted; and the rigour of the restriction is illustrated by an incident that happened recently on the Congo, where "one man, who

(*Australian Aborigines*, p. iv.), who are sometimes ranked as the lowest of savages: "It may be truly said of them, that, with the exception of the low estimate they naturally place on life, their moral character and modesty—all things considered—compare favourably with those of the most highly cultivated communities of Europe"; if those who doubt this were themselves "to listen to their guileless conversation, their humour and wit, and their expressions of honour and affection for one another," they would have to admit "that they are at least equal, if not superior, to the general run of white men." Still lower in the scale of humanity are the Shoshones (California): "Those who have seen them unanimously agree that they of all men are lowest . . . having no clothes, scarcely any cooked food, in many instances no weapons" (Bancroft, *Native Races*, i. 440). Yet one traveller says, "They are very rigid in their morals," and "honest and trustworthy, but lazy and dirty"; another, that they are "frank and communicative"; another, "highly intelligent and lively . . . the most virtuous and unsophisticated of all the Indians"; another, "the most pure and uncorrupted aborigines . . . scrupulously clean . . . and chaste in their habits." Of the Dinka, Schweinfurth says (*Heart of Africa*, i. 169), "Notwithstanding that certain instances may be alleged which seem to demonstrate that the character of the Dinka is unfeeling, these cases never refer to such as are bound by the ties of kindred . . . the accusation is quite unjustifiable that family affection, in our sense, is at a low ebb among them."

[1] *Supra*, p. 161.

[2] Captain Hinde, speaking at the British Association, 1895.

[3] *Folk-Lore*, June 1892 (Hartland, *The Sin-Eater*).

was placed on sentry-go, shot his own father, and then expressed regret, because by the rule of the tribe he could not eat the body of his parent."[1]

Finally, there are instances in which only members of the tribe are eaten. This practice is reported by Herodotus[2] of the Padæi—probably the Gônda of the Northern Dekkan, who still maintain the custom—and his statement, that few of them attain to old age, because a man is at once killed when he shows symptoms of illness, is curiously confirmed by the words of Captain Hinde, speaking of a different race: "On the Lomami River no grey hairs were to be seen, because the adults were eaten when they began to manifest signs of decrepitude." We may therefore believe Herodotus when he makes the same statement of the Massagetæ,[3] especially as the mode of consumption described by him reappears amongst the Bangala;[4] and of the Issedones,[5] whose treatment of the bones of the deceased finds its parallel in the remarkable discoveries made just now in Egypt by Dr. Flinders Petrie; and whose invitations to friends to partake in the feast are paralleled by a similar custom in Luzon.[6] It is not, therefore, *à priori* improbable that the Irish followed the custom, as Strabo reports,[7] especially as it is said to have been found amongst another branch of the Aryan peoples, the Wends.[8] It occurs also in the Uaaupés Valley, South America,[9] amongst the Battas of Sumatra, the Kookies, the inhabitants of Sindai and of the Floris Islands,[10] and the Australians.[11] The Quissamas kill and eat criminals of their own tribe.[12] In Francis Island, "thieves were killed and their bodies eaten—only in such cases was there cannibalism."[13]

To understand the custom, we must place ourselves at the savage point of view. We must remember the savage's habitual disregard for human life, and that amongst nomads, compelled by the severity of the struggle for existence to abandon the aged who cannot keep up with the enforced

[1] Captain Hinde, *loc. cit.* [2] Hdt. iii. 99. [3] Hdt. i. 216.
[4] Schneider, *Relig. d. Afrik. Naturvölker*, 135. [5] Hdt. iv. 26.
[6] Bastian, *Oest. Asien*, v. 272. [7] Strabo, iv. v. 4. [8] Bastian, *loc. cit.*
[9] Wallace, *On the Amazon*,[3] 346. [10] Bastian, *loc. cit.*
[11] *Journal of the Anthropological Institute*, xxiv. 182, 196.
[12] *Ibid.* *i.* 187. [13] Turner, *Samoa*, 300.

marches of the tribe, the aged meet their fate voluntarily, manfully, and without any sense of hardship. Next, strange as at first sight it may appear, eating aged relatives neither implies want of respect to them nor prevents them from being worshipped after death. The evidence is clear on both points. Strabo says of the Irish that they regard it as an honour; Herodotus, that the Massagetæ consider it "the happiest issue," and count it a misfortune when disease prevents them from "attaining to sacrifice"; the Issedones gilded the skull and made yearly offerings to it.[1] Throughout, the words of Herodotus, as Stein remarks *ad locc.*, imply ceremonial killing and the solemnity of sacrifice. In fine, the custom is probably simply one of the savage's attempts "to make sure that the corpse is properly disposed of, and can no longer be a source of danger to the living, but rather of blessing."[2] By this disposal of it, the life of the clan is, according to savage notions, kept within the clan; the good attributes of the dead man are communicated to his kin; and his spirit is not set adrift to wander homeless abroad—if it were so cut off from the ties uniting it to the clan, it would become dangerous: hence, even when inhumation has become usual, the ancient practice of eating survives, amongst the Quissamas and in Francis Island, in the case of criminals, whose spirits, owing to their dangerous propensities, are especially likely to give trouble, if they are not treated in the ancient and more respectful manner. Where the dog was the totem animal —and as the dog is the commonest and earliest domesticated animal, he must have been a common totem—these same ends would be secured by making him, as a member of the clan, consume the body; and this may be the origin of the practice of giving corpses to be devoured by dogs, a practice which is common to the Northern Mongolians,[3] the Parthians,[4] the Hyrcanians,[5] the ancient Persians,[6] and has left its traces amongst the Parsis: "their funeral ritual requires that when a corpse is brought to the Dakhmá, or the place where it is to be given up to the vultures, it should first be exhibited to one or more dogs . . . this ceremonial is called

[1] Hdt. iv. 26.
[2] Robertson Smith, *Religion of the Semites*, 370.
[3] Prejvalsky, *Mongolia*, i. 14.
[4] Justin, xli. 3.
[5] Cic. *Quart. Tusc.* i. 45.
[6] Hdt. i. 140.

Sagdíd (Vendidad Farg. vii. 3). That this is a relic of the former detestable custom, is evident from the fact of the said Scriptures enjoining the exposure of corpses that dogs and carrion birds may see and devour them (Vendidad Farg. v. 73, 74)."[1]

Where the relatives could not or would not adopt either of these modes, the corpse, which is one of the things inherently taboo,[2] had to be isolated in some manner. There were various ways of effecting this isolation: inhumation—which prevented the ghost from swelling the "inops inhumataque turba" of spirits—and cremation need no illustration. The practice of abandoning the house or room in which the corpse lay, and thus isolating it, has been illustrated already.[3] But the custom of suspending the corpse between heaven and earth for the same purpose is not so familiar. It is found, however, amongst the Australians: "a stage consisting of boughs is built in the branches of a tree, the corpse placed thereon and covered with boughs."[4] It is practised by the Aleuts,[5] the Mandans, the Santa Fé tribes, the Dacotahs, the Western Ojibways, the Assiniboins, and on the Columbia River.[6] Amongst the Samoyedes, the bones of a dead shaman are put in a tree; and in Equatorial Africa, Mbruo, a rain-maker, "selected for his tomb an old tree, being possessed by an idea that it was indecorous for a prince to be placed in contact with the earth; and he gave orders that the upper part of the tree was to be hollowed out lengthwise, and his body placed inside it in an upright position."[7]

In conclusion, the reader may have noticed that there is one class of offerings (weapons, implements, utensils, etc.) of which no mention has been made in this chapter. The fact is they differ in nothing from the offerings, *e.g.* of food, which have been discussed: the ghost requires them, as he does food, and is dependent for them on the living. Eventually, however, owing to the analogy of certain features in the ritual of the gods, they come to be interpreted as gifts to

[1] Rajendralála Mitra, *Indo-Aryans*, ii. 162.
[2] *Supra*, p. 76. [3] *Supra*, p. 77.
[4] *Journal of the Anthropological Institute*, 178; cf. 182, 186, 195.
[5] Bancroft, *Native Races*, i. 93. [6] Dorman, *Prim. Superstitions*, 168.
[7] Casati, *Equatoria*, i. 170.

appease the manes. But these features, and the "gift theory of sacrifice" to which they give rise, cannot be adequately explained until we come to see the influence of agricultural beliefs on religion—the subject of our next chapter. Here, therefore, we will content ourselves with noting that the theory that the things so given to the deceased are things which belonged to him and to which his ghost might cling, does not account for the fact that in neolithic interments the flint implements, etc., are perfectly unused, and that the Ojibway Indians place new guns and blankets on the grave in case the deceased's own are old or inferior.[1] The motive, therefore, is not fear of the clinging ghost.

[1] *Journal of the Anthropological Institute*, 112.

CHAPTER XVI

TREE AND PLANT WORSHIP

THE savage's theory of causation is animistic; that is to say, he regards everything, animate or inanimate, which acts or produces an effect as possessing like powers and passions, motives and emotions, with himself. That trees and plants especially possessed like parts and passions with himself, was an inference in which he was confirmed not merely by the fact that they possess (vegetable) life, but by the blood-like sap which many exude when cut, and by the shrieks which they utter when felled. But animism is rather a primitive philosophical theory than a form of religious belief: it ascribes human, not superhuman, powers to non-human beings and things. When, however, the attention of the savage is directed by the occurrence of some incomprehensible or strikingly unexpected and unaccountable event to the sentiment of the supernatural latent in his consciousness; when he ascribes irresistible power over his own fortunes to some animate or inanimate object, then that object becomes marked off from other things and is distinguished from them by the possession of superhuman powers, and by the fact that in it the savage sees the external source of that sentiment of the supernatural of which he is conscious within himself. That the savage in his blind search for the supernatural amongst external objects was frequently in all lands led to believe that trees and plants exercised supernatural powers, is a well-known fact. That he would then seek to establish an alliance between his tribe and the species which he believed to possess any especial power over his own fate, is an inference which the existence of animal totems would justify us in drawing *à priori*. And as a matter of fact we have good evidence of the existence of plant and tree totems. "The Karama tree is the totem of the Dravidian Kharwárs and Mánjíhs."[1] Kujur is the name both of a Dravidian sept and of a jungle herb which the sept does not eat.[2] "The *Bara* sept is evidently the same as the *Barar* of the Oráons, who will not eat the leaves of the *bar* tree or *Ficus indica*. In Mirzapur they will not cut this tree. . . . A Tiga sept takes its name from a jungle root which is prohibited to them."[3] In Berar and Bombay "it is said that a betrothal, in every other respect irreproachable, will be broken off if the two houses are discovered to pay honour to the same tree—in other words, if they worship the same family totem."[4] These family totems are called Devaks (guardian gods), and are animals or trees. "The Devak is the ancestor or head of the house, and so families which have the same guardian cannot marry. . . . If the Devak be a fruit-tree . . . some families abstain from eating the fruit of the tree which forms their devak or badge."[5] In North America, "the Red Maize clan of the Omahas will not eat red maize,"[6] and they, like the Dravidian septs, seem to have believed themselves descended from their totem.[7] On the Gold Coast of Africa, there is a clan called Abradzi-Fo, "plantain-family," and "in the interior members of this family still abstain from the plantain."[8]

We have already seen[9] that animals may be chosen as totems of individuals as well as of tribes: thus, in Central America, "nagualism is one of the ancient forms of worship, and consists in choosing an animal as the tutelary divinity of a child, whose existence will be so closely connected with it that the life of one depends on that of the other."[10] So, too, in Europe, amongst Aryan peoples, Romans[11] and Teutons,[12] there is evidence enough to show the existence of a belief that the fate and life of a man may be mystically involved with that of his "birth-tree," *i.e.* a tree planted at his birth:

[1] Crooke, *Popular Religion and Folk-Lore of Northern India*, 22.
[2] *Ibid.* 283. [3] *Loc. cit.* [4] *Ibid.* 286.
[5] *Ibid.* 287. [6] Frazer, *Totemism*, 11. [7] *Ibid.* 6.
[8] Ellis, *Tshi-speaking Peoples*, 207. [9] *Supra*, p. 182.
[10] Bancroft, *Native Races*, iii. 458.
[11] Mannhardt, *Antike Wald und Feld-kulte*, 23.
[12] Mannhardt, *Baumkultus*, 32 and 50.

his life depends on and terminates with that of the tree; he grows or withers as his tree grows or withers.

To return, however, to the clan totem. We may expect to find the history of the tree totem passing through much the same stages as that of the animal totem: thus an individual tree or some few individuals may come to enjoy the whole of the worship which was originally bestowed upon all the members of the species; and this was the case with the sacred olive of Athênê at Athens, and with the maypole of the Teutons, which was to the village what the "birth-tree" was to the individual, "it was the *genius tutelaris*, the *alter ego* of the whole community,"[1] which afforded an asylum to every member of the village community,[2] protected the villagers from all harm,[3] and brought them all blessings.[4] Or, again, the species may continue to be worshipped; but, owing to the relaxation of the blood-tie consequent upon settled life and political development, the worship may be thrown open to all and not confined to the clan: thus in Greece and Rome the laurel and the ivy, in Assyria the palm-tree, were species of plants whose worship was general and not in historic times restricted to any one tribe; in India, "among the sacred trees the various varieties of the fig hold a conspicuous place . . . the various fig-trees hold an important part in the domestic ritual. . . . The *pipal* is worshipped by moving round it in the course of the sun . . . this regard for the pipal (*Ficus religiosa*) extends through Africa, New Zealand, Australia, Sumatra, and Java."[5]

As the animal totem eventually in some cases assumes human form, and, after passing through various intermediate shapes, becomes an anthropomorphic god, so we may expect the tree totem to be anthropomorphised; and this is often the case. The Dryads or tree-nymphs of the Greeks will occur to the reader at once; and amongst the Aryans of Northern Europe, Mannhardt has shown conclusively that the tree-spirit was represented by a human being or a human figure tied to a tree or set on a tree-top, or enveloped in tree-leaves ("Jack in the green"), or otherwise associated with the tree. When, then, we find a *Ζεὺς ἔνδενδρος* or a

[1] Mannhardt, *B. K.* 182. [2] *Loc. cit.* [3] *Ibid.* 53. [4] *Ibid.* 37.
[5] Crooke, *op. cit.* 247–9.

Διόνυσος ἔνδενδρος, and that in Greece "images of the gods were set on trees,"[1] and that the Ephesian Artemis was believed to dwell within the stem of an oak, we are justified in believing that these deities were either originally tree totems or that their worship has absorbed that of some tree totem; and the same conclusion holds good, when we find that a species of tree or plant is "associated" with some god, *e.g.* the laurel with Apollo or the ivy with Dionysus.

As totem tribes name themselves after their animal totem, and continue to be designated by the name even when they have left the totem stage behind, so with plant totems. On the Gold Coast, the Abradzi-fo or Plantain family still abstain from the plantain, as the Leopard, Dog, and Parrot families abstain from leopards, dogs, and parrots respectively.[2] We can therefore hardly refuse to believe that the Corn-stalk family and the Palm-oil Grove family had the corn-stalk and palm-tree for totems originally, though we do not happen to have evidence to show that they continue to show respect to the plants from which they take their name. Amongst the Greeks and Romans tree and plant worship may probably account for such names as *Φηγαιεῖς*[3] and Fabius; and in North Europe there are instances which may possibly be remote survivals of this practice.[4]

As the animal totem was at certain seasons taken round the settlement in order to fortify the inhabitants with supernatural powers against supernatural dangers, *e.g.* the python procession in Whydah, so in North Europe "the begging processions with May-trees or May-boughs from door to door had everywhere originally a serious and, so to speak, sacramental significance; people really believed that the god of growth" [rather the tree totem] "was present unseen in the bough; by the procession he was brought to each house to bestow his blessing."[5] So, too, the god presumably was originally present in the switch of rowan with which the Scottish milkmaid protects her cattle from evil spirits; and,

[1] Schrader, *Prehistoric Antiquities*, 278.
[2] Ellis, *Tshi-speaking Peoples*, 206–7.
[3] *Corp. Inscrip. Att.* ii. 108, 435, etc.
[4] Mannhardt, *B. K.* 51. [5] Frazer, *G. B.* i. 86, translating *B. K.* 315.

on the same principle, in India "most Vaishnava sects wear necklaces and carry rosaries made of holy basil."[1]

As in death the clansman was believed to rejoin the animal totem, so "the Orâons of Bengal revere the tamarind and bury their dead under its branches."[2] This is probably a contributing cause to the practice of suspension burial mentioned in a previous chapter.[3] "Some of the semi-Hinduised Bengal Ghonds have the remarkable custom of tying the corpses of adult males by a cord to the *mahua* tree in an upright position previous to burial."[4]

Finally, tree totems, like animal totems, make their appearance in the marriage rite. Amongst some of the Dravidian races a branch of the sacred *mahua* tree "is placed in the hands of the bride and bridegroom during the ceremony,"[5] evidently to bring them under the immediate protection of the totem-god, and by way of worship "they also revolve round a branch of the tree planted in the ground," just as in Northern Europe amongst the Wends the bride had to worship the "life-tree" of her new home.[6] Or the bride and bridegroom are married first to trees and then to each other.[7]

Much more important, however, than tree totems for the history of religion and of civilisation in general are plant totems, for it was through plant-worship that cereals and food-plants came to be cultivated, and it was in consequence of their cultivation that the act of worship received a remarkable extension. With regard to the origin of cultivation, "it has usually been held that cultivation must have taken its rise from the accident of chance seeds being scattered about in the neighbourhood of the hut or of the domestic manure heap—the barbaric kitchen-midden."[8] But something more, considerably more, than this is necessary to account for the origin of cultivation: seeds must be retained from one year to the next for the purpose of sowing them, and such retention implies, first, that primitive man was aware of the necessity of saving seeds, and, second, that he had the self-control to save them instead of eating them. To account

[1] Crooke, *op. cit.* 257. [2] *Ibid.* 256. [3] *Supra*, p. 204.
[4] Crooke, 251. [5] *Loc. cit.* [6] *B. K.* 161, 174, 182.
[7] For examples, Crooke, 258 ff. [8] Grant Allen, *The Attis*, 45.

for such self-control in the savage, whose habit is "to eat and destroy with lavish prodigality whatever he possesses in the pure recklessness of the moment,"[1] we must suppose some exceptionally powerful motive. Without some such stimulus, "primitive man, careless of the future as he is, would scarcely be likely deliberately to retain seeds from one year to the next for the purpose of sowing them."[1] That motive could only have been religious. Our argument therefore in outline will be to show, first, that cereals and food-plants are actually totems amongst savages; next, that the treatment of totem-plants generally is such that the seeds are necessarily preserved from one year to the next, simply because the plants are totems, and without any view to their cultivation; third, that amongst civilised peoples the rites and worship connected with cereals and agriculture are exactly what they would have been if the cereals had been totems.

That savages do adopt food-plants and cereals as totems, we have already seen. We need only mention the Red Maize clan of the Omahas in North America, and the Plantain and Corn-stalk clans of the Gold Coast. We have also seen that the tree-spirit or totem-god was supposed to be actually present, not only in the tree, but in any branch of it, and that the presence of the god in the branch brought blessing and protection to his worshippers. We have next to note that amongst the European Aryans it was customary not only to carry such branches in procession, as already described, but also to plant them on the roof or in front of the door of a house,[2] in order to secure the permanent presence and supernatural protection of the tree-spirit. Planting the branch in this position was an annual ceremony, and the branch was preserved from one year to the next, and then a fresh one was substituted with the same ceremonies. We may infer, therefore, that those savages whose totems were plants adopted much the same means for obtaining the constant protection of their god as those whose totems were trees. Just as in the case of animal totems the god was supposed to dwell or manifest himself in any and every individual of the species, and consequently the death of any

[1] *Loc. cit.* [2] *B. K.* 605.

individual is not the death of the god, so, according to the belief of the North European Aryans, a vegetation spirit inhabited not a single plant, but several individuals or the whole species, and consequently did not perish in the autumn with the individual.[1] Hence any sheaf would, like any branch, contain the god; and if preserved in the house or tent from one year to the next, it would secure the presence and protection of the god in the interval between the autumn and the spring, during which there was no growth or life of plants in the field. But the preservation of the sheaf would also teach primitive man the fact—of which in the beginning he must have been ignorant—that food-plants are produced from seeds, and can be produced from seeds which have been kept from one year to the next. It would also form in him the habit of preserving seeds to sow them.

That our Aryan forefathers in Europe were in the habit of thus preserving a sheaf and worshipping it, has been conclusively proved by Mannhardt[2] from an examination of harvest customs still surviving. Several ears of corn are bound together, worshipped, preserved for the year, and supposed to influence the next harvest. In Great Britain the ears are still sometimes bound together, made into the rude form of a female doll, clad in a paper dress, and called the Corn Baby, Kern Baby, or the Maiden,[3] sometimes also, in England and elsewhere in Europe, the Old Woman or Corn Mother.[4] That the practice is not peculiar to the Aryan peoples, and that its explanation must be sought in some world-wide belief, is shown by the existence of the custom in the New World, both in Central and in South America. Thus in Peru "they take a certaine portion of the most fruitefull of the Mays [maize] that growes in their farmes . . . they put this Mays in the richest garments they have, and, being thus wrapped and dressed, they worship this Pirua and hold it in great veneration, saying it is the Mother of the Mays of their inheritances, and that by this means the Mays augments and is preserved";[5] and in Mexico "the damsels that served Chicomecoatl carried each one on her shoulders seven ears of

[1] *B. K.* 4.
[2] *B. K.* 209 note, 212, 213.
[3] Frazer, *G. B.* i. 344.
[4] *Ibid.* 338 ff.
[5] Lang, *Custom and Myth*,[2] 19, quoting Grimston's translation of Acosta.

maize rolled in a rich mantle."[1] After the festival in which they carried this maize in procession, "the folk returned to their houses, and sanctified maize was put in the bottom of every granary, and it was said that it was the heart" [life, spirit] "thereof, and it remained there till taken out for seed."[2]

Originally a clan that had a plant or animal for its totem worshipped the actual plant or animal as a being possessed of supernatural powers. Then the totem-god was conceived as a spirit manifesting itself in any and every member of the species; then, again, gradually this spirit was conceived as having human shape; and, finally, the anthropomorphic god becomes so detached from the species that his origin is quite forgotten, and the plant or animal is merely sacred to him, or a usual sacrifice to him, or simply "associated" with him in art. In the examples cited in the last paragraph, the food-plant is still itself worshipped, but the first step towards anthropomorphism has been taken. The female dress which it wears is evidently intended to indicate that the indwelling spirit would, if seen, appear in human shape. So in Bengal the plantain tree is "clothed as a woman and worshipped."[3] This transition stage in the development of the goddess out of the plant may be compared to the half-human, half-animal shape of the animal totems of Egypt. The next stage in the evolution is completed when the goddess is represented in purely human form, but expresses her connection with the plant by her functions, attributes, or name so clearly that her origin is undisguised. Thus the origin of the Mexican goddess of maize, Xilonen, is expressed without any possibility of disguise by her name (from xilotl, "young ear of maize") as well as by her function; and the same may be said of the Peruvian Saramama or Maize-mother and the Hindoo Bhogaldái or Cotton-mother. Finally, the Mexican goddess Chicomecoatl and the Greek Demeter are representatives of the stage in which it is forgotten that the goddess was originally a plant, and her origin is indicated only by the fact that the former is represented as carrying stalks of maize in her hand, the latter as wearing a corn-garland, and both as having cereals offered to them.

[1] Bancroft, *Native Races*, iii. 358. [2] *Ibid.* 362. [3] Crooke, 255.

The primary object of a totem alliance between a human kin and an animal kind is to obtain a supernatural ally against supernatural foes. Annually the totem clan sacrifices its animal god, and by partaking of the sacrificial meal fortifies its members against supernatural dangers for the forthcoming year, renews the alliance, and enters into fresh and closer communion with the totem-god. In the case of clans having for their totems trees and plants which do not produce edible fruits or seeds, communion with the god was sought by another means, which we reserve for separate discussion hereafter. In the case, however, of totem trees and plants which do produce edible seeds and fruits, the sacramental meal was possible; and its evolution, which we now have to trace, followed lines so parallel in the Old World and the New, that it is evident that the causes at work to produce it were not exceptional or peculiar to any one race or time or clime, but were general causes yielding general laws for the history of early religion.

The first stage in the development of this form of the sacramental meal is that in which the plant totem or vegetation spirit has not yet come to be conceived of as having human form. In this stage the seeds or fruits are eaten at a solemn annual meal, of which all members of the community (clan or family) must eat, and of which no fragments must be left—two conditions essential, as we have seen,[1] in the sacrificial meal of the animal totem. Of this stage we have a survival in the Lithuanian feast Samborios. Annually in December, in each household, a mess, consisting of wheat, barley, oats, and other seeds, was cooked; of it none but members of the household could partake, and every member must partake; nothing might be left, or if left, the remains must be buried.[2] A similar survival was the Athenian Pyanepsion, an annual feast (occurring at the end of the procession in which the eiresionê was carried) in which also a mess of all sorts of cereals (*πάνσπερμα*) was cooked and consumed by the household.[3] In Sicily, the Kotytis feast had degenerated considerably. Like the Athenian feast, it began with a procession in which the branch of a tree was carried round the community, but the only trace of the original

[1] *Supra*, p. 145. [2] *W. F. K.* 249; cf. *supra*, p. 149 ff. [3] *W. F. K.* 227.

meal of which all were expected to partake was the practice of throwing the fruits, which had been attached to the branch, to be scrambled for by the people.[1] In the New World, Chicomecoatl's feast in April began with a procession of youths carrying stalks of maize and other herbs through the maize-fields; and then a mess of tortillas, chian flour, maize, and beans was eaten in the goddess's temple "in a general scramble, take who could."[2]

The second stage is that in which the plant totem has come to be conceived of as a spirit having human form. At this stage the custom is to represent the spirit by a dough image of human form. Thus in Mexico "they made out of dough an image of the goddess Chicomecoatl, in the court-yard of her temple, offering before it all kinds of maize, beans, and chian."[3] Father Acosta describes the image more particularly. "Presently there stepped foorth a Priest, attyred with a shorte surplise full of tasselles beneath, who came from the top of the temple with an idoll made of paste, of wheat and mays mingled with hony, which had the eyes made of the graines of greene glasse and the teeth of the grains of mays. . . . Then did he mount to the place where those were that were to be sacrificed, showing this idoll to every one in particular, saying unto them, This is your god."[4] That the dough image was sacramentally eaten in Mexico, we shall see shortly. It was also so eaten in the Old World. "In Wermland the House-mother makes a dough doll, in the shape of a little girl, out of the corn of the last sheaf garnered, and it is distributed between and consumed by the assembled members of the household."[5] In Bourbonnais "a fir-tree is planted in the last load of corn, and on the top is fastened a man of dough. Tree and dough-man are taken to the mairie, and there kept till the end of the vintage, when a general harvest festival is celebrated, and the mayor divides the dough figure and distributes it amongst the people to eat."[6] This "contamination" of tree-worship and the worship of the vegetation spirit has its parallels in the New World. "Every year, at the season of the maize harvest,

[1] Bancroft, iii. 258. [2] *Ibid.* 360. [3] *Ibid.* 421.
[4] Acosta, Grimston's translation (Hakluyt Soc.), ii. 347.
[5] Mannhardt, *Mythologische Forschungen*, 179. [6] *B. K.* 205.

the mountaineer Peruvians had a solemn festival, on which occasion they set up two tall straight trees like masts, on the top of which was placed the figure of a man, surrounded by other figures and adorned with flowers. The inhabitants went in procession, armed with bows and arrows, and regularly marshalled into companies, beating their drums, and with great outcries and rejoicings, each company in succession discharging their arrows at the dressed-up figures." [1] (This ceremony corresponds to the solemn slaughter of the animal totem, in the responsibility for which every member of the community must take his share, *Religion of the Semites*, p. 284.) In Mexico we have a similar "contamination" combined with the sacrifice and sacramental eating of the god: at a festival in the tenth month of the Mexican year, a tree was felled and the trunk erected. A paste figure, representing Xiuhtecutli, was placed on the top, and young men vied with each other in climbing up the ropes which maintained the tree trunk in position, but very few reached the top. The first to do so seized the figure, stripped it of its insignia, broke it in pieces (as the mayor in Bourbonnais does), and scattered the fragments amongst the crowd below, who disputed and fought for them.[2]

In the next stage, the dough or paste, which was an appropriate material for the image of a cereal goddess, spreads to the rites of other deities; and a dough image (of animal or human shape) takes the place of the animal or human victim which originally furnished forth the sacramental meals of non-cereal deities. In the Old World this extended application of the dough image seems to have been confined to local cults, and not to have been adopted into the State ritual. Thus amongst the Greeks the use of cakes in the shape of animals as offerings at the Diasia is mentioned as a peculiarly local use.[3] Amongst the Semites there are indications that the image assumed human form. According to Ibn Kutaiba, the Banu Hanifa, before their conversion, made an image of their god out of a paste of dates, butter, milk and meal, and consumed

[1] Zarate, *Conquest of Peru*, 361 (in Kerr, *Voyages*, iv.).

[2] Sahagun, bk. ii. c. 19. Climbing the May-pole is a European custom also; see *B. K.* 209.

[3] θύματα ἐπιχώρια Thuc. i. 126 (rightly explained by the scholiast).

it sacramentally.[1] In the New World the use of dough for the images of non-cereal deities was adopted in the State ritual, and became quite common. Thus the human images of the Tlalocs,[2] or mountain-gods, and of Omacatl,[3] the god of banquets, were made of dough, and were consumed sacramentally. Further, the rite of sacrifice was accomplished upon these paste idols, *e.g.* once a year a dough statue was made of Huitzilopochtli, and a priest hurled a dart into its breast. This was styled "killing the god Huitzilopochtli, so that his body might be eaten."[4] Father Acosta's account, though it omits the "killing of the god," is worth quoting:—"The Mexicaines in the moneth of Maie . . . did mingle a quantitie of the seede of beetes with rosted Mays, and then they did mould it with honie, making an idoll of that paste in bignesse like to that of wood." It was conveyed in procession from the temple to the court by maidens "crowned with garlands of Mays rosted and parched"; and then to various places in the neighbourhood of the city by young men "crowned after the same manner like vnto the women." On their return, "all the virgins came out of their convent, bringing peeces of paste compounded of beetes and rosted Mays, . . . and they were of the fashion of great bones." Then "certaine ceremonies with singing and dauncing" were used, "by meanes whereof they [the peeces of paste] were blessed and consecrated for the flesh and bones of this idoll" (Vitzilipuztli). "The ceremonies, dancing, and sacrifice ended, . . . the priests and superiors of the temple tooke the idoll of paste, which they spoyled of all the ornaments it had, and made many peeces, as well of the idoll itselfe as of the tronchons which were consecrated, and then they gave them to the people in maner of a communion, beginning with the greater, and continuing vnto the rest, both men, women, and little children, who received it with such teares, feare, and reverence, as it was an admirable thing, saying that they did eate the flesh and bones of God, wherewith they were grieved. Such as had any sicke folkes demaunded thereof for them, and carried it with great reverence and veneration."[5]

[1] Bastian, *Der Mensch*, iii. 157. [2] Sahagun, ii. 16 and i. 21. [3] *Ibid.* i. 15.
[4] Sahagun, bk. iii. c. 1, § 2, and Bancroft, *Native Races*, iii. 299.
[5] Acosta (Grimston's trans., pp. 356–361 in the Hakluyt Society's edition).

The final stage is that in which the use of dough or paste has become so firmly established in the sacramental meal, that it is no longer felt to be necessary to give them the shape of the deity, whether human or animal. Thus in the New World annually amongst the Mayas, consecrated wafers were broken, distributed, and preserved as a protection against misfortune for the year.[1] In Peru, in August, four sheep were offered to four divinities, and "when this sacrifice was offered up, the priest had the *sancu* ['a pudding of coarsely ground maize'] on great plates of gold, and he sprinkled it with the blood of the sheep. . . . The high priest then said in a loud voice, so that all might hear: 'Take heed how you eat this *sancu*; for he who eats it in sin, and with a double will and heart, is seen by our father the Sun, who will punish him with grievous troubles. But he who with a single heart partakes of it, to him the Sun and the Thunder will show favour, and will grant children, and happy years and abundance, and all that he requires.' Then they all rose up to partake, first making a solemn vow, before eating the *yahuar-sancu* ['*yahuar*, blood; *sancu*, pudding'], in which they promised never to murmur against the Creator, the Sun, or the Thunder; never to be traitors to their lord the Ynca, on pain of receiving condemnation and trouble. The priest of the Sun then took what he could hold on three fingers, put it into his mouth, and returned to his seat. In this order and in this manner of taking the oath all the tribes rose up, and thus all partook, down to the little children. . . . They took it with such care that no particle was allowed to fall to the ground, this being looked upon as a great sin."[2] Acosta's account is as follows:—"The Mamaconas of the Sunne, which were a kind of Nunnes of the Sunne, made little loaves of the flower of Mays, died and mingled with the bloud of white sheepe, . . . then presently they commanded that all strangers should enter, . . . and the Priests . . . gave to every one a morcell of these small loaves, saying vnto them that they gave these peeces to the end that they should be vnited and confederated with the Ynca; . . . and all did receive and eate these peeces, thanking the Sunne infinitely for so great a favour which he had done

[1] Waitz, *Anthropologie*, iv. 330.

[2] Markham, *Rites and Laws of the Yncas*, 27.

them. . . . And besides this communion (if it be lawfull to vse this word in so divelish a matter) . . . they did likewise send of these loaves to all their Guacas, sanctuaries, or idolls."[1] In the Old World the use of wafers or cakes not in human or animal shape has not left many traces. In Tartary they were used, as one eye-witness, Father Grueber, testifies: "This only do I affirm, that the devil so mimics the Catholic Church there, that although no European or Christian has ever been there, still in all essential things they agree so completely with the Roman Church as even to celebrate the sacrifice of the Host with bread and wine: with my own eyes have I seen it."[2] As for the Aryan peoples, we find these consecrated cakes associated, amongst the ancient Prussians, with the rite which we have already[3] quoted as a typical instance of the sacrificial meal. Whilst the flesh of the animal victim was cooking, rye-cakes were made and were baked, not in an oven, but by being continually tossed over the fire by the men standing round, who threw it and caught it.[4] These consecrated wafers survive also in "Beltane cakes." These cakes are made on the evening before Beltane, May 1 (O. S.); in Ross-shire they are called *tcharnican*, *i.e.* "hand-cake," because they are made wholly in the hand (not on a board or table like common cakes), and are not to be put upon any table or dish; they must never be put from the hand[5]—like the Peruvian *sancu*, to allow which to fall from the hand was a great sin.

On the other hand, the ritual appropriate to animal totems came in course of time to be applied sometimes to tree-totems. Thus the Esthonians once a year smeared their trees with blood.[6] "Castrén tells us that the Ostiaks worshipped a larch-tree, to the branches of which they hung the skins of animals as offerings";[7] and the Totonacs made a dough of first-fruits and the blood of infants, of which men and women partook every six months,[8] much as the Peruvians mingled the blood of sheep with the *sancu*, and as the Hebrews were forbidden to offer the blood of sacrifice

[1] Acosta, 355.
[2] Grueber, in Thevenot, *Divers Voyages*, iv.
[3] *Supra*, p. 144.
[4] Bastian, *Der Mensch*, iii. 156.
[5] *Folk-Lore*, VI. i.
[6] Bastian, *Oest. Asien*, iv. 42.
[7] D'Alviella, *Hibbert Lecture*, 1891, p. 109.
[8] Bancroft, iii. 440.

with leavened bread.[1] Another way in which the ritual of plant deities came to be affected by and assimilated to that of animal deities, was that when the plant deity ceased to be regarded as immanent in the plant species he did not at once come to be regarded as having human form: as a matter of fact, he is commonly conceived to have animal shape.[2] The explanation of this, I suggest, is that at the time when vegetation-spirits were thus invested with animal forms, the only gods (other than plant totems) known to their worshippers were animal totems, and consequently the only shape which a plant deity could assume, different from the plant, was that of an animal—the only shape which totem-gods at the time were known to have. When, then, vegetation spirits were supposed to appear as animals, it was fitting that those animals should be sacrificed to them; and in the Old World we find that a cereal deity like Demeter has an animal, the pig, sacred and sacrificed to her.

But the rite of worship with which tree-worshippers usually approached their god, and placed themselves in communion with him and under his protection, was of a different kind. There were two ways in which early man sought to effect an external union between himself and the god he worshipped: by the sacrificial meal he incorporated the substance of the god into his own body; by blood-letting rites and the hair-offering, he, so to speak, incorporated himself with the god. Now, though the former method is not absolutely impossible for the tree-worshipper — for throughout Northern India the worshippers of the sacred *nīm* tree chew its leaves in order to gain the protection of the deity against the death-pollution, and "the Kauphatas of Cutch get the cartilage of their ears slit and in the slit a *nīm* stick is stuck,"[3] and thus the substance of the god is incorporated in the body of the devotee—still the practical inconveniences are so great, that it is the second method that is generally used; and Mr. Hartland, in the second volume of his *Legend of Perseus*, has demonstrated learnedly and conclusively not only that the union may be effected by the incorporation of any portion of the worshipper (blood,

[1] Ex. xxiii. 18. [2] For instances, see Frazer, *G. B.* ch. iii. § 10.

[3] Crooke, *Folk-Lore of Northern India*, 253.

hair, saliva) with the god, but that, according to primitive modes of thought (*i.e.* thought guided by the association of ideas and not by reason), anything worn by or belonging to, or even merely handled by a man, is part and parcel of the man. Hence the widespread "practice of tying rags or leaving portions of clothing upon a sacred tree or bush"[1] is a sacramental rite. "Our examination of the practices of throwing pins into wells, of tying rags on bushes and trees, of driving nails into trees and stocks, of throwing stones and sticks on cairns, and the analogous practices throughout the world, leads to the conclusion that they are to be interpreted as acts of ceremonial union with well, with tree, or stock, or cairn,"[2] *i.e.* with the water-spirit, tree-spirit, etc. "My shirt or stocking, or a rag to represent it, placed upon a sacred bush, or thrust into a sacred well—my name written upon the walls of a temple—a stone or a pellet from my hand cast upon a sacred image or a sacred cairn—a remnant of my food cast into a sacred waterfall or bound upon a sacred tree, or a nail from my hand driven into the trunk of the tree—is thenceforth in continual contact with divinity; and the effluence of divinity, reaching and involving it, will reach and involve me. In this way I may become permanently united with the god."[3]

The characteristic of the things chosen, all over the world, for thus placing the worshipper in communion with his god, is that they are things having no commercial value, rags, nail-parings, hair, stones, etc.,—they may be "offerings," if so we choose to term them, but they are not gifts. Still, occasionally, articles of value are included amongst them, and gifts of value are commonly made to the gods of civilised communities. In ancient Greece, where offerings were hung upon sacred trees, as is shown by the results of the excavations in Olympia[4] and discoveries in Cyprus,[5] the practice of making gifts of great value was well established even in Homeric times.[6] But this was not the original practice anywhere, as Mr. Hartland has conclusively proved, and

[1] Hartland, *Perseus*, ii. 200. [2] *Op. cit.* 228. [3] *Op. cit.* 214-5.

[4] Helbig, *Homerische Epos*, 314. [5] Cauer, *Homerkritik*, 197.

[6] *Od.* iii. 273: πολλὰ δ' ἀγάλματ' ἀνῆψεν (*i.e.* fastened to trees or altar), ὑφάσματά τε χρυσόν τε.

we have now to trace the origin of the idea and practice of making presents to the gods. To do so, we must return to our plant totems.

Our argument, to show that it is to totemism we owe the cultivation of plants as well as the domestication of animals, may be summed up thus far as follows: food-plants are adopted by savages as totems; that the savage ancestors of civilised races took cereals for their totems is a point of which we have not, and under the circumstances could not, expect to have, direct evidence; but we have proof that they treated cereal plants in the same way as savages treat their totem-plants, *i.e.* they kept from one year to the next a bundle of plants, for the sake of the protection afforded by the immanent spirit, just as a branch of a sacred tree was kept for the same purpose; that the sheaf thus preserved would yield seeds and suggest sowing is clear, and it is certain that the sacred sheaf was used for that purpose. But if the cereal was a totem, then originally it must have been forbidden as food (except at the solemn annual sacramental meal), just as the animal totem was taboo, and just as in Africa the Plantain-family abstain from the plantain. How then did it come to be a staple article of food? In all probability in the same way as the animal totem: originally the animal totem was sacrificed and eaten only once a year; then, as flocks and herds multiplied, and the taste for flesh-meat developed, trivial pretexts for slaughtering victims were frequently found or invented, until at last the only traces to be found of the original taboo are, *e.g.*, the ceremonial rite which, amongst Mohammedans, the butcher is expected to observe, or the small offering to the gods which, amongst the Hindoos of Manu's time, the consumer had to make before eating, or the Tartars' practice of not beginning a meal until they have first smeared the mouth of their god Nacygai with fat,[1] *i.e.* until the god has himself eaten of the meat.

Now, if cultivated plants were originally, like domestic animals, forbidden food, we should expect to find some traces of the original taboo in the case of cereals as we do in the case of flesh-meat; and such traces, I suggest, we find in the widespread reluctance to eat the new corn, etc., until some

[1] Bastian, *Der Mensch*, iii. 154.

ceremony has been performed with the first-fruits to make it safe to eat the new crop. Further, as the ceremony which made the animal victim's flesh safe to eat consisted in assigning to the god the share of the food which fell to him of right as a member of the clan, we should expect to find that the ceremony which made the corn lawful food consisted in inviting the god to partake of the first-fruits; and as a matter of fact we do find indications that this was actually the case. In the Tonga Isles the first-fruits of yams, etc., are offered to the divine Tooitonga.[1] In Mexico, no one dared eat of the green maize before the festival in honour of the Maize-maiden, Xilonen;[2] and although we are not told that the goddess was supposed to consume the offerings, we may perhaps infer it from the fact that in Mexico new wine was taboo until the god of wine had in person (*i.e.* in the person of a man clad in the god's insignia, and supposed to be the earthly tabernacle of the divine spirit) visited the house and opened the cask.[3]

But though we can thus catch a glimpse of a time when the first-fruits of the earth, like the flesh of the animal victim, furnished forth the joint meal of which both the god and his worshippers partook, and by which the bond of fellowship between them was renewed, still, the prevailing view in civilised times was that the first-fruits were a tribute paid to the deity. According to this relatively late view, the deity is no longer a spirit immanent in the corn, etc., but a god to whom mankind are debtors for the boon which he bestows upon them by causing the plant to grow: he is no longer one of a body of clansmen, all of whom have rights (if not equal rights) to share in the joint produce of the community; he is now the lord of the soil from which he causes crops to be yielded. In a word, the comparatively modern idea of property has been introduced into religion, and the relations between the gods and their worshippers have been adjusted to the requirements of the new conception,[4] and have been placed upon a property basis. Henceforth offerings of all kinds continued to be made as they had

[1] Mariner, *Tonga Islands*, ii. 127. [2] Sahagun, ii. c. 28.

[3] *Ibid.* i. c. 21.

[4] Robertson Smith, *Religion of the Semites*, 390; cf. 111, 222, 241, 261.

been made before this new social institution, but the tendency now was to interpret them as gifts from man to god. The animal which originally had been the god, and for long after was sacred in its own right as a member of the clan, was now property, and only became holy by being presented as a gift —"consecrated"—to the god. The "offerings" by which the worshipper had united himself with his god became property; and to be accepted as gifts must be valuable. Hence in the long run arose religious difficulties: the traditional ritual showed that the animal was consumed as food by the deity; the new view made that food a gift from the worshipper; thus the god had to be fed by man. The traditional custom of attaching offerings to tree or altar had for its object "the attainment of some wish or the granting of some prayer";[1] the new view required that the offering should be a gift. Thus religion was in danger of becoming the art of giving something in order to get more in return, a species of higgling in the celestial market,[2] ridiculed by Lucian, denounced by the Psalmist, and exposed in the *Euthyphro*. Amongst the Hebrews this danger was met by the teaching of the prophets that God requires no material oblation, but justice, mercy, and humility. Amongst the Hindoos the notion that sacrifice consists in the voluntary loss of property, and that thereby merit is acquired, reduced religion to mere magic; sacrifices of sufficient magnitude gave man the same power of absolute command over the gods as in folk-tales Solomon exercises over the djinn. It is true that, both in India and in Greece, philosophers argued for a higher view of sacrifice: thus Isocrates maintained that the truest sacrifice and service was for a man to make himself as good and just as possible;[3] and throughout the Upanishads the idea recurs that "there was something far better, far higher, far more enduring, than the right performance of sacrifice; that the object of the wise man should be to know, inwardly and consciously, the Great Soul of all; and

[1] Hartland, *Perseus*, ii. 200.

[2] Ἐμπορικὴ ἄρα τις ἂν εἴη, ὦ Εὐθύφρον, τέχνη ἡ ὁσιότης θεοῖς καὶ ἀνθρώποις παρ' ἀλλήλων, Plato, *Euthyphro*, 14 E.

[3] Isoc. *Nicoc.* 20: ἡγοῦ δὲ θῦμα τοῦτο κάλλιστον εἶναι καὶ θεραπείαν μεγίστην, ἐὰν ὡς βέλτιστον καὶ δικαιότατον σαυτὸν παρέχῃς.

that by this knowledge his individual soul would become united to the Supreme Being, the true and absolute self."[1] But it is also true that this teaching remained practically sterile; and the reason of the sterility seems to lie in the fact, the general law, that it is only by, and in the name of, religion that reforms in religion have been accomplished: it is only by a higher form of religion that a lower is expelled.

Finally, the gift-theory of sacrifice has in modern times contributed to a fundamentally erroneous conception of the history of religion. It has been supposed that all offerings were from the very beginning gifts, whereas in truth the earliest "offerings" were but means for placing the worshipper in physical contact and permanent communion with his god. This erroneous supposition has then been combined with the theory that to primitive man all supernatural powers were malevolent; and the conclusion has been drawn, that the offerings were intended to appease these malevolent gods, that religion had its origin in fear—whereas a god is a friendly power from whom man expects aid and protection, and with whom he seeks communion. Sometimes the two fallacies—the gift-theory of sacrifice and the fear-theory of religion—are combined with the further error that ancestor-worship is the earliest form of religion, thus: "The basis or core of worship is surely offering—that is to say, the propitiation of the ghost by just such gifts of food, drink, slaves, or women as the savage would naturally make to a living chief with whom he desired to curry favour."[2] But the core of worship is communion; offerings in the sense of gifts are a comparatively modern institution both in ancestor-worship as in the worship of the gods; and ancestor-worship is later than, and modelled on, the worship of the gods.

[1] Rhys Davids, *Hibbert Lecture*, 1881, p. 28.

[2] Grant Allen, *The Attis*, 93.

CHAPTER XVII

NATURE-WORSHIP

WHAT raised man from savagery to civilisation was the transition from a natural to an artificial basis of food-supply, *i.e.* was the domestication of animals and cultivation of plants; and such domestication and cultivation was, as we have endeavoured to show, the outcome, not the designed but none the less the inevitable outcome, of the earliest form of religion, that is, totemism, the worship of plants and animals. Having shown that religion gave the first impetus to material progress, we have now to show how material progress reacted on religion, how the widening circle of human activity brought man into more extensive contact with the forces of nature, rendering their co-operation with him more necessary, and giving him fresh reasons to establish friendly relations and a permanent alliance with the powers on whose goodwill the increase of his flocks or the fertility of his fields depended.

The hunter must have a knowledge of the habits of the quarry; the herdsman must know not only where to find pasture for his flocks, but, to some extent, the conditions which favour the growth of herbage: he has a very direct interest in the rains and the streams which water the earth. Further, he must be able to see some distance ahead, to be ready with his preparations to take care of the younglings of his herd when born; he must be able to compute time. Now, though it may appear to us that no very extensive observation would be required on the part of primitive man to discover that the same amount of time always elapsed between one new moon and the next, or to calculate how many days that period consisted of, yet when we remember that there still are savages unable to count more than five, and many who cannot count more than twenty, we shall see that very considerable mental effort must have been necessary before the savage could determine with certainty that the lunar month consisted of twenty-eight days; and from what we know of the natural man's aversion to exertion of any kind, we may be sure that he would not have taken this trouble except for some practical end and some manifest benefit to be derived from it. For the nomad, dependent on roots, berries, and the chase, the computation of time has no inducement. For the herdsman there is an evident advantage in being able to calculate in how many months he may expect his flocks to bring forth their young. Thus there are several natural forces with which, and on which, the herdsman has to reckon: streams, fountains, clouds, the sky and the moon. In the pastoral stage, man's interests have become wide enough to make him desire the co-operation of all these forces; and all, it is hardly necessary to remark, came to be worshipped by him in consequence.

For the agriculturist, even greater powers of prevision are necessary. "The cultivator must so arrange his labours that his land may be in tilth, and ready for the seed, at a time favourable to germination; the time of the growth of the plant must coincide with the season of rain, its blossoming with warm weather, and its maturity with the hottest sunshine."[1] To count by lunar months, in making all these calculations, would inevitably lead to error, for the interval from one midsummer to another is greater than twelve lunar months, and not so great as thirteen. We may conjecture that it was the loss and damage caused by the errors consequent on counting by lunar months that awoke early man to the necessity of better calculation, and led him to notice that from spring to summer the days grew longer, from summer to winter shorter, until eventually he discovered that the shadow of a familiar object cast by the noon-day sun is longest on the shortest day, the winter solstice; shortest on the longest day, the summer solstice, and then calculated the vernal and autumnal equinoxes. Hence the four great festivals of the agricultural stage of

[1] Payne, *New World*, i. 348.

civilisation are the winter solstice (*brumalia*, Yule, Christmas), the vernal equinox (Easter, A.S. Eostra, a goddess), the summer solstice (the great festival of Olympian Zeus), and the autumn equinox. But the importance of the sun, as the cause of all growth, was to the cultivator even greater than its importance as a measurer of time. At the same time, the varying qualities of soil must have impressed man in the agricultural stage with the idea that the earth could yield or refuse increase to the crops at will. Thus the cultivator was compelled to feel his dependence on these two nature-powers, to seek their co-operation, and add two more to the list of deities inherited by him from the pastoral stage.

That this was the actual order of events, at any rate in the case of our own forefathers, seems to be indicated by the results of linguistic palæontology; the undivided Indo-Europeans were acquainted with the moon as the "measurer" of time,[1] they worshipped a sky-spirit,[2] and they had not yet passed out of the pastoral stage;[3] they had not learnt to calculate the solar year[4]—that was reserved for the agricultural stage, *i.e.* the period after the separation of the Indian from the European branch.

That man in the pastoral and agricultural periods would be impressed with the desirability of winning the permanent favour of the spirit of the river, or clouds, earth, moon, sun, or sky, will hardly be doubted; nor can it be doubted, if the argument of our previous chapters be admitted, that the ritual employed by the totemist to unite himself with the new supernatural powers whose favour he desired would be formed on the analogy of the rites with which he worshipped his plant or animal totem—he knew no other way of worship. Those rites were first the sacrificial meal, by which the substance of the god was incorporated in the worshipper; second, the offerings by which the worshipper was placed in contact with the god. In the case of streams and fountains, it is the second method which obviously commended itself, and, as we have seen in the last chapter, it has actually left abundant survivals all over the world.

[1] Schrader, *Prehistoric Antiquities*, 306 ff.
[2] *Op. cit.* 417.
[3] *Op. cit.* 287.
[4] *Op. cit.* 309.

Here we need only add that it is not merely offerings which the worshipper immerses, but on occasion his own body: "bathing is throughout India regarded as a means of religious advancement";[1] and the world-wide use of water for purposes of (ceremonial) purification was in its origin, we may conjecture, simply a means of gaining for the worshipper the protection of the water-spirit against the consequences of pollution. From the practice of immersion, the stream or pool becomes a place of oracle and divination, the will of the deity being indicated according as the water swallows or rejects the offering cast into it[2]—the origin of the ordeal of water as applied to witches. The principle of the sacramental meal is not indeed inapplicable to the water-spirit, but instances are not common: traces of it may be found in the belief that drinking the sacred water proves fatal or injurious to the criminal or the perjurer, as in Mexico or on the Gold Coast "eating fetish," *i.e.* eating sacred soil, does.[3]

In the case of non-totem deities which, like sun, moon, and sky, are beyond the reach of physical contact, it might be supposed that neither form of totem rites could be applied, that external, physical union was impossible, but this is not the case; there were various means of getting over the difficulty. In the first place, it is to be remembered that the basis of totemism is primitive man's discovery that, as men are united to one another in kindreds, so natural objects can be classed in natural kinds—hence the totem alliance between a human kin and a natural kind. Now, the waters on the earth and those in the sky obviously belong to the same kind, and communion with one member of the species is, according to the belief on which totemism is based, communion with all. Hence the worshipper who, wishing a river-god to grant a vow, unites himself with the god by throwing some "offering" into the water, follows exactly the same process when he wishes to commend himself to the waters above the earth. In Estland, when rain was wanted, something was cast into a certain sacred brook: "streams or lakes which, the moment wood or stones are

[1] Crooke, *Folk-Lore of Northern India*, 20.

[2] Robertson Smith, *Religion of Semites*, 178.

[3] *Supra*, p. 64.

thrown into them, cause rain and storm clouds to appear, occur all over Europe."[1] On the same principle, in times of drought the agriculturist seeks to place his plants under the protection of the spirit of waters by immersing in a stream the representative (human or otherwise) of the vegetation spirit.[2]

But if communication could thus be effected with the spirits of sky and cloud, then neither were sun and moon inaccessible to would-be worshippers, for they are of the genus fire, and whatever is cast into a fire on earth would establish communion with the greater and the lesser lights in the sky, as in the case of the waters on and over the earth. It is, at any rate, in this way that the Ainus make their offerings to the sun—all fire, including that of the sun, being divine to them.[3] The parallel thus drawn between fire and water is confirmed by the purificatory powers of both; the person or thing that passes through or over a fire is brought in contact and in communion with the fire-god.

When totemism has become so far disintegrated that it is forgotten that the animal sacrificed is the god himself, then animal sacrifice can be and is extended by analogy from totem to non-totem deities; the sacrifice of an animal is then the traditional mode of approaching certain deities, and is inferred to be the proper mode of worshipping all deities. Hence we get a second means of establishing union between man and gods who are spatially remote from him: animals are sacrificed to them as to other gods, but whereas tradition determined what animals should be sacrificed to totem gods, analogies (more or less fanciful) had to be sought to determine the proper sacrifices to non-totem gods,—horses were sacrificed to the sun, perhaps because of his motion, and also to the sea, perhaps from the shape and movements of its waves; river-gods were supposed to appear, often as bulls, often as serpents. The blood of sacrifice, in the case of non-totem as well as of totem gods, is then dashed upon an altar or stone, and the gods of both kinds are supposed to visit or

[1] Mannhardt, *W. F. K.* 341, note 1, who, however, regards these as instances of sympathetic magic.

[2] *B. K.* 356, note, for instances.

[3] Howard, *Trans-Siberian Savages*, 172.

manifest themselves in the stone. Hence it is that the Peruvians "in their temples adored certain stones, as representatives of the sun."[1] But though this would be the natural and obvious mode of sacrifice to the sun, there was a manifest propriety in combining this with the first-mentioned mode (viz. casting "offerings" into fire), and casting not only offerings, but also sacrificial victims into the flames, for thus the essence of the victim's flesh was wafted into the air, and rose upwards to the divinity in the sky above. This mode was in harmony with the tendency which, from other causes,[2] had arisen to burn those portions of the victim which were intended for the god; and when not only sun and sky gods, but all the gods, were supposed to reside aloft and at a distance, and when the spirits of the dead also were relegated to a distant other world, the practice of burnt offerings had even more to recommend it.

There remains yet a third way in which the worshipper could place himself in communication with distant and non-totem gods; and it is one of some importance both in the history of religion and for the right comprehension of that history. The origin of animal sacrifice is not the desire of the worshipper "to curry favour" with the deity by offering him a present of food, but is due to the fact that the animal was the god, of whose substance the worshipper partook. The god was himself the victim that was offered in the sacrificial rite. Ultimately that fact was indeed forgotten, but whilst the true comprehension of the fact remained it must have appeared essential to the act of worship that the god should be the sacrifice to the god; and we shall see hereafter, in the chapter on the Priesthood, that, as a matter of fact, this mystic principle has left many traces behind it. Here, however, we have only to suggest that this principle afforded in early times a solution of the problem, with what sacrifice should a god, like the sun, belonging to the genus fire, be approached? Obviously, with fire. And as the totem-animal was sacrificed annually to the totem-god, so fires would annually be kindled as an offering to the Sun. That the summer solstice should be chosen, when the sun's power was greatest, is natural enough. Hence, then, the fire-

[1] Zarate, *Conquest of Peru* (in Kerr, *Voyages*, iv. 360). [2] *Supra*, p. 160.

festivals on Midsummer Eve or Midsummer Day which survive so generally all over Europe,[1] and the African custom of worshipping the moon by shooting flaming arrows towards her.[2] Mr. Frazer, however, who apparently inclines to regard religion as developed out of magic, consistently enough says, "The best general explanation of these European fire-festivals seems to be the one given by Mannhardt, namely, that they are sun-charms or magical ceremonies intended to ensure a proper supply of sunshine for men, animals, and plants;"[3] and, following Mannhardt, he also explains the custom of burning the representative of the vegetation spirit as a piece of sympathetic magic, having the same object as the Midsummer bonfires. But sympathetic magic implies that an effect is produced in virtue of the similarity between that effect and its cause, and without the intervention of any supernatural being—there is nothing religious about it. Now, neither is there anything religious in the Midsummer rites as at present practised by European peasants; but then these rites are survivals, and in religion a survival consists in the continued performance of acts, originally having a religious significance, after all religious significance has departed from them. Thus no one doubts that streams and wells were once considered supernatural powers, or the abodes of supernatural spirits, having, amongst other powers, that of curing disease. Nor can it be doubted that originally the worshipper placed himself in contact with, and under the protection of, the spirit by bathing in the water. That the "sacred" wells, which are common enough now, were originally worshipped as gods is tolerably clear. But the practice of resorting to them is now a survival—it is, in the proper sense of the word, a superstition; that is to say, those who believe that water from a certain well will cure diseases of the eye, believe so, not because they suppose any spirit to dwell in the water, but simply because it is the tradition that that water does, as a matter of fact, cure eye-disease. But it would be erroneous to infer that, because now no spirit is supposed to effect the cure, therefore the belief never had a religious element in it; and in the same way it is not safe to

[1] For instances, see Frazer, *G. B.* ii. 58 ff., and Mannhardt, *W. F. K.* 309.

[2] Réville, *Peuples non-civilisés*, i. 58.

[3] *G. B.* ii. 267–8.

infer that because there is now no element of religion in the Midsummer rites, therefore there never was. Rather, I would suggest, the inference is that the fire-festivals, occurring as they do at the summer solstice, are like other festivals occurring on that day, survivals of early sun-worship; while the burning of the vegetation spirit's representative is the early cultivator's method of commending his crops to the sun-spirit, as immersion is his method of placing them under the care of the sky-spirit or rain-god. On the other hand, if we regard these fire-festivals and water-rites as pieces of sympathetic magic, they are clear instances in which man imagines himself able to constrain the gods—in this case the god of vegetation—to subserve his own ends. Now, this vain imagination is not merely non-religious, but anti-religious; and it is difficult to see how religion could have been developed out of it. It is inconsistent with the abject fear which the savage feels of the supernatural, and which is sometimes supposed to be the origin of religion; and it is inconsistent with that sense of man's dependence on a superior being which is a real element in religion.

CHAPTER XVIII

SYNCRETISM AND POLYTHEISM

The material progress made by man, as he advanced from the material basis of subsistence on roots, fruits, and the chase, first to pastoral and then to agricultural life, required that he should make an ever-increasing use for his own ends of natural forces. These forces were to him living beings with superhuman powers, of whom he stood in dread, but whose co-operation he required. Without some confidence that it was possible, if he set about it in the right way, to secure their favour and assistance, his efforts would have been paralysed. That confidence was given him by religion; he was brought into friendly relations with powers from which, in his previously narrow circle of interests, he had had little to hope or to gain; and thus the number of his gods had been increased.

Pastoral life and even a rudimentary form of agriculture are compatible with a wandering mode of existence, in which the sole ties that can keep society together are the bonds of blood-kinship and a common cult. But the development of agriculture is only possible when the tribe is permanently settled in a fixed abode; and then it becomes possible for neighbours, not of kindred blood, to unite in one community. In a word, political progress becomes possible; and political progress at this stage consists in the fusion or *synoikismos* of several tribes into a single State. This process also had its effect upon religion: a clan is a religious community as well as a body of kinsmen, and the fusion of two clans implied the fusion of their respective cults. In many cases the resemblances of the two cults may well have been so great as rather to promote than hinder the alliance; thus when we find, as occasionally happens, that in some villages two May-poles (survivals of tree-worship) are used at a harvest festival instead of one, the inference[1] rightly seems to be that two communities, both worshipping trees, if not the same species of tree, have in neighbourliness united their worship. Or, again, when we find that the branch which the tree-worshipper annually carries round the community, in order that the spirit present in it may confer blessings on all to whom it is presented, is hung with various kinds of fruits and associated with cereals, we may infer that tree-worshipper and plant-worshipper have found no difficulty in uniting in a joint festival and common act of worship. So, too, in the Lithuanian Samborios, the Athenian Pyanepsion, and the Mexican offering to Chicomecoatl, the common feature is that cereals and leguminous plants of all kind are combined in one offering; and the implication is that the festival was one common to all the cultivators and worshippers of the various plants represented in the offering.

Again, two communities might happen to agree, though for different reasons, in offering the same kind of animal in their annual sacrifice. Thus the moon-worshipper seems very generally to have believed that the moon-spirit manifested herself on earth in the shape of a cow, and that a cow was therefore the proper victim to offer, on the principle that the deity is to be offered to himself. A fusion, therefore, between a family of moon-worshippers and a family whose original totem and traditional deity was the cow, would meet with no difficulty on the ground of religion, if prompted by neighbourliness or political reasons. So, too, the clan that bred horses would be prepared to recognise fellow-worshippers in a clan that was in the habit of offering horses to the sun; one that owned bulls, to unite with one whose river-deity was bull-shaped.

Or neighbourhood and neighbourliness might lead to the use of a common altar and sacred place by two or more clans, each offering a different victim, because having different totems, and each sacrificing at different times; until the fusion became complete, and nothing more would be required but a myth to explain how it was that the one god worshipped

[1] Mannhardt, *W. F. K.* 260.

at the altar appeared in different animal shapes, or had different animals offered to him.

Fusion of this kind—syncretism—would be materially facilitated at first by the fact that the gods had originally no proper names. As long as the clan had only one god, no name was required, the gods of hostile clans were sufficiently distinguished by the fact that they were the gods of other clans: "the deity" was the deity of our clan, just as "the river" is that near which I dwell, and whose geography-book name I may not know. But the possession of a proper name gives more individuality to a god; and fusion between two gods, each possessing this higher degree of personality, is more difficult than between two nameless spirits. On the other hand, fusion is not impeded, if of the two gods one possesses a name and the other does not, only the advantage is with the one having a personal name. He readily absorbs the nameless one: thus the cult of the Greek god of wine was a combination of the worship of a vegetation spirit and of the spirit of the vine, but the former was nameless, and therefore it was the latter, Dionysus, that gave its name to the god. So, too, when we find that in different places half a dozen different animals—wolf, roe, goat, ram, mouse, grasshopper, lizard, swan, hawk, eagle—to say nothing of plants (*e.g.* the laurel), were associated with or offered to Apollo, we are justified in inferring that as many different nameless totem gods, plant or animal, have been absorbed by the spirit which was fortunate enough to possess the personal name Apollo. Whether that spirit was or was not a sun-god is a question to which no decisive answer is forthcoming. But it is clear that fusion between the cult of the sun-god and the worship of other gods would be considerably facilitated by the fact that burnt-offerings played a part in the ritual both of the sun-god and of other gods. The agriculturist, whose crops required sunshine, acknowledged his dependence on the sun and worshipped him. In many cases the sun-god might continue to be consciously distinguished from the plant totem or vegetation spirit, but in many, perhaps most, cases the agriculturist would worship both gods in a common festival, and combine their ritual: he had to make offerings to both, and to both it was possible to convey his offerings by casting them into a fire. Thus the Druids, at their great quinquennial festival, constructed a colossal Jack of the Green, placed inside it both animal victims and human criminals (captives, or, in default thereof, clansmen), and burnt the whole.[1] That in course of time their festival might come to be regarded as a feast in honour of some one god, is readily intelligible; and as long as the different gods concerned were nameless, none could appropriate the festival. A similar combination of cults is indicated by the fact that before temples were known,[2] and, for the matter of that, after they were common, the altars of the gods—whether Aryan or Semitic or Hamitic—were usually to be found in the neighbourhood of a sacred tree, or trees, and a sacred stream. Now the cultivator whose crops required watering (and the herdsman whose pasturage was dependent on the water-spirit) had an interest in worshipping the spirit of waters as well as the vegetation spirit; and, as the common association of sacred grove and sacred stream shows, he sought, for the place of his worship, a spot in which he could at one and the same time approach both spirits in a joint act of worship, and there he set up the altar-stone on which he dashed the blood of sacrifice. To this spot he resorted at the fixed festivals of the agricultural calendar—the solstices and equinoxes—and also on extraordinary occasions, when drought, sterility, or disease awoke in him a consciousness of the necessity of renewing the bond with the gods to whose protection it was the custom of the clan to resort with confidence in cases of emergency. On such occasions there was a fixed ritual to be observed: some "offerings" must be cast into the river, others hung upon the trees, the blood of sacrifice be sprinkled on the stone, and the victim's flesh be solemnly consumed by the assembled clan. It was on the exact and punctilious performance of all these various proceedings that the success of the act of worship (*i.e.* a sense of reconciliation with the god, and the termination of the drought, or the staying of the plague) depended. The omission of any one of them, or the failure to perform them in the exact manner prescribed by custom and tradition,

[1] *B. K.* 526; Cæs. *B. G.* vi. 16; Strabo, iv. c. 198; Diod. v. 32.

[2] *Supra*, p. 135.

would invalidate the whole. In a word, the proceedings, from the time of entering to the moment of leaving the sacred place, tended to present themselves to the worshipper's mind as one single act of worship. That the various constituent parts of that act had had different origins, was a fact which would inevitably tend to be obscured and eventually forgotten. That the various rites composing the one act of worship had been originally addressed to different spirits, would *pari passu* also tend to be forgotten; indeed, if the spirits were nameless, it would be difficult for several generations of worshippers to hold them clearly apart in their minds. What would be present to the consciousness of any given worshipper would be, that on certain occasions, *e.g.* when danger of any kind threatened, it was the customary thing to resort to the sacred place of the clan, and there to perform certain external acts, and that, if those acts were performed in the proper way, the danger would be averted by the supernatural power or powers friendly to the clan and haunting the grove. Whether one or more spirits were concerned in granting the prayers of the community might be matter for speculation; the unity of the act of worship, however, would be a presumption in favour of the unity of the power worshipped. Thus in Aricia there was a sacred grove or forest, *the* forest of the inhabitants, *Nemus*, which was thus resorted to; and the numen of the spot was known simply as "the forester," Nemorensis. Eventually, "the forester" was identified with a goddess having a more individual name and a higher degree of personality—Diana. On the analogy, therefore, of Diana Nemorensis, we may conjecture that deities with double names, Phœbus Apollo, Pallas Athene, and so on, were originally distinct deities whose cults have been combined by syncretism.

But it is not here alleged that even spirits whose abodes were so closely associated together as were those of tree-spirits and river-spirits necessarily or generally blended together, or were absorbed by a god with a more developed personality. Each of the gods might have such a marked personality that fusion was impossible. The Dryads, the Nereids, the Naids, the nymphs of trees and streams, continued to exist side by side with the greater gods of Greece.

In a word, where syncretism did not take place, polytheism arose. And it is with polytheism that we have now to deal. The development of polytheism is in the main the outcome of early political progress, as was indicated at the beginning of this chapter; the political union of two or more communities involved religious union also. Thus, the southern tribes of the Gold Coast, Fantis, form one confederation; the northern tribes, Ashantis, a rival and more powerful confederation. Each has its own federal god—Bobowissi the god of the southern, Tando the god of the northern federation; and whenever a tribe revolts from the Ashantis it renounces the Ashanti god Tando, and is admitted to the southern federation by joining in the worship of Bobowissi.[1]

But though the development of polytheism is in the main the outcome of political causes and of the *synoikismos* by which a State and a nation are made, still a tendency to polytheism manifests itself in even earlier times. The sky-god, whose favour is essential to the herbage which supports the herdsman's cattle, as well as to the farmer's crops, may be worshipped concurrently with the totem plant or animal, and retain his independence, as the Dyaus, Zeus, Jupiter, of the Aryans, did. Again, as the worship of two spirits at one festival sometimes results in a combination of the two cults and in the syncretism of the two deities, so, conversely, the worship of one deity at two different festivals sometimes ends in the production of two deities: at the spring or Easter festival of the agricultural calendar, the rites appropriate to the green corn or maize are celebrated, and later in the year the worship of the ripe ear takes place, with the result that the Corn-Maiden, or Kern Baby, is differentiated from the Old Woman or Corn-Mother—Korê from Demeter, Xilonen from Chicomecoatl.

In this connection we may note that amongst savages there are sex-totems,[2] and amongst civilised peoples what we may call sex-mysteries: sex-totems are animals which are exclusively sacred to the women of the tribe, or exclusively to the men; sex-mysteries are those from participation in which one or other sex is excluded. Now, the mysteries

[1] Ellis, *Tshi-speaking Peoples*, 33. [2] Frazer, *Totemism*, 51–3.

which are celebrated exclusively by women, and from which men are excluded, are generally connected with agriculture and agricultural deities, *e.g.* the Thesmophoria, the rites of the Bona Dea, and sundry Hindu ceremonies.[1] Further, it is a well-known fact that amongst savages agriculture is left to the women: amongst the Niam-Niam "the men most studiously devote themselves to their hunting, and leave the culture of the soil to be carried on exclusively by the women;"[2] amongst the Kafirs "the women are the real labourers, the entire business of digging, planting, and weeding devolves on them;"[3] "whilst the Monbuttoo women attend to the tillage of the soil and the gathering of the harvest, the men, except they are absent, either for war or hunting, spend the entire day in idleness."[4] In fine, it may be said of Africa generally, that "the wife has the chief share of the hoeing and cultivation of the soil;"[5] as it was said of the ancient Peruvians, "these women give great assistance to their husbands in all the labours belonging to husbandry and domestic affairs, or rather, these things fall entirely to their lot."[6] It is therefore an easy guess that the cultivation of plants was one of woman's contributions to the development of civilisation; and it is in harmony with this conjecture that the cereal deities are usually, both in the Old World and the New, female. The agricultural or semi-agricultural mysteries, therefore, from which even in civilised times women continued to exclude men, may be survivals of early times, when agriculture was a cult as well as a craft, a mystery as well as a ministerium, and when, further, the craft (and therefore the cult) was the exclusive prerogative of the wives of the tribe. That cultivated plants were originally totems we have already argued. If women were the first cultivators, it will follow that cereals were originally sex-totems. Agriculture, however, when its benefits became thoroughly understood, was not allowed, amongst civilised races, to continue to be the exclusive prerogative of

[1] Crooke, *Folk-Lore of Northern India*, 41 and 43.
[2] Schweinfurth, *Heart of Africa*, ii. 12 (E.T.).
[3] Shooter, *Kafirs of Natal*, 17. [4] Schweinfurth, ii. 90.
[5] Duff Macdonald, *Africana*, i. 137.
[6] Zarate, *Conquest of Peru* (Kerr, *Voyages*, iv. 351).

women; and the Corn-goddess, Maiden or Mother, had to admit to the circle of her worshippers the men as well as the wives of the tribe. Hence, though the corn-spirit continued to be of the sex of her original worshippers, and though women continued to play a part in the myths about the goddess as well as in her worship (*e.g.* the maidens who carried the ears of maize in Mexico and Peru, and those who are represented on Greek monuments as carrying ears of corn), still Demeter took her place with the other deities; the men of the tribe participated in her worship (though the youths who figured in the Eiresione procession at the Pyanepsion had to dress up as women [1]), and the Eleusinian mysteries were open to men as well as to women.

Political development in early times—to turn to the main cause of polytheism—depends on two conditions: first, the causes which tend to induce neighbouring communities to act together and blend together in one political whole, or State, must be more powerful than the causes which tend to keep them apart; and next, the causes which tend to keep them apart are two, namely, first the tie of blood, which unites the members of a community together and marks them off from strangers, and next the tie of a common worship, to which none but members of the community are admitted. Both these dividing influences must be overcome, if a State of any size and political importance is to grow up. In a word, in early times polytheism is the price which must be paid for political development. The loyalty to the clan and to the clan-god, the conviction that the religious community formed by the tribe constitutes it a peculiar people, is essential to monotheism and inconsistent with political growth: politically the Jewish State was insignificant and at the mercy of its neighbours; at the present day the Jews are scattered and form no political community; but they retain their original loyalty to the blood-bond and to the God of their fathers.

That different tribes would exhibit different degrees of attachment to their ancestral faith, different degrees of jealousy for their clan-god, follows from the variety of

[1] *κατὰ γυναῖκας ἐστολισμένοι*, Photius, *Biblioth.* c. 239, p. 322; Mannhardt, *W. F. K.* 216.

human nature. But when the first step towards polytheism has been taken, when once the tribe's worship has been finally divided between the totem and another deity—though this does not take place probably without many relapses, by the process of syncretism, into the old custom of a single sanctuary and a single totem to a single tribe—the development of polytheism is easy and rapid; the need for friendly relations with all the natural forces by which man's fortunes are or can be supposed to be affected is so great that one after another all are gradually brought within the circle of his worship. But this is a process which cannot take place without affecting the nature, character, and position of the gods. For instance, the original clan-god was omnipotent: the worshipper appealed to him in any and every need, with confidence that he could, if he so willed, save him. But when, by the fusion of several communities, the members of the new State found themselves the worshippers of several omnipotent gods, some adjustment of their relations was necessary. That adjustment often took the form of a division of labour, and we can see clearly in some cases how a god originally all-powerful would come to be a merely departmental god. In the view of early man war is a holy function: before going into battle, sacrifice is offered to the clan-god, the warriors are consecrated to him and are placed under the taboos ordinarily imposed on those who are in direct and special communion with the clan-god. Whether the clan-god be an animal totem or a vegetation spirit, or what not, he is all-powerful, and only exercises this power of protecting his warriors by the way, so to speak. But if of several tribes uniting in a political federation one is distinguished for its success in war, the inference inevitably will be that its god has special powers of conferring victory in war; and the other clans federated with it will worship its god more especially and rather than their own in time of war. Thus a god who, like Mars, was admittedly in the beginning a vegetation spirit, may end by becoming the war-god of a nation. Again, the sacred trees [1] and sacred stream [2] of a holy place are habitually used as oracles; and if some sacred place for some reason or other gains repute as a place for

[1] Robertson Smith, *Religion of the Semites*, 194. [2] *Op. cit.* 187.

oracles, the god of the spot may, like Apollo in Delphi, come to be specially the god of divination and of prophecy.

It may perhaps be thought that if Mars was, as is now generally admitted, originally a vegetation spirit, he must also originally have been a functional deity, and not an all-powerful god; and so, generally, that all gods were at first departmental or functional, and that the conception of omnipotence was only gradually built up in the history of religion. But on the hypothesis that vegetation spirits were plant totems, this is not so. That at a certain stage of development it was considered to be the special business of the Corn-mother, or Maize-mother, or Cotton-mother, to look after the growth of their respective plants, and see that they prospered, is not denied. The importance of the plants to man is quite sufficient reason for his requiring a supernatural power to tend them, and none was so proper as the spirit originally supposed to be immanent in them. And the same observation will apply to animals of economic importance. But obviously the case is different with plants and animals of no value to men for food or any other purpose: man has no interest in the multiplication of crocodiles, sharks, snakes, and insects, or plants and trees which he can neither eat nor otherwise make use of. When, then, he worships the supernatural beings immanent in such plants and animals—and he does adopt all of them as totems—the purpose of his worship is not to secure their multiplication, for he has no interest therein, and, consequently, the immanent deities must be worshipped because of their possession of supernatural powers other than purely functional. If the only thing the crocodile totem could do was to increase the number of crocodiles, there would be—to borrow a word from the Political Economist—a positive "disutility" in his worship. Nor would the utility of the butterfly, in that case, be sufficient to induce men to adopt it as a totem, as some tribes do. Now, the original wild ancestors of our domesticated plants and animals did not differ in any obvious way from other wild animals and plants: the savage could not foresee that the oyster would and the turtle would not come to be cultivated; and if he adopted them both as totems, it was not in order to eat them, for he adopts, in the same way, plants and animals which he cannot eat, and moreover the totem-plant or animal is precisely the species which he abstains from eating. In fine, he worshipped plant totems for the same reason as he worshipped animal totems, and he worshipped totems which eventually turned out to possess economic utility for the same reason as he worshipped those which eventually proved to have none; and that reason was that he believed them to be supernatural beings possessing the power to protect him from all dangers, and to confer on him all blessings. That eventually the prayers which he addressed to the Corn-spirit or Maize-spirit came to be mainly prayers for good crops, was due to the various causes which we have already suggested: the growth of polytheism led to a division of labour amongst deities, the economic importance of food-plants made their multiplication a matter of especial desire, and the spirit immanent in them, being their life, naturally came to be considered to be the spirit that made them grow. But even so there are clear traces enough in late times that the vegetation spirit, though mainly concerned with vegetation, continued to exercise other powers: the tree-spirit of the Lithuanians had control over rain and sunshine,[1] and amongst the northern Europeans generally the vegetation spirit brought blessings of all kinds, and not merely prosperity to the crops.[2] Therefore also the general supernatural powers exercised by Demeter, Dionysus, Chicomecoatl, etc., may have been inherited and not extended to them in late times on the analogy of the other gods of the pantheons to which they belonged.

But when once the conception of departmental deities had been developed by polytheism, it extended widely. The animistic belief that everything was a living being, and the root-conception of totemism, that things are united in kinds as men are united in kins, was combined with the new idea that the spirit immanent in any species of beings or class of things had the functional power of promoting the utility of that class. Hence a large number of new, minor deities, whose co-operation man must secure. That worship was necessary for this end was self-evident. That the worship of the new deities should be modelled on that of the old was

[1] *B. K.* 37. [2] *B. K.* 52.

inevitable. But to understand the difficulty in the way of extending the old rules of worship to cover the new instances, some explanation is required. In the earliest form of sacrifice a theophany of the totem-god was procured by dashing the blood of the totem-animal on the altar-stone: the victim was the god, the blood was the life, the spirit of the species to which the animal belonged. No invocation, therefore, was required, no naming the god was necessary; the god had no name, indeed, and the only god who could pass into the altar was the spirit immanent in the animal, that is to say, the totem-god of the clan. To this day, survivals of this state of things may be found: the Kureks at irregular times slaughter a reindeer or a dog, put its head on a pole facing east, and, mentioning no name, say, "This for Thee: grant me a blessing."[1] But when polytheism grew up, when one clan worshipped several gods, it would be necessary to distinguish. Especially, when the same animal might be offered to different gods, would there be nothing to guarantee that the right god passed into the altar. Hence the advantage of having different names for the different gods, and the custom of invoking a god by his name before slaying the victim that was intended for him. Those who did not know the name of the god could not offer him a sacrifice, could not enter into communion with him, could not gain his ear for any prayer. Hence the profound and successful secrecy with which the name of the tutelary deity of Rome was guarded, that no foe might induce him to abandon Rome. Finally, we may note that savages generally believe that knowledge of a man's name confers power over the man himself; a man's name—or, for that matter, a god's name—is part of himself in the savage's opinion, and consequently, just as hanging clothes on a sacred tree places the wearer in contact with the divinity of the tree, just as writing a name on temple-walls puts the owner of the name in continual union with the deity of the temple, so for early men the knowledge, invocation, and vain repetition of the deity's name constitutes in itself an actual, if mystic, union with the deity named.

To return to our minor and departmental deities, of

[1] Bastian, *Der Mensch*, ii. 109.

whom the Roman Di Indigetes are the most remarkable example, it is clear, first, that for the worship of these generic deities it was essential that their names should be known, and second, that, when known, the mere repetition of their names would be an act of worship sufficient for the purpose, though not, of course, excluding sacrifice as well, if it were deemed advisable. Hence in Rome the pontifices kept registers (indigitamenta) of the names of all these Di Indigetes. From what is said by writers quoting from or basing themselves on Varro, who had access to the indigitamenta, it seems probable that there were four classes of these functional deities: the first consisted of those in-dwelling in articles of food, clothing, and other necessaries of life, and the second of those in certain parts of houses (door, hinge, threshold, etc.); but the other two classes are the most interesting, because the *di* comprised in them are all immanent, not in material things, but in processes—the various processes, (1) of farming, (2) of human life—and they showed that the Roman had reached the conclusion that anything whatever to which a class-name could be given had a real existence, affording a sphere for the function of a spiritual being. Examples of Di Indigetes are the spirit of sowing (a satione Sator), harrowing (ab occatione deus Occator), dunging (a stercoratione Sterculinius), of doors (Forculus a foribus), hinges (Cardea a cardinibus), of the threshold (Limentinus), of talking (Locutius), of the cradle (Cunina), etc. The most probable derivation of the word *indiges* is from *indu* (cf. ἔνδον and *indu-perator* = *im-perator*) and *ag* (the stem of *agere*), in the sense of the god that acts, manifests himself, or is immanent in a thing.

But though it is the Di Indigetes of Rome with which we are most familiar, it is not to be inferred that it was in Rome alone that polytheism worked with disintegrating effect, and produced these functional deities. We meet with them in every quarter of the globe. In Africa, the negro has "tutelary deities, each of which is for a special purpose. These also are inanimate objects, possessing indwelling spirits. One perhaps watches that no quarrel or division takes place," like the Latin Concordia, "another may watch over them when dancing or holding a festival, and a third may take care of the drums. Each of these minor guardian gods has, as it were, a special duty."[1] To turn to the New World, in Mexico there were similar gods of black maize, roasted maize, banners, metal objects, bucklers, etc.[2] In Asia, we find that "the sword was worshipped by the Rájputs; . . . in Bengal, the carpenters worship their adze, chisel, and saw; and the barbers their razors, scissors, and mirror; . . . the writer class worship their books, pens, and inkstands. . . . In Bombay, jewellers worship their pincers and blow-pipe; carriers worship an axe, and market gardeners a pair of scales,"[3] and so on. The corn-sieve is sacred in India, as was the *mystica vannus Iacchi* in Greece; and the worship of the plough, which is carried on still in India, and used to be practised by the ancient Teutons, survives in England in the customs of Plough Monday. This kind of worship, therefore, sometimes called fetishism, so far from being the origin of religion, is later than, and a degeneration from, the original state of things.

The last development of polytheism is anthropomorphism. This was a stage which had not been reached in ancient Italy in historic times: before the invasion of that country by the anthropomorphic gods of Greece, the Italians neither conceived their many gods to have human form, nor had human-shaped idols, nor imagined their gods to marry and give in marriage. To this stage of religious belief, to distinguish it from polytheisms such as those of Greece and Mexico, of which the deities are anthropomorphic, and have a correspondingly higher degree of personality, the name polydæmonism, as it has been suggested,[4] might be given rather than polytheism. At any rate, it is well to bear in mind the fact that a people may have many gods, and none of them in human form.

With the effects which anthropomorphism produced on the general course of civilisation we have not here to deal: it produced and perfected the two forms of art which the nineteenth century has been able to appreciate but little, and to produce, not at all—sculpture and architecture. In

[1] Ellis, *Tshi-speaking Peoples*, 86, 87.
[2] Sahagun, I. xxii.
[3] Crooke, *Folk-Lore of N. India*, 305 ff.
[4] Jevons, *Plutarch's Romane Questions*.

religion, anthropomorphism made it possible to bring polytheism into something like a system, to bring all the gods to dwell together in one Olympus, to organise them into a society framed on the model of human society, and to establish their relations to one another by means of mythology. It is therefore of mythology that our next chapter must treat.

CHAPTER XIX

MYTHOLOGY

As long as man is on the natural basis of subsistence, as long as he lives on roots, fruits, and the produce of the chase, so long it takes him the whole of his time to scrape together enough food to live on, and progress is impossible. It is the domestication of plants and animals which enables him to produce a greater food supply in a shorter time, which gives him leisure, sets free a large part of his energies, and gives him time to meditate the further appropriation of natural powers to his own purposes, and so makes material progress possible. The consequent increase of wealth brings in its train the institution of private property. This development of material civilisation—itself due to religion—reacts upon religion. In every cult there are two tendencies or impulses, the mystic and the practical, the need of the blessings which the supernatural power can bestow and the desire for communion with the author of those blessings. The latter manifests itself from the first, as we have seen, both in the sacrificial meal and in the sacramental offerings, by means of which the worshipper seeks to unite himself with the object of his worship. But it tended to be obscured, and material progress tended to emphasise the practical object of cult, in two ways. Polytheism disintegrated the totem-god and gave birth to functional deities, thus suggesting and fostering the idea that as these deities had only one function to perform—and that one of material benefit to man—their only function was to perform it for man's benefit. At the same time, the conception of property was introduced into the relations between God and man in such a way that sacrifice tended to appear as a bargain in which the latter had so much the better that he got everything and practically gave nothing. Thus the practical impulse in worship was gradually exaggerated till its absurdity became gross; and the mystic impulse had been thrust into the background until it was almost entirely lost to view. How it came to reassert itself we shall have soon to inquire, but we can now no longer delay to recognise that in religion, besides the mystic and practical tendencies, there is also the speculative tendency, and whereas the former manifest themselves in cult, the latter finds expression in mythology. It is indeed true that in early religions, while it was absolutely incumbent on a man to perform exactly and punctiliously the external acts which constituted the ritual and cult of the clan or state to which he belonged, yet "belief in a certain series of myths was neither obligatory as a part of true religion, nor was it supposed that, by believing, a man acquired religious merit and conciliated the favour of the gods."[1] It is also true that there is a conspicuous absence of religious feeling from most myths. Still it is impossible for us to exclude the consideration of mythology.[2]

Myths are not like psalms or hymns, lyrical expressions of religious emotion; they are not like creeds or dogmas, statements of things which must be believed: they are narratives. They are not history, they are tales told about gods and heroes, and they all have two characteristics: on the one hand, they are to us obviously or demonstrably untrue and often irrational; on the other hand, they were to their first audience so reasonable as to appear truths which were self-evident. Many myths are (or in their original form were) designed to explain some name, ritual, or whatever seemed to require explanation: the name of Shotover Hill is explained to be due to the fact that Little John once shot over it. Other myths explain nothing and point no

[1] Robertson Smith, *Religion of the Semites*, 17.

[2] The view of mythology in this chapter is that of a disciple of Mr. Andrew Lang; and the student is referred to Mr. Lang's article on Mythology in the *Encyclopædia Britannica*, his *Myth, Ritual, and Religion*, and his *Custom and Myth*. The most comprehensive account of the various theories which have been held on the subject of mythology is to be found in Gruppe, *Die griechischen Culte und Mythen* (the English reader will find a briefer account by the present writer in the article on Mythology in Chambers's *Encyclopædia*).

moral: they are tales told for the sake of the telling and repeated for the pleasure of hearing, like fairy-tales.

A fundamental article in the totem faith is that the human kin and the animal kind are one flesh, one blood, members of the same clan, bound by the sacred tie of blood to respect and assist each other. Then the question naturally arises, if the human and the animal members are brothers, how is it that they wear such different shapes? and the answer obviously is that they were not always different: once upon a time they were the same, and then something occurred to make them different. Thus, "the Cray-fish clan of the Choctaws were originally cray-fish and lived underground, coming up occasionally through the mud to the surface. Once a party of Choctaws smoked them out, and, treating them kindly, taught them the Choctaw language, taught them to walk on two legs, made them cut off their toe-nails and pluck the hair from their bodies, after which they adopted them into the tribe. But the rest of their kindred, the cray-fish, are still living underground."[1] In course of time, as we have seen, it comes to be believed that the totem-god is the father of his worshippers, and the question again arises, how can human beings be descended from an animal forefather? and the answer is on the same principle as before. "Thus the Turtle clan of the Iroquois are descended from a fat turtle, which, burdened by the weight of its shell in walking, contrived by great exertions to throw it off, and thereafter gradually developed into a man."[2] Later, again, in consequence of the development of anthropomorphism, it comes to be believed that the proper and original shape of the gods is human; and then the belief that the family is descended from a god in animal form requires explanation; and the obvious inference is that as the god's real and normal shape is human, he must have transformed himself temporarily on this occasion and for some especial purpose: thus Zeus changes himself into a swan to win Leda, into a bull to win Europa.

In art and ritual the gradual process by which the originally animal or vegetation god became eventually human in form can be clearly traced, with all the intermediate steps.

[1] Frazer, *Totemism*, 4. [2] *Ibid.* 3.

The god appears occasionally on Egyptian monuments in purely animal form; the skin of the animal totem, a branch of the god-tree, some actual ears of wheat or maize, are worshipped as very god. Then the semi-human nature of the god is expressed by clothing a human image in an animal skin,[1] or placing a human figure (of dough, etc.) on a tree, or clothing a tree or a sheaf of ears in human dress, or a human being in a sheaf or leaves. Then, when the animal or plant origin of the god has been altogether forgotten, the god is simply "associated" in art with the plant or animal: Demeter wears a garland of wheat-ears, Chicomecoatl carries maize-stalks in her hand, Apollo stands beside a dolphin; and finally, even these symbols are dropped. The same evolution is abundantly illustrated in mythology: the Turtle of the Iroquois corresponds to the purely animal form of the Egyptian gods; Zeus, who is at one time human and at another animal, corresponds to the *misch-bild*, the human body with animal head, which is the most common Egyptian mode of representing the gods, or to the half-human, half-vegetable deity represented by a sheaf wrapped in human raiment. The "association" of a deity with a plant appears in the myth of the Red Maize clan of the Omahas, who say that "the first man of the clan emerged from the water with an ear of red maize in his hand."[2] Finally, even the "association" disappears in the myth of the Pima Indians about the maize-spirit: "one day, as she lay asleep, a rain-drop fell on her naked bosom, and she became the ancestress of the maize-growing Pueblo Indians."[3]

In course of time, the clan may forget that their animal god was their ancestor, and then a fresh reason is required to account for the alliance between the human kin and the animal kind, and so "some families in the islands Leti, Moa, and Lakor reverence the shark, and refused to eat its flesh, because a shark once helped one of their ancestors at sea."[4] Or the clan may remember that it was descended from an animal, but—owing to the general disappearance of animal-worship—forget that the animal was a god, in which case

[1] Ἄρτεμις ἕστηκεν ἀμπεχομένη δέρμα ἐλάφου, Paus. viii. c. 37.

[2] Frazer, *op. cit.* 6.

[3] Payne, *New World*, i. 414 note 4.

[4] Frazer, *op. cit.* 7.

"transformation" still appears as a feature in the story, but it is no longer due to divine agency: "the Kalang, who have claims to be considered the aborigines of Java, are descended from a princess and a chief who had been transformed into a dog."[1]

Now, we began by noting that, though many myths are ætiological, *i.e.* designed to explain something, many are not, but are rather like fairy-tales; and it is evident that we are now, after starting with the former, rapidly approaching the latter class: the transformation of the Kalang chief reminds us of the enchanters and enchantresses of the *Arabian Nights*; the helpful Papuan shark belongs to the same order of creatures as Arion's dolphin and the "friendly animals" of numerous nursery tales. What then are the relations between the two classes?

To begin with—granted that the tendency to ask the reason why, the desire "rerum cognoscere causas" (provided the things be interesting), is characteristic of man generally—it is clear that curiosity would be inevitably aroused by the totemistic beliefs that human beings are descended from animals and that animals help men: some explanation would eventually be felt to be necessary, and as a matter of fact explanations of the kind already illustrated are forthcoming. It is clear also that when the beliefs were dead and forgotten, the stories which had been invented to account for them would, if they survived, *ipso facto* be dissevered from the beliefs; and would now appear no longer as reasons or explanations, but as statements of facts which occurred "once upon a time,"—incidents, anecdotes. And, as still happens with anecdotes, there was nothing to prevent them from being appropriated to (or by) the wrong persons: the original dolphin-myth was attached to the historic Arion, whilst the totem-dolphin, the original of the myth, was absorbed by the god Apollo. But a single incident does not make a story. "There was once a man and he was changed into a dog," is not a statement of sufficient interest to live long in the memory; but it may have the requisite interest if either I believe that the man in question was an ancestor of my own, or if I know something about the man, other-

[1] Frazer, *op. cit.* 6.

wise, *e.g.* if I know him as the hero of other incidents. So that, granted that the incidents which compose myths are explanations which have survived the beliefs they were invented to explain, we have yet to learn why they came to be grouped together—a point of first-rate importance, because they would not have survived if they had not been combined together. We cannot suppose that they were first dissevered from the beliefs on which they originally depended for their existence, and then were subsequently combined so as to obtain a renewed existence, because they would probably have perished in the interval. We must therefore suppose that they were combined into tales ere yet the beliefs or institutions which gave them their first lease of life had perished. This means that the various parts of one institution, for instance, must have had each its separate explanation, and that these explanations were combined into one whole, the unity of which corresponded to the unity of the institution. An illustration will make this clearer, and we will choose one which shall serve to remind us that the relations of men to their totem-animal and to their animal kindred are not the only things for which early man required an explanation, and are not by any means the only source of the incidents to be found in myths and fairy-tales.

Ceremonies may continue to be performed as a matter of custom and tradition long after their original purpose and object have been forgotten; but they will not continue to be performed unless some reason or other is forthcoming, and usually the reason which commends itself is some inference from the nature of the ceremony itself, which is indeed an incorrect inference but is so easy and so readily understood that various people can arrive at it for themselves, and all can appreciate it at once. The explanations which thus come to be given of religious ritual form an important class of ætiological myths, and have the further interest for us that they afford instances of myths which from the beginning were tales and not merely single incidents: a single rite might consist of a series of acts, each of which demanded its own explanation; and the unity of the rite might produce a unity of interest and action in the resulting myth. For an instance we must obviously turn to a complex ritual, and we will take the ritual which resulted from the syncretism of the wine-god Dionysus and a vegetation spirit. It is probable that the festival of Dionysus at Thebes and elsewhere [1] began with a procession in which a branch, or something else originally representative of the vegetation spirit, was carried round the cultivated fields adjacent to the city, in the same way as the ears of maize were carried at the feast of the Mexican Chicomecoatl, or branches by the European Aryans generally on similar occasions—the purpose being the same in all cases, namely, to place the crops under the blessing of the vegetation spirit. The branch or image or what not was carried by a man dressed up as a woman, just as the *εἰρεσιώνη* was carried by youths dressed up as women—perhaps, as previously hinted, because the worship of the vegetation spirit was originally confined to women. This is the first act of the ceremony: the carrying of the symbol of the god by a man dressed as a woman. Then, by a custom common in Europe and exactly paralleled in Mexico, a human figure was attached to the top of a tree-trunk previously felled and prepared, and the trunk was hoisted by ropes into an upright position. This, as we have seen, is an indication of the presence of the anthropomorphic vegetation or tree-spirit in the tree.[2] The image was then pelted with stones until it fell, when it was torn in pieces by the crowd of women celebrating the festival. Stoning was the mode adopted of killing first the animal and afterwards the plant totem, because by means of it the whole community could share jointly and equally in the responsibility of killing the god. In the third and final act of the ritual, the woman who in the scramble secured the head of the image raced off with it, and nailed it to the door or roof of the chief house of the town or of the temple, just as the branch is fastened, after its procession round the fields, to the door or roof of the landlord's house, in northern Europe, and just as the *εἰρεσιώνη* was similarly attached to the temple of Apollo.

Now there came a time when the original meaning of all

[1] For what follows I am largely indebted to Mr. A. G. Bather's original and exhaustive paper on "The Problem of the *Bacchæ*," *Journal of Hellenic Studies*, 1894, vol. xiv. ii. 244–64.

[2] *Supra*, p. 215.

three parts of the festival was forgotten, and the spectators were reduced to their own conjectures. The leading fact and the starting-point for all attempts at explanation was that the festival was in honour of the god Dionysus, and whatever was done or represented in it must be something redounding to his glory. Then who was represented by the figure on the tree-top which was treated with such hostility and hatred, pelted and pulled to pieces by the women? It must be some enemy of the god, whose destruction was a triumph for Dionysus and was therefore commemorated in this festival. The women evidently were on the side of the god—must have been his worshippers—therefore the man was *not* one of Dionysus' worshippers. Perhaps that accounts for the opposition between him and the god: he would not bow down to Dionysus, whereas the women accepted the god cheerfully—the women of a community would be more likely to welcome a novelty in worship than the head of the family and representative of the old worship. But why is the man dressed in woman's clothes? no man in his senses would go about in public dressed up like a woman. No; but it is just one of the powers of the wine-god that he makes men lose their senses—and that may account, too, for the women killing their own king, they must have been frenzied to do that. So there only remain two things not clear now, why is the god not represented at his own festival? and what is the meaning of the tree being suddenly hauled up erect? Perhaps the god is supposed to be present, invisible but directing everything; and in that case it is he who causes the tree-top to rise, after inducing his foe to mount it, in order that, after exposing him to ridicule, he may cause him to perish at the hands of the women of his own family.

We have only now to fill in the proper names in order to have the myth of Pentheus which affords the framework of Euripides' play, the *Bacchæ*. Pentheus is the king who resists the introduction of the worship of Dionysus,[1] and is consequently bereft of his senses and led in woman's clothes as a laughing-stock through his own town by Dionysus.

[1] I explained the similar myths of Lycurgus, Eleutheræ, and Tiryns in much the same way in *Folk-Lore*, June 1891, vol. ii. ii. 238–41.

The women of Thebes, headed by Agave, the mother of Pentheus, are the women who accept the god, and become mænads. It is to enable Pentheus to spy their worship that Dionysus bends down a pine-tree, sets him on the top, and then lets it go. Finally, it is Agave who, with the other bacchæ, pelts and pulls to pieces her own son and carries off his head and sets it on his own palace-gable.

The tendency of syncretism to yield myths is not confined to Greece. Let us take a pair of instances from the New World. The Chibchas of New Granada had a goddess who dwelt as a serpent in Lake Iguaque, but whose name, Bachuê, "simply means 'she who suckles the maize,'"[1] *i.e.* she was a maize-mother, a plant totem, from whom the Chibchas traced their descent. Evidently the worshippers of this maize-mother had united their worship with that of a clan having an animal, a serpent, for totem; and the worship of the water-spirit had further been incorporated with that of Bachuê, with the result that a myth had to be invented to account for it all, and was to the effect that "on the first day of the world there emerged from its [Lake Iguaque's] waters a beautiful woman named Bachuê or Fuzachagua [= the good woman], carrying in her arms a child three years old. These were the ancestors of the race: when the world was peopled, they returned to the lake, and disappeared in its waters in the form of serpents."[2] The syncretism of a maize-goddess and a bird-totem has given rise to the myth told by the Cañari Indians, in the district southward of Quito. There were once two brothers whose provisions were exhausted; "the herbs and roots which they were able to collect scarcely sufficed for their sustenance, and hunger sorely pressed them, until two parrots entered their hut in their absence and prepared them a meal of cooked maize, together with a supply of the fermented liquor (chicha), which is made by steeping it in water. This happened day by day, until at length one of the birds was made captive by the brothers. When thus captured, it changed into a beautiful woman, from whom the brothers obtained the maize-seed and learned the art of cultivating it, and who ultimately became the ancestress of the Cañari nation."[3] Possibly the maize

[1] Payne, *New World*, i. 455. [2] *Ibid.* [3] *Ibid.* 327.

was originally the totem of the women, the parrot of the men, of the tribe; for the cultivation of maize, Mr. Payne adds, "was in the earliest times the exclusive task of the women of the tribe. It is only in a later stage that it is shared by the men," and then the men would be admitted to the worship of the maize-goddess, and the maize totem would be placed by the side of the parrot totem, till the worship of the two blended in one whole, and required a myth to explain it.

There was a time in the history of man when as yet the first tale had not been told, and the very idea of story-telling had not yet occurred to his mind. When it did occur, it was probably due to suggestion and not to his own unaided invention; and probably also it was an idea of very slow and gradual growth. The explanations which primitive man found for the various problems which perplexed him were of course, to him, actual facts, not pieces of imagination; and they were mostly single incidents, usually destitute of interest except for the community for whom they were originally designed—they might and did supply materials for tales, but they were not themselves tales. Some of these explanations, however, being designed to explain a series of phenomena, would spontaneously form a series of incidents, forming a true tale, *e.g.* as in the case of the myth of Pentheus; and some, as for instance the Cañari myth, would have a charm of their own which would win and delight other people besides the actual descendants of the bird-maiden. The man whose memory affectionately retained as many of these myths as he could gather, and who could repeat them well, would always command an audience. When he had told all he could easily remember, the tribute of praise couched in the appealing imperative, "Go on!" would stimulate him to rack his memory, with the result that semi-consciously he might substitute for the original incident or character some analogous one—the transformation into an animal instead of a bird, a god for a goddess, a jealous Hera for an irate Dionysus—and when what was first done semi-consciously came to be done with full consciousness and deliberation, the art of story-telling would be accomplished. Again, tales with a permanent human interest would easily spread beyond the limits of the original audience, and so would tend to become detached from the belief or ritual or other institution which they were first invented to explain. But in such circumstances statements which were in the first place explanations of something come themselves to require explanation: the Kalang chief was transformed into a dog, or a maiden into a bird, but why? The question was inevitable, and the answer would add a fresh incident to the story, a fresh complication to the plot. Further, the answer would be sought amongst incidents already familiar to the narrator and his audience, or would be framed on the analogy of one of them. Now, of such incidents there would be plenty that had been framed by early man to account for the numerous problems which interested him. One such problem was raised by taboos: to approach certain persons under certain circumstances, mourners, women, and others, was tabooed, but why? because once someone violated the taboo, and he or the tabooed person suffered a certain dreadful thing—in folk-tales the tabooed wife is often changed into a serpent or a bird.[1] Now, deities who confer benefits on man, teach him to cultivate maize for instance, frequently disappear, when they have completed their beneficent work—sometimes, like Bachuê, disappear in animal form. Here we have a series of very easy "chances" for the story-teller ransacking his memory: the parrot-maiden who married a human being eventually departed as she came in the shape of a bird, and so departed because her husband violated a certain taboo. Such a story would be interesting even to those who did not claim to be descended from the heroine, and were not interested in the cultivation of maize. It would be interesting enough to spread, *vivu' volitare per ora virum.* And as a matter of fact it is the type of a class of tales found all over the world, and known as Swan-maiden tales, from the best-known example, the *Arabian Nights'* tale of "Hasan of Bassorah."[2]

The incidents which compose the Swan-maiden story are such as have been familiar probably to every race at a certain stage of its development, and accordingly—unless we make the somewhat arbitrary and certainly unproved assumption

[1] Lang, *Custom and Myth,*[2] 75 ff.

[2] See Hartland, *Science of Fairy Tales,* cc. x. and xi.

that there was only one race of men capable of telling tales —those incidents may have been put together in this particular combination at any place in the inhabited world. But it does not follow that this particular combination would be formed by every race which was familiar with the separate incidents. The Cañari combination might indeed spring up independently in several centres, for a number of tribes trace their descent to the maize-mother or a cereal goddess, and the circumstances which would lead to a belief in the transformation of the goddess into an animal are fairly common also; and the particular animal might be a bird in several cases; or, if it was a serpent, then we should get a tale of the Mélusine class. But the further incidents of the departure of the beneficent deity, and in animal form, and that form a bird (or serpent), and that departure in consequence of a violation of taboo—though they might conceivably have been combined in this particular sequence more than once, probably are not, on the theory of chances, likely to have come together in this particular form. When, then, we find the story with its full complement of incidents (or in a form which clearly postulates the previous existence of the full complement) in several different places, we should conclude that it has spread to them from its place of origin. We have, then, now to consider the problem of the diffusion of myths.

One way in which a myth might be diffused is the dispersion of the people to whom it was known. The Indo-Europeans spread from their original home, wherever that was, until they covered Europe and part of Asia; and if they had any tales interesting enough to live, those tales may well have been diffused over all the area eventually covered by the Indo-Europeans. But it is quite certain that the circulation of those tales would not be confined to the Indo-European public: they would find their way to all peoples with whom the Indo-Europeans had dealings, and there would be an international exchange of tales as well as of goods. In other words, borrowing is a factor in the diffusion of myths as well as tradition. And when we reflect that the Oceanic or Malay race has come to extend from the Sandwich Islands on the west to Madagascar on the east, and from Formosa on the north to New Zealand on the south, we shall be inclined to believe that it may well have exchanged tales with the negroes of Africa and the Mongols and Aryans of Asia, if not also with the peoples of Central America.

When, then, we find any given myth widely diffused, there are three ways in which its diffusion may be accounted for, namely, borrowing, tradition, and independent origin. Of these three the two latter are of somewhat restricted operation. The theory that a myth has originated independently in several different places is applicable mainly where the myth is a single incident or simple combination of two or three incidents; and where the incident or combination is such that it would or might easily arise in consequence of the action of causes known to exist in the supposed places of origin. Amongst the problems which savages speculate on, the cause of lunar eclipses is one; and a fairly common solution hit upon is that the moon is swallowed by some monster. To postulate borrowing or tradition to account for the fact that different peoples believe the moon's disappearance to her being gradually swallowed up, seems superfluous. Or, again, the regularity with which the sun moves along his allotted path calls for explanation, and the inference that he does so because somebody compels or has compelled him is so easy and obvious that various people may well have hit upon it independently of each other. But when the myth is even moderately complex, the theory of independent origin seems to become inapplicable.

The difficulties in the way of applying the tradition-theory are so great, that it has almost entirely been given up. A story common to several different branches of the same race may have been inherited by them from their undivided forefathers, but it may also have originated after the dispersion, and have spread by borrowing from one branch to another long after they had dispersed from the original home. There is little agreement amongst experts as to what, indeed whether any, myths can be traced back to the original home of the Indo-Europeans, for instance. As for tracking back a myth by the hypothesis of tradition, from the uncertain home of the Indo-Europeans to the cradle of the human race, the attempt is not to be made. Myths that are world-wide are either such as by their relative complexity show that they have spread by borrowing, or such as by their absolute simplicity show that they may have originated amongst any race in the earliest stage of culture discernible by palæontology. That stage was not confined to any one portion of the globe —the Stone Age gives us no clue to the place of man's origin on earth.

There remain two classes of myths to which we have not yet alluded, those about the origin of the world and of man, and flood-myths. The myths about the origin of man, so far as they have any uniformity at all, seem to be constructed on the analogy of the totemist's belief about the ancestor of his clan: the first man grew out of an animal—"belched up by a cow," say the Zulus—or out of a tree, or out of the ground like a tree, or out of a rock or mountain. The cosmogonic myths include some which regard the universe as "the hollow of a vast cocoa-nut shell, divided into many imaginary circles, like those of mediæval speculation"[1]—these seem to be borrowed; others regard "many of the things in the world as fragments of the frame of a semi-supernatural and gigantic being, human or bestial, belonging to a race which preceded the advent of man"[2]—and these too are perhaps not above the suspicion of being borrowed; and others, again, credit the totem-ancestor, whether in animal or human form, with having something to do with the construction of the world as known to the particular myth-maker. Of flood-myths—as of cosmogonic myths—some are not native to the peoples amongst whom they are reported as having been found, but are due to Christian influences. Others have not been derived from European settlers, and may be genuine native productions: the mythical descent of the tribe from a mountain—*e.g.* the Babylonian "mountain of mankind"—involves the necessity of explaining how the ancestor came to be on the mountain from which he issued, and the savage hypothesis is that he must have been compelled to go there, and compelled obviously by a flood. Others are possibly not myths at all, but traditions of a local inundation.

[1] Lang, *Myth, Ritual, and Religion*, i. 194. [2] *Op. cit.* i. 166.

Myths, then, it seems, are in their origin attempts to explain things—the phenomena of nature, the constitution of the universe, and the descent of man—which in later times form the subject-matter of science and of philosophy. They are the first outcome of the speculative tendency in man, the first application of the reason and of the scientific imagination to the solution of problems which have never ceased to engage the attention of man. In a word, mythology is primitive man's science and philosophy, and is the first ancestor of the philosophy and science of the modern *savant*. But further, these primitive speculations on perennial problems took the shape of narratives: their common form is that so-and-so takes place or took place because somebody once did such-and-such a thing. These narratives, relating, as facts which took place, what were really only inferences, could not be and were not distinguished by primitive man from the traditions of his time which were more or less historic. In fine, mythology was largely primitive man's history as well as his science and his philosophy; and the impossibility of his distinguishing these narratives from actual traditions accounts for the fact that the early history of all peoples contains some admixture—greater or less—of mythology. Further, again, some of these explanatory narratives become, as we have seen, tales told for the sake of the telling, works of the poetic imagination. Thus mythology was primitive man's romance as well as his history, his science, and his philosophy.

Now, explanations of all kinds inevitably take their colour and character to a large extent from the character of their author: in seeking to account for a person's conduct, the uncharitable and unchristian man finds an unchristian explanation, and imputes uncharitable motives. In astronomy even, allowance has to be made for "the personal equation," and modern histories reflect the political or personal prepossessions of the modern historian. Poetry reflects or rather expresses the tone and morality—austere or sensual—of the poet; successful poetry, of the poet's generation. Literature reveals the religion or want of religion of the age. And this brings us to the relation of mythology to religion.

The narratives in which primitive speculations were embodied were not merely intellectual exercises, nor the work of the abstract imagination: they reflect or express the mind of the author in its totality, for they are the work of a human being, not of a creature possessing reason and no morality, or imagination and no feeling. They will therefore express the morality of the author and his generation; the motives ascribed to the heroes of the narrative will be such as actuated the men by whom and for whom the narrative was designed; they may be high or low according as the standard of the time is high or low, but they cannot be higher than the best which the author could find in his own heart. In the same way, then, as the moral tone and temper of the author and his age makes itself felt in these primitive speculations, so will the religious spirit of the time. In fine, mythology is not religion. Mythology is not the source of religion, though it is the source of science, philosophy, poetry, and history. Mythology is no more the source of religion than it is of morality; but just as the latter is expressed in a man's thoughts—in what he likes to dwell on and how he likes to imagine himself faring—in a man's actions, in a people's poetry, so mythology is one of the spheres of human activity in which religion may manifest itself, one of the departments of human reason which religion may penetrate, suffuse, and inspire. Hence we may expect that the early narratives, in which the science and poetry, the history and philosophy, of early peoples are embodied, will in different peoples differ in religious spirit. For instance, if we grant for a moment that the cosmogonies which appear with such similarity in early Hebrew and Chaldæan records, were a piece of primitive science attempting to account for the constitution of the universe, then we have in them a striking example of the vast difference between primitive narratives which are inspired by the religious spirit and primitive narratives which are not so penetrated. The same considerations will apply to the various narratives of the Flood, or to a comparison of the Paradise of the Book of Genesis with the Babylonians' Garden of Eden or the Persians' Eran Vej. It is the differences in these early narratives, not their resemblances, which are important on this view. The resemblances are due to the human reason, which in different places working on the same material comes to similar inferences. The difference which distinguishes the Hebrew from all other primitive narratives testifies that the religious spirit was dealt in a larger measure to the Hebrews than to other peoples.

In a previous chapter[1] we have seen that primitive man starts with a fundamental conviction that there are certain things which must not be done; and the human reason, in the endeavour to determine what are the things which must not be done, goes as far astray as it did in its primitive attempts to solve the problems of science. Primitive logic, at the mercy of the association of ideas, tended to multiply the number of things forbidden, until man's every step in life was entangled in a network of taboo. Some of these prohibitions were required in the interests of mankind, others not; and progress, in this respect, consisted in the survival of the fittest of these restraints and the rejection of the rest. The share of religion in this process consisted in what we have called the supernatural selection of the fittest of these restraints: the religious spirit rejected those which were repugnant to the religious consciousness, and retained those which were essential to the moral law and to the conception of "holiness." Now, as the human reason, by its very constitution, was impelled to interpret the fundamental feeling that there are certain things which must not be done, so it was impelled to interpret the phenomena of nature, society, and life, in order to furnish an answer to the problems which those phenomena suggested. And as the restraining and selective agency of the religious spirit was required to criticise the interpretations put forward by the reason in the one case, so it was required in the other. Thus, in the primitive pieces of science, to which reference was made in the last paragraph, the conspicuous fact is that in the Hebrew narratives there has been what we have called a supernatural selection, and a rejection of the elements which are inconsistent with monotheism and the higher religion of the Hebrews. But we can trace the action of supernatural selection even

[1] *Supra* p. 85.

further, and gain a still further confirmation of the fact that the primitive science of these early narratives was the work of the human reason, and proceeded from a different source from that whence the religious elements in them came. As those features of a primitive hypothesis which were repugnant to the religious consciousness were rejected by it, so might the whole of such a hypothesis be repugnant and be rejected accordingly *in toto*. The selective process could not be confined to portions of a myth; it would inevitably be applied to discriminate one myth from another, and result in the rejection of those which were inconsistent with the particular stage of religious development of the time. Explanations of the kind familiar in primitive science might occur, and be rejected by the mind to which they occurred, or fail to obtain any vogue in the community, because they were below the spiritual level of the community; or they might commend themselves to the community, but be repugnant to the religious consciousness of the more spiritual members, and be rejected by their influence. The result would be twofold: the imagination would be more and more excluded from the region of speculation which produced the ordinary myths of early peoples; and more and more restricted to the path of religious meditation. Now, these two features are both characteristic of the Hebrew Scriptures: their poverty in myths has struck every inquirer; their richness in devotional poetry is familiar to all.

The extraordinary notion that mythology is religion is the outcome of the erroneous and misleading practice of reading modern ideas into ancient religions. It is but one form of the fallacy that mythology was to the antique religions what dogma is to the modern—with the superadded fallacy that dogma is the source, instead of the expression, of religious conviction. Mythology is primitive science, primitive philosophy, an important constitutent of primitive history, the source of primitive poetry, but it is not primitive religion. It is not necessarily or usually even religious. It is not the proper or even the ordinary vehicle for the expression of the religious spirit. Prayer, meditation, devotional poetry, are the chosen vehicles in thought and word; ritual in outward deed and act. Myths originate in a totally different psychological quarter: they are the work of the human reason, acting in accordance with the laws of primitive logic; or are the outcome of the imagination, playing with the freedom of the poetic fancy. In neither case are they primarily the product of religious feeling: it is not the function of feeling to draw inferences. It is for moral feeling, or religious, to reject what is alien to it, to penetrate what is compatible with it. Hence the selective function of the religious consciousness depends upon the sensitiveness of that consciousness. Where its sensitiveness was great, only those pieces of primitive science survived which were capable of being informed by the religious spirit. Far different was the case with those nations in whom the religious spirit was late in waking. The explanations which savages invent to account for things that puzzle them are of necessity, like their inventors, savage. If, then, a nation advances from savagery, through barbarism and semi-barbarism, to civilisation, and if the myths which were invented in the savage stage are not rejected by the religious consciousness, but continue to live, in virtue of their connection with the institutions which also are transmitted from the earlier to the later stages of the national life, the result will be that a civilised generation will find itself saddled with myths that attribute to the gods actions of a savage, irrational, and even disgusting description. Philosophers like Plato, then, may argue that tales of this kind, which cannot be true and must be demoralising, ought to be thrown overboard altogether; but the majority of people, to whom these tales have been taught as part of their traditional religion, cannot away with them in this fashion. At the same time they cannot accept them wholly and literally. A *via media*, therefore, has to be sought, and this *via media* has always been found in allegory: the obvious meaning of the myths cannot be the true one, but they must have some meaning, therefore they must contain a hidden meaning, intentionally concealed by the authors of the myth. This was the explanation given of Sanskrit mythology in early times in India, and of Greek mythology by Anaxagoras and Empedocles in Greece and by the Stoics of Rome.

The assumption at the base of all forms of the allegorical theory is that in early times there existed a class of philosophers teaching profound philosophy, and conveying it in the form of fables. Now the existence of this caste of philosophers, if it is a historic fact, ought to be capable of being demonstrated in accordance with the ordinary canons of historical criticism; and it is Lobeck's contribution to the science of mythology that he proved, once and for all, the entire absence of any proof, or even presumption, in favour of the historical existence of these philosophers. Since Lobeck's time—his *Aglaophamus* was published in 1829—the application of the theory of evolution to the science of man has enabled us to trace back civilised peoples through the Iron Age and the Bronze Age to the time when their ancestors had only flint implements, and were unacquainted even with the rudiments of agriculture. At the same time the study of savages still in the Stone Age has revealed the fact that not only are the implements made and used by them the same all over the world, but that the institutions and conceptions by which they govern their lives have an equally strong resemblance to one another. The presumption, therefore, that our Indo-European forefathers of the Stone Age had beliefs and practices similar to those of other peoples in the same stage of development, is very strong; and it is confirmed by the fact that amongst the most backward members of civilised communities, amongst those classes which have made relatively little advance in civilisation, folk-lore discovers abundant traces of superstitions which find exact analogues in savage customs. For the proof, however, that the irrational elements in the mythology and folk-tales of civilised nations—the taboos and metamorphoses, the incest and bestiality—are survivals from savagery, we must refer the reader to the works of Mr. Andrew Lang mentioned at the beginning of this chapter.

That the allegory theory of mythology survived to the present century, until it received its deathblow from Lobeck, was due partly to the belief that the inner, esoteric meaning of the myths was taught to the initiated at the Eleusinian and other mysteries by the priests, to whom it was handed down by their predecessors, the inventors of this mode of teaching. This belief, which we shall have to examine shortly, derived considerable sustenance from two fallacies. One was based on the illicit importation of modern ideas into ancient institutions: it was naturally but erroneously inferred that because in modern religions great stress is laid upon what a man believes, the same importance was ascribed to this side of religion in ancient times, whereas "the antique religions had for the most part no creed; they consisted entirely of institutions and practices."[1] Hence, then, the first fallacy, that of believing that the business of the ancient priest was to teach. There was no authoritative dogma for him to teach, and as a matter of fact he did not teach. The other fallacy consisted in the assumption that mythology was the work of the priests—which is but a form of the wider and coarser fallacy that religion is the invention of priestcraft.

It seems, therefore, to be desirable that, before resuming the direct thread of our argument, and showing how the mystic tendency, obscured under polytheism, was revived by the mysteries, we should indicate the place of the priesthood in early religion, and show that it was not the priest that made religion, but religion that made the priest.

[1] Robertson Smith, *Religion of the Semites*, 16.

CHAPTER XX

PRIESTHOOD

In all early religions, priests are marked off from other worshippers, partly by what they do, and partly by what they may not do; and there is so much agreement between the different religions on both points, that we obviously have to do with the effects of a cause or causes operating uniformly in all parts of the world. At the same time there are certain features of the priesthood which, though they recur in various religions, are not uniformly present in all: they are not essential parts of the antique conception of priesthood. It is clear, therefore, that any general theory on the subject must account for both the uniformity in certain characteristics and the want of uniformity in the other characteristics. The general cause which a theory postulates must be such that its operation would produce the complete uniformity of the one class and the only partial uniformity of the other class of features.

The most important point in which only partial uniformity prevails is tenure of office. Some priesthoods are annual, some tenable for five years, some for twelve, some for life; of some the tenure is terminable on certain contingencies; others are hereditary. Sometimes priests form an order apart, and in that case the order in some places consists of priests appointed for life, sometimes of hereditary priests. In one country there may be only one form of priesthood, *e.g.* an order of hereditary priests as in Israel, or an order of priests chosen for life, as amongst the negroes of the Gold Coast. In another, life-priests, annual and quinquennial priesthoods, and priesthoods terminable on certain contingencies, may all exist side by side, as, *e.g.*, in ancient Greece. And the tenure of even hereditary priesthood may be made terminable—as far as the individual is concerned—on certain contingencies, or on attaining a certain age, *e.g.* manhood; for, whereas some priesthoods could not commence before manhood, others could only be held before that period.

Having illustrated the want of uniformity in this feature of the priesthood, and having noted that it will require explanation, we may proceed to examine the features in which uniformity prevails. First, we will take the fact that in all religions there are certain things which priests may not do: there may be, there is, a want of agreement in details, as to the particular things, but the general principle is universal. When, however, we come to examine the details, we find that, though the particular things which are thus forbidden in antique religions vary, they all agree in certain points: they are prohibitions which have no spiritual value (*e.g.* the priestess of Athênê at Athens might not eat cheese[1]), no ethical import (*e.g.* the prohibition of attendance at funerals[2]), and no practical utility (*e.g.* the prohibition of seeing an army under arms[3]); in fine, they constitute the "irrational element" in the conditions of priesthood, and have exactly the same value for the historian as the irrational element of myth has: they indicate that the institution has been transmitted to civilised man from ancestors who were in a less advanced stage of culture than he, and to whom, consequently, these prohibitions appeared, when they made them, perfectly reasonable. It is clear, then, that any general theory of the priesthood must account for these prohibitions; and to be a satisfactory theory must account for them all. The nature of the class of facts requiring explanation may be inferred from the summary Mr. Frazer gives[4] of the prohibitions or rules of life observed by the Flamen Dialis at Rome; "they were such as the following: the Flamen Dialis might not ride or even touch a horse, nor see an army under arms, nor wear a ring which was not broken, nor have a knot on any part of his garments; no fire except a sacred fire might be taken out of his house;

[1] Strabo, ix. 395. [2] Lev. x. 6, xxi. 1–5; Plato, *Laws*, 947 C.

[3] Festus, 249*b*, 22 for the Flamen Dialis, and Schömann, *Antiquities Grecques*, II. ii. 507 for Greek priests.

[4] *G.B.* i. 117.

he might not touch wheaten flour or leavened bread; he might not touch or even name a goat, a dog, raw meat, beans, and ivy; he might not walk under a vine; the feet of his bed had to be daubed with mud; his hair could be cut only by a free man and with a bronze knife, and his hair and nails when cut had to be buried under a lucky tree; he might not touch a dead body, nor enter a place where one was burned; he might not see work being done on holy days; he might not be uncovered in the open air; if a man in bonds were taken into his house, he had to be unbound, and the cords had to be drawn up through a hole in the roof and so let down into the street. His wife, the Flaminica, had to observe nearly the same rules, and others of her own besides. She might not ascend more than three steps of the kind of staircase called Greek; at a certain festival she might not comb her hair; the leather of her shoes might not be made from a beast that had died a natural death, but only from one that had been slain or sacrificed; if she heard thunder she was tabooed till she had offered an expiatory sacrifice." The theory that priestly taboos were symbolical of the religious qualifications required of the priest, can hardly be stretched to cover all the facts. It may explain partly why some taboos were retained in advancing civilisation; it cannot explain their original imposition. We shall have, therefore, to find another explanation of their origin. Their abolition it is which is due to the religious sentiment, not their origin; and the same selective process which gradually weeded out the irrational prohibitions permitted the survival of those which could be explained as the outward and visible symbols of higher things.

We now turn from the things which priests may not do, to the other feature characteristic of and common to all priests in early religions, namely, the things which they do. Here, too, in the midst of what at first sight appears to be endless variety, we find a principle of uniformity: the priest had charge of the ritual of the sanctuary in which he served. It was his business to see that the various external acts which constituted that ritual were performed in the order and manner prescribed by custom. The prescribed details might and did vary greatly in different places: thus in Sicyon a pig might not be offered to Aphroditê; in Megara she was the only deity to whom it could be offered. But uniformly the priest's office was to draw near to the god and to introduce the worshipper to him. The central feature of the priestly function, the key to his position and place in the ritual, was that by inviolable custom he and he alone could kill the victim which the worshipper brought and on the sacrifice of which the worshipper's hope depended of commending himself to the god and renewing the bond with him. The priest alone dealt (actually or formally) the first and fatal blow at the victim: hence his power of rejecting a worshipper who brought the wrong kind of victim or failed to fulfil any of the preliminary conditions (of fasting, purification, etc.) which the custom of the sanctuary exacted. It is the power and duty of dealing the first blow which is universally characteristic of the antique priesthood; and as this duty is involved with the act of sacrifice which is the centre and origin of ancient religious institutions, we may reasonably consider that in it we have an indication of the direction in which we must look for the origin of the priesthood. What was it that caused a primitive community to agree in looking upon one particular man as peculiarly qualified or privileged to strike the first blow?

To answer this question, we must note that in civilised communities the priest as a rule only intermediates between the god and the worshipper, in the sense that by sacrificing the victim which the latter brings he puts him into communication with the former, and so enables him to make his prayer. The priest may, from his constant attendance upon the sanctuary and the zeal with which he looks after the interests of the deity, have, as Chryses in the *Iliad* has, some personal influence with the god; but, as a rule, in civilised times the priest does not himself exercise supernatural powers. But to this rule there are exceptions, well established in civilised countries and more common amongst uncivilised peoples. For instance, a supernatural power of foreseeing the future may be exercised by the priest or priestess, who is then believed to be temporarily inspired or "possessed" by the god. Two instances must suffice for us. In Fiji, "one who intends to consult the oracle dresses and oils himself . . .

there is placed before the priest a dish of scented oil, with which he anoints himself . . . in a few minutes he trembles; slight distortions are seen in his face and twitching movements in his limbs. These increase to a violent muscular action, which spreads until the whole frame is strongly convulsed, and the man shivers as with a strong ague fit. . . . The priest is now possessed by his god, and all his words and actions are considered as no longer his own, but those of the deity who has entered into him. Shrill cries of 'It is I! it is I!' fill the air, and the god is thus supposed to notify his approach. While giving the answer, the priest's eyes stand out and roll as in a frenzy; his voice is unnatural, his face pale, his lips livid, his breathing depressed, and his entire appearance like that of a furious madman. The sweat runs from every pore, and tears start from his strained eyes; after which the symptoms gradually disappear. The priest looks round with a vacant stare, and as the god says, 'I depart,' announces his actual departure by violently flinging himself down on the mat."[1] The other instance is contained in Virgil's description of the "possession" of the Sibyl:—

> "Ventum erat ad limen, cum virgo 'Poscere fata
> Tempus' ait; 'deus, ecce deus!' cui talia fanti
> Ante fores subito non vultus, non color unus,
> Non comptæ mansere comæ; sed pectus anhelum,
> Et rabie fera corda tument; maiorque videri,
> Nec mortale sonans, adflata est numine quando
> Iam propiore dei . . .
> At Phœbi nondum patiens immanis in antro
> Bacchatur vates, magnum si pectore possit
> Excussisse deum; tanto magis ille fatigat
> Os rabidum fera corda domans fingitque premendo."[2]

But the Apollo who entered the Sibyl and prophesied through her lips could also in the same way give supernatural strength;[3] and in the orgiastic worship of Dionysus the worshippers were supposed by the Greeks to be endowed with superhuman physical power by the god on whose body they had fed. Amongst savages even more extensive powers are believed to be exercised, not temporarily, but permanently, by human beings of whom a god has taken not temporary

[1] Williams, *Fiji and the Fijians*, i. 224.

[2] *Æn.* vi. 45 ff., 77 ff.

[3] Paus. X. xxxii. 6.

but permanent possession. Thus in the Marquesas Islands there was a class of men who "were supposed to wield a supernatural power over the elements; they could give abundant harvests or smite the ground with barrenness; and they could inflict disease or death."[1] In South America, the Chibchas had a high pontiff, and "by a long and ascetic novitiate this ghostly ruler was reputed to have acquired such sanctity that the waters and the rain obeyed him and the weather depended on his will."[2] From Africa Mr. Frazer gives a long list of kings who are consulted as oracles, and can inflict or heal sickness, withhold rain, and cause famine; and from Cambodia he quotes the two kings of Fire and of Water, who control those elements respectively; and again, "the Buddhist Tartars believe in a great number of living Buddhas, who officiate as Grand Lamas at the head of the most important monasteries."[3] In the semi-civilisations of the New World "the Mexican kings at their accession took an oath that they would make the sun to shine, the clouds to give rain, the rivers to flow, and the earth to bring forth fruits in abundance,"[4] and the Incas of Peru were revered like gods. In the Old World the kings of Egypt were deified in their lifetime, and the Mikado belonged to the same class of sacred potentates, who are (or were) also to be found in Ethiopia, Southern India, Siam, Sumatra, Babylon; and of whom probable traces were to be found even in Europe.

Of these wielders of supernatural power, some, it will have been noted, are high priests, some kings, and some, like the Incas of Peru and the kings of Egypt, both kings and high priests. This creates a presumption that originally these possessors of supernatural power united in their own person the functions which afterwards came to be held by separate officials: originally there was but one supreme institution, and it was only in course of time that the priestly function and the royal were separated, and that the one institution became two. This presumption is both confirmed and explained by the taboos which attach to the institution. Not only priests but kings are subject to taboos, and the royal taboos are of the same kind as the priestly. To take a parallel which recent investigation has made possible, the Flamen Dialis, it will be

[1] Frazer, *G. B.* i. 38. [2] *Ibid.* 44. [3] *Ibid.* 42. [4] *Ibid.* 49.

remembered, was limited as to the food he might eat or even see, as to the garments he might wear; he might not ride, or see work done on holy days. Now, not only was "the Sabbath known, at all events in Accadian times, as a *dies nefastus*, a day on which certain work was forbidden to be done," but "the king himself, it is stated, must not eat flesh that has been cooked over the coals or in the smoke, he must not change the garments of his body, white robes he must not wear, sacrifices he may not offer, in a chariot he may not ride."[1] In civilised communities the restrictions imposed upon both kings and priests have usually decreased in number and dwindled down to mere survivals—therein keeping pace with the diminution of the sacred powers ascribed to each. In less advanced stages of culture, where high priests and kings each exercise the divine powers deputed to them more extensively, the restrictions are more numerous and more real; and both the powers and the limitations are united and more extensive in the case of rulers who are, like the Egyptian, at once high priest and king. The parallel between the royal and the priestly office further extends to the conditions of tenure—kingship may be hereditary or elective, annual or lifelong, etc.—and, as we shall hereafter see, to the manner of consecration. At this point, however, our business is to see how the natural operation of the taboos would tend to differentiate the primitive institution into the two separate institutions of royalty and priesthood.

The infectiousness of taboo is such that the energies of primitive society are devoted to isolating the tabooed person or thing. A human being in whom the divine afflatus is permanently present is highly taboo, and the most stringent measures are taken to isolate him; and that is the original reason of the restrictions imposed on priests and kings. But the isolation acts or tends to act in a way not originally contemplated: even if it does not lead to the permanent and absolute seclusion of the ruler in his palace (as was the case with the Mikado and other sacred kings, in Ethiopia, Sabæa, Tonquin, and in Corea and Loango at the present day[2]), still the number of prohibitions to which he is subjected is enough (as the taboos on the Flamen Dialis may show) to hamper and restrict him in such a way that he is as effectually cut

[1] Sayce, *Higher Criticism*, 75.

[2] *G. B.* 164.

off from intercourse with his subjects and the discharge of the active duties of kingship as if he were absolutely confined to his palace. The result is that all real power passes out of the hands of a man in such a helpless condition. For a time the institution of king-priest may endure, because there are found men who are content to enjoy the power without the glory of ruling. But generally the pressure of external foes eventually makes it necessary for the king-priest to entrust the command of his subjects to a war-king. The office of war-king may be intended to be temporary [1]—annual, or terminable at the end of the campaign—but it usually results in becoming lifelong and frequently hereditary.[2] If the war-king, further, is not content with military power, but arrogates to himself the rest of the temporal power that originally belonged to the priest-king, and then succeeds in founding a family, the result will be the existence side by side of two institutions—one, the kingship, in which the temporal power is centred; the other, the pontificate, in which the spiritual powers remain.[3] But the divinity which hedged in the priest-king was inevitably transferred with the transference of part of his functions to the temporal king. Even when the latter was, like the Tycoon of Japan, a mere usurper, the same fate eventually overtook his descendants as had befallen the Mikado, whose functions they usurped: "entangled in the same inextricable web of custom and law, they degenerated into mere puppets, hardly stirring from their palaces, and occupied in a perpetual round of empty ceremonies, while the real business of government was managed by the council of state."[4] When, then, the war-king was not a unsurper but was duly consecrated by the king-priest, the divine character of the original office would be likely *à fortiori* to be transmitted to the new institution (as in Mexico), wholly or in part. If the divine character was transmitted only in such degree that the king was not impeded in his work, the institution of royalty was safe from the danger which deprived the original institution of half its power; but if in a greater degree, then some means of evading the hampering restrictions of the

[1] So in Mangaia, *ib.* 120.

[2] So in Tonquin, *oc. cit.*

[3] So in Mexico and Colombia, *ibid.* 44, 113.

[4] *Ibid.* 119.

office had to be found. One such means was that adopted by the Mikado: it consisted in abdicating on the birth of a son and doing homage to the child, on whom thus fell all the restrictions, while the father, acting in the infant monarch's name, exercised all the power.[1] It is in a similar way, we may conjecture, that the priesthoods administered by young men or children were transferred to them by their fathers; for the rules which would hamper the father in his daily life and work could be observed with less practical inconvenience in the case of the young or infant son. For, it need hardly be remarked, the priest, even when temporal power had passed to the kingship, still retained the divine character, and with it the incapacity for mixing in the affairs of daily life, which attached to the priest-king. Thus in Tartary, we find Father Grueber saying, "Duo hoc in Regno Reges sunt, quorum prior Regni negotiis recte administrandis incumbit, et Dena dicitur; alter ab omni negotiorum extraneorum mole avulsus, intra secretos palatii sui secessus otio indulgens, Numinis instar adoratur . . . hunc veluti Deum verum et vivum, quem et Patrem æternum et cœlestem vocant, . . . adorant."[2]

In this connection we may note it as a further indication of the original indivisible unity of the office of priest and king, that even when the two functions have come to be exercised by different persons there is a perpetual tendency to revert to the old organic unity: it is not merely that each of the separate offices retains some part of the divine character that attached to the undivided office, but the functions themselves tend to reunite—reverting in their unity sometimes to the priest and sometimes to the king. If, for instance, the priesthood becomes (or remains) hereditary, and temporal rulers are appointed *ad hoc* and from time to time, the temporal functions naturally relapse into the priesthood in the intervals (longer or shorter) when no judge or war leader is forthcoming. Indeed, even in the latest times, the consecration of the king by a priest testifies to the original source of the king's office. On the other hand, if the kingship becomes hereditary but the priesthood not, then, in spite of the existence of priests, priestly functions tend to attach themselves to the kingly office; hence it is a

[1] *Loc. cit.* [2] Thevenot, *Divers Voyages*, iv. 22.

very general feature of the kingship in ancient times that the king can offer sacrifice, like a priest. If this reunion of the two functions becomes so intimate as to amount to a reversion to the ancestral organism, so to speak, then the same process of fission which originally gave birth to the king will be repeated; and the temporal ruler, whose office originated in a delegation of power from the king-priest, will himself have to appoint a delegate to do those warlike duties which the sanctity of his office prevents him from discharging himself—by the side of a βασιλεύς we shall find a πολέμαρχος, by the side of the "king" a *heretoga*. The tendency to reversion, however, which manifests itself particularly when either of the derived offices is hereditary, may be averted without danger to the hereditary principle, if the hereditary priest (or king) delegates his temporal (or priestly) functions to his brother, or other relative and his descendants.

A further and remarkable fact which tends to connect kingship and priesthood together, and to prove their common origin, is the common fate to which divine kings and divine priests alike were liable: at the end of a certain period of time the king had to commit suicide or was put to death. In India, the king of Calicut had to cut his throat in public at the end of a twelve years' reign; so, too, the king of Quilacare in South India.[1] The divine kings of Meroe in Ethiopia could be ordered to die whenever the priests chose.[2] In various parts of Africa, kings and priests having supernatural powers are put to death, sometimes when old age threatens, sometimes when they have developed the least bodily blemish, such as the loss of a tooth; and the executioner may be the destined successor of the king. Amongst the ancient Prussians, the ruler, whose title was God's Mouth, might commit suicide by burning himself in front of the sacred oak.[3] Amongst other peoples[4] death seems not to have been insisted on at all unless drought or pestilence or other calamities occurred. But even so, a difficulty was found in obtaining persons willing to take office. In Savage Island, "of old they had kings, but as they were the high priests as well, and were supposed to cause the

[1] Frazer, *G. B.* i. 224.
[2] *Ibid.* 218.
[3] *Ibid.* 223.
[4] *E.g.* the Swedes, *ibid.* 47.

food to grow, the people got angry with them in times of scarcity, and killed them, so the end of it was that no one wished to be king."[1] On the other hand, it is clear that peoples who wished to retain the institution of kingship would have to give up requiring suicide of the king. The requirement, however, would not have been made in the first instance if there had not been a very powerful motive—whatever the motive might have been—for making it; and the motive operated against the abolition of this condition of holding royal office, as also it must have operated in inducing the occupants of the office to comply with it. Eventually the condition was evaded. Amongst the Western Semites, in Babylon, the tenure of office seems to have been annual—the original term, as we shall hereafter argue—and at the end of the year the king was put to death. In course of time the community seem to have consented to an evasion: when the time for execution came, the king abdicated, and a criminal was allowed to reign in his stead for five days, at the end of which time the criminal was executed and the king resumed his throne.[2] Elsewhere the king abdicates annually, and a temporary king is appointed but is not killed, he is only subject to a mock execution.[3] In two places (Cambodia and Jambi) the temporary kings come of a stock believed to be akin to the royal family.[4] Sometimes the mock king is not appointed annually, but once for all for a few days at the beginning of the reign, which seems to indicate that in this case the custom of annually executing a substitute for the king had given way to the practice of executing one, once for all, at the accession of the king. Finally, it is suggested by Mr. Frazer that a criminal would probably not at first have been accepted by the community as an adequate substitute: hence possibly the original substitute was the king's firstborn son.[5] The practice of sacrificing the firstborn to the gods is well known.

It seems probable that originally the office of divine priest-king was held for a year, because in that case the difficulty and cruelty of insisting on the fulfilment of the condition of tenure would naturally lead to an extension

[1] Turner, *Samoa*, 304. [2] Frazer, *op. cit.* 227. [3] *Ibid.* 228–31.
[4] *Ibid.* 234. [5] *Ibid.*

first to some definite period, as for instance to twelve years (or, since as some priesthoods were quinquennial, perhaps to five years), then for life, provided that natural death was not allowed to interfere with the suicide or execution which was in the bond. To prevent this last contingency, some peoples made the appearance of the first indication of old age, the first physical blemish, a sign for execution, and to the end a physical blemish in a priest was widely deprecated: "sacerdos non integri corporis quasi mali ominis res vitanda est."[1]

It seems, then, that the functions habitually performed by the priest in the civilised states of ancient times, and the powers which he exercised less frequently, and the restrictions which were laid upon him, were all inherited by him from his predecessor the divine priest. It seems also that the similar restrictions and the similar sanctity of the ordinary king of historic times were inherited by him from his predecessor the divine king. And the existence of these divine priests and divine kings—in all quarters of the globe, as the instances accumulated by the learning of Mr. Frazer show—points to the fact that in the early history of the race, in patriarchal times, each wandering community of fellow-tribesmen had over it a person who was in some sense divine, both priest and king, and whose death, voluntary or imposed, at the end of a year, was regarded by the community and accepted by the victim as imperative in the highest interests of the community. We have therefore to inquire why this was believed; and it is only proper that we should begin by stating Mr. Frazer's answer to the question.

Mr. Frazer thinks that men began by believing themselves to be possessed of magical powers, and consequently that the distinction between men and gods was somewhat blurred—apparently that it was difficult or impossible for primitive man to tell whether a certain person, his own ruler in this case, was a very great magician or a god. Further, apparently the primitive community seem to have come to the conclusion that their chief was a god, and that, having got hold of a god, it was desirable to retain him for purposes of their own. But the god might grow old and feeble, which

[1] Seneca, *Controv.* So in Mexico, Sahagun (pp. 62 and 97 of the French trans.).

would be a pity, and he might die and so slip through their hands altogether. Both misfortunes, however, could be averted by inducing his soul to migrate into another healthy young body. This was effected by killing the god: his soul then had perforce to leave its old body, and by some means, not quite clear, it was supposed to enter the body of the murderer, who thus became the new god. Eventually, however, according to Mr. Frazer, men learned to distinguish between magic and religion, and then they placed their faith in the former no longer, but in prayer and sacrifice—not now deeming themselves indistinguishable from gods.

The doctrine that magic is prior to, or even in origin coeval with, religion has already failed to win our assent,[1] and we have also argued that the idea of man's coercing the gods for his own ends belongs to a different set of thoughts and feelings from those in which religion originates, and must be later in point of development, because gods must exist first before coercion can be applied to them.[2] We do not, therefore, propose to repeat our arguments on the general question of the priority of religion or magic. Nor do we propose to traverse the statement that divine power can be transmitted by the person who possesses it to someone else. What we are here concerned to show is that, apart from these questions, there is evidence to show, first, that these kings and priests were not gods, and, next, that the divine powers they possessed were not native to them and inherent in them, in virtue of their magic, but communicated to them or derived by them from the gods.

This may take us a step further towards the answer to the main question of this chapter, namely, how and why did the community come to regard it as the privilege or duty of some one particular member to exercise the priestly function of dealing the first and fatal blow at the sacrificial victim? To answer that it was because that person was the chief of the tribe, will not advance us much now that we recognise the

[1] *Supra*, p. 177-9.

[2] If it be argued that the magical means of coercion may have existed before the gods did, we must refer the reader again to our attempt to show that all such magic is derived from, or rather a distortion or parody of, the worship of the gods.

original unity of the kingly and the priestly office: the king was the person who exercised the priestly function, and the priest was the person who discharged the kingly office. In other words, we have seen how kings came to exist, and how priests came to be: our problem now is how did a man come to be king-priest? Not by inheritance, because the office was originally annual, and was terminated by the death, voluntary or imposed, of the king-priest at the end of the year. Nor by election, because the office was open to anyone who chose to take it with the penalty attached—hence it died out in some cases for want of volunteers. Mr. Frazer's solution apparently is that it was originally the greatest magician, or, what in consequence of the primitive incapacity to distinguish between men and gods comes to the same thing, a god. We have therefore to inquire whether the divine priests and kings were gods or indistinguishable from gods.

To begin with, it will be conceded that the Sibyl, who temporarily possessed supernatural knowledge, was distinguishable and distinct from Apollo who "possessed" her; the worshippers of Dionysus, who were endowed with superhuman strength, different from the god whom they worshipped. The more extensive powers of causing food to grow which were exercised in Savage Island by the king—until the office fell and remained vacant—were exercised by him as high priest, and therefore he too seems to be a priest as distinct from a god. And Father Grueber spoke of the Lama as "*veluti* Deum verum et vivum," and says "numinis *instar* adoratur." Now, in Mexico, where the priest was allowed to evade the violent death which attached to his office, on condition that he found a substitute (a war-captive), the distinction between the human victim and the god was always steadily preserved, in spite of the fact that for the year preceding the sacrifice the captive was dressed in the insignia of the god and styled by the name of the god, just as in Greece the priestesses of the Leukippides were themselves called the Leukippides.[1] Thus Father Acosta says: "They tooke a captive such as they thought good, and afore they did sacrifice him vnto their idolls, they gave him the name of the idoll, saying, he did represent the same idoll.

[1] Paus. III. xvi.

And during the time that this representation lasted, which was for a yeere in some feasts . . . they reverenced and worshipped him in the same maner as the proper idoll; . . . the feast being come and hee growne fatte, they killed him, opened him, eat him, making a solempne sacrifice of him."[1] The presumption therefore is that the South Indian king in Quilacare who at the end of twelve years of reigning had to kill himself in public, in front of an idol, and who "performed this sacrifice to the idol and undertook this martyrdom for love of the idol,"[2] like the Aztec victim, "did represent the same idoll." But though most or all of the Aztec deities had human representatives of the kind described, the distinction is always maintained between the human "image," as he was called in Mexico, and the actual idol or god to whom and before whom he was sacrificed. And the Mexican idea doubtless was all that was intended by the king of Iddah when he told the English officers of the Niger Expedition with unintentional offensiveness: "God made me after His own image; I am all the same as God; and He appointed me a king."[3] At any rate his concluding words do not lend much support to Mr. Frazer's theory that it is by being magicians that men come to be divine kings and priests. On the contrary, they constitute an explicit statement of the king of Iddah's consciousness that his sacred office was bestowed upon him and his powers delegated to him from above. Now, this belief, that the divine spirit can and does enter into men and fill them in a greater or less degree, is universal. On the truth of the belief the historian has not to pronounce: he has only to note that the universality of the consciousness, if it cannot demonstrate, neither can it impair, the truth of the belief. Nor does it follow that, because man has often mistaken the conditions under which the Holy Spirit descends upon man, or the tokens of its manifestation, therefore the belief is untrue. The belief in the universality of causation is none the less true because particular things have been and often are supposed to stand as cause and effect to each other and are not really so related.

[1] Acosta, *History of the Indies* (Grimston's translation in the Hakluyt Society's edition, ii. 323).

[2] *G. B.* i. 224.

[3] *Ibid.* 42.

The sacrificial and sacramental meal, which from the beginning has been the centre of all religion, has from the beginning also always been a moment in which the consciousness has been present to man of communion with the god of his prayers—without that consciousness man had no motive to continue the practice of the rite. In the beginning, again, the sacramental meal required, for the annual renewal of the blood-covenant, that the worshipper should partake of the body and blood of the victim: this participation was the condition and cause of the communication of spiritual and supernatural protection to the worshipper against the supernatural dangers by which primitive man was surrounded. It was by drinking the blood of sacrifice that the priestess of Apollo in Deiras obtained the power of prophecy and became "possessed" by the god.[1] Amongst the Scandinavians a blood-offering gave even the sacred altar-stone the power of prophecy;[2] and the Balonda and Barotse have a similar "medicine" with which they can make images of wood and clay prophesy.[3] But the blood or the fat of the victim or the oil obtained from it might be sprinkled or smeared on the altar-stone or on the lintel of a house to indicate the presence and protection of the god; and in the same way the oil used in the consecration of the king indicated that it was not in virtue of his own merits—still less of his magical powers—but of the entry in him of the divine spirit that "divine right" was bestowed upon him and that he became king. Again, it was of the skin of the victim that the first idols probably were made: the Kuriles make their idols by wrapping an image in the skin of an animal they have slaughtered for the purpose,[4] and the custom of dressing an idol thus was known to the Greeks. In all these cases the use of the skin was probably not merely symbolical but was supposed to ensure the god's actual presence in the idol, just as in Northern Europe enveloping the human representative of the vegetation spirit in a sheaf or green leaves probably imparted a divine character to him. In the same way, when the human "image" of an Aztec deity was dressed in the insignia of the god, it was not merely a ceremonial attire but was

[1] Paus. ii. c. 24: γευσαμένη τοῦ αἵματος ἡ γυνὴ κάτοχος ἐκ τοῦ θεοῦ γίνεται.
[2] Bastian, *Der Mensch*, ii. 269. [3] *Ibid.* 258. [4] *Ibid.* 258.

thought to invest him with some of the divine powers; and when the priest, after sacrificing him, clad himself in the skin of the human victim,[1] he undoubtedly resumed the divine powers which at the beginning of the year he had resigned to the "image" of the god, for thus clad he ran through the streets to sanctify them, as the Luperci ran for the same purpose, though not in the same guise.

When tree and plant worship prevails, the tree or plant is figured as the body of the god, and eating some part thereof continues to be regarded as the cause or condition of divine possession. In India, the leaves of a sacred tree are eaten to obtain supernatural protection against the death-pollution.[2] In ancient Greece, Apollo's priestess was inspired not only by drinking the blood of sacrifice, but equally by eating the leaves of the laurel.[3] The sacramental eating of the body of cereal deities we have already enlarged on.[4] Here we have to note that the blood of vegetation spirits consisted in the sap of the tree or juice of the plant; and if the plant worshipped happened to be one the juice of which was a poison or an intoxicant, the clan would find itself in possession of a particularly potent deity. Ordeal by poison, in which the deity recognises and spares the innocent, sprang up in the one case; the orgiastic rites of the wine-god in the other, for the intoxication, being due to the juice of the vine (the blood of the god), was evidently due to the action of the divine substance on the worshipper; and his strange behaviour was taken as a manifestation of divine "possession." Hence in course of time any man who behaved in this way, without having drunk wine, was considered to be "possessed" by a god. It need perhaps scarcely be remarked that as plant-worship has been universal, every plant capable of producing intoxication in every part of the globe has been discovered and has been employed for the purpose; and so the idea that frenzied conduct indicates "possession" is universal. A few instances must suffice.

Among the northern Indians of Chili, it was the case that "such as happen to be subject to epilepsy or St. Vitus' dance are considered as especially marked out for the service"

[1] Sahagun, i. c. viii.
[2] *Supra*, p. 220.
[3] Lucian, *Bis accus.* 1.
[4] *Supra*, ch. xvi.

of the priests.[1] A man becomes a Shamán by being "possessed"; he is generally by nature a nervous, hysterical subject, easily sent into a trance; sometimes Shamáns select such a subject, sometimes he declares himself.[2] Where the symptoms do not naturally exist, they may be artificially induced, as, *e.g.*, by the dancing Dervishes. In course of time violent symptoms may cease to be expected of the man who is to be a priest, but still the diviner, seer, or priest is expected to be marked off by his nature from other men: thus amongst the Amazulu a man is so set apart, when "he dreams many things, and his body is muddled and he becomes a house of dreams."[3] In the Tonga Islands the native term (*fahe-gehe*) for priest means a "man who has a peculiar or distinct sort of mind or soul, differing from that of the generality of mankind, which disposes some god occasionally to inspire him."[4]

Admission to the priesthood may be perfectly unorganised, or it may be a hereditary privilege, or it may be obtained by initiation at the hands either of an individual or a corporation; but the one indispensable condition of admission in all cases is that there shall be some outward and visible indication or guarantee that a god has entered him. Thus in the Tonga Islands "a god is believed to exist at that moment (*i.e.* the moment of inspiration) in the priest and to speak from his mouth" (in the same way the Peruvian word for priest means "he who speaks," *i.e.* by inspiration[5]), "but at other times a priest has no other respect paid to him than what his own proper family rank may require,"[6] and "those only in general are considered priests who are in the frequent habit of being inspired by a particular god. It most frequently happens that the eldest son of a priest, after his father's death, becomes a priest of the same god who inspired his father."[7] So, too, in the Pelew Islands, a god can take possession of any man he pleases, temporarily or permanently; if permanently, the "possessed" is recognised and installed as

[1] Kerr, *Voyages*, v. 405.
[2] Bastian, *Allerlei*, i. 124.
[3] Callaway, *Religious System of the Amazulu*, 259.
[4] Mariner, *Tonga Islands*, ii. 80.
[5] Garcilasso de la Vega, *Royal Commentaries of the Incas* (Hakluyt Society's edition, i. 277).
[6] Mariner, *loc. cit.*
[7] Mariner, ii. 127.

priest, and as such exercises great political power, however low his origin. When he dies, the god is unrepresented until some one begins to go about in a wild, ecstatic, "possessed" manner, with sufficient pertinacity eventually to convince the community, which at first laughs at him.[1] In Guiana, "the office of peaiman was formerly hereditary. If there was no son to succeed the father, the latter chose and trained some boy from the tribe—one with an epileptic tendency being preferred," and "the peaiman, when in the midst of his frantic performance, seems as though overcome by some fearful fit, or in the extreme of raving madness."[2] The Tinneh "have no regular order of Shamáns; anyone when the spirit moves him may take upon him their duties and pretensions."[3] Among the Thlinkeets, shamánism is mostly hereditary, but the son must be initiated, *i.e.* he must fast, kill an otter and keep the skin (it not being lawful to kill an otter save for this purpose), and his hair is never cut.[4] Amongst the Clallams the initiation takes the form of a pretended death and resurrection, which elsewhere is the condition of initiation into various mysteries: the candidate fasts till apparently dead, his body is plunged into a river (this they call "washing the dead"), he then runs off into a wood, and reappears equipped in the insignia of a medicine-man.[5]

Where the priesthood forms a corporation, as for instance in the Sandwich Islands, where "the priests appear to be a distinct order or body of men, living for the most part together,"[6] some form of initiation is always required. The priests of the Batta tatoo themselves with the figures of beasts and birds, and eat buffalo flesh during the ceremony.[7] A Roman Catholic missionary among the Suahili, describing the initiation of candidates for the priesthood, observes that a leading feature in the ceremony consisted in the candidate's eating a sacramental meal—a fact which, as the sacramental meal is the essence of every form of early religion, is not surprising, but which to him appeared "a satanic imitation of the Communion." He could not, however, smile contempt

[1] Bastian, *Allerlei*, i. 31.
[2] Im Thurn, *Indians of Guiana*, 334.
[3] Bancroft, *Native Races*, iii. 142.
[4] *Ibid.* 145.
[5] *Ibid.* 155.
[6] Mariner, *Tonga Islands*, ii. 127.
[7] Bastian, *Oest. Asien*, v. 45.

at the parody, the solemnity with which the proceedings were conducted was too awe-inspiring: a victim was slain, the blood sprinkled on the candidate, and the flesh eaten, before the morning dawn, by the priests and those who had previously partaken of a similar meal.[1] Finally, the selection of a candidate may be made, as in the case of the Dalai Lama, by lot: this also is a direct expression of the divine will. Divination by water, *i.e.* by consultation of the water-spirit, we have already explained.[2] Here we have only to add that our word "lot" is etymologically identical with κλάδος, twig, small stick, from which comes the Greek word for "lot," κλῆρος;[3] and that the use of pieces of wood for drawing lots is due to the presence of the tree-god therein.

This review of the modes in which admission to the priesthood is obtained lends no countenance to the theory that it is by being a magician that a man becomes a priest or king or king-priest. On the contrary, it is inspiration by the god of the community which makes a man a priest; and this conclusion is confirmed by the fact that a clear line is drawn between priest and magician. In those who believe that the idol is an elaborated fetish, it is consistent to maintain that the priest is a successful sorcerer; but we have seen reason to reject the former idea, and the latter is not borne out by the facts of the case. Those facts are sometimes obscured by the European traveller's habit of applying the terms conjurer, witch, sorcerer to any native who professes to exercise supernatural powers, without inquiring as to the use or source of those powers, or even when he knows that the conjurer is the priest of the community, as, *e.g.*, when it is said that "the *jugglers* perform the offices not only of soothsayers and physicians but also of *priests*."[4] Fortunately, however, it is quite clear on examination in most cases that there are two distinct classes of men comprised under these undiscriminating epithets, one bringing about disease and death in the community, the other counteracting the machinations of the first class, and also bringing positive blessings to

[1] Bastian, *Allerlei*, i. 142. [2] *Supra*, p. 229.

[3] Schrader, *Prehistoric Antiquities*, 279.

[4] Dobrizhoffer, *History of the Abipones*.

the community in the way of good crops, etc. This distinction is generally recognised by travellers in Africa, when they speak of the witch and the witch-finder; and amongst the Indians of Guiana we find *kenaimas* who cause mischief, and the *peaiman* who cures it: "it is almost impossible to overestimate the dreadful sense of constant and unavoidable danger in which the Indian would live, were it not for his trust in the protecting power of the *peaiman*."[1] Further examination shows that the one class derive their powers from the god who protects and is worshipped by the community, the other from spirits who are bound by no ties of fellowship or goodwill to the community. Thus the Australian "sorcerer" is universally believed to get his powers from the good spirit who lives beyond the sky.[2] In the Pelew Islands, besides the tribal and family gods, there are countless other spirits of earth, mountains, woods, and streams, all of which are mischievous, and of which the islanders are in daily fear. It is with these spirits that the sorcerers deal. The priests live generally in peace with the sorcerers, but the attitude of the community is shown by the fact that sorcerers are liable to be put to death for exercising their powers.[3] The fact that it is in the interests of the community that the powers derived from the tribal god are exercised, is shown by the frequent combination of the office of chief and priest in one person: amongst the Murrings (Australia) the "sorcerer" is respected highly, is chief at once and "sorcerer."[4] Amongst the Damaras "the chiefs of tribes have some kind of sacerdotal authority—more so than a military one. They bless the oxen."[5] As for the Haidahs, the chief is the principal "sorcerer," and "indeed possesses but little authority save from his connection with the preter-human powers."[6] The chief of the Salish "is *ex officio* a kind of priest."[7] Amongst the Eskimo the Angakuts (priests) are "a kind of civil magistrates," amongst the Zulus "'the heaven is the chief's,' he can call up clouds and storms . . . in New Zealand every Rangatira has a supernatural power . . . among the Zulus 'the Itongo (spirit) dwells with the great man; he who

[1] Im Thurn, *Indians of Guiana*, 333.
[2] Bastian, *Allerlei*, i. 248.
[3] *Ibid.* 46.
[4] *Ibid.* 248.
[5] Galton, *South Africa*, 189.
[6] Bancroft, *Native Races*, iii. 150.
[7] *Ibid.* 154.

dreams is the chief of the village' . . . the Kaneka chiefs are medicine men."[1]

Thus we are brought round once more to the priest-king and to our question, how did a man come to be invested with the office? Negatively, we have urged reasons to reject Mr. Frazer's theory that it was by becoming so great a magician that his fellow-tribesmen thought he was a god. Positively, we have argued that in all cases the human "image" of the god is distinguished from the god, and that the divine spirit must enter the man before he can be the human representative of the god, just as the altar-stone must be dashed with blood, anointed with oil, clad in the skin of the sacred animal, etc., before the god can be considered to be present in it. Further, the modes of consecration—whether of priest or king—are various, but they can all be traced back to the primitive idea of the sacrificial meal, namely, that it is by participation in the blood of the god that the spirit of the god enters into the worshipper. It is therefore to some feature of the ritual of the primitive sacrificial meal that we must look for the solution of our problem. Now, the mere drinking of the blood would not suffice to mark off one of the worshippers, for all the clansmen drank of the blood, and all so far became possessed of the divine spirit. But on the man who was to be the king-priest that spirit descended in a larger measure; and it was some act performed by him, and him alone, during the rite, that marked him off as thenceforth more holy than his fellow-men.

Now we have seen that in historic times the distinguishing function of the priest, and the key to his priestly power, is that he deals the first and fatal blow at the victim. Unless the victim is slain there can be no sacrifice, no drawing near to the god, and the community must be left defenceless against its supernatural foes. But the victim is the animal whose life the clan are bound to respect as the life of a clansman, to kill it is murder (as in the Bouphonia at Athens), nay! it is killing the god. The clansman, therefore, whose religious conviction of the clan's need of communion with the god was deepest, would eventually and after long waiting be the one to strike, and take upon himself the issue,

[1] Lang, *Custom and Myth*, 237.

for the sake of his fellow-men. "The dreadful sacrifice is performed not with savage joy but with awful sorrow."[1] So great was the difficulty of finding anyone to strike the first blow, that the practice of stoning the victim to death was frequently adopted, as thereby the responsibility was divided amongst all the clansmen—a practice which survived in the custom in Northern Europe of pelting the representative of the vegetation spirit, in the similar λιθοβολία of the Greeks (*e.g.* in the Pentheus myth) and a New World custom already referred to.[2] That shedding even human blood is a crime, the responsibility of which must be shared by all the community, appears from the fact that, when a criminal has to be executed, it is a negro custom to tear him to pieces. Amongst the Hottentots the chief gives the first blow, and then the rest fall on the criminal and beat him to death;[3] and amongst the Tuppin Imbas, when a captive is to be eaten, the man who deals him the first blow incurs the guilt, and, as blood must have blood, the king draws blood from his arm, and for the rest of the day he must remain in his hammock.[4] But the fact that the priest in all religions slays the victim suffices to show that the earlier custom of stoning must have given place universally to that which gave rise to the priesthood.

That blood-guiltiness would attach to the man who struck the first blow is evident. But the king-priest is distinguished from his fellows by his superior holiness, and it is not clear that the act of dealing the blow would *ipso facto* give him that larger measure of the divine afflatus which marked the priest off from his fellow-worshippers. In the Philippine Islands it does indeed seem to have been the belief that the slaying of the victim was, if not the cause, at any rate the occasion of the god's entering into the slayer, as appears from

[1] Robertson Smith, *s.v.* "Sacrifice" in the *Encyclopædia Britannica*.

[2] *Supra*, p. 215–6. For other instances, see *G. B.* i. 264; *B. K.* 413; *Myth. Forsch.* 209; *Journal of Hellenic Studies*, xiv. ii. 252–3; the λιθοβολία in Troezen (Paus. ii. xxxii. 2), at the Eleusinia, the Lupercalia, and Nonæ Caprotinæ; and cf. the stoning of the φάρμακος (Harp. *s.v.*).

[3] So too the scapegoat in Asia Minor, the Mamurius Vetus in Rome, and the slave at the Chæronean festival, were beaten—not as a piece of sympathetic magic.

[4] Bastian, *Der Mensch*, iii. 3.

the account of an old traveller (who when he says "le Diable" means the god of the savages): "Il y a de ces prestres qui ont vn commerce particulier auec le Diable . . . il passe quelquesfois dans le corps de leur Sacrificateurs & dans ce peu de temps que dure le Sacrifice, il leur fait dire & executer des choses qui remplissent de crainte les assistans . . . le Sacrifice . . . se fait en frappant la Victime, auec certaines ceremonies, que le Sacrificateur fait en cadance, marquée par vn tambour ou par vne cloche, c'est dans ce temps-là que le Diable les possede, qu'il leur fait faire mille contorsiōs & grimace et à la fin, ils disent ce qu'ils croyent auoir veu ou entendu."[1] But against this we have to set the universal belief that it is by drinking the god's blood that the god enters the worshipper. It is therefore to this part of the rite we must look. Now, the slayer of the victim would naturally be the first to drink of the blood; and it is entirely in accord with primitive ideas to suppose that the first blood was considered to contain more of the sacred life than the rest—we need only recall to mind the universal reluctance to partake of the first-fruits of the field, as containing the divine life in its most potent form. So by the European custom the man who ate the first apple from the tree in which the vegetation spirit dwelt became the human representative of the spirit for the year.[2] Thus it was the man who greatly daring first killed the victim and drank the first draught of the sacred life who thereby became the human "image" or representative or vicegerent of the god, priest and king for a year, by which time the blood-covenant required to be renewed, and again a victim had to be slain, a slayer found.

There remains the question why the priest-king forfeited his life at the end of the year. Now the forfeit attached to the office: the moment the office was undertaken, the forfeit was incurred. But it was by a man's own voluntary act that the office was assumed; and that act had two elements, the office two sides. There was the blood-guiltiness attaching to the killing of the god, and there was the sanctity brought by the drinking of the sacred blood. It must therefore have

[1] Thevenot, *Divers Voyages*, iv., "Relation des Isles Philippines."
[2] *B. K.* 409.

been in one of these two characters that the king-priest was slain. Mr. Frazer's view is that he was slain as being the god. This, however, is unsatisfactory from our point of view, for two reasons. The first is that the evidence, as we have argued, seems to indicate that the king-priest was as a matter of fact regarded, both by himself and others, as the god's vicegerent, rather than as himself the god. The other is that if he was regarded as the god and slain as such, then there would from that time on have been no further need or possibility of *animal* sacrifice: the priest who slew the slayer would in turn be slain, and so human sacrifice and cannibalism would have been the universal type of the sacrificial meal, whereas, first, cannibalism as a ritual is the exception, not the rule, and next, every religious institution, and every survival in religion which has a bearing on the question, points to the sacramental eating first of totem-animals and then of totem-plants.

We are therefore forced back on the other hypothesis, that it was as the shedder of divine blood that the king-priest's blood was shed, that it was the blood-guiltiness attaching to his original act which made his life forfeit from the first. For a year the sanctity of the divine blood in his veins ensured his safety; at the end of that time the penalty was exacted. If it be asked why at the end of a year, the only answer is that in early times the community seem to have felt the need of an annual renewal of the blood-covenant with their god; the yearly sacrifice is the oldest; at the end of a year they felt that the sacred blood that was in them had departed from them; and if from them, then from the king-priest, whom accordingly it was now safe to slay, and their duty to slay. That the exaction of the penalty would eventually come to be deferred, is probable enough, and is confirmed by the historic instances in which it was only enforced at the end of a twelve years' reign. Then it would be deferred indefinitely to the appearance of the first physical blemish indicative of old age, or until famine or disaster warned the community that the spilling of divine blood had not yet been avenged. But, in the absence of such monitions, the penalty might even be evaded altogether, with the consent of the community, by the substitution of the priest-king's firstborn son,[1] for whom again a substitute might be found in a criminal or a captive, until even the taking of such lives was felt to be a stumblingblock. By this time the office may have become hereditary; and thus would arise the necessity on occasion of devolving some of the functions, *e.g.* war (for war is, as we have seen, a sacred function in primitive times) or legislation upon a younger brother or other relative less hampered by the divinity and the restrictions which hedged in the priest-king. Or the sanctity of the office might extend to the whole family of the priest-king, in which case his descendants would constitute a hereditary order of priests, the eldest representative being high priest. Then, too, a war-king would have to be sought outside the limits of the priestly family. To his office also sanctity would attach; he too would require consecration and receive a τέμενος. But whereas political progress tended to give the king a larger kingdom and greater powers, all concentrated in his one person, it tended to diminish the importance of the priest, for it brought polytheism in its train, and so multiplied the number of the priests, proportionately dividing their power.

The growing tendency, which the above view postulates, to defer and then to remit the forfeit of the king-priest's life, can hardly be dissociated from the change which gradually took place in men's view of animal sacrifice. At first, sacrifice was the killing of the god manifested in the animal. Then the rite came to be regarded as a sacrifice to the god, now conceived to be present in the altar-stone on which the blood was dashed. Finally, the sacrifice was a meal in which the god took part, and the animal's life was no longer considered sacred—the animal was but the chattel of the tribe that bred it. Now these changes must have materially assisted the tendency to remit the king-priest's penalty: as long as the animal was the god, the blood-guiltiness of the slayer called for his death; when the animal was rather a sacrifice to than of the god, the death of the priest would be required

[1] In view of the existence of a survival of annually killing the king-priest in Babylon, it may be well to note that an Accadian text expressly states that sin may be expiated by the vicarious sacrifice of the eldest son (Sayce's Appendix, p. 418, to his edition of *Hdt.* i. and ii.).

rather by tradition than by any living sentiment of necessity. When the animal was a mere chattel, the execution even of a captive would be unmeaning; of a firstborn son, shocking. Nor can we fail in this connection to note that, whereas drinking the blood was of the essence of the rite originally, in course of time it came to be generally dropped or prohibited—possibly on grounds of refinement, but possibly also on religious grounds, on the ground that no man should be allowed to communicate so closely with the divine life. Finally, we may note that the original idea of taboo is identical neither with that of holiness nor that of uncleanness, but is the root-idea out of which both these were subsequently differentiated and developed: it is simply that which must not be touched or approached. Now the king-priest was strictly taboo in the original sense: both as the shedder of blood and as the partaker in divine life, he was not to be approached, during his year.

We have endeavoured to show that the institution of the priesthood was the natural, necessary, and inevitable outcome of the primeval rite of the sacrificial meal; and that from the beginning the priest had no other means of drawing near to his god than those open to all his fellow-worshippers; he was distinguished from them only by his greater readiness to sacrifice himself for their religious needs. We have found nothing to support the notion that religion is the invention of priests, and we have been obliged to dissent both from the view that primitive man was uncertain whether he was a god or not, and from the view that the priest was a sorcerer who had got on in the world.

We have next to show how the mystic view of sacrifice, as communion, struggled to reassert itself against the commercial view of sacrifice, as giving in order to get something, which had overlaid it; and how this affected man's view of the future state. But first we must understand what his view of the other world was, to begin with.

CHAPTER XXI

THE NEXT LIFE

As to man's future state many very different views have been held and are held by different peoples. To some it appears but a continuation of the present life, for others it involves a retribution for what has been done in this world; and each of these theories has many varieties. The retribution may consist in a simple reversal of this life's lot, so that those who have fared ill here will be well off in the next world, and *vice versâ*; or the better lot in the next world may be reserved either for those who in this were persons of quality, or for those who distinguished themselves by their valour, or by their virtue, or by their piety. Or the next life may be for all men alike a continuance of this, under more pleasant conditions, or under more gloomy conditions, but in either case the rank and occupation of the deceased will be what they were in this life, even the scars and mutilations of the body surviving with the other marks of personal identity. Or, again, life may be continued, but in such a way that personal identity is concealed, as for instance by the transmigration of the soul into an animal body, or is forgotten, as by the souls that drink the waters of Lethe before being reborn, or merged in the divine essence. Or the soul may not survive death at all—only the fruit of its moral or immoral acts may be transmitted.

An equally great variety of opinion prevails as to the situation and topography of the next world. It may be on the earth's surface, or under it or above it. If on it, then it is a far-off land, a garden behind far distant hills, a land beyond a distant river, an island across the sea, a far-off western world. Or it may be above the earth, in the sun, the moon, the stars, or above the solid firmament of the sky. If below the earth, it may be one vast and gloomy realm, or it may be mapped out into many various divisions. If the retribution theory is held, then the heaven may be above the earth, or it may be underground. If it is underground, then the places of bliss and punishment are topographically distinguished; if the heaven is above the world, then it may or may not be locally distinguished from the abode of the gods. The underground hell may or may not have places of torture; if it has, they too may be more or less numerous. The number of heavens may extend to the third, the seventh, or even go as high as thirty.

Into the mass of bewildering details, of which these are but a few, some order has been introduced by the labour of various writers, especially Professor E. B. Tylor, in his *Primitive Culture.* He has shown, for instance, that the retribution theory appears generally at a later stage of culture than the continuance theory; and that the conceptions of the next world as a far-off land, a western world, an underground abode, or as located in the sun, moon, stars, or sky, are of common occurrence amongst different peoples, and are conceptions such as might be formed independently by different peoples, and need not have been borrowed by one from another. These conclusions may be regarded as well established, and we shall make them the basis for an attempt to trace the growth of the belief in a future state.

Whether the funeral rites practised by man in the lowest stage of culture known to us, and also in the earliest times from which we have interments, were prompted by love or fear, by the desire to detain the spirit of the one loved and lost, or by the wish to drive off the ghost, may be a disputed question. But that these rites show primitive man to have believed that the ghost lingered for some time in the neighbourhood of the survivors, is universally admitted. Nor can there be any doubt as to the cause of the belief: the memory of the departed is still fresh in the minds of the survivors, and the occasions are frequent which suggest to their minds the picture of the deceased engaged in his familiar guise and occupations. As time goes on, the memory of him is revived less often and at longer and longer intervals, and it is in occasional dreams that he appears most vividly to mind. Such appearances are regarded by the savage as visits of the dead man; and the fact has to be accounted for that such visits, at first frequent, gradually become separated by longer and longer intervals. The obvious explanation is, in part at any rate, that the ghost is now further off, and it takes him longer to make the journey. Hence the belief in a far-off land on the surface of the earth is, I suggest, the first hypothesis as to the dwelling-place of the dead. In Borneo, it is situated, for the Idaan race, on the summit of Kina Balu; in West Java, on the mountain Gungung Danka; the dwelling-place of the dead, according to the Chilians, was Gulcheman beyond the mountains; "hidden among the mountains of Mexico lay the joyous garden of Tlalocan."[1]

Whether burial is the oldest mode of disposing of corpses, or is later than cremation—as seems indicated by the fact that in the oldest interments known to archæologists the body is always partially burnt—burial is and long has been universally known and practised, and no one doubts that it is the burial of bodies underground which has given rise to the belief that the abode of the dead is also underground. The belief is widely spread: "in North America, the Tacullis held that the soul goes after death into the bowels of the earth . . . among rude African tribes, it is enough to cite the Zulus, who at death will descend to live among the Abapansi, 'the people underground.'"[2] Amongst the Karens, a rude Asiatic tribe, the land of the dead is held to be below the earth. The Aryan peoples undoubtedly held the same view: the Roman Orcus and the Greek Hades are underground. The Babylonians placed "the land whence none return," as it was termed by them, in the bowels of the earth; and the Hebrew Sheol is the name both for the grave and for the subterranean abode of the departed. As to the nature of this realm and the kind of life spent by its inhabitants, there is a unanimity which is a striking illustration of the fact that under similar conditions similar minds will reach similar conclusions. In it, according to the Hurons, "day and night the souls groan and lament";[3] the region of Mictlan, the subterranean land of Hades in Mexico, "was an abode looked forward to with resignation,

[1] Tylor, *Primitive Culture*, ii. 60 and 61. [2] *Ibid.* 66. [3] *Ibid.* 79.

but scarcely with cheerfulness."[1] The Yoruba proverb runs: "A corner in this world is better than a corner in the world of spirits." The ghost of Achilles rejected consolation: "Nay! speak not comfortably to me of death, O great Odysseus. Rather would I live on ground as the hireling of another, with a landless man who had no great livelihood, than bear sway among all the dead."[2] "The Hades of the Babylonian legends closely resembles the Hades of the Homeric poems. It is the gloomy realm beneath the earth, where the spirits of the dead flit about in darkness, with dust and mud for their food and drink, and from whence they escape at times to feed on the blood of the living. Here the shades of the great heroes of old sit each on his throne, crowned and terrible, rising up only to greet the coming among them of one like unto themselves . . . good and bad, heroes and plebeians, are alike condemned to this dreary lot; a state of future punishments and rewards is as yet undreamed of; moral responsibility ends with death. Hades is a land of forgetfulness and of darkness, where the good and evil deeds of this life are remembered no more; and its occupants are mere shadows of the men who once existed, and whose consciousness is like the consciousness of the spectral figures in a fleeting dream."[3] For the Sheol of the Old Testament we may quote Smith's *Dictionary of the Bible*: it is "the vast hollow subterranean resting-place which is the common receptacle of the dead. It is deep (Job xi. 8) and dark (Job xi. 21, 22); in the centre of the earth (Num. xvi. 30; Deut. xxxii. 22), having within it depths on depths (Prov. ix. 18), and fastened with gates (Isa. xxxviii. 10) and bars (Job xvii. 16). In this cavernous realm are the souls of dead men, the Rephaim and ill-spirits (Ps. lxxxvi. 13, lxxxix. 48; Prov. xxiii. 14; Ezek. xxxi. 17, xxxii. 21). It is all-devouring (Prov. i. 12, xxx. 16), insatiable (Isa. v. 14), and remorseless (Cant. viii. 6). . . . Job xi. 8, Ps. cxxxix. 8, and Amos ix. 2 merely illustrate the Jewish notions of the locality of Sheol in the bowels of the earth. . . . Generally speaking, the Hebrews regarded the grave as the final end of all sentient and intelligent existence, 'the land where *all things are*

[1] *Loc. cit.*
[2] *Od.* xi. 486 (Butcher and Lang's trans.).
[3] Sayce, *Hibbert Lecture*, 364.

forgotten' (Ps. vi. 5, lxxxviii. 10–22; Isa. xxxviii. 9–20; Eccles. ix. 10; Ecclus. xvii. 27, 28)."

In this view of the future life there is no room for the retribution theory: all men alike go to Hades or Sheol, the all-devouring. Indeed, the continuance theory is generally clearly involved in it. In the Babylonian underworld, those who were in their lifetime heroes, retain their thrones. In the Greek Hades, Achilles is still a king, and the phantom Orion hunts phantom beasts; and "there the soul of the dead Karen, with the souls of his axe and cleaver, builds his house and cuts his rice; the shade of the Algonquin hunter hunts souls of beaver and elk, walking on the souls of his snow-shoes over the soul of the snow; the fur-wrapped Kamchadal drives his dog-sledge; the Zulu milks his cows and drives his cattle to kraal; South American tribes live on, whole or mutilated, healthy or sick, as they left this world, leading their old lives."[1] So, too, in Virgil, the ghost of Deiphobus shows its ghastly wounds to Æneas. In Sheol the kings of the nations have their thrones,[2] and the mighty their weapons of war.[3]

The idea that, in the underground ghost-land, the soul continues to follow the same pursuits as in life, gave rise to the custom of burying with him the necessary weapons, implements, pottery, clothes, etc.; and, as habits are less easily changed than opinions, this custom continued to be practised even when the continuance theory which originated it had given way to the retribution theory. It was, however, impossible that the custom should continue without affecting belief; and the way in which it affected the retribution theory was twofold: it modified men's conception first of the nature of the blissful state, and second of the means by which it is to be attained. It made, that is to say, future bliss to consist simply in pursuing earthly occupations under more delightful conditions than exist in this life, or existed in the dreary shadow-land to which the continuance theory first gave birth; and, in the next place, the persistence of ancestor-worship made it appear that the soul's attainment to future bliss depended in part at any rate on something that the survivors could do for it. Thus,

[1] Tylor, 75-6. [2] Isa. xiv. 9. [3] Ezek. xxxii. 27.

in the Scandinavian Walhalla, the warriors ride forth to the fight as they did on earth, only at the end of the day and the fray those who have been killed go back to the banquet and enjoy it, just as much as their victors do. In Egypt, where the heaven was also one of material, though more peaceful, delights, access to it depended quite as much upon the due performance of the elaborate funeral rites by the survivors, as upon the virtue and piety of the deceased himself. It is clear, then, that ancestor-worship was a considerable hindrance to the acquisition or reception of a purer and more spiritual conception of the future life. It is therefore important for the historian of religion to note that ancestor-worship was forbidden to the Jews: the worship of God did not permit of ancestor-worship. This prohibition, however, was not in itself either the cause of or a stimulus to a higher view of man's future state: it only cleared the ground of weeds which might have choked its growth. As a matter of fact, though the soil was thus prepared, it was not until the time of the Captivity that the first seeds were sown in it.

Here too, perhaps, it will be well to note that in these early speculations as to ghost-land, whether it be placed in an underground region or in some far-off land upon the earth's surface, there is nothing religious: they have nothing to do with the service of the gods, they are totally unconnected with the sacrificial meal by which communion with the god of the tribe is sought: they are purely philosophical speculations. Religion did not originate from ancestor-worship, nor ancestor-worship from religion. It is important also to remember that complete consistency is not to be found or expected in these or any other speculations indulged in by man when in a low stage of culture. Impressed by the broad fact that the dead do not return to life, he may describe the underground abode as one from which there is no return. But this cannot, with him, weigh against the fact that ghosts are occasionally seen; and that fact in its turn in no wise impairs his belief that there is a distant world which is the proper abode of departed souls. Indeed, at the present day, in Christian countries, the superstitious believe that graveyards are haunted, though they would not deny that the souls of the dead are really in heaven or in hell.[1] So too the Zulu, who believes that the dead join the Abapansi, the underground people, none the less recognises the soul of an ancestor in the snake which visits his kraal. And, generally speaking, we may say that the belief of the totemist, that the dead man rejoins his totem and is transformed into the shape of the animal totem, may live for a long time by the side of the belief in a ghost-land.

Indeed, just as the key to the origin of species is the persistence, transmission, and development of qualities originally peculiar to an individual, and constituting it a mere "sport" or "variety," so the key to the evolution of the many forms of religion is in many cases to be found in the persistence, side by side, of beliefs that were originally but "sports" or "varieties" of the same stock. Thus the belief in the appearance of ghosts is but a form of the continuance theory, or rather is the continuance theory in its original form: the ghost, as it appears in dreams or in visions, continues to have the same outward presentment as the man himself had in life. The belief that ghosts continue their favourite occupations in a ghost-land, whether underground or on a remote part of the surface of the earth, is equally a form of the continuance theory. But when the original form of a belief persists by the side of a later form, a certain inconsistency is felt between them; and if it be such as to be felt very strongly, the result will be that what were originally but varieties of the same idea will become two different species of belief. An example may make this clearer. The original form of the belief in a ghost-land simply postulated that that land was far away: the belief that it was far down in the bowels of the earth, in depth below depth, was but a slight variation on the original belief—the essential was that ghost-land was far away, in which dimension of space did not matter. But though the conception of ghost-land as an underground world established itself, we may say, universally, and gradually drove out the older

[1] This simple consideration seems to me to be fatal to Rohde's extravagant idea that the Hades of Homer is a sort of "fault" in the strata of Greek belief, and is different from the tenets held by the Greeks both before and after the Homeric period. To say that because there is, according to Homer, no return from Hades, therefore there were, in Homer's opinion, no ghosts to haunt the living, betrays want of sympathy with primitive modes of thought.

belief in a far-off land, still the older belief, or rather a reminiscence of it, still lingered here and there; and, being different from the now dominant faith in an underworld, it called for explanation. That explanation was fairly obvious and easily forthcoming. Here were old men declaring that in their time, or in times they had heard of, the spirits of the dead used to go to a far-off land, not to the underground world as they do now. Obviously, therefore, things have changed: in the good old times men did not go to the dreary, gloomy nether land; they went to a garden beyond the hills, lighted and cheered by the rays of the sun, very different from the sunless abodes of Hades. But that is over now; to this generation the gates of that bright land are closed; and if they were open to the men of yore, that is because men were heroes in the brave days of old. This, I submit, is the origin of Hesiod's myth [1] of the fourth and last of those ages of which the Golden Age was the first. The heroes who fell at the siege of Troy or of Thebes were placed by Zeus, after death, in a land at the uttermost bounds of the earth,[2] where they continue in happiness.[3] In Babylon also there were "blissful fields beyond Datilla,"[4] to which in bygone times a few persons, *e.g.* Xisuthros and his wife, not heroes but pious persons, had been admitted, though the gates were closed to all else. Sometimes the explanations, invented to account for the difference in the treatment of this generation and of bygone generations, do not invoke the superior valour or piety of the latter to account for the change—indeed, such ideas belong to the retribution theory, and probably were comparatively late additions to the original form of explanation, which contented itself with the simple fact that the first man or men dwell there, and all other souls go to the homes of underground. Thus in Iranian mythology, Yima, the first man, and his generation, live and have lived from the beginning of history in the Far-off Land, Eran Vej, an earthly paradise.[5] Even here, however, the original

[1] Hesiod, *Works and Days*, 156–73.

[2] 168, Ζεὺς Κρονίδης κατένασσε πατὴρ ἐς πείρατα γαίης.

[3] 170, καὶ τοὶ μὲν ναίουσιν ἀκηδέα θυμὸν ἔχοντες.

[4] Sayce, *Herodotus*, i.–iii. App. 392.

[5] For this, see Mr. Alfred Nutt in *The Voyage of Bran*, 309–11.

explanation has been adapted and altered to supply material for cosmological speculation. Eran Vej is said to have been created by Ahura Mazda, whereas the Far-off Land, as we have seen, had nothing to do with religion, and was not supposed to have been created by, or to be in any way connected with, the gods. In this respect we get a truer view of the Far-off Land in certain tales which go back to the time when its delights—so bright by comparison with the underground world—were still matter of tradition, when its existence (if only it could be discovered) was still believed in, but its origin, as ghost-land, was forgotten. These are those tales of a land of Cockaigne, with which even antiquity was acquainted,[1] which a Solon could describe in verse,[2] and which are the earliest types of many a subsequent Utopia.

We may then take it as a general law that the human mind is capable of holding, simultaneously, beliefs which are inconsistent up to a certain (undefinable) point; but if, by the force of circumstances, the inconsistency becomes too great, an explanation will be invented; and that explanation will exaggerate and stereotype the difference, so that what were but two varieties of the same original opinion will become two quite different beliefs, capable of being logically held by the same person. Let us apply this canon to the belief in the underground ghost-land.

Inasmuch as the abode of the dead is underground, the entrance to it must be through some hole in the ground, cave, etc. Thus the souls of the Baperi in South Africa go down through the cavern of Marimatlé; in Mexico there were two such caverns, Chalchatongo and Mictlan, which were the entrances to the nether world; "North German peasants still remember, on the banks of the swampy Drömling, the place of access to the land of departed souls"; [3] in ancient Rome the mundus or opening through which the spirits of the dead came up thrice a year for their offerings was in the Comitium; in Ireland it was believed in the fifteenth century A.D. that Sir Owain descended into the nether world with the monk Gilbert through St. Patrick's purgatory, a cavern in the

[1] See Mr. Nutt on the "Happy Other World," *op. cit.*
[2] Frag. 38 (Bergk [4]).
[3] Tylor, ii. 45.

island of Lough Derg, County Donegal;[1] in Timor earthquakes are dreaded, because the souls may escape through the chasms thus opened;[2] the entrance to the Accadian underworld "was believed to be in the marshes beyond the mouth of the Euphrates."[3] Many peoples can tell of living men who, before Sir Owain, have descended by those openings, and have returned to describe the underworld.

But these openings, being of necessity local, are known only to the neighbouring inhabitants. There is, however, one entrance to the nether world which is familiar to many different peoples; and it is known to many, because the facts which prove it to be a gate of the underworld are patent to all. Those facts are that the sun disappears below the surface of the earth in the west, and emerges again from it in the east; therefore in the night he must have travelled from west to east below the earth, *i.e.* through the realm of the dead. Among the natives of Encounter Bay the sun is feminine: "every night she descends among the dead, who stand in double lines to greet her and let her pass."[4] Amongst the Magyars it is day in Kalunga, the land of the dead, when it is night on earth, because the sun passes through it by night, as it is also believed to do by the people of Mangaia,[5] and was believed to do by the ancient Egyptians to the end. "The New Zealander who says 'the sun has returned to Hades,' simply means that it has set";[6] and it was an Aztec saying that the sun goes at evening to lighten the dead.[7] The hole in the ground, therefore, through which the sun descends below the earth is the entrance through which, according to many peoples, the souls of the dead have to gain admission to the underworld. In Australia they travel for that purpose to Nynamnat, the sunset; in Torres Strait, to *kibuka*, the western world;[8] in Polynesia, too, they go west; to the west, likewise, the spirits of the Iroquois, of the Fijians, and of the Brazilians; in Virginia the cave Popogusso lies west, west the Gulchinam of the Chilians.[9] Odysseus found the entrance to

[1] Tylor, ii. 55–7.
[2] Bastian, *Die Verbleibs-Orte der abgeschieden Seele*, 52.
[3] Sayce, *Herodotus*, i.–iii. App. 392.
[4] Lang, *Myth, Ritual, and Religion*, i. 129.
[5] Bastian, *op. cit.* 52.
[6] Tylor, 66.
[7] *Ibid.* 72.
[8] Bastian, 39.
[9] *Ibid.* 54.

Hades in the west. In Babylonia "the mountain of the west, where the sun set, was a pre-eminently funereal place," and "the entrance to Hades was near this mountain of the west."[1]

But though the belief in an entrance in the far-off west is common and widely spread, it did not occur to every people, or did not always find favour. For instance, it did not become known to the Aryan peoples until after they had settled in the countries occupied by them in historic times; and even then it did not dawn upon all of them, for it was unknown to the Romans, who until late times were quite satisfied with the opening in the Comitium, and regularly continued to roll away the stone, the *lapis manalis*, which blocked it, in order to allow the manes to come up for their offerings, on August 24th, October 5th, and November 8th. In other countries, as in Greece and Babylonia, the western gate remained only one of several entrances to the underworld, with nothing to distinguish it particularly from the rest. And neither Greeks nor Romans (by their own unaided efforts) nor the Babylonians got beyond the old belief in a gloomy, sunless Hades or Orcus, the common destination of all men, good or bad.

Elsewhere, however, the glowing west of the sunset became the place where the souls of the departed assembled to wait for the moment when the sun's arrival would open the portals of the nether world and let them in. According as the sun set beyond a plain, the sea, or mountains, the bright gathering-place was an island across the sea, a place behind the hills or beyond some distant fields. In any case, what was the constant gathering-place of the continually dying came necessarily to be a place in which spirits of the dead were constantly to be found, and so a permanent abode of the dead. But the old belief in the underground world of ghosts was much too firmly rooted in the minds of men to be ousted by this new view; and accordingly an accommodation was found—both the nether world and the western world were abodes of the dead. Then the existence of two such different abodes, one gloomy and sunless, the other suffused with light and warmth, called for explanation; and this demand was, I conjecture, if not the cause, at any-

[1] Lenormant, *Chaldean Magic* (E. T.), 168.

rate the occasion of the retribution theory. The question became pressing, which souls went to the cheerful western home, which to the dreary world below? Probably it was taken for granted at first that the chiefs, who took the best things here, had a right to the more attractive region after death; then, that the best warriors would claim an entrance. The two views were combined by the Ahts: "In Vancouver's Island, the Ahts fancied Quawteaht's calm, sunny, plenteous land in the sky as the resting-place of high chiefs, who live in one great house . . . while the slain in battle have another to themselves. But otherwise all Indians of low degree go deep down under the earth to the land of Chay-her, with its poor houses and no salmon and small deer, and blankets so small and thin, that when the dead are buried the friends often bury blankets with them."[1] "The rude Tupinambas of Brazil think the souls of such as had lived virtuously, that is to say, who have well avenged themselves and eaten many of their enemies, will go behind the great mountains, and dance in beautiful gardens with the souls of their fathers; but the souls of the effeminate and worthless, who have not striven to defend their country, will go to Aygnan."[2] In the Tonga Islands it is only aristocratic souls that go to Bolotu, the western and fortunate isle, "full of all finest fruits and loveliest flowers, that fill the air with fragrance, and come anew the moment they are plucked; birds of beauteous plumage are there, and hogs in plenty, all immortal save when killed" to be eaten, and even then "new living ones appear immediately to fill their places."[3]

There was, then, in the west, at the entrance of the sun's nether domains, a happy other-world to which the souls of the valiant and the virtuous went; and there was the old, cheerless, unhappy other-world to which went the cowards and the bad. To call the one Heaven and the other Hell, would be misleading, for these terms bear a reference to religion, and the latter further implies a place of torment. Now, as we have said, early speculations on the other-world were philosophical rather than religious: it was only in course of time that the happy other-world came to be adopted into antique religions. The Jews were cut off

[1] Tylor, 85. [2] *Ibid.* 86–7. [3] *Ibid.* 62.

by their primitive prohibition of ancestor-worship from the philosophical speculations which resulted in a happy other-world of bodily delights; and it was only by degrees that the cheerless nether ghost-land came to be a place of active torment. Egyptian religion is instructive on both points. The righteous soul went to the happy fields of Aalu, where the height of the corn, we are told, "is seven cubits, and that of the ears is two (in some readings four) cubits,"[1] but the reward of the righteous is not spiritual, it is earthly; and, as depicted on the monuments of the old Empire, it has not risen above the level of peoples in the continuance-stage of development—except that their dead do not enjoy their occupations much, and the Egyptian did enjoy his: "the tomb of Ti at Sakkarah, for instance, presents us with pictures of the after-world, in which the dead man lives over again his life in this; he farms, hunts, superintends his workmen and slaves, and feasts, just as he had done on earth."[2] A more naïve confession of the fact that the happy other-world of the Egyptian was only an improvement on the original ghost-land, and not a place of spiritual bliss superior to the delights of this world, could not be found than that which is contained in the rubric to the first chapter of the *Book of the Dead*, describing the lot of the righteous soul: "There shall be given to him bread and beer, and flesh upon the tables of Rā; he will work in the fields of Aaru, and there shall be given to him the wheat and barley which are there, for he shall flourish *as though he were upon earth*"[3] —no higher or more spiritual ideal entered or could enter into the composition of the Egyptian abode of bliss, because its origin was essentially non-religious. But if the happy world had not been developed into a heaven, neither on the monuments of the old Empire had the cheerless underground world become a place of torment: "we should look in vain in them for those representations of the torments and trials which await the dead below, of the headless souls and horrible coils of the monstrous serpent Apepi, that startle us on the pictured walls of the royal tombs at Thebes."[4]

In India, too, the underground world originally, like

[1] Renouf, *Hibbert Lecture*, 181.
[2] Sayce, *Hdt.* i.-iii. 346.
[3] Renouf, *Hibbert Lecture*, 192-3.
[4] Sayce, 347.

Hades and Sheol, was the land to which went the souls of all, good and bad; but then the happy other-world drew off a portion of its population, namely, the souls of those who in their lives had been worshippers of Soma, and left only the bad to go to the world below. At first, apparently, the contrast between the cheerlessness of the old ghost-land and the delights of the happy world, where soma could be drunk for ever, seems to have constituted sufficient punishment for the bad. But in course of time, in India, as in Egypt, torments were added, and "the ultimate outcome of this evolution," in the sixth and fifth centuries B.C., "is a series of hell visions, which for puerile beastliness and horror outvie anything perhaps that even this hideous phase of theological fancy has pictured."[1]

The idea that the place where the sun went down was the entrance to the nether world, led, as we have seen, to the belief that there was a happy other-world in the west. But it also led men to find a happy other-world elsewhere, *e.g.* in the sun or in the sky. How it might naturally do so will be clear, if we reflect that it was the sun's descent below the horizon which was supposed to open the western entrance to ghost-land: thus the funeral dirges of the Dayaks describe how the spirits of the departed have to run westward at full speed, through brake and briar, over rough ground and cutting coral, to keep up with the sun, and slip through the clashing gates by attaching themselves to him.[2] Now, though holding on to the sun in order to win through the momentarily open entrance was at first simply a means by which the ghost might reach its underground abode, yet it was indispensable and all-important, and so might easily come to be considered the only thing necessary for the ghost who was to be at peace, and to be released from the cruel race after the sun. The ghost, it should perhaps be said, who could not keep up with the sun and arrive at the entrance simultaneously with him, has to recommence the race next day: hence rest and release for the departed spirit were only to be found in catching up and joining the sun—after that came peace. Thus the sun was the resting-place of the departed. But the old belief in the underground

[1] Nutt, *op. cit.* 323.

[2] Bastian, *op. cit.* 25.

spirit-land still continued to exist; and the fact that there were two other-worlds was explained by the retribution theory. The sun was the abode of departed chiefs and warriors among the Apalaches of Florida and the Natchez of the Mississippi; the sun or the bright sky generally was the happy other-world assigned in India to the soma devotee.

The idea that the souls of the righteous went to the sun was one of the many different and inconsistent beliefs for which accommodation was found, somehow or other, in the state-religion of ancient Egypt. But as provision was already made in the blissful fields of Aalu for the departed, an abode in the sun was superfluous; and it never succeeded in displacing the former, because it held out no particular attractions, whereas in Aalu the departed was just as well off as if he were alive. Hence, union with the sun continued to be simply an alternative—not the only alternative, as we shall see—to Aalu. Attempts, however, were made to bring the sun theory into organic relation with the other elements of Egyptian religion. In the Middle and New Empires, the Osiris myth gave rise to those ideas of after-death torments which find such ample expression on the monuments of the period and in the *Book of the Dead*;[1] and it was by union with the sun, Osiris, by becoming an Osiris, that the deceased was enabled to pass by and triumph over all the horrible monsters and dangers which beset his path through the underworld. Now this provided the Egyptian with a motive for desiring to become an Osiris, but it did not diminish his desire for the earthly and agricultural delights of Aalu, and it did not entirely clear up the relations of these two forms of beatification. Philosophy therefore came to the rescue: all things and beings are made of certain elements, or rather they are but different compounds of one element, different modes of one essence, for there is but one thing real in all the universe, and that is the divine essence, God. Eventually, all things and beings must be resolved into their constituent parts, must revert to the original essence of which they are but transient modes. The divine essence was the god Osiris; to become an Osiris

[1] Sayce, *loc. cit.*

was to be merged in the divine essence. This view afforded a reconciliation of the belief in Aaru and the Osiris doctrine: the soul first went to Aaru, and then became an Osiris; the soul entered "the blissful fields of Aalu, there to be purified from all the stains of its early life, and, after becoming perfect in wisdom and knowledge, to be absorbed into the divine essence."[1]

Finally, we may note that the happy western world under certain circumstances shared the fate which overtook the far-off land. As we have seen in the chapter on Mythology, a primitive hypothesis, if detached from the belief or custom, etc., which it was invented to explain, becomes a myth. It may be so detached from its basis, either because the belief, etc., on which it was based has changed or perished, or because it has sufficient romantic interest in itself to be worth telling and hearing, quite apart from its "topical allusions." In this way the far-off land, when it was depopulated, so to speak, by the introduction of the underground world as the abode for the dead, became first a place to which none now go or can go, and then an earthly paradise, and finally a land of Cockaigne, Utopia. Now, though the belief in the happy western world never perished wherever it became known, still it might become detached from its basis, inasmuch as rumours of it as a place of high delight might spread to peoples who had as yet not advanced to the conception of a happy other-world. To such a people, having no conception of the retribution theory, and having only one ghost-land—and that a dreary one—for the reception of all ghosts, righteous or unrighteous, alike, the rumour might penetrate of a happy land in the bright west, the inhabitants of which dwelt in fabulous delights and never died. The wonder and romance of the tale would be heightened by the added fact that all the inhabitants were righteous. And the natural objection of the sceptic, that if there were such a happy land everybody would go there, would be met by the statement, made on the same authority as the original rumour, that the place is over the western sea, an island, a fortunate island, to which only those favoured by the gods are carried, and the

[1] Sayce, 345.

road to which no living man ever yet discovered. A tale so romantic would be readily caught up by story-tellers, ever as eager as their hearers for some new thing, and by them be worked into their tales. In some such way as this, I suggest, the rumour of the blissful fields of Aalu spread from Egypt to Greece. The resemblance of the name of the Egyptian fields to that of the "Elysian" plains of Homer may be accidental, but it is perhaps more than fortuitous that it was in Egypt that Menelaus heard for the first and only time of the Elysian plains to which he was ultimately to be carried by the deathless gods, according to Proteus.[1] Be this as it may, there are other imaginary and romantic happy lands in Greek literature, and all are what we should expect on the hypothesis sketched above: there is the isle of Syria, at the turning-place of the sun, where death never enters and sickness is unknown; there is the land of the Hyperboreans (west as well as north), to which man never found his way by sea or land;[2] there are the islands of the Hesperides, the islands of the Blest, and the dwellings, in the east and in the west, of the righteous Ethiopians, who once more bring us to the neighbourhood of Egypt. From the Greeks the rumour of this wonderland spread to the Celts; and Irish literature is full of tales telling, as *The Voyage of Bran* tells,[3] of a happy island from which the man who discovers it cannot return—an island in which, according to the Adventures of Connla, there was no death and no sin; and, according to the tale of Cuchulinn's Sick Bed, there are all manner of delights. When, however, the western world has thus become a mere wonderland, it inevitably becomes confused with the far-off land, which also in course of time becomes a merely romantic conception; and fairy islands and enchanted mountains become the scene of exactly the same kind of romantic adventures.

[1] Homer, *Od.* xv. 403.
[2] Pindar, *Pyth.* x. 30.
[3] K. Meyer, *The Voyage of Bran*, 142; cf. *Classical Review*, x. ii. 121-5 (March 1896).

CHAPTER XXII

THE TRANSMIGRATION OF SOULS

THUS far we have been engaged in tracing the evolution of the primitive philosophical theory of a ghost-land, and have seen it successively assume the shapes of a far-off land, an underground world, a western island or other abode of the blessed, a happy other-world in the sun or sky, until at last ghosts and ghost-land alike are dissolved by an advanced philosophy into the ocean of divine essence. It is time, therefore, to recall to mind that, even when the belief in ghost-land first arose, there was another view as to man's future state, inconsistent indeed but coexistent nevertheless with the ghost-land theory: it was that after death man rejoined his totem and assumed the shape of, the plant or animal that he worshipped. We have therefore now to trace the career of this view. In most, the vast majority, of cases it had no career. The people which held the view were either progressive or they were not. If they were not, then *ex hypothesi* no development in their views took place: the two views as to the future state remained, as amongst the Zulus, inconsistent and coexistent. On the other hand, if the people were progressive, then everything in totemism that was capable of being taken up into the higher forms of religion which supervened was so transformed, and the rest—including this particular feature of totemism—lingered on as a mere survival, in the shape of tales of men being changed into animals, and, in out-of-the-way and backward places, in the belief that such changes still take place. It may therefore seem at first sight as though in no case could there be any development of this particular feature of totemism, namely, a belief in the posthumous transformation of man into a plant or animal (a different belief from that in metempsychosis or the transmigration of souls—as different as an acorn is from an oak). As a matter of fact, there is only one combination of circumstances under which the development in question has ever taken place; that is, the contact of a more advanced religion, holding the doctrine of retribution in a developed form, with a less advanced religion, adhering to the belief that after death man rejoins his totem. That contact, moreover, must take place under peculiar circumstances: the two religions must exist side by side in the same community, political or social; and the higher religion must be one bent on finding room within itself for the beliefs of all sections of the social or political community in which it is the dominant force. Now, in the ancient world there were, from the nature of the case, only two countries in which this peculiar combination could occur. They were Egypt and India. Let us begin with Egypt.

Ancient religions knew no dogma and consequently no heresies. The only one which was an exclusive religion and whose God was a "jealous" God, was the Hebrew religion. To this exclusiveness and jealousy is due the fact that the Jews remained monotheists; while the toleration which other peoples showed to foreign worships, though it led to polytheism, facilitated political growth by means of *synoikismos*.[1] In any large community, and particularly in a state formed, like Egypt, by the amalgamation of many small states, there will be found various strata of belief, from the lowest superstition to the highest form of religion capable of existing in the given time and place. The beliefs which are held by the wealthiest and most cultured classes will find expression in the literature and on the monuments of the nation; the beliefs of the masses will go unrecorded. Thus, the monuments of ancient Egypt express the hopes, the fears, the beliefs of the ruling classes. Those beliefs might or might not be shared by the common people; they certainly would not and could not be forced on them either by a Church—which did not exist—or by the State. And if the fellaheen had beliefs and rites of their own, they would find no place on the monuments, but they would not therefore

[1] *Supra*, Ch. XVIII. "Syncretism and Polytheism."

cease to exist. Thus, totemism continued to flourish, until Greek and Roman times, in the rites and customs of the common people, though the religion of the ruling classes had more than half emerged from the totemistic stage even in the time of the earliest monuments.

Now, just as the animal names and half-animal forms of the gods depicted on the monuments betray their totemistic origin,[1] so the representations of the future state betray the existence of a large number of persons who had not yet cast aside the belief that after death they would rejoin the totem, in favour of the newer belief that they would go to the plains of Aalu. The older totemistic belief must have been shared, at this time, by some proportion of the more cultured classes, for we find from the monuments that, as many departed souls preferred going to Aalu to union with Osiris, so many preferred—and were allowed, in the opinion of their class—to migrate into some animal. But what marks this belief as different from and an advance upon the simple totemistic faith, is, first, that the deceased may migrate into any animal he pleased—this was evidently because there were many different totems, and each man would be sure to choose his own ; and, next, that it was only the good who were allowed to do this. Thus the retribution theory held by one portion of the community has influenced and modified the totemism of another section : it is only on condition of conforming to the moral standard of the time—a high one—that the totemist was allowed to conform to the practice of his fathers and join them in animal shape. On the other hand, it is clear that as yet we have by no means reached metempsychosis. Let us go on.

In the long course of advancing civilisation, the cultured classes of ancient Egypt all dropped the belief that a man ought to rejoin his totem after death. Aalu and Osiris triumphed, and the belief that souls migrated posthumously into plants and animals survived amongst the educated no longer as a religious conviction, but simply as an echo of what once had been an ordinary thing, but now was simply an incident of romance. Of such a romance we have an example in the tale of Batta, contained in a papyrus of the

[1] *Supra*, pp. 124 ff.

nineteenth or perhaps the eighteenth century: as often as Batta is killed in one shape he reappears in another—a flower, a bull, a tree, a man. With the decay of totemism amongst the cultured, first the moral obligation to migrate into the totem animal had relaxed and the permission to assume any form whatever had been acted on; and then the belief had lost its religious character and passed into the nature of romance.

Amongst the uneducated, however, totemism still continued to exist; and—whether it was that the ranks of condemned souls were supposed to be recruited most largely from amongst the uneducated, or that the assumption of animal shape was at last thought an unworthy reward of virtue—the doctrine came to be held that the wicked soul "was sentenced to the various torments of hell, or to wander like a vampire between heaven and earth, or else doomed to transmigrate into the bodies of animals, until permitted to regain its original body and undergo a fresh trial."[1] Thus in Egypt the artificial combination of the retribution theory with totemism at last produced a real theory of metempsychosis; and, for the purpose of avoiding confusion between the Egyptian and the Indian forms of the belief in the transmigration of souls, it is important to note three things: the first is that it is only the wicked who are doomed by the Egyptian theory to transmigration; the next is that Egyptian transmigration is a circular process—the soul of a man migrates into animals, birds, fish, but finally returns to its human form; the third is that there is no escape from the cycle when once it has started, it is only after reaching human form again that the soul has another trial and another chance of becoming an Osiris. Bearing these facts in mind, let us turn to India.

A happy other-world in the sun or sky was known in India as early as the time of the Vedas,[2] and by the sixth century B.C. an elaborate hell had been worked out by the dominant religion. In India, totemism was to be found; indeed, well-marked traces of it survive to the present day.[3] In India, as in Egypt, the dominant religion and the lower

[1] Sayce, *Hdl.* i.–iii. 345. [2] Nutt, *op. cit.* 320.

[3] Crooke, *Folk-Lore of Northern India*, ch. viii.

forms acted and reacted on one another, with the result that the retribution theory of the former had to be reconciled with the belief of the totemist in a posthumous transformation into the shape of the plant or animal totem. "Thus in the Chāndogya Upanishad we read: 'Those whose conduct has been good will quickly attain some good birth, birth as a Brāhmaṇa or as a Kshatriya or a Vaiṣya; . . . 'and in the Kaustutaki Brāhmana Upanishad: '. . . he is born either as a worm, or a grasshopper, or a fish, or a bird, or a lion, or a boar, or a serpent, or a tiger, or a man, or some other creature, according to his deeds and his knowledge.'"[1] Here we have a genuine theory of transmigration of souls: the simple totemist belief has been enlarged so as to meet the views of those who, not being totemists, were not bound to be changed into any one particular animal, and man has been introduced into the list of metamorphoses. But though, in India as in Egypt, the totemist faith has been generalised and dissociated from the totem animal, and though in both countries the migrating soul may return to human form, here all resemblance ceases. In Egypt, metempsychosis was first made a means of rewarding the righteous exclusively, and then exclusively an instrument for punishing the wicked. But in India it was applied to both good and bad alike: the retribution theory was infused into metempsychosis—all men were born again, but the good got a good birth, the bad a bad one, according to their deeds and deserts. In the next place, there was a cycle of transformations in Egypt, with the possibility of escape on the completion of the cycle. But in India there was no cycle and no escape: the good got a good birth, and then bad behaviour might cause him to be reborn lower in the scale—but whether the soul behaved well or ill, it always had to be born again.

Now, to the pessimist the prospect of living for ever, in one form or another, is an evil. It was a pessimist, therefore, Gotama, who revolted against the Brahminist doctrine of the transmigration of souls. Gotama, the "enlightened," the Buddha, struck at the root of the theory he attacked by denying the existence of the soul altogether—he also denied the existence of a God—therefore there could be no trans-

[1] Rhys Davids, *Hibbert Lecture*, 81.

migration of souls. What did take place, according to the Buddha, was transmission (not transmigration) of *karma*, character (not soul). The good and evil that men do live after them—not in the changes, good or bad, which their actions bring about during their own lifetime, or in the effects they produce on their contemporaries or in the memory of those who come after them, but—in a fresh individuality, a fresh ego, which never would have come into being at all, had it not been for the desire of existence entertained by the previous member of the chain, and which is good or bad according as he was good or bad. Plato's doctrine—based upon the Egyptian view—is similar and simpler: he allows the existence of a soul, which is enamoured of the delights of the body, and so even when it has escaped from one body returns to another, because it craves after existence and the bodily delights that go therewith. According to Buddhism, there is no soul: it is the craving after existence and corporeal pleasures which results in renewed existence; and therefore it is the extinction (nirvana) of this craving (not the extinction of the soul, for there is no soul) which is the Buddhist's object.[1] This extinction of the desires men can accomplish by being righteous. Thus the motive of the Buddhist is annihilation, the giving up of the craving for a future life of any kind, even in heaven. In any given chain of existences, the karma of that chain is transmitted; and if the karma take the form of an ever-weakening desire for existence and ever-increasing righteousness, there will come a time when the desire will cease, and "then no new link will be formed in the chain of existence; there will be no more birth; for birth, decay, and death, grief, lamentation, and despair, will have come, so far as regards that chain of lives, for ever to an end."[2]

Thus the goal of Buddhism was the extinction of existence, just as in Egypt the transmigration of the soul was terminated by the dissolution of the individual in the vague of the One, the All, the divine essence, Osiris. But this external resemblance must not blind us to the real difference between the two theories. In Egypt it was only the bad, not all men, who were doomed to transmigration. In Egypt

[1] Rhys Davids, *Hibbert Lecture*, 88–109. [2] *Ibid.* 99.

there was a cycle of changes to be suffered; in Buddhism karma is transmitted in a direct line, which may be continued to infinity. In Egypt escape is possible only on the completion of the cycle, and then it is, first, conditional on the favourable judgment of the god Osiris, and is, next, effected by union with Osiris; whereas in Buddhism, which denies the existence both of the soul and of God, escape neither depends on divine judgment nor consists in the absorption of the soul into the divine essence.

In connection with the theory of metempsychosis, and as a preliminary to our investigation of the subject of the Mysteries, it remains for us to give a short account of Pythagoreanism.

The unanimous voice of antiquity proclaimed that Pythagoras (in the sixth century B.C.) taught the doctrine of the transmigration of souls, and—with how much truth may be questioned—that he derived the doctrine from Egypt, and that he himself remembered his experiences in his previous states, which, if true, would have made it unnecessary, we might suppose, for him to learn the fact of transmigration from anyone else, Egyptian or other. Empedocles, a follower of Pythagoras, taught—doubtless in accord with his master's teaching—that the cause of transmigration was sin, that the term of transmigration was thirty thousand years, that he himself had served that term, and that finally his soul, like others in the same case, would become a god—which indeed it had been from the beginning.[1] Pindar, who was a contemporary of Empedocles, and picked up some Pythagoreanism on his visits to Sicily, also lets us see that it was only the wicked who were doomed to transmigration, the good went straight to a happy otherworld; and that, after transmigration and return to human form, the soul had to be judged by Persephone, and might then enter the abodes of bliss. In quite recent years there have been discovered in graves near Thurii and Petelia, that is in the home of Pythagoreanism, three golden tablets bearing inscriptions.[2] These inscriptions contain directions to the deceased Pythagorean with whom they were buried, to

[1] Jevons, *History of Greek Literature*,[2] 105.
[2] Dieterich, *Nekyia*, 85.

enable him to find his way about in the underworld, thus: "On the left you will find a stream and near it a white poplar: go not near that stream; you will find another, cool water flowing from the mere of Memory; in front of it are guards. Say, 'I am the child of earth and starry sky; I am of heavenly origin, as ye yourselves know full well. I am parched and perishing with thirst; give me at once cool water flowing from the mere of Memory,' and they will give you of the divine stream to drink."[1] The tablets were buried with the deceased, because they possessed a magical power to direct and protect him. The name of Persephone occurs on two of them, thus confirming what Pindar says; the cause of transmigration is said to be sin, its nature a cycle (*κύκλος*), and the soul that escapes from the cycle becomes a god—thus confirming Empedocles. To this we must add that when the soul is said to become a god or God,[2] and still more when it is said to be a child of earth and starry sky,[3] the expression was one which could be taken in two senses, a religious sense and a philosophical sense. It could be taken by the Pythagorean to mean either that his individual personality would be dissolved in the One, the All, the sky; or that his personal identity would continue in a blissful life in a happy other-world. The latter is the view which commends itself to Pindar (in his second Olympian), the former makes itself felt in Euripides,[4] and is expressed in the funeral inscription on the grave of the Athenians who fell at Potidæa in B.C. 431.[5] But the average man did not distinguish the two views very clearly: whether the place was the sky, or the ether, or Olympus, or Elysium, he did not curiously inquire—he used all the terms convertibly.[6]

This brief sketch will suffice to show that Pythagoreanism is very different, not only from Buddhism, which is not a belief in the transmigration of souls, but also from the Indian doctrine, which is. The idea that Pythagoreanism was

[1] The inscription is in Kaibel, *I. G. S. I.* 641, and Dieterich, *loc. cit.*

[2] *θεὸς ἐγένου ἐξ ἀνθρώπου*, Kaibel, *I. G. S. I.* 642.

[3] *γῆς παῖς εἰμι καὶ οὐρανοῦ ἀστερόεντος*, Kaibel, 641.

[4] *Supp.* 531.

[5] *C. I. A.* i. 442.

[6] This is apparent from the various funeral inscriptions given in Dieterich, 100–7.

borrowed from India is impossible: it differs from the Indian doctrine in all four of its cardinal points, namely, the cause of transmigration (sin), the nature (a cycle), the fact of escape, and the mode of escape (trial before a deity). Next, if Pythagoreanism were as independent, in its origin, of the Egyptian doctrine as it is of the Indian, it ought to differ equally in its character. But the four points in which it differs from the Indian theory are four points (not the only points) in which it is identical with the Egyptian. This, combined with the tradition of antiquity that Pythagoras derived his doctrine from Egypt, would suffice to prove its Egyptian origin. But there are further resemblances. The Egyptian philosophy which taught that the soul returns to the divine essence from which it sprang, is reproduced in the Pythagorean teaching that the soul emanated from and finally returns to the ether, the starry sky. And just as the Egyptian philosophers adopted religious terminology to convey their speculations, and taught that to become God or a god, Osiris or an Osiris, was the same thing as being merged in the divine essence, so Pythagoreanism taught that for the soul to become *θέος* or *δαίμων* was the same thing as for it to dissolve into ether or into the starry sky, of which it was the offspring. But even granting that Pythagoras could and did invent out of his own head a theory exactly resembling in its cardinal points a doctrine which in Egypt was the result of slow centuries of evolution, still we must think it strange that the minor details and non-essential accessories should be the same. Let us illustrate this point. In the Pythagorean inscription already quoted, the departed soul is represented as anxiously eager to drink of cool, flowing water. No such anxiety is ever expressed in literature, as far as I am aware, by any Greek ghost not holding Pythagorean doctrines.[1] But in the inscriptions on tombs in ancient Egypt[2] the deceased commonly prays for this lustral water. This may, however, be a fortuitous agreement, for libations of water are offered in ancestor-worship by the Hindus. But the Hindus did not

[1] In Homer, ghosts are offered water (*Od.* x. 520), but they prefer blood (*Od.* xi. 49).

[2] For examples, see Renouf, *Hibbert Lecture*, 127–41.

conceive some supernatural being as giving the water to the deceased, whereas, as we have seen, the Pythagoreans did. And, oddly enough, so did the Egyptians. And again, though such an idea as the Pythagorean notion of supernatural "guards" giving the ghost water to drink is unknown elsewhere in Greece, it is an ordinary feature of the pictures on Egyptian tombs: "the most usual representation of this is the picture in which the goddess Nut pours out the water of life to the deceased, from the interior of a sycamore-tree. In a picture published by M. Chabas, the deceased kneels before Osiris, and receives from him the water of life from a vessel under which is written *ānch ba*, 'that the soul may live.'"[1] Again, in the Egyptian *Book of the Dead* the deceased is directed to protect himself, in his long and perilous journey through the underworld with its monsters of all kinds, not only by the use of amulets and talismans, but by proclaiming "I am Osiris."[2] So the Pythagorean ghost is to proclaim that he is divine. Again, it is not likely that the idea of issuing a guide to the underworld occurred straight off to Pythagoras, whereas the Egyptian *Book of the Dead* took centuries to form. If it be said that a small gold tablet is not to be compared with the *Book of the Dead*, which has hundreds of chapters, the answer is that the verses on the Pythagorean tablets are but extracts from a greater work;[3] and that in Egypt the most important of the talismans which were buried (like the Pythagorean tablets) with the deceased was one which had an extract from the *Book of the Dead* (namely, chapter xxx.) engraved upon it: "the rubric directs it to be placed upon the heart of the deceased person."[4]

The foreign origin of Pythagoreanism is further attested by the fact that its attachments to native Greek beliefs are so few, so slight, and so forced. Thus, in order to find a footing for the doctrine that the soul of man emanated from the divine essence, that man was a compound of earth and ether, and so returned, body to earth and soul to ether,[5]

[1] Renouf, 141.

[2] *Ibid.* 192.

[3] Dieterich, *Nekyia*, 85.

[4] Renouf, 192.

[5] *C. I. A.* i. 442 (the Potidæan inscription): *αἰθὴρ μὲμ ψυχὰς ὑπεδέξατο, σώματα δὲ χθών.*

the Pythagorean was forced in despair to clutch at a text in Hesiod which taught not that men but that gods were first created from the union of Earth and Sky.[1] Again, in Egypt it was right that the supreme god, Osiris, should judge the departed; and he could properly be present in the nether world, because the Egyptians believed that he, the sun, travelled every night through the underworld. In Greece, however, Zeus, the supreme god, had nothing to do with the nether world; the god Hades was already appropriated to the old dreary ghost-land; so the Pythagorean had to be content with Persephone as the deity who regulated admission to the abodes of bliss. Again, the idea that souls had anywhere to go to, except to the old cheerless, sunless ghost-land, was absolutely unknown to the Greeks. So, in order to form a conception of an abode of bliss for the righteous dead, Pindar and other poets drew upon the descriptions of Elysium and the fortunate isles,[2] contained in epic poetry; and thus eventually the plains of Elysium came to be, what in Greece they had never been before, namely, the abode of the dead.

In fine, there is nothing in Pythagoreanism which is not to be found in the religion of ancient Egypt; and there is much which is unintelligible, if taken by itself, but is at once seen to have a meaning when restored to the Egyptian context from which it was taken. The doctrine which in Egypt took centuries to develop, cannot have been invented in Magna Græcia by one man, though one man might well bring back from Egypt a mixture of the leading doctrines and some unimportant accessories and introduce them in the form of a "mystery" into his own country. Again, the theory of the transmigration of souls is not a simple but a complex idea. It is not an idea which could spring up wherever totemism existed, else it would be as widespread as are the animal and half-animal gods which totemism has everywhere left behind it. Metempsychosis is a complex idea, it is a combination of the retribution theory with a

[1] The phrase in the Pythagorean inscription, *γῆς παῖς εἰμὶ καὶ οὐρανοῦ ἀστερόεντος*, is from Hesiod, *Theog.* 105:

ἀθανάτων ἱερὸν γένος αἰὲν ἐόντων,
οἳ Γῆς τ' ἐξεγένοντο καὶ Οὐρανοῦ ἀστερόεντος.

[2] *Supra*, pp. 312, 313.

living belief in the transformation of men into animals; and this combination is one which could not have taken place in Magna Græcia, because neither of the elements of which the theory is composed was in existence there. Totemism had been transmuted into a higher form of belief even in Mycenæan times; the retribution theory was as yet unknown. In the time of Homer and Hesiod, the souls of all men, good and bad alike, went to one and the same place, the underground ghost-land. Even after their time there is no hint of any difference in the future state of the good and of the bad, until the time of the Pythagorean and other mysteries; and then such references are always made in connection with the mysteries, and as part of the doctrine taught at the mysteries. Why this should be, and why the retribution theory should have begun to stir the minds both of the Greeks and of the Jews about the same time, *i.e.* from the time of the Captivity of the Jews onwards, are the questions to which we must address ourselves in the next chapter. Let us therefore sum up and conclude this.

There are certain elements of the belief in a future world that recur so constantly and under such different circumstances in the various religions which we have examined in this chapter, that we must regard them as latent in the human mind, and ready to manifest themselves whenever the conditions requisite to evoke them are brought into play. They are, that the soul continues to exist after death, that its fate then depends upon its deeds in this life, that it must undergo a transformation of some kind and rejoin the object of its worship. In two of the religions that we have mentioned, those of the Greeks and the Jews, these elements had not been synthesised before the sixth century, and we have yet to see whether and how far they were combined subsequently. In other religions, *e.g.* those of India and of Egypt, the synthesis had been effected to some extent; but that the synthesis was not one which could permanently recommend itself as satisfactory to the religious consciousness, is demonstrated by the fact of its leading in the one country to the Buddhist denial of the existence both of the soul and of God, and in the other to a pantheism which equally denied personal immortality. If we seek for reasons why these attempts failed to produce a faith capable of satisfying the religious consciousness, the first fact that strikes us is that they were premature. While the continuance theory was still so strong in its hold upon the minds of men that they could conceive no future life except as an exact reproduction of the conditions and activities of this life, the retribution theory was fused with it, so that the rewards and punishments were pictured in the grossest and most materialistic fashion. On the other hand, before the belief that man must undergo a posthumous transformation had been dissociated from the idea of transformation into animal or plant form, it was infused with the retribution theory, so that the soul could not escape from a material body on this view, any more than from its material occupations and delights on the other. A further reason why these attempts failed to satisfy the religious consciousness, is that they did not proceed from it: they were in their origin the speculations of primitive philosophy. They were indeed adopted into religion, but, in the case both of India and Egypt, they were fatal to it. The after-death communion with God which they offered was either purely formal and external, as must be the case when there are many gods for the soul to meet; or absolute absorption and extinction. That communion during life was at once a condition and an anticipation of what was to be hereafter, was a conception which could not arise where sacrifice had degraded into the giving of something in order to get more. In other words, no religious synthesis of the elements of belief in a future state could be effected as long as, on the one hand, that belief was out of relation to the central act of worship, the sacrificial meal; or as long, on the other hand, as the sacramental character of that act was obscured. We have therefore to consider in the next chapter how far these two conditions were fulfilled by the religious movements amongst the Greeks and Jews from the sixth century B.C. onwards.

CHAPTER XXIII

THE MYSTERIES

The sixth century B.C. shows a hitherto unheard-of and inconceivable innovation in religion. Hitherto the only circle of worshippers conceivable had been one the members of which were united by blood; the only religious community to which a man could belong was that into which he had been born. In the nomad stage of society the tribal god was worshipped by the members of the tribe and by them alone: the same hostility to all other tribes which made "strangers" synonymous with "enemies" made it impossible for any but the tribe to approach the tribal god. The tribe, and therefore the worshippers of the god, consisted only of those born into the tribe. Even when circumstances compelled the tribe to abandon its nomad habits, to settle finally in one local habitation, and to form a permanent fusion, social, political, and religious, with its neighbours, the new and enlarged community thus formed consisted exclusively of the members of the amalgamating tribes and their blood-descendants: citizenship—membership of the new political community—was an inherited privilege; and the only gods whose cults were open to a man were those of the state to which he belonged by birth. On the one hand, the local cults were jealously closed to all but citizens of the place. On the other, the citizen was not free to choose his religion: the only gods to whom he had access were those of the community into which he was born.

But in the sixth century B.C. we find in the ancient world new rites and cults arising which differ from all previous ones, first in that they were open to all men, and next in that membership was voluntary and spontaneous. They were not always or necessarily new religions, for in them the old gods of the nation might still be worshipped, though with new rites. They can scarcely be called sects even, for their members were not required to give up the ordinary hereditary worship of the state to which they belonged. But the idea was now for the first time expressed in action that a man could belong to a religious community which was distinct from the state. The possibility of choice between the worship to which he was born and another was now before him. Freedom of choice entails personal responsibility for the choice made, and makes it necessary that the man should decide between competing claims in the tribunal of his own heart and conscience. Such reflection and judgment in matters religious eventually deprive a traditional and hereditary religion of much of the advantage which, in its competition with newer forms, it derives from the fact that it is hereditary and traditional; and the habit of reflection, even if it finds none of the newer forms acceptable, cannot fail to reveal some of the weak points in the older. Thus the innovations of the sixth century in course of time contributed their share to the disintegration of the antique religions and to the preparation of the soil for the reception of Christianity; and no one who reflects how great is the strength of custom and tradition, and how slow is the growth of the critical faculty, will consider the time too long for the effect. Rather the marvel is, first that a new form of religious communion should ever have arisen, and next that it should have been allowed by the dominant religions to exist for so long. These, then, are the two points that we must begin with.

The new movement had its origin in the Semitic area of the ancient civilised world, and in the national calamities which befell the Northern Semites in the seventh and sixth centuries B.C.[1] The strength of the national religions of antiquity lay largely in the fact that they were national. But in that fact there also lurked the possibility of danger. As long as the nation prospered, the relations between the national gods and their worshippers were taken to be satisfactory; but when political disaster overtook the state,

[1] Robertson Smith, *Religion of the Semites*, 357 ff.

the inference was that the national gods were unwilling or unable to protect their worshippers. The worshipper might therefore seek to avert the divine wrath or he might seek to flee it; but either course was bound to introduce modifications into the national religion and to mark a new departure, for in either case the worshipper sought for closer communion, whether with the national or other and more powerful gods. The consequences of the closer attention thus concentrated on the facts of the religious consciousness and the inner revelation thereby gained were twofold. First, in the place of the gloomy anticipations of a dismal abode after death in Sheol, a confidence and hopefulness with regard to the future life began to manifest themselves, which find their highest expression, "with extraordinary splendour,"[1] in the Psalms. The second consequence was one which affected in various ways and degrees the conception and performance of the central rite of religion, the act of sacrifice.

Amongst the Hebrews, the effect produced upon the more spiritual minds took the form of the conviction that animal sacrifice was valueless and meaningless. The gift theory of sacrifice, the idea that the worshipper presented offerings in return for which he was entitled to receive blessings, already stood condemned. Now it became clear that communion with God was not to be effected by the blood of bulls and rams, or by any physical, mechanical means; and the necessity of the sacrifice of a broken and contrite spirit was inculcated. This, however, did not satisfy the yearnings of those whose faith required for its support the performance of some outward and visible act of worship. They felt, as men always have felt, that sacrifice, to be real, to be perfect and complete, must be in some sense external to themselves. They were warned by their national calamities, the tokens of divine wrath, that the sacrifices which they had customarily offered were not an adequate means of communion. But the Northern Semites were incapable of rising to the height of the more spiritual minds amongst the Hebrews, and of casting aside animal sacrifice; and they followed a *via media*. The customary sacrifices they abandoned, and they sought for other forms of sacrifice,

[1] Mr. Gladstone in the *North American Review* for March 1896.

unusual, extraordinary, and therefore presumably more potent. Such sacrifices, owing to the uneven rate at which religion progresses in different districts, were forthcoming. Even where religion generally had advanced far beyond the stage of animal-worship, survivals of such worship were to be found here and there in out-of-the-way and backward places. Generally, all that was left of the religious respect paid to the original animal god was a vague feeling that the creature was not to be touched by man—was "unclean." But at some obscure sanctuaries and in some unprogressive rituals the animal still continued to be offered in sacrifice; and though the fact that the animal had once been a god might have disappeared from memory, the sacrifice of an animal almost universally held to be unclean would be deemed mysterious by all and by some even offensive. It was therefore to such "abominations" as the sacrifice of dogs, swine, mice, and horses that the Northern Semites resorted in order to avert the divine wrath. In some cases this revival of ancient modes of religion was carried still further; and a direct reversion to the primitive conception of sacrifice produced a new form of religious community. Where the bond of blood-relationship is the only tie which holds a community together, such expressions as that the tribesmen are of one blood or one flesh are understood literally, in the most concrete, physical sense; and it is to the joint meals of the clansmen as much as to their common origin that this physical unity of the kin is ascribed. To the Arab the life of the stranger who partakes of his meal is, for a time at anyrate, sacred, because for the time he becomes of one blood with him. The same view as to the effect of commensality is at the bottom of the Roman *confarreatio,* and is implied in the Greek worship of Zeus Xenios. In the case of the sacrificial meal the bond created between the participants was one of peculiar force and sanctity, because all became partakers in the divine life of the sacred animal. This conception had indeed, as a rule, been obliterated in course of time by the growth of the gift theory of sacrifice and the degradation of the animal from its original sanctity to the level of a mere chattel. But the spread of the gift theory had not been so uniform or so complete as entirely and everywhere to destroy the original sacramental character of the sacrificial meal, and accordingly it becomes a prominent and indeed in its consequences the most important feature of the religious revivalism of the sixth century B.C. Hitherto the only religious organisation to which a man could belong had been the kin or community into which he was born; and now that the political disasters which threatened the very existence of the political community testified to the permanent estrangement of the gods of the community from their worshippers, men's minds were roused to look about for some other religious community in which to find shelter from the divine wrath. No such organisation was in existence, or rather those which existed were not available, for strange gods had each his own circle of worshippers closed to all outside it and open only to those born into it. But though no open circle was in existence, the unifying efficacy of the sacrificial meal made it possible to form one; and in it we have the principle of voluntary religious associations, which were (unlike that of the community) open to all, and membership in which did not depend upon birth, but was constituted by partaking in the divine life and blood of the sacred animal.

Thus in the Semitic area the characteristic features of the new movement of the sixth century B.C. were, first, a tendency to discard the gift theory of sacrifice and seek a closer communion with God; next, a more hopeful view of the life after death. The gift theory might be discarded in favour either of the sacrifice of a contrite heart, or of the mystic sacrifice of a divine animal, or of religious association constituted by the participation in the divine life of the sacred animal; but in any case the effort to draw nearer to God was accompanied and marked by the greater confidence with which man looked forward to the next world. In a word, a religious basis was henceforth provided for that belief in immortality which in its original shape had rather belonged to primitive philosophy. In that respect the new movement rose superior to the eschatology of the Egyptian and Indian religions, for the eschatology of both was not generated by the religious spirit, but was due to the incorporation of early philosophical speculations into those religions—an incorporation which eventually in Egypt led to the denial of individual immortality, and in India to the Buddha's denial of the existence of the soul at all. But though hopefulness as to the future world was now associated with and conditional on spiritual communion in this life, the attempt to bring the religious belief in the future life into relation with the central rite of religion, sacrifice, was either not made or was made prematurely. Where animal sacrifice was discarded, no external sacrificial rite was left with which the belief could be connected. Where mystic sacrifices were revived, the belief was indeed associated with the rite, but the association was premature, because the rite itself had no permanent vitality: the reversion to mystic sacrifices merely escaped from the error of the gift theory to fall into a recrudescence of barbarous ritual acts, such as those of dismembering the divine animal and drinking its blood.

The wave of religious revivalism which had its centre of diffusion in the Semitic area, was speedily propagated over the Greek cities of Asia Minor, over Hellas itself, and finally over Italy. The widespread conviction amongst the Northern Semites that divine wrath could be averted by extraordinary, piacular sacrifices, was one easily communicated and readily picked up and conveyed to Greece by individuals. And it was probably in the form of purificatory ceremonies and sacrifices that the new movement first travelled to Greece. Thus it was from Crete that the Athenians, for instance, in B.C. 596 summoned Epimenides[1] to purify their city, when they wished to cleanse themselves from the pollution caused by the murder of Cylon's followers at the altars of the gods. He ordered sheep, black and white, to be driven in all directions from the Acropolis; and when they had wandered as far as they would, they were to be sacrificed wherever they lay down; and the altars on which they were to be immolated were not to be dedicated to any known god by name, but simply to the proper deity.[2] Hence, long after, altars might be found in various places in Attica which bore no dedication, and were therefore popularly known as the nameless altars or as altars of the unknown gods.

[1] Aristotle, Ἀθ. πολ. c. 1.

[2] Τῷ προσήκοντι, *Diog. Laert.* i. 110 and 112.

It was, however, not only cities that required purification from pollution; private individuals also might need to be reconciled with the offended gods; and ministers to their spiritual wants were forthcoming, though they have not, like Epimenides or Empedocles after him, bequeathed their names to posterity. Collectively they were known as *agyrtæ*, a Greek substantive derived from a verb,[1] meaning to beg alms or make a collection, in order to defray the expense of the sacrifice which was an essential part of their mysteries. The *agyrtes* professed by means of his rites to purify men from the sins they had themselves committed, or from an ancestral curse or hereditary guilt, and so to secure to those whom he purified an exemption from the evil lot in the next world which awaited those who were not initiated. The *agyrtes* travelled from city to city with his apparatus—a pile of sacred books, a tame serpent, a drum, a chest, a magic mirror, etc.—laden on a donkey's back.[2] Arrived at his temporary destination, he pitched his tent, which also was carried by the donkey, and in which the mysteries were to be celebrated; and then, with attendants to carry a portable shrine, *i.e.* "a miniature temple on a salver or board,"[3] and to beat the drum, he proceeded to parade the streets in procession, he himself dancing ecstatically to the sound of the drum, and either carrying the sacred serpent or else gashing his legs or cutting his tongue till the blood flowed from it.[4] Thus he succeeded in attracting a crowd, which he drew after him to his tent, where those who chose consulted him, and by the aid of his books and his magic mirror, which probably he used in the same way as it is used in Egypt at the present day, he replied to them.

But in all this there was nothing to make any such permanent change in Greek religion as did actually follow upon this invasion of Greece by Oriental rites. The calamities which befell Greek states were at this time merely casual, not catastrophic, as in the Semitic area; and there

[1] *ἀγείρειν*.

[2] Ὄνος ἄγων μυστήρια, Ar. *Frogs*, 159.

[3] Ramsay, *Church in the Roman Empire*,[2] 127. Such were the silver shrines of Diana of Acts xix. Cf. the *θεοφόροι* and *ναόφοροι* in Ignatius, *Ephes.* § 9; and for a picture of them, Schreiber, *Kulthist. Bilderatlas*, xvii. 10.

[4] Lucian, *Lucius*, 35.

was therefore no permanent demand for the services of such men as Epimenides and Empedocles. On the other hand, the *agyrtæ* were itinerant, and their ministrations intermittent. In a word, to account for the permanent changes wrought in Greece by the wave of revivalism which spread from the Northern Semites over Hellas, it is obvious, first, that there must have been some more permanent motive at work upon the Greek mind than the fear inspired by casual political disasters, and next, that there must have been some more stationary and permanent organisation for the propagation of the new movement than was provided by the itinerant and intermittent agency of the *agyrtæ*. Now the Greek with his joyous nature had no abiding sense of sin, and if he welcomed the strange sacrifices and stirring rites from the East, it was partly because there was in them the promise of a more satisfactory sacrament than the gift-sacrifices of the traditional religion provided, and partly because they opened up a brighter and more hopeful view of the life after death. It is beyond doubt that other and less worthy motives were also at work: love philtres, charms for bewitching enemies, and spells generally, were both demanded and supplied; and for the *agyrtes* who supplied them an itinerant life was a necessity, if only for the sake of escaping detection and exposure. But with the *agyrtes* who settled definitely in one place, founded a permanent religious association, and so gave a guarantee of earnestness and faith in his mission, the case is different—and it is with him that we now have to deal.

Amongst the religious associations of the Greeks [1] there were certain societies, known variously as *thiasi*, *erani*, or *orgeones*, the constitution of which is fairly well known to us from inscriptions (usually votes of thanks to the officials). The inscriptions do not carry us further back than the fourth century B.C., but we have plenty of literary evidence of the existence of these associations in the fifth century, and *thiasi* are recognised even as early as B.C. 594, in the legislation of Solon, as legal societies, the bye-laws of which were acknowledged and enforced by the state, so far as they were not in conflict with the law of the land.[2] These *thiasi* were

[1] For what follows, see Foucart, *Des Associations Religieuses chez les Grecs.*

[2] Gardner and Jevons, *Greek Antiquities*, 560.

voluntary associations for religious purposes, which differed from the cult of the national gods in the fact that only members of the state were admitted to the worship of the state's gods, whereas the *thiasi* were open to all, to women, to foreigners, to slaves, and to freed men; and all members of the society, whatever their origin, enjoyed the same rights. But though all, without distinction of sex or origin, might become members of a *thiasus*, there were certain conditions to be fulfilled first: there was an entry-fee to pay, and the officers of the society had to satisfy themselves that the candidate for admission was suitable. The affairs of the society were regulated by its "law" (*i.e.* its articles of association) and by the decrees of the general assembly of the members. The "law" laid down the conditions of admission into the society and the circumstances under which members might be expelled; the times at which the assembly was to hold its regular meetings; the amount of subscription to be paid by members, the means for enforcing payment, and the circumstances under which delay in payment was allowed; the dues to be paid in money or kind by those who offered sacrifices in the society's temple; the purposes on which the society's revenues might be expended; the terms on which money might be lent to members, and the security they were to offer; the nature and value of testimonials voted to benefactors; the steps to be taken to enforce this "law," to carry out the decrees of the assembly, or to punish those who injured the society.[1] The general assembly, consisting of all the members of society, had absolute control over the affairs of the society, and met once a month for the transaction of business. It elected annually the officers of the society, who took an oath of obedience to it on entering office, and on quitting office were again accountable to it. Where the "law" of the society prescribed the duties of an officer, he had only to obey it; when cases arose not foreseen by the law, he had to seek instructions from the assembly. The officers included, besides a secretary and a treasurer, a president,[2] who represented the society when

[1] Foucart, 13. The Greek terms are νόμος, ψηφίσματα, and ἀγορά.

[2] ἀρχιθιασίτης at Delos, ἀρχερανιστής at Rhodes and at the Peiraeus, ἀρχέρανος at Amorgos; Foucart, 27.

necessary in the law-courts, but whose power is otherwise vague and was probably rather honorific than real; and certain officials, sometimes called *episcopi*, sometimes *epimelētæ*,[1] who in some places had the right of convoking the assembly, and in others shared the functions of the treasurer or the secretary. All these officials were, so to speak, civil officers, and were elected by the votes of the assembly. The religious functions were discharged by a priest, priestess, or sacrificers,[2] who were chosen by lot—a recognised mode of consulting the divine will. The duties of the priest (or priestess) were to conduct the sacrifices and the rites, to open and close the temple at the proper times, to preside over the purification and initiation of members, and to celebrate the mysteries, for the performance of which the society existed. The funds of the society were devoted, first to the purchase and maintenance of a sanctuary,[3] or sacred enclosure, containing a temple, a hall in which to hold the sacred banquet, and other buildings; next, to defraying the cost of the monthly sacrifices; third, to the payment of salaries; and last, not unfrequently to the burial of deceased members. These societies were usually in debt or in danger of it, and the treasurer (who was, when the society could so contrive it, a man of means and generosity) not uncommonly came to the rescue of the society with his private purse. When the poorer members were assisted by the society, it was not as a matter of charity but on the principle of a mutual benefit society: the money was advanced on security, and had to be repaid by the borrower. On the other hand, an inscription recently published shows that the poorer members of a society were sometimes charitably assisted by the wealthier.[4]

The constitution of these societies, as described in the last paragraph, is obviously modelled on the republican institutions which prevailed in many of the Greek states of the fourth century B.C., and cannot be earlier than that period. In previous times it must have been different, and

[1] *ἐπίσκοποι, ἐπιμεληταί*, also *σύνδικοι* or *λογισταί*. [2] *ἱεροποιοί*.

[3] Τέμενος.

[4] *Corp. Inscr. Atticarum*, iv. ii. 624*b*, 12: *ἐφρόντισεν δὲ τοῦ καὶ τοὺς δημοτικοὺς μετέχειν τῶν δεδομένων ὑπὸ τῶν ὀργεώνων φιλανθρώπων*. The inscription is not later than B.C. 159.

naturally much simpler. Probably in the beginning there was only one official, the priest: the finances of the society were not so great as to require a treasurer, nor its archives so extensive as to call for a secretary. It was only with the growth of the society, if it did grow (for many of these associations probably never got beyond a rudimentary stage of existence), that the number of members increased, the revenues swelled, and the expenses of the ritual developed so much that the priest became unable to manage the whole, and that a division of labour became necessary between a secretary, treasurer, president, and priest.[1] The ease and simplicity with which an *agyrtes* could found one of these associations in their simplest form may be seen from an inscription,[2] which, though it is in date as late as the second century of our era, is yet probably in spirit and essentials true to its type. The inscription was discovered in 1868 near the silver mines of Laureion in Attica, and it shows how the worship of an Oriental deity, in this case Mên Tyrannos (*i.e.* the Sovereign Moon), might be introduced into Greece. The worship of Mên was widely spread over Asia Minor: the image of the god figures on the coins of nearly all the towns of Phrygia, Lydia, and Pisidia, as well as on some of the monuments of Pamphylia, Caria, and Thrace. The author of the inscription was a Lycian slave, working in the mines for his owner, a Roman proprietor; and it was the god Mên himself, who, in a vision or dream, bade Xanthos establish his cult: "I, Xanthos, a Lycian, belonging to Caius Orbius, have consecrated the temple of Mên Tyrannos, in conformity with the will of the god." To erect a temple was an undertaking beyond the resources which Xanthos had at his disposal, so he simply appropriated a deserted heroön and adapted it to his own purposes. As founder and priest of the cult, he himself composed and engraved (as the style and spelling sufficiently show) the "law" of the new cult. In it he laid down the conditions under which the temple might be used, sacrifices offered, and *erani* or banquets held: no one who was "unclean" might approach the temple, sacrifices might not be offered without the co-operation of the founder, Xanthos, and in

[1] Foucart, 26. [2] No. 38 in Foucart, *op. cit.*

case of his death or absence his functions could only be discharged by someone nominated by him in person.[1]

The "law" thus laid down by Xanthos was probably somewhat simpler than that which formed the basis of the earliest *thiasi*. Plato talks of the piles of books which itinerant *agyrtæ* carried about with them,[2] and they were doubtless handed down by the original founder of a *thiasus* to his successors. These books contained, as we learn from Plato, instructions as to the ritual to be observed in sacrifice; and, according to Demosthenes,[3] it was from such sacred books, belonging to the *thiasus* of Sabazios, that Æschines read the formulæ which had to be recited during the purification and initiation of those who wished to be admitted to these mysteries.

In these private mysteries, as in the public mysteries which we shall have to describe hereafter, we have to distinguish between the preliminary ceremonies of purification and preparation and the actual rite for the celebration of which the religious organisation, public or private, existed. For the private mysteries we get our information mainly from the passage of Demosthenes already referred to. The exact order of proceedings, the precise acts to be performed by the novice, his very attitude and gesture at each stage of the proceedings, seem to have been prescribed in the ritual-book; and the function of the youthful Æschines was to read out these instructions so that the novice might know what next to do. The first step in the preliminary ceremony was to place the candidate under the protection of the god, and this was done by throwing a fawn-skin round him. In this act we note the survival or revival of one of the oldest beliefs connected with animal-worship, namely, that the animal god may reside in the skin of the animal just as a tree-god may reside in the bough of a tree. In this faith, totem tribes on solemn occasions clothe themselves in the skin of the totem animal, and more advanced peoples made idols of animal-gods by stuffing the hide, or later (as in Greece) clothed a human-shaped idol with the skin.[4] When the

[1] Foucart, 119 ff.

[2] *βίβλων δὲ ὅμαδον παρέχονται . . . καθ' ἃς θυηπολοῦσι*, *Rep.* 364 E.

[3] *De Cor.* § 259.

[4] Paus. viii. c. 37.

candidate had been thus commended to the god, the next thing was that he should be purified. To this end, he was stripped and made to crouch down upon the ground, and then bowls of water were poured over him. In some mysteries this purification by water was such a prominent and important feature in the ceremony, that those who practised it took their name from it, and were known (and derided) as Baptæ. In others, however, a more startling and paradoxical mode of purification was in vogue: the novice was cleansed with a mixture of clay and bran. When these ceremonies, which were made the more awe-inspiring by ecstatic ejaculations from the attendants, were completed, the candidate was bidden to rise from his kneeling, crouching position, and to cry out, Bad have I escaped and better have I found—words which were intended to express the conviction that he was now purified in heart and spiritually prepared for the actual mystery, *μυστήριον*, the solemn rite by which he was to be admitted into fellowship with the god and his worshippers. That this rite was in the nature of a sacramental meal, is obvious. The main expenses of these private religious associations are shown by the inscriptions to have consisted in the sacrifices and sacred banquets, and in the building and maintenance of the edifices in which to celebrate them. The leading characteristic of the religious revival of the sixth century B.C., both in the Semitic area and as transplanted into Greece, is a reaction against the gift theory of sacrifice, and a reversion to the earlier sacramental conception of the offering and the sacrificial meal as affording actual communion with the god whose flesh and blood were consumed by his worshippers. To try to discover anything else in the case of the more respectable of the private mysteries, to seek for something secret and mysterious, is *chercher midi à quatorze heures.* That sacrifices were offered and eaten was a fact about which there was no concealment. The feeling of reverential awe with which the worshipper partook of the sacrament doubtless could not be conveyed in words: so far, indeed, there may have been secrecy, though not concealment.

After participation in the sacred meal, the candidate was a novice no longer, but a member of the religious confraternity, united by a mystic bond with his fellow-worshippers. As such it became his duty to promote the interests of the association, to gain new members for it, and to extend its influence. He therefore took part in the procession of the society which paraded the streets in order to attract fresh followers, and wearing a garland of fennel or poplar, and bearing the sacred cist or the mystic winnowing fan, or carrying a tame serpent in both hands above his head, he danced wildly along, testifying to his membership by shrieking the words, Evoe Sabœ! Hyês Attês! Attês Hyês! But this method of proselytising was probably limited to the poorer and more struggling associations, which could not afford to build temples, but met in the private house of one of the wealthier members, or of the promoter of the organisation, and did not offer sacrifice of animals, but partook of sacred wafers or cakes, such as came to furnish forth the sacramental meal both in the New World and the Old, when cereal gods took their place by the side of animal gods.[1]

In spite of the fact not only that these "private" mysteries were open to all, but also that the most strenuous efforts were made by the members to obtain the largest possible number of adherents, these associations at the best were sects, and narrow ones; and as such they were exposed to the same dangers as are all sects, that is to say, being withdrawn, by the nature of the case, from the sane and healthy action of public opinion, they were liable to run into extravagance and excess. The danger was in this case all the greater, because the essence and the attraction of the rites which these associations were formed to celebrate lay in the fact that the ritual was different from that of the ordinary cult, was strange, unusual, mysterious, and therefore more

[1] The passage of the *De Corona* (259, 260) on which the above account is based runs as follows: *ἀνὴρ δὲ γενόμενος τῇ μητρὶ τελούσῃ τὰς βίβλους ἀνεγίγνωσκες καὶ τἄλλα συνεσκευωροῦ, τὴν μὲν νύκτα νεβρίζων καὶ κρατηρίζων καὶ καθαίρων τοὺς τελουμένους καὶ ἀπομάττων τῷ πηλῷ καὶ τοῖς πιτύροις καὶ ἀνιστὰς ἀπὸ τοῦ καθαρμοῦ κελεύων λέγειν· Ἔφυγον κακόν, εὗρον ἄμεινον, ἐπὶ τῷ μηδένα πώποτε τηλικοῦτ' ὀλολύξαι σεμνυνόμενος . . . ἐν δὲ ταῖς ἡμέραις τοὺς καλοὺς θιάσους ἄγων διὰ τῶν ὁδῶν τοὺς ἐστεφανωμένους τῷ μαράθῳ καὶ τῇ λεύκῃ, τοὺς ὄφεις τοὺς παρείας θλίβων καὶ ὑπὲρ τῆς κεφαλῆς αἰωρῶν, καὶ βοῶν· Εὐοῖ σαβοῖ, καὶ ἐπορχούμενος Ὕης ἄττης, ἄττης ὕης, ἔξαρχος καὶ προηγεμὼν καὶ κιστοφόρος καὶ λικνοφόρος καὶ τοιαῦτα ὑπὸ τῶν γρᾳδίων προσαγορευόμενος, μισθὸν λαμβάνων τούτων ἔνθρυπτα καὶ στρεπτοὺς καὶ νεήλατα.*

potent as ritual. Again, the very object of the strangeness of these new rites, of the whirling dances, the frenzied shrieks, and the streams of blood which flowed over the devotees as they scourged or gashed their limbs or their tongues, was to work upon the worshipper's emotions until he had no control over them, and was swept away by the tide of ecstasy which was shared, as he saw, by his fellow-worshippers. Add to this that an essential feature of these revivalist rites consisted in returning to the primitive fashion of offering the solemn and awful sacrifice of the totem-god by night, and we shall understand that these private mysteries were both morally and spiritually at the best in a state of unstable equilibrium, and might easily lapse into the excesses and debauchery which attended the spread of the Baccanalia in Italy. The very freedom with which the organisation of these societies was permitted worked in the same direction. It is doubtful whether there was in Athens any restriction on the formation of these societies: foreigners were not, as a rule, allowed to acquire or possess land in Attica, but when they wished to purchase a site for a temple in which to worship their own gods after their own fashion, they were allowed to do so, as we know from the stone-record of the decree which gave permission, on the express ground that there was no law to forbid the proceeding:[1] the purpose to which the site was to be applied constituted actually a reason in favour of allowing the foreigners to acquire Athenian soil. But whether this Attic law allowed Athenian citizens to partake in such foreign worships is another and disputed question. It has been both asserted and denied[2] that the legal penalty for the introduction of new gods (in the sense of inducing citizens to worship other than their ancestral gods) was death; but, without undertaking to settle this obscure point, we may note that there is no instance on record in which anyone was even prosecuted, much less condemned, on the sole charge of introducing new gods: there were always other counts in the indictment, which seems to indicate that for some reason or other there was no prospect of getting a jury to convict on the ground simply

[1] The Citians, *ἔδοξαν ἔννομα ἱκετεύειν*, *C. I. A.*

[2] Gardner and Jevons, *Greek Antiquities*, 219 and 560.

of worshipping strange gods. Whatever danger there may have been for the Athenian citizen in such worship, could be to some extent, if not wholly, averted by a demonstration of the mythological identity of the foreign deity, say Sabazios or Cybele, with some Greek god or goddess, as Dionysos or Rhea; and it is possible that fear of the law as well as the desire of commending a strange god by proving him to be merely an old deity under a new name, may have helped to give the gods of the Orphic mythology the haziness of outline and want of definition which at once marks them off from the genuine gods of Greece, and enables any one to be identified with any other. Be this as it may, it is certain that no penalty attached to the private worship of the established gods with the new ecstatic ritual, and that no permission or licence had to be obtained from the state in order to organise a *thiasus* or *orgeon* for the purpose. Consequently any adventuress who chose might set up as priestess, and, under the pretence of orgiastic worship, might make her house the scene of "orgies" in the modern sense of the word.

That this actually was done in some cases is certain, but that all private mysteries were a mere excuse or occasion for debauchery is improbable in itself, and is contradicted by the evidence. If any charge of this kind could have been brought or even insinuated with any degree of probability by Demosthenes against the mother of Æschines, we may be sure that it would not have been omitted. There is not in the speech of Demosthenes any suggestion that Glaucothea's *thiasus* was anything but respectable from the moral point of view: there is contempt for the semi-menial functions performed by Æschines in the ritual, there is a satirical juxtaposition of the barbarous rites and the solemn formula, Bad have I escaped and better have I found, to emphasise the absurdity and folly of people who imagined that spiritual regeneration was to be effected by the external application of a mixture of clay and bran, but even Demosthenes does not venture to hint at anything worse than folly in the members of the *thiasus*, and perhaps semi-conscious imposture on the part of the promoters of the organisation. In a word, the attitude of the better class of Athenians towards these private mysteries was very much that taken by many educated people at the present day towards spiritualistic séances, or towards the methods adopted by the Salvation Army.

In the case of the larger and more permanent associations, which were wealthy enough to possess investments, to build and maintain temples, halls, and dwellings for their officials, and which were not exploited in the interests of a promoter, but were managed by the free votes of all the members, it is obvious that we must set aside the theory of imposture, conscious or semi-conscious, and of inordinate folly: if the number of members could be maintained at the level necessary to keep such a voluntary organisation in working order, it must have been because this particular form of religious society provided some spiritual satisfaction which was not otherwise to be obtained. Nor on this point are we confined to *à priori* reasoning: we have the evidence of the inscriptions to show that the members of these societies were largely foreigners and slaves, in other words, to show that the worship was a genuine worship, such as they were familiar with in their own country, and welcomed in a strange land. That such "barbarous," *i.e.* foreign, worship should be despised by the better class Greek, and that contempt and distrust should be the feelings manifest in Greek literature towards this importation from abroad, is perfectly natural, but is not an absolutely final verdict in the matter, nor a condemnation from which there is no appeal. For one thing, religious progress may outstrip the advance of material civilisation; for another, it was not in the domain of religion that ancient Greece rendered its service to the cause of civilisation. We cannot therefore accept the literary Greek as a specially qualified judge in matters religious, but must endeavour to form our own opinion.

At the outset, however, it must be noted that there is in our own day and circumstances a cause at work which tends to make our judgment unduly unfavourable to these early attempts to escape from the gift theory of sacrifice, and to bring the belief in a future life into some living relation with religion. In the conviction that spiritual regeneration or conversion, to be real, must manifest itself in making the man a better man morally, so much stress is now laid on the necessity of moral improvement, that the spiritual change is frequently regarded merely as a particularly efficacious, perhaps the only really efficacious, means of effecting a moral change. The identity of the spiritual life and the moral is emphasised; their difference, and the wider area of the former, tends to be lost from view. When, then, we find that in the antique religions there was a lively, if intermittent, sense of the need of a reconciliation between God and man, and a craving for a spiritual life and communion with Him, but at the same time find, though many external acts and ceremonies were prescribed, no moral amendment was insisted upon, we are apt to infer that there was no real religious force at work either. Whereas the truth would rather seem to be that the force was religious, but was misdirected. The aspiration to communion with God, not only in this life but in the next, can only be described as religious; and it was misdirected, not merely because erroneous conceptions of the Godhead were entertained, but because there was no consciousness that it was in the direction of moral purity that satisfaction for the spiritual aspiration was to be sought. It would, however, be rash to infer that because a consciousness of the connection between moral reform and spiritual progress was wanting, therefore the connection itself was wanting. That would be much the same as arguing that because Socrates, Plato, and Aristotle had no name for the conscience or the will, therefore they possessed no conscience and no will. In fine, many must have failed to obtain even the degree of spiritual communion which was open to them, who would have attained to it had they been taught the necessity first of amending their lives. Of the rest, those who regarded the mere acts of ceremonial purification as all-important and of sole importance, derived no more spiritual benefit from them than they would have derived from the rites and ceremonies of a higher religion; but those who considered them merely as aids in their search for the better, cannot have failed in some measure to escape from evil. Doubtless the purificatory acts themselves were very barbarous and puerile, and especially do they seem so to us who would rather they had purified their hearts; but, trivial as the acts were, their spirit and intent were religious; mistaken though the rites were, the desire of the worshipper was to fit himself to approach his God; and though we may despise or deplore the means he adopted, we may also hesitate to assert that the yearnings of his heart were wholly defrauded in the result, or that his spiritual travail brought forth no moral fruits.

We can, however, go a step further than this. We need not rely exclusively on the *à priori* argument that the genuine desire for closer communion with God, in both worlds, must result in a more godly and righteous life. We have direct and explicit evidence to show that in the private mysteries moral amendment was actually laid down as the condition of such communion and of future bliss. In the second book of his *Republic*,[1] Plato wishes to insist on the fact that righteousness is desirable in itself and without regard to consequences, that the truly moral man is he who loves and does what is right for its own sake, and simply and solely because it is right. He therefore denounces the common, vulgar teaching that honesty pays, because so many people at once jump to the conclusion that the only reason for doing what is right is the material advantages which ensue from right-doing; in a word, that it is not reasonable or sensible to do what is right for its own sake. But if the bourgeois doctrine, that prosperity in this world is the proper motive for honesty, appears immoral to Plato, much more monstrous does it seem to him that the doctrine of future rewards and punishments should be used to bribe men into doing what is right and frighten them from doing wrong. And it was precisely this doctrine which, according to Plato, was taught in the private mysteries by Musæus and Orpheus: in the next world the righteous received blessings[2] and a life of happiness as a reward for their virtue[3] in this life; whereas evil-doers were punished in Hades.

In the face, therefore, of this explicit testimony from a hostile witness, it seems impossible to maintain[4] that the wide diffusion and permanent success of the private mysteries in

[1] 363 C. [2] *Ibid.* νεανικώτερα τἀγαθὰ . . . παρὰ θεῶν διδόασι τοῖς δικαίοις.

[3] *Ibid.* ἀρετῆς μισθόν.

[4] As, *e.g.*, M. Foucart does at the end of his otherwise excellent work, already quoted.

Greece can be wholly accounted for by the supposition that they required a lower standard, moral and spiritual, than that attained by the ordinary religion of the Greek citizen, and were consequently welcomed by the lower members of Greek society, as affording an escape from the exacting demands of the state religion. Nor can we accept as completely satisfactory the view that the ecstatic ritual merely supplied a spur and stimulus to the grosser natures, and gave them a pseudo-spiritual, sensual excitement. That this was the effect in some cases is true; but the influence of public opinion and the force of the law were quite strong enough both in Greece and Italy to purge out such depravities; and we must not form our judgment of antiquity solely by the revelations of its law courts. The majority of the private mysteries, certainly those that had the element of permanence in them, cannot have lived solely on the unhealthy tendencies of society, or have thriven for centuries on outbursts of excitement which in their nature are necessarily spasmodic and transitory. The doctrine that future happiness depended upon righteousness in this life—whatever its intrinsic value from the point of view of moral philosophy—was a great advance upon anything previously known in Greek religion; and the extent to which it had spread in Plato's time is shown both by the alarm which it caused in his mind and by the vast amount of "Orphic" literature which it rapidly called into existence. If it be asked why then did the mysteries not effect the moral regeneration of Greece, we may suggest two reasons. First, the morality which was taught was simply the ordinary morality of Greek life: no new moral truths were revealed. On the best natures no fresh demand was made: they *ex hypothesi* were already living up to the highest moral standard of the time; and so for them the message had nothing new. If they were dissatisfied and uneasy, without knowing why, the mysteries could not help them: St. Clement tried them all and found all empty. In the next place, the spirit of exclusiveness was wanting from these organisations: their members were not expected to renounce the worship of the state gods. Thus those members who had been living below the ordinary standard of morality, and who were induced by participation in the mysteries to amend their lives, were liable to relapse to their old level, which was so much easier to maintain, and with which the state gods, at anyrate, had no quarrel to find.

So far from trying to sever themselves from the traditional religion, the members of the new organisations endeavoured to show the fundamental identity of the two; and they succeeded in their attempt because the two were fundamentally identical. The belief in a happy other-world was indeed something unknown to traditional Greek belief, which regarded Hades as a dismal abode, equally dreary for all men. But the rites and ceremonies which were thought essential for that closer union with God on which future bliss was conditional were not new to Greece: they were in Greece as in the Semitic area, revivals of a ritual which, though it had disappeared in most places, still lingered in old-world out-of-the-way sanctuaries, and which, because it was archaic and unfamiliar, was regarded as particularly potent. This fact is of cardinal importance for the right comprehension of the mysteries. If the new movement spread so rapidly and widely over Greece, and took such firm root everywhere, it was because, in addition to its promise of future bliss, there was nothing really foreign about its rites and ceremonies: they were absolutely in harmony with the spirit of the customary religion of Greece, for they belonged to a stage of its development which it had not yet outgrown. This is, again, the element of truth in the modern view which would see in the movement nothing but a relapse from the civilisation the Greeks had reached, and a return to semi-barbarous practices which they had abandoned: the rites and ceremonies were a reversion, but the doctrine of future happiness was an advance. Finally, the fact that the movement was a revivalist movement explains both its original success and its ultimate failure as a religious movement—its success, because it was a reversion to the original sacramental character of sacrifice; its failure, because the conviction that some sacrifice external to man was necessary to the reconciliation of God and man, could not be permanently satisfied by animal sacrifice.

The archaic religious practices which were revived in and by the mysteries, though not new to Greece, were not, of course, confined to Greece; on the contrary, they are or have been world-wide, and though they belong to a particular stage of religious development, they are confined to no particular century or country. Ceremonial purification by water, which plays a large part in the mysteries, is to be found everywhere, and was known to the Homeric Greeks long before the time of the mysteries. The practice, again, of placing a person or thing in direct communication with an animal-god by wrapping the person or thing in the skin of the animal, is, as we have already seen, world-wide: it was practised by the European branch of the Aryans from prehistoric times. The crouching posture which the novice had to assume during the preliminary purification may or may not have been known to the Semites, but it was certainly part of the archaic Greek ceremony of purification known as *Δίος κῴδιον*.[1] The ceremonial use of clay is a point of sufficient importance to require rather closer examination. In the mysteries, daubing the novice with clay was part of the process by which he was cleansed and purified; and pouring water over him was another. Now, as it is not obvious at first sight how rubbing a person with mud can clean him, and as symbolism affords an easy explanation even of things which never had any symbolical meaning, some modern writers have explained that the candidate was first plastered with clay and then washed clean with water, to express symbolically and by outward act the internal and spiritual purification which he was undergoing. But, unfortunately for this explanation, the actual order of proceedings was otherwise: the novice was first soused with water, and then made clean with mud. The words of Demosthenes[2] are quite explicit upon both points. The clay it was that possessed the cleansing properties; and that is what is meant by Plutarch when he speaks[3] about "cleansings unclean and purifications impure." Hence, too, according to the teaching of the mysteries, sinners were in the next world buried in clay[4]

[1] Daremberg et Saglis, *Dict. des Antiquités*, s.v.

[2] *Supra*, p. 340.

[3] *De Superstitione*, 12.

[4] Plato, *Rep.* 363 C: τοὺς δὲ ἀνοσίους αὖ καὶ ἀδίκους ἐς πηλόν τινα κατορύττουσιν ἐν Ἅιδου; *Phæd.* 69 C: ὃς ἂν ἀμύητος καὶ ἀτέλεστος εἰς Ἅιδου ἀφίκηται, ἐν βορβόρῳ κείσεται.

—obviously to cleanse and purify them of their wickedness.

Now, there are at the present day plenty of people who plaster themselves with clay. The negroes of the West Coast of Africa, when engaged in the service of a god, notify the fact by dressing in white and covering themselves with white clay if the service be of a festal character, with red if it be of a more serious kind. This reminds us of the Polynesian custom of painting things which are taboo red, the colour of blood; and, in point of fact, persons who are about to undertake some sacred function, or who are actively engaged in the service of the gods, are very generally considered taboo, and are marked off as such, in order that other people may abstain from contact with them, and that so they may neither carry pollution into the worship, nor communicate the "infection of holiness" to others. The most familiar instance of this precaution is (I submit) afforded by savage warfare: to the savage, war is a sacred function, the tribal god himself fights for his clan, the warriors are engaged in his service, as such they are taboo and dangerous, and they notify the fact by donning "war-paint." Thus the Ethiopians who served the great king in his invasion of Greece, painted half their bodies with white clay when they were going into battle, and the other half with red.[1] That the Greeks themselves had once followed this practice, is proved by an odd instance of its survival or rather revival in historic times. The Phocians, who were always at war with the Thessalians, and were always getting the worst of it, at last, in despair, sent to Elis for a seer (*μάντις*), Telliês by name, to help them; and he put them up to a device. He took six hundred of their bravest men, made them plaster themselves and their armour all over with white clay, and then sent them to make a night attack upon the foe, which they did with such success that they killed four thousand Thessalians.[2] Now, Herodotus regards this as nothing but

[1] *Hdt.* vii. 69: *τοῦ δὲ σώματος τὸ μὲν ἥμισυ ἐξηλείφοντο γύψῳ ἰόντες ἐς μάχην, τὸ δὲ ἄλλο ἥμισυ μίλτῳ.*

[2] *Hdt.* viii. 27: Telliês *σοφίζεται αὐτοῖσι τοιόνδε· γυψώσας ἄνδρας ἑξακοσίους τῶν Φωκέων τοὺς ἀρίστους, αὐτούς τε τούτους καὶ τὰ ὅπλα αὐτῶν, νυκτὸς ἐπεθήκατο τοῖς Θεσσαλοῖσι.*

a clever and somewhat humorous device on the part of the holy man: the Phocians recognised each other in the darkness by their war-paint, and the Thessalians were terrified by six hundred apparitions in white. But it seems more likely that if the Phocians sent to Elis for a seer, it was because they wanted some advice as to the way in which they might win the favour of the gods; and Telliês must have had a reputation for knowing the proper ritual to be observed in the conduct of war. Evidently, amongst the traditions stored up in his mind, one was that warriors should be prepared for battle by previous purification and by dedication to the gods. Whether Telliês was aware that the war-paint was but the outward sign that the warriors were dedicate and so taboo, or whether he regarded the daubing as part of the purificatory ceremony, there is nothing to show. But in the mysteries, by the time of Plato, the daubing, though it still did not take place until after the novice had been purified by water, and so had become fit to be dedicated, was regarded as but a second and more potent means of cleansing. In fine, if we divide the preliminary ceremonial of the mysteries into two parts, namely, (1) purification, and (2) dedication, the plastering with clay, which originally was the first stage in (2), came eventually to be regarded as the last stage in (1).

To cover the whole of the body with clay is a process which, though effectual, naturally tends to be abridged if possible. Mourners, who are highly taboo, and are bound to notify their condition in order that no one may inadvertently touch them, in various countries substitute white clothing for white clay, and either (like the West Coast negroes on festal days) only daub their faces, or dispense with the daubing altogether. In Greece, it can be shown that the *mystæ* only daubed their faces. For the various strange acts which the *mystæ* had to perform, reasons had to be given; and the reasons took the form of myths—the *mystæ* had to do the thing because once some god or hero or supernatural being did it. Hence from the myths we can sometimes gain important information as to the ritual. Now, the myth in this case is that the Titans, when about to murder the infant Bacchus, plastered their faces in order that they might not be recognised: therefore those who worshipped the mystic

Bacchus were to daub their faces also with white clay. If the ritual had been for the worshippers to plaster themselves all over, we may be sure the Titans would have done the same.

The idea that play-acting may be a sacred function is not quite so unfamiliar to the modern mind as the sanctity of war: it is pretty generally known that in Greece tragedy and comedy were part of the worship of Dionysus. It need not therefore surprise us to find that the actor, like the warrior, was a sacred person during the discharge of his function, and that his sanctity was notified to the world in much the same way. The satyric chorus, out of which tragedy was developed, wore goat-skins, and were called goats (τράγοι), to mark their intimate relation with the goat-god,[1] just as the novice in the mysteries was clad in a fawn-skin. The actor had his "war-paint" with which he smeared his face, to indicate that he was under the protection of the wine-god, and therefore inviolable. But as regards the colour of his paint, he adopted, not the Phocian but the Polynesian use: he smeared his face blood-colour, with the lees of wine. The blood of the vine and the vine-god was thus put to the same use as the skin of the animal-god. The actor smeared his face with wine-lees, not for practical or utilitarian but for religious reasons—for exactly the same reasons as other persons dedicated to the gods painted their faces with white clay or red.

It seems, then, that the rite of painting the face was not imported into Greece. It had existed from of old amongst the Greeks as well as amongst the Semites. It was revived first amongst the latter and then in Greece by the new movement of the sixth century B.C., by the conviction that a better lot in the next world was to be obtained by a reversion to archaic and potent ritual. And the same holds good of the other rites of purification and dedication in the mysteries by which the candidate was prepared to partake of the sacramental meal, participation in which admitted him to the new society, and bound him with a mystic bond to the god and to his fellow-worshippers. It also holds good of the sacramental meal itself: that the worshipper who ate

[1] Gardner and Jevons, *Greek Antiquities*, 662–5.

of the meat of sacrifice was partaking in the divine life of the sacred animal was a conception which had largely disappeared from view, especially in the cities, the centres of civilised life. But in the country, where things change more slowly and ideas move less rapidly, the old notion, together with the old and more or less barbarous ritual of drinking the blood and scrambling for the victim's flesh (or for the sacred wafers and cakes), still lingered on, until the sixth century wave of revivalism made it once more a potent factor in the development of religion. Doubtless the revived conception and the revived ritual, as taught and practised by the *agyrtæ*, and in the *thiasi* and *orgeones*, at first appeared to the Greeks who dwelt in cities as something new and foreign. But they were not long in discovering that the supposed foreign novelty had the sanction and authority of some of their own native and venerable sanctuaries. One Greek god there was with whose worship the supposed new rites could be seen by everybody to be fundamentally identical, namely, Dionysus. And accordingly the cult of Dionysus, who hitherto, as a god of vegetation and harvest generally, and of the vine and the vintage in particular, had been almost exclusively a rustic god, now spread from the country to the towns. It was in the middle of the sixth century, in the time of the Pisistratidæ, that tragedy, the worship of Dionysus, found its way from the country into Athens, and was taken under the patronage of the state.

In these circumstances, it is not surprising that the deities Sabazios, Zagreus, and Iacchus, who were worshipped with the revived rites in the East, should have been identified by their Greek worshippers with Dionysus. At the same time the differences as well as the resemblance between say Zagreus and Dionysus had to be explained; and the explanations of the likeness in unlikeness necessarily took the form of myths. Further, as there was no priesthood whose function was to teach, as there were no revealed books, no Church to formulate a creed or enforce a dogma, the field was open to all-comers, and every worshipper was at liberty not merely to believe, but also to frame any explanation he chose. Many explanatory myths accordingly were framed, some of which were more and others less plausible. The more convincing soon spread beyond the limits of the first audience — of *thiasotæ* or *orgeones* — to whom they were addressed: as we have already seen, the founder of a *thiasus* provided the sacred books which prescribed the ritual and gave its explanation, and the successful establishment of a *thiasus* probably depended largely on whether the myths were of a satisfactory and convincing character. Hence a wide circulation for those which commended themselves to the average Greek: they were essential to the successful propagation of the new worship. But explanatory myths were required not only to prove the fundamental identity of the new god with the old, but also to give a reason for the peculiar character of the purificatory and dedicatory rites and for the remarkable ritual of the sacrifice. Finally, the new teaching of hope with regard to the life to come had to be brought into some connection with the customary religion, to be grafted on it, if it was to grow. Now, the same tendency which made both Greeks and Romans take it for granted that in foreign deities they could detect their own gods under different names, made the religious Greek, who recognised Dionysus in Zagreus, take it for certain that the new teaching about the next life must have once formed part of his own religion, if only he could rediscover it, just as the new rites turned out to have been preserved in certain out-of-the-way sanctuaries. The only question was which of the great men of old had taught the doctrine. Plainly it must have been someone who had visited the other world, and so could speak on the subject with authority. That person could only have been Orpheus. The teaching therefore was the teaching of Orpheus; and from that position it was but an easy step to ascribe to Orpheus not only the substance but the actual words of any particular metrical myth which, owing to its popularity, had detached itself from the circle of worshippers for which it was originally intended and had circulated widely but anonymously. Such literature, of which inconsiderable fragments have survived to our own day, accordingly came to be known as Orphic, and the religious associations whose worship these myths were composed to explain and justify came to be spoken of as Orphic mysteries. In the second half of the sixth century B.C., this literature was "edited" in some sense or other at the court of Pisistratus (whose patronage of tragedy shows his favourable inclination to the cult of Dionysus) by Onomacritus. Then the Pythagorean doctrine of the transmigration of souls spread from Lower Italy to Greece, and Pythagorean pantheism was imported into Orphic literature. The change thus brought about in the character and tendency of Orphic literature is important for the history of the mysteries, and especially (as we shall see in the next chapter) for the right comprehension of the public mysteries, the Eleusinia.

The tyranny of Pisistratus lasted from B.C. 560 to B.C. 527, and the literary activity of Onomacritus must accordingly be placed before the latter date. The floruit of Pythagoras is agreed to be about B.C. 530, and accordingly the Pythagorean brotherhoods can scarcely have spread from Lower Italy to Greece in time to have influenced Onomacritus in his work (whatever its nature) in connection with Orphic literature and the new movement. Now, before the appearance of Pythagoreanism in Greece, the Orphic mysteries, whether disseminated by itinerant *agyrtæ* or taking local and permanent form in the shape of *thiasi*, were a religious innovation struggling for recognition; and the object of their adherents was to prove that the apparently new rites and new objects of worship, so far from being alien or offensive to the traditional religion and established gods, were fundamentally identical with them and more venerable forms of them. The proof of these statements consisted in the production of myths, of religious legends, associating the new deities and rites with the deities of the accepted Greek mythology. After the introduction of Pythagoreanism into Hellas, these very myths are themselves taken as a basis and are explained as allegorical or symbolical statements of a pantheistic philosophy. In the pre-Pythagorean period, that is to say, the object aimed at was religious and practical, namely, to secure the recognition and acceptance of the new rites and the new faith. But the aim of the later literature was philosophical and speculative, namely, to show that the Orphic myths led to some particular theory of the origin of man, of evil, or of the world. Now, these philosophical theories differed, according to the taste and tendencies of the particular theoriser, in the speculations which they evolved out of the Orphic myths, but they all agree in taking the same myth for their basis; and this indicates that, before Pythagoreanism reached Greece, one of the religious legends that were invented to reconcile the new Orphic movement with the customary religion had been so successful that it had driven out all its competitors and had established itself as the orthodox explanation of the new worship. The myth or legend which could do that must, we may be sure, have had in it something of the charm which has enabled certain folk-tales and fairy-tales to find a home in every quarter of the globe, and to outlive the mightiest empires of the world. And as a matter of fact, the myth in question is a folk-tale, belonging to the type known to folk-lorists as the Transformation-Conflict, of which the oldest variant is the Tale of Batta, told in an Egyptian papyrus of the nineteenth century B.C., and the most familiar variant is that which occurs in the *Arabian Nights*. The wide distribution of the tale is proved by Mr. Hartland in the first volume of his learned *Legend of Perseus*, but as he does not give our variant, it shall be set forth here. The "motives" of the Orphic adaptation of the tale are several: to connect Zagreus with the traditional Greek mythology, to show his real identity under apparent difference with Dionysus, to prove that Zagreus is the real, original Dionysus, and not a new-comer or colourable imitation, and finally to explain the ritual of his worship.

Zagreus was the son of Zeus by Persephone, and even in his childhood the government of the world was destined for him by Zeus. This promise aggravated the natural jealousy which since the time of Homer had been the most prominent feature in Hera's character; and she conspired with the Titans, the ancient enemies of Zeus, for the destruction of Zagreus. They accordingly disguised themselves by smearing their faces with clay, and made friends with the infant Zagreus. They showed him various things (which accordingly were shown in the sacred cist to his worshippers in the mysteries), and when he was engaged in looking at himself in the mirror which they had presented to him, they fell upon him. Thereupon Zagreus goes through a series of transformations in his conflict with the Titans in his endeavours to escape from them; but finally, when he was in the shape of a bull, the Titans overpowered him, tore him piece-meal, and devoured his flesh (wherefore his worshippers also were to consume his flesh). The heart of Zagreus, however, was rescued by Athênê and conveyed by her to Zeus, who swallowed it; and so Zagreus was born again as "the new Dionysus," the son of Zeus and Semelê. This last incident—in which someone by swallowing a portion of the bodily substance of the hero becomes the parent of the hero in one of his re-births—has at first sight a fantastic, Oriental air; but it is a widespread incident in folk-tales, and must have been familiar to the average Greek, else it would not have proved so successful as an explanation of the fundamental identity of Zagreus and Dionysus.

Thus far we have been dealing with myth and with a genuine folk-tale. We now proceed to the philosophical speculations which individual thinkers endeavoured to read into this folk-tale, and we find ourselves in a very different atmosphere. Zeus in his anger smote the evil Titans with his thunderbolts, and reduced them to ashes. From those ashes sprang the human race. Hence the two elements in man, the Titanic and the Dionysiac, the evil and the divine, the material and the spiritual. Thus the folk-tale of early Orphic literature was made to afford a basis for the Pythagorean teaching of the opposition of the body to the soul, and the efforts of the latter to escape from imprisonment in the former and to rejoin the world-soul, the divine essence, which was sometimes by accommodation termed Ouranos, sometimes Zeus. In the same vein the Orphic myth of the dismemberment of Zagreus by the Titans was made to bear witness to Pythagorean pantheism: the body of Zagreus was the one reality, the divine essence of all things, which is robbed of its divine unity by the action of the Titanic or evil element and split up into the manifold of the phenomenal world. But the longing of the soul to escape from its fleshly prison, to merge itself in the divine essence and so shuffle off its individual existence, is a testimony at once to the original unity which existed before its harmony was broken by the intrusion of evil, and to the ultimate destiny of the soul when purified.

It is, however, no part of our task to pursue further these speculations, which, indeed, are rather philosophical than religious. Rather we have to inquire how the original Orphic doctrine of the future life was modified by its fusion with Pythagoreanism. But to do this we must know what the Orphic doctrine, not later than the time of Onomacritus, was. That, however, is a question which can only be answered when we have some notion of the teaching on this subject associated with the great public mysteries, the Eleusinia. Meanwhile it is hoped that enough has been said to show how the new worship was grafted on to the old religion, and how the way was made easy for a man to join the new movement without ceasing to worship the state gods.

CHAPTER XXIV

THE ELEUSINIAN MYSTERIES

In the last chapter we were concerned with religious associations which were founded and organised by private individuals, which to the end remained as they had been from the beginning in the hands of private individuals, and so may be called "private mysteries." But there also arose in Greece, as a consequence of the wave of revivalism which spread over that country in the sixth century B.C., "public mysteries," and it is of importance that the meaning of the term "public" in this connection should be clearly understood. The term does not imply that these mysteries were more widely open to the general public than the "private" mysteries were: both alike were open to all who chose to go through the ceremony of initiation. Nor does the distinction consist merely in the fact that more persons availed themselves of the permission in the one case than in the other; for, though it is true as a matter of fact that a greater number did go to the "public" mysteries, yet that was simply because they were more widely known, and their wider fame was due to the fact that they were under the management of some famous State. This, however, indicates that in some cases the State's attitude towards the new movement was not one merely of tolerance but one of actual participation: for some reason or other the State adopted the new principle of initiation, *μύησις*, instead of the old principle of birthright, of citizenship, as the qualification for admission to the worship of the State gods. Now, this was a violation of all the traditional ideas, according to which none but the members of a tribe or state would be listened to by the gods of that state or tribe, and the human members of the community were as jealous as the divine of strangers. It is therefore important to note that it was only in the case of one State, Athens, that the sixth century wave of revivalism broke through this jealous exclusiveness—though in after years other States imitated Athens—and it was only one cult in that State which was thus thrown open to all Greeks, bond or free, men or women. The worship of Demeter in Eleusis became a "mystery," *i.e.* was thrown open to all who chose to become initiated, become *mystæ*, but the worship of the same goddess elsewhere, *e.g.* at the Athenian Thesmophoria, was not thrown open thus.

What distinguishes then "public" or State mysteries both from the ordinary public worship and from "private" mysteries is that in the State mysteries, by an exception wholly alien to the spirit of the antique religions and strictly confined to an exceptional case, the State adopted initiation as the qualification for joining in the national worship of a national god, as the qualification for admission to a cult hitherto confined to citizens. Private mysteries, on the other hand, were not attached to an ancient cult; they sprang up independently; membership in them conferred admission to their own rite, not to any State-sanctuary or State-worship. But State mysteries threw open some one particular cult and adopted exceptionally *μύησις* as the qualification for admission to that one cult and that alone. But an innovation which might have led to the substitution of an international religion for the hitherto prevailing national worships, an innovation which certainly accustomed men who were dissatisfied with their customary religion to project their thoughts beyond their local gods, an innovation which at the least is a strange and unparalleled departure from the prevailing traditional ideas, is a change which, it might be thought, requires some explanation. The Athenians themselves in later times were quite aware of the necessity of some explanation, and found it in the comfortable doctrine of their own "liberality."[1] We may, however, be sure that that is not the right reason to be given for so great a departure from the very essence and life of antique religion. And why did their liberality extend no further? why did it choose this particular cult rather than

[1] Isoc. *Paneg.* 28: οὕτως ἡ πόλις ἡμῶν . . . φιλανθρώπως ἔσχεν.

any other in which to display itself? There is no reason in the nature of the cult itself to account for its being singled out. The probability is that its selection was purely accidental and wholly undesigned. The great changes in institutions and constitutions are rarely deliberately planned; they generally spring from some accidental departure from the traditional path, so slight as originally to be overlooked altogether, or condoned, if challenged, as of no practical importance. The variation may die out altogether; it may soon prove so mischievous as to call for complete repression; or, from unforeseen circumstances, it may bring unforeseen advantages and commend itself by its success in spite of its irregularity. The Athenian explanation of the conversion of the cult of the Eleusinian Demeter into a "mystery" is obviously unhistorical. Modern scholars have paid little or no attention to the point; and it is a problem which we shall have to endeavour to solve for ourselves in this chapter.

That little regard has been paid to this important point, is probably due to the long prevailing but now slowly dissolving view that the chief characteristic of the mysteries was secrecy, and that the most important problem was to discover their secrets.. Hidden wisdom and esoteric doctrines were supposed to have been handed down from priest to priest, and by them communicated under a vow of secrecy to the initiated. But the mysteries were not secret societies: they were open to all without distinction; and all could be initiated into every grade, even the last and the highest. The priests, again, formed no secret order, but were plain citizens, having no such superiority in education or political or social position that they could be in exclusive possession of any sublime religious knowledge—and, as we have said, the whole Greek world was at liberty to learn the whole of what they had to teach. But the priests were not preachers or teachers: their official duties consisted simply in knowing and performing the traditional ritual. About the doctrine of immortality and the future blessedness of those who partook in the mysteries, there was no concealment whatever: Pindar, Æschylus, and Sophocles openly refer to it; Aristophanes parodies it; the Homeric Hymn to Demeter, which was an official publication, so to speak, states it expressly and explicitly. It is therefore not surprising to find that no oath of secrecy was required of the candidate for initiation. The herald called indeed for silence,[1] but it was for silence during the sacred ceremonies, the silence that befits religious worship, and naturally accompanies the concentration of the mind upon higher things. It is true also that silence was observed afterwards as to the ceremonies by the initiated, but this too was a reverential silence rather than an attempt at concealment, and the motive which prompted it was the same as that which required the candidate to be prepared by fasting and purification before participating in the mysteries: things sacred must not be polluted by contact with things or persons unclean; indeed, such contact is, owing to the infection of holiness, dangerous to the unclean. Hence, if participation in and knowledge of the mysteries were withheld from all who were not duly initiated, the object of such exclusion was not a desire to keep the mysteries a secret, but fear of the danger which contact between the holy and the unclean would bring upon both. So, too, the silence observed after initiation was not for the sake of concealment, but in order to prevent pollution and its consequent dangers. The identity, or at least the close connection between a thing and its name, not only makes the utterance of a holy name an invocation which ensures the actual presence of the deity invoked, it also makes the holy name too sacred for common use or even for use at all. Thus even to speak of the mysteries to the uninitiated, the profane, would be just as dangerous as to allow such unclean persons to take part in the sacred ceremonies. Hence the revelation of the mysteries was a crime which the State undertook to punish—not because of any violation of secrecy, but because of the danger to the unclean, and in order to avert the divine wrath which such pollution might bring on the community at large.

The secrecy, then, which shrouded the celebration of the mysteries was accidental, and not deliberately designed for purposes of concealment. Failing to observe this, however, many modern scholars have supposed that, where so much concealment was practised, some marvellous secret must have been hid; while other scholars, arguing from the fact that

[1] ἐπιτάττει τὴν σιωπήν, Sopater in Waiz, *Rhet. Gr.* 8. 118. 24 ff.

nothing marvellous in the mysteries has ever been discovered, have concluded that the secret was so well kept simply because there was nothing to reveal. The truth may well lie between these extremes: there must have been something to reveal, else Æschylus, for instance, could not have been prosecuted for revealing it; but that something need not have been anything marvellous—it probably simply consisted in certain ancient ritual acts which appeared mysterious to the worshipper because their original meaning had been forgotten, and which were chiefly impressive because the worshipper believed that through them he reached closer union with the Divine Nature, and received the hope of eternal life. It will therefore be necessary to attempt not only to ascertain the nature and original meaning of this archaic ritual, but also to guess how the new doctrine of future bliss came to be attached to the worship of Demeter. The latter problem is sometimes solved by the simple assertion that Demeter was a "chthonic," *i.e.* underground deity; and as such naturally exercised an influence over the underground world to which the souls of the dead departed. But not all deities are chthonic that are simply asserted to be so; and the proposed solution fails to explain how it is that of the many places in which Demeter was worshipped, Eleusis was the only spot in all Greece in which Demeter was sufficiently "chthonic" to be connected with the doctrine of a future life. Another way out of the difficulty is sometimes found by the aid of mythology: the daughter of Demeter is Persephone, the seed-corn, which descends below the earth only in due time to be raised again to life, and it is from this mythical analogy that the Greek belief in immortality arose. But this explanation fails to explain the very thing which requires explanation. It is not the Greek belief in a future life which requires explaining—that existed from of old. It is the belief in future blessedness, in a "heaven," as distinct from the weary, dreary Hades of Homeric times, that requires to be accounted for; and the analogy of the seed-corn, the myth of Persephone's rape, could not have produced that.

Neither Persephone, then, nor Demeter had originally any connection with the belief in a happy other-world: both were goddesses long before the retribution theory made its appearance in Greece. Neither had Demeter or her daughter

Korê, the Maiden, anything originally to do with Persephone: in Homer, Demeter is a goddess, but not the mother of Persephone, and Persephone is wife of the god Hades and queen of the dead, but is not the daughter of Demeter, and was not carried off by Hades against her mother's will. Yet in the "Homeric" Hymn to Demeter, which is much later than the Iliad and Odyssey, but is certainly not later than the middle of the sixth century B.C., Persephone has become identified with Korê, and it is participation in the worship of Demeter and Persephone which confers the better lot in the next world. But it was in the sixth century B.C. that Greece was invaded by the teaching that the next life was not necessarily and for all men the shadowy, empty, weary existence which it had hitherto been supposed to be, but that there were rites of purification and sacrifices of a sacramental kind which gave man a better hope of the next world. Sanctuaries, therefore, in which archaic ritual still prevailed, were eagerly sought out; and it so happened that just at this time one sanctuary, of which the rites were peculiarly ancient and striking, was now first thrown open to the Athenians—it was the sanctuary at Eleusis. To it, then, those Athenians who were touched by the new movement repaired, being convinced that its antique and mysterious ceremonial offered the kind of worship of which they were in search, and on participation in which future blessedness was conditional. But though the strange and unfamiliar rites satisfied the emotions, the mind still required to understand how and why the worship was connected with the doctrine of happiness in the next world. The necessary explanation took, as usual, the form of a myth, *i.e.* of a hypothesis such as the facts themselves seemed to point to. This myth is contained in the Hymn to Demeter, which accordingly is the source to which we must look for information as to the Eleusinian rites in their earliest form.

The soil of Attica was as a rule poor and thin, but there was one spot of exceptional fertility—the Rarian plain, the territory of the small State of Eleusis. The wealth which the fertility of its soil gave to Eleusis enabled it to maintain its independence long after all the other village-communities in Attica had been merged in the Athenian State; it was not until the time of Solon[1] that Eleusis was brought into political union with Athens, and the goddesses of Eleusis took their place amongst the deities of the Athenian State. The long resistance to this political synoikismos and religious fusion which the Eleusinians offered was probably due to religious causes. Like other primitive agricultural communities, the Eleusinians worshipped the corn which they cultivated, both the ripe ear the Corn-Mother, and the green blade or Corn-Maiden.[2] Their cultivation of the corn was to them no mere agricultural operation, but a religious worship. Their abundant crops were due in their eyes not to their own skill in farming, or to the chemical properties of the soil, but to the favour which the Corn-Goddess showed to her true and faithful worshippers. Now that favour was earned by the minute and punctilious performance of the traditional rites and ancient worship of the goddesses; and it was not to be expected that the Eleusinians would either forsake their own goddesses, who blessed them exceedingly, for strange gods, or admit foreigners as fellow-citizens, fellow-worshippers, and partners in the blessings which the Eleusinian goddesses had the power to bestow.

The nature of the Eleusinian goddesses was obviously the same as that of cereal goddesses all over the world; and their ritual identical with that everywhere used in the worship of plant totems. Originally every ear of corn was sacred to the tribe which took corn for its totem, just as every owl was sacred to an Owl-clan. Then some one particular ear or sheaf of ripe corn was selected to represent the Corn-Spirit, and was preserved until the following year, in order that the worshippers might not be deprived during the winter of the presence and protection of their totem. The corn thus preserved served at first unintentionally as seed, and suggested the practice of sowing; and even when a larger and proper stock of seed-corn was laid in, the one particular sheaf was still regarded as the Corn-Mother, which, like the Peruvian Mother of the Maize,[3] determined by her supernatural power the kind and quantity of the following harvest. In Eleusis this sheaf was dressed up as an old woman,[4] and was pre-

[1] *Hdt.* i. 30.

[2] Cf. *supra*, p. 239, 241, 243.

[3] *Supra*, p. 212.

[4] *H. H.* v. 101: γρηΐ παλαιγενέϊ ἐναλίγκιος.

served from harvest to seed-time in the house of the headman of the village originally, and in later times in a temple. This sheaf was probably highly taboo, and not allowed to be touched or even seen[1] except on certain occasions, and then only by those who had elaborately purified themselves of their uncleanness: the whole future harvest depended on the sheaf in question, and its sanctity would naturally be great and anxiously protected. It was at the time of sowing, after the seed had been committed to the ground, and during the period of uncertainty as to whether the young plant, the Maiden or Corn-Maiden, would ever appear above ground, that the favour of the Corn-Mother was especially necessary, and that her protection was particularly invoked. The rites by which the Eleusinians on this occasion annually sought to place themselves in close communion with their goddess, were rather solemn than joyous, more in the nature of a fast than a festival. They purified their fields by fire, running over them in all directions with lighted torches for this purpose.[2] Their children they purified in the same way, passing them through the fire by night,[3] or making them jump over it, in a way which survives here and there in Europe even to the present day. The adults prepared themselves for the crowning ceremony by fasting[4] and abstaining from washing[5] for nine days. They also "renewed the bond" with their deity by offerings of their own blood, which they made to flow, not as in Polynesia by beating each other's heads with clubs, but by pelting each other with stones.[6] At the end of this trying time of preparation and preliminary purification, they were ritually "clean" and prepared for the two great and solemn acts of worship by which they were to be united to their deity and to become recipients of her favour. The first was a sacrament. As the worshippers of animal totems at their annual sacrifice consumed the flesh of their god and thus partook of his divine life, so the worshippers of the Corn-Goddess annually partook of the body of their deity, *i.e.*

[1] For the consequences of seeing things taboo, see *supra*, pp. 59, 60.

[2] *H. H.* v. 48: *στρωφᾶτ' αἰθομένας δαΐδας μετὰ χερσὶν ἔχουσα.*

[3] *Ibid.* 239: *νύκτας δὲ κρύπτεσκε πυρὸς μένει.*

[4] *Ibid.* 49.

[5] *Ibid.* 50: *οὐδὲ χρόα βάλλετο λουτροῖς.*

[6] For this practice elsewhere in Greece, see *supra*, p. 292.

of a cake or paste or posset made of the meal of wheat and water.[1] The joint participation in this by all the worshippers not only renewed the bond between them and their deity, it also once more united the fellow-worshippers in a mystic bond with one another; and for the younger members, now taking part in the ceremony for the first time, it was an initiation, *μύησις*. Thus fortified by this sacramental meal, the worshippers were considered to be properly prepared for the second great act of worship. This consisted in the presentation to the eyes of the worshippers of the actual ear or sheaf which was the Corn-Mother herself, and which might now be seen without danger, because her worshippers were no longer "unclean." This manifestation of the Corn-Goddess afforded not merely a visible hope and tangible promise that the sowing of the seed should be followed by a harvest of ripe corn, but in itself constituted a direct communion with the deity; and it was in the confidence inspired by that communion that the worshipper ventured to breathe the simple prayer for the fall of rain and the growth of the crops[2] with which the ceremony terminated.

Those were the rites on which the prosperity of Eleusis and the welfare, both spiritual and material, of its citizens depended. They were the rites which, with whatever additions, constituted the Eleusinian mysteries. Their meaning may have been obscure even to the Eleusinians of the sixth century B.C. To the town-bred Athenian of Solon's time, whom the Eleusinians had hitherto jealously and successfully excluded from any share in the worship of their powerful goddesses, the ritual now thrown open must have appeared even more mysterious, and by its gloomy and in some respects even savage character must have been unusually impressive. But though the vagueness of the rites made it easy for the Athenian to read into them a meaning which was not theirs originally; and although the rites were archaic enough to carry conviction to those who started with the belief that happiness in the next world was to be secured by the performance of mysterious rites in this; still something more definite than this, some explicit statement, was necessary. At the same time the relation of the Eleusinian goddesses

[1] *H. H.* v. 208: ἄλφι καὶ ὕδωρ.

[2] ὗε, κύε.

to the company of the Athenian deities into which they were now received, had to be defined to the popular satisfaction; and the myth which did this explained also why it was that the worship of the two goddesses conferred future bliss on the worshippers.

Whether the etymological meaning of the name Demeter is or is not "corn-mother," whether Demeter was originally a cereal goddess or a chthonic deity, it is certain that her form and functions were such as to allow of her being readily identified with the various nameless corn-goddesses who were worshipped locally in various parts of Greece, and that the cereal goddess who was probably known in Eleusis, as in various parts of Europe still, as the Old Woman, was at once identified by the Athenians with the Demeter of Homer and of their own Thesmophoria. The only point that required any explanation here was that whereas Demeter certainly dwelt with the other gods and goddesses in Olympus, the Old Woman of Eleusis equally certainly dwelt, for part of the year, in the house of the head-man of the village of Eleusis, and was actually seen there once a year by the whole body of worshippers. There was, of course, no difficulty in imagining that Demeter did actually descend from Olympus and dwell for a time in Eleusis, and that she appeared in the guise of an old woman to the Eleusinians, who accordingly did not recognise in her the goddess Demeter; *χαλεποὶ δὲ θεοὶ θνητοῖσιν ὁρᾶσθαι.*[1] But Demeter must have had some motive for thus withdrawing herself from Olympus and seeking for a home in the abodes of men, as she first did, according to Eleusinian tradition, in the house of Keleos, a mythical king of Eleusis. If she withdrew from the courts of Zeus and the company of her fellow-gods and goddesses, it obviously was because she had some cause of quarrel with them. Equally plain was it that the quarrel had some reference to her daughter the Corn-Maiden, for the time at which Demeter appeared at Eleusis in the disguise of an old woman was the time during which the young corn was below ground: when the green blade at length shot up, the old woman was no longer seen in Eleusis—she returned to Olympus. In other words, Demeter's wrath terminated

[1] *Il. H.* v. 111.

with her daughter's reappearance on the shores of light. It must then have been her daughter's disappearance which caused Demeter's wrath, and Olympian Zeus must have had some share in her daughter's disappearance or some responsibility for it.

The fact that Korê the Maiden, Demeter's daughter, spent part of her life below the earth's surface would probably in itself have been quite sufficient reason for identifying her with Persephone, the wife of Hades. But in the sixth century B.C., when the doctrine of future bliss was finding its way into Greece, and rites as strange and imposing as those of Eleusis appeared to the Athenians, were supposed to carry with them a special hope of future happiness, it was inevitable that an attempt should be made to identify one of the Eleusinian goddesses with Persephone, in whose power it was, as queen of Hades, to make or mar man's lot after death. Further, this identification was confirmed on reflection by several considerations. It accounted in a satisfactory way for the Eleusinian belief that Demeter had resided with them: if Demeter descended from Olympus, it was obviously in quest of her daughter; for, as Persephone was the wife of Hades, she must have been carried off by him to his underground abode. Again, when the ritual acts performed traditionally in any cult required explanation, it was the common form in mythology to say that they were performed by the worshippers because the deity himself had originally performed them. It was therefore self-evident that Demeter had originally fasted and abstained from washing for nine days; and as these were recognised modes of expressing mourning, they plainly indicated the grief she felt at the loss of her daughter. And since Demeter, like her worshippers, rushed wildly about in all directions, carrying torches in her hand, it must have been because she did not know what had become of her daughter, or whither she had gone—Hades must have carried off Persephone without Demeter's knowledge or consent.

Although the Athenians might concede to the Eleusinians that Demeter dwelt for a time in Eleusis in the house of Keleos, they could not admit that that was her permanent abode: she must have eventually returned to Olympus; and if so, then there must have been a reconciliation effected between her and the denizens of Olympus. But the only reconciliation possible was the restoration of her daughter. That her daughter was restored to the upper world was a fact about which the Eleusinians had no doubt, for they themselves saw and worshipped the Corn-Maiden when she reappeared from underground. At the same time it was beyond doubt that Persephone's proper home was in the house of Hades. The only inference, therefore, which could be drawn from these facts was that both were true, and that she spent part of her time with Hades and part with Demeter in Eleusis. To some Eleusinians, jealous for the honour of their local goddess, this arrangement may not have appeared a worthy compromise or a sufficiently great triumph for Demeter; but this difficulty was got over by the adaptation of an incident so common in folk-tales and so familiar, that its adequacy for the purpose could not be doubted. Persephone was ill-advised enough to partake of food—a pomegranate—in the house of Hades; and, as everyone knew, to do so was to put herself into the power of Hades for ever: joint-eating establishes, according to primitive ideas, a sacred bond between guest and host, which not only makes (as amongst the Arabs) the guest's life inviolable, but also (as in the case of mortals who partake of fairy food) makes him one of the host's clan, and, as such, subject to the customs of the clan. This was a law which even Zeus himself could not override, so Demeter felt it no ground of complaint against him that her daughter was only restored to her for part of the year; and though it had been with Zeus' connivance that Hades originally carried off the maiden, Demeter relaxed her wrath against Olympus. As long as Persephone was with Hades underground, Demeter refused her gifts to mankind, no crops grew,[1] and no sacrifices could be offered by mortals to the gods in Olympus.[2] But with the restoration, through Zeus' intervention, of Persephone to her mother, *i.e.* with the first appearance of the green blade above ground, the period of fasting, of sorrow and anxious expectation, was over, reconciliation was effected not only between Zeus and Demeter, but between man and his gods; and the goddess, revealing herself to the Eleusinians as now no longer the Old Woman but as

[1] *H. H.* v. 306. [2] *Ibid.* 312.

Demeter,[1] bade them henceforth worship her, with rites commemorative of her sufferings, and with the hope of that future bliss which her daughter had it in her power to bestow upon man after death.[2]

Thus the political union of Eleusis with Athens entailed the admission of all Athenian citizens to the worship of the Eleusinian goddesses. But the Athenians thus admitted imported their own ideas, religious and mythological, into the worship. This widening of the circle of worshippers would under any circumstances have deprived the cult of some of its local narrowness and have expanded its religious significance; for Athenians would not take part in the Eleusinian worship merely to secure the favour of these powerful goddesses to the Eleusinians: the Athenian worshipper resorted to the Eleusinian sanctuary for the blessings, spiritual or material, which he might himself derive thence. It was, however, no part of the original design of the Eleusinian cult to bring blessings on the Athenians, but simply to secure fertility to the Rarian plain. The inclusion, therefore, of Athenians in the Eleusinian circle of worshippers necessarily involved the expansion of the cult from a purely local and agricultural worship into an element of national religion. This development was effected not by any change in the ritual—to alter that would have been to forfeit the favour of the two goddesses—but in the feelings and beliefs with which the new worshippers performed the rites. And this change in feeling and belief found its expression in the Homeric Hymn to Demeter, which is evidently composed in the attempt to pour new wine into the old bottles, and to show that the new Athenian doctrine as to the real personality of the Corn-Mother and Maiden, so far from being at variance with the Eleusinian tradition, is presupposed by it and gives it a far higher religious significance.

But though the Eleusinian cult in becoming Athenian would have become broader, it would not have attained the

[1] *H. H.* v. 268:

εἰμὶ δὲ Δημήτηρ τιμάοχος, ἥτε μέγιστον
ἀθανάτοις θνητοῖσι τ' ὄναρ καὶ χάρμα τέτυκται.

[2] For an analysis of the Homeric Hymn to Demeter, see Appendix, p. 377 below.

religious importance it did attain, had not the opening of the Eleusinian sanctuary to the Athenians just coincided with the first marked stirrings of the new movement in religion which spread from the Semitic area to Greece in the sixth century B.C. And though the association of the Eleusinian ritual with the doctrine of future happiness gave it the potency of great importance, the Eleusinian cult would never have exercised any influence on Greek thought and Greek religion, if admission to it had been confined, as it was at first, strictly to Attic citizens. It is to this, therefore, the next point in the history of the Eleusinian mysteries, that we must next turn.

The new movement of the sixth century spread first in the form of a belief in the possibility of closer communion with the gods than was afforded by the gift theory of sacrifice. There was a revival of the sacramental view of sacrifice and a reversion to a more primitive form of ritual. The immediate consequence was that those sanctuaries of the national gods which, like the Eleusinian, had for some reason or other adhered faithfully to an archaic form of ritual, became thronged with worshippers who had come under the influence of the new movement. These, however, were but the first ripples of the wave from the East which was speedily to invade Greece: wandering *agyrtæ* introduced the rites and the worship of foreign gods; religious organisations, *thiasi*, were formed by the *agyrtæ* and sanctioned by the legislation of Solon, for the worship of Iacchus, Zagreus, Sabazios, Cybele, and other deities unknown before in Greece. The spread of these new cults was facilitated first by their resemblance to that of Dionysus, and next by the Orphic mythology which sought to prove the identity of Iacchus, Sabazios, or Zagreus with Dionysus. The attitude of the tyrant Pisistratus towards the new movement was one of favour and protection. It was at his court and with his countenance that Onomacritus organised the Orphic literature which was to prove that these foreign gods were not foreign but the originals of the god known to the Greeks as Dionysus. It was by Pisistratus that tragedy, part of the ritual of Dionysus, was welcomed from the country into the town. And it was by Pisistratus that the cult of Iacchus was incorporated into the Eleusinian rites.

The consequence of this incorporation was an expansion of the cult of the Eleusinian goddesses even greater than that which followed on the union of Eleusis with Athens. The ritual was enlarged: the image of Iacchus was conveyed in procession by his worshippers from his temple in Athens, along the Sacred Way, to Eleusis, and there placed in the Eleusinion by the side of the two goddesses. This was an expression in outward act of the union of the two cults, and constituted an addition to the Eleusinia, but not a modification of them. But the introduction of Iacchus did also modify the Eleusinia: Iacchus was identified with Dionysus, and the dramatic performances which were part of the worship of Dionysus now became part of the ritual of Eleusis. The original, primitive agricultural rites were not dropped: the sacrament of the *κυκεών* was still administered, and the ear of corn was still exhibited. Indeed, these were always the most sacred part of the whole ritual. But to this ritual other things were added. It was the promise of future bliss which drew worshippers to Eleusis; and this promise had no original or intimate connection with the primitive agricultural rites of Eleusis. But it was connected with the myth which, owing to Athenian influence, had entirely transformed the meaning and purport of the rites. It was therefore naturally the myth which was emphasised; and the requisite emphasis was given when the introduction of Iacchus enabled the principle of dramatic representation to be transferred from the worship of Dionysus to that of Demeter and Persephone. The sacred drama performed at Eleusis consisted mainly, probably entirely, of choral odes and dances, as was the case with tragedy itself in its earlier stages of development and at the time when the Dionysiac element was first introduced into the Eleusinia. The excavations on the site of Eleusis have shown "that at Eleusis there was no provision for the production of strange stage-effects. Never at any time was there in the shallow stage of a Greek theatre any room for those elaborate effects in which modern stage-managers delight. All was simplicity and convention. But at Eleusis there was not even a stage. The people sat tier above tier all round the building, and whatever went on had to go on in their midst. If they were dazzled by strange sights, these strange sights must have been very simply contrived. If they saw gods descending from the sky or rising from the ground, they must have been willing to spread round the very primitive machinery, by which such ascents and descents would be accomplished, an imaginative halo of their own."[1]

Whether the infant Iacchus played any part in the Eleusinian drama is matter for conjecture. The birth, *Γοναί*, of various deities appears as the title of various lost comedies; and, according to the Orphic theology, Iacchus was the child of Persephone. It may be, therefore, that the birth of Iacchus formed the subject of some of the choral odes and dances. Persephone was made in Orphic mythology to be the mother of Iacchus, chiefly because thus the reception of the foreign god was facilitated. That the cult of Iacchus had gained a footing in Athens before it was incorporated with the Eleusinia, is shown by the fact that there was a temple of Iacchus, an Iaccheion, in Athens, in which the image of Iacchus was kept always, except for the few days when it was taken to Eleusis to take part in the Eleusinia. That the cult of Iacchus was introduced into Athens by private individuals, as a private worship, and was carried on by means of one of the ordinary private religious associations, or *thiasi*, may be considered as certain on the analogy of all the other Eastern cults, which without exception were introduced in this way. But this *thiasus* of Iacchus, like all other *thiasi*, would be open to all who chose to become members of it, and probably large numbers did choose to join it. When, therefore, Pisistratus ordained that the circle of the Eleusinian deities should be enlarged by the addition of Iacchus to their number, and that the statue of Iacchus should accordingly be carried in solemn procession by its worshippers from Athens to Eleusis, and there by them be placed by the side of the two goddesses, he not only enlarged the number of the Eleusinian deities, he also enlarged the circle of their worshippers. Indeed, the object of Pisistratus may have been to draw to Eleusis worshippers who might otherwise have preferred to place their hope of future blessedness in the worship of Dionysus. If his object was to increase the number of worshippers at

[1] Gardner and Jevons, *Greek Antiquities*, 283.

the sanctuary of Eleusis, he succeeded beyond his expectation. Since this *thiasus*, like all other *thiasi*, was open to all who chose to become members of it, whether native Athenians or foreigners; and since all members of this *thiasus* were qualified to follow the procession of Iacchus, and present themselves at Eleusis, a foreigner who wished to see the Eleusinian rites had only first to join the *thiasus* of Iacchus. Thus the rites of Eleusis now for the first time came to be "mysteries" in the proper sense of the word, that is to say, they became rites which were open to all who chose to be initiated, to become *mystæ*—they were no longer a local cult, admission to which was confined as a birthright to citizens, they were potentially catholic; and initiation, *μύησις*, not *civitas*, was the qualification for membership. Initiation into the worship of Iacchus took place at the lesser mysteries,[1] and eventually was required of all who wished to be admitted to the greater mysteries at Eleusis; but a memory of the time when the lesser mysteries of Iacchus were peculiarly the portal by which foreigners obtained admission to the Eleusinia, still survives in the myth that the lesser mysteries were invented for the benefit of Heracles, who wished to be admitted to the Eleusinian rites, but could not be initiated because he was a foreigner; therefore the lesser mysteries were invented and thrown open to all foreigners[2] (Greeks, not barbarians).

The popularity of Iacchus and of the Eleusinian mysteries was enormously increased in B.C. 480 — half a century after the expulsion of the Pisistratidæ—by the fact that the great and glorious victory over the Persians at Salamis was won on the very day appointed for the procession of Iacchus from Athens to Eleusis; and when Athens, in consequence of her self-sacrifice and devotion in the Persian wars, became the leading state in Greece, the mysteries of Eleusis grew yet more famous, and became the chief agent in the conversion of the Greek world from the Homeric view of Hades to a more hopeful belief as to man's state after death. We have therefore now to trace the several stages through which the belief passed.

[1] Steph. Byz. s.v. Ἄγρα, Nonn. *Dion.* xxvi. 307.

[2] Schol. ad Aristoph. *Plut.* 1014.

In the Homeric Hymn to Demeter, which presents us with the belief as it existed before the intrusion of Iacchus and of Orphic doctrines into the Eleusinia, both punishments and rewards await men after death; but it is not for their morally good or bad deeds that men are rewarded and punished respectively. The doctrine is not ethical, but ritual: the man who offers to Demeter and Persephone the worship which is grateful to them is rewarded with prosperity in this world[1] and happiness in the next;[2] the man who slights the goddesses in this world, and neglects the opportunity of salvation offered by the Eleusinian rites, is punished in Hades by the offended Persephone for the indignity put upon her.[3] The punishment is purely retributive, not reformatory; and there is no attempt to describe the nature of the happy life—the man who has partaken of the sacrament of the *κυκεών* and who has enjoyed the communion conferred by the sight of the mysteries is "blessed," ὄλβιος, that is all.

It is not likely that the incorporation of the cult of Iacchus into the Eleusinia would be effected without ultimately modifying the original belief as presented in the Homeric Hymn; and one such modification can be traced with some certainty. The Orphic mysteries, which laid weight on ceremonial purification, especially cleansing by mud, as a preparation without which no one could partake of the sacramental sacrifice and the blessings which it ensured, taught that if a man failed to purify himself thus in this world he would have to be purified hereafter; and hence they represented the wicked as being plunged into mud in the next world,[4] while the good enjoyed "everlasting"[5] happiness. Thus the idea that the life after death must be eternal, which had not occurred to the writer of the Homeric Hymn, had now become established, in Orphic literature at least; and the rewards had become eternal, but the punishment purgatorial. And that this view eventually was adopted by the worshippers at Eleusis, is shown by Aristophanes' parody, in which[6] evil-doers are represented as buried in mud.

[1] *H. H.* v. 488. [2] *Ibid.* 480. [3] *Ibid.* 365–9.

[4] ἀδίκους ἐς πηλόν τινα κατορύττουσιν ἐν Αἵδου, Plato, *Rep.* 363 C.

[5] αἰώνιος, *ibid.*

[6] Ar. *Frogs*, 145 ff. and 273 ff.

Both in the passage from Aristophanes and in the passage from Plato referred to in the last paragraph, the wicked who are punished are offenders against morality; and here we may probably see the influence of Pythagoreanism on the original Orphic doctrine. Pythagoras borrowed from Egypt the idea of a day of judgment after death, on which the future fate of man would be decided, according to the good or evil he had done; and it is clear from the Pythagorean tablets that it was Persephone who, according to the Pythagoreans, sat in judgment on the souls of the departed, and dismissed them to bliss or woe. Hence, when Pythagoreanism blended with the Orphic theology, the theory of ethical retribution would easily be imported into Orphic literature; and it is not to be supposed that the Eleusinian mysteries would remain at a lower moral level than the Orphic, or reject a conception which so readily commends itself to the conscience of man.

Thus by the beginning of the Christian era the mysteries had permeated the Greek world with several ideas of great importance for the subsequent development of religion. They were, first, the doctrine of future punishments and rewards; next, that happiness hereafter is conditional on communion with some deity in this life; third, that such communion, with its hope of future bliss, was freely open to all (Greeks and Romans), whether men or women, bond or free, who chose to avail themselves of the grace thus offered by the mysteries; and finally, the conception of a religious community the bounds of which were not limited by those of any political community, and the members of which were knit together not by the tie of blood or a common citizenship, but by the bond of spiritual fellowship and the participation in a common religious worship.

Owing to the influence of the Neo-Platonic philosophy, it is possible that philosophical pantheism may have come to be read into the mysteries by both worshippers and officials, but there is no reason to believe that the mysteries at any time taught monotheism.

APPENDIX TO CHAPTER XXIV

ANALYSIS OF THE HYMN TO DEMETER

1–21. THE daughter of Demeter is carried off by Aidoneus, with the permission of Zeus, but without the knowledge of her mother. She was gathering flowers on the Nysian plain, and had stretched out her hands to pluck a marvellously beautiful narcissus, when the earth yawned, Hades appeared, and carried her off shrieking in his chariot to his underground abode.

The name Persephone is carefully avoided by the poet, until line 56, because by the phrase "daughter of Demeter" Eleusinians would naturally understand Korê to be meant, whereas if the name Persephone had been used they might not have realised that it was Korê who was being spoken of. So, too, the Athenian auditor, not yet accustomed to the idea that Persephone was the daughter of Demeter, only finds out incidentally in 56, when it is, so to speak, too late to protest (for his sympathies are by that time enlisted) that the daughter of Demeter is Persephone. The permission of Zeus is put in the forefront of the story, in line 3, because otherwise there would be no reason why Demeter should be angry with Zeus, and then it would be impossible to account for Demeter's forsaking Olympus and residing in Eleusis, which is one of the most important facts that the poet had to provide an explanation for.

22–87. Demeter hears the cries of her daughter as she is carried off, and rushes to seek her, but can find no trace. For nine days she seeks her everywhere, carrying torches in her hand, abstaining from eating, drinking, and washing, in her grief. On the tenth day Hecate tells her that she heard Persephone's voice, but knows not who carried her off; and Demeter and Hecate together go to Helios, who informs them that Hades, with Zeus' consent, had carried off Demeter's daughter.

It was necessary that Demeter should not at first know what had become of her daughter, because the torch-rite showed that the goddess had wandered about (else her worshippers would not have done so); and she would not have wandered, if she had known where to look for her daughter. At the same time it was necessary that she should discover Zeus' complicity, else there would be no motive for that residence of the Corn-Goddess in Eleusis which was an article of firm faith with the Eleusinians. All-seeing Helios therefore is naturally introduced into the story; but Hecate is so useless for the action of the story that we may conjecture she was introduced for purely ritual reasons.

88–183. Wrathful with Zeus, Demeter forsook Olympus and descended to earth, in disguise; and no mortal who saw her knew that she was Demeter.[1] At length she drew near to the house of Keleos, who was then lord of Eleusis; and took her seat, in the guise of an old woman, by the Parthenian Well. There the four daughters of Keleos came to draw water, saw the Old Woman, and inquired her story. She had been carried off from her Cretan home by pirates, but had escaped from them, and would be grateful to find employment such as might befit a woman of her age, *e.g.* as nurse. They declared that any of the citizens (some of whose names are mentioned, *honoris causâ*) would welcome her, but especially their own father and their mother, who had a young son to nurse. After consultation with their parents, they conduct her to the house of Keleos.

Throughout this section, for a hundred lines, the poet carefully avoids all mention of the name Demeter. The reason is that the Eleusinians originally only knew the cereal goddess as the Old Woman; and there would be an obvious impropriety of feeling in the poet's thrusting his new doctrine

[1] Line 94 : οὐδέ τις ἀνδρῶν
εἰσορόων γίνωσκε βαθυζώνων τε γυναικῶν.

in just here, for he would naturally wish, in describing what happened at Eleusis, to adhere as closely as possible to the Eleusinian point of view. Further, the object of the poet was not to deny that the goddess dwelt as the Old Woman in the house of the head-man, but to account for the fact; nor did he wish to deny that the Eleusinians were ignorant of the identity of the Old Woman with Demeter—he only wished to show that their ignorance was natural, excusable, indeed the doing of the goddess herself, and does not afford any presumption that the Old Woman was not Demeter. The prominent part which the women, the wife and daughters of Keleos, play, and the fact that it is they who first meet the Corn-Goddess and introduce her to Eleusis, points to a tradition that it was the women of Eleusis who first cultivated corn,[1] and, like the women of Athens in the Thesmophoria, worshipped the Corn-Goddess by themselves.

184–300. Demeter entered the house of Keleos and sat down in silence and sorrow, and smiled not, and neither ate nor drank, in her grief for her daughter, until Iambe by her drollery brought a smile to her lips. Then Metaneira, the wife of Keleos, offered her wine, but she declined it, saying it was forbidden her; but she bade meal and water be mixed and offered her. Then she nursed the young son, Demophoön, and at night would pass the child through fire, to make him immortal, but her beneficent design was frustrated by Metaneira, who once saw her, and exclaimed that she was killing her son. In her anger Demeter revealed who she was, pronounced that Demophoön, though he could not now become deathless, should become famous, and that in his day the Eleusinians should ever shed each other's blood.[2] Then, having bidden that a shrine and altar be erected to her, she departed. All night long the women did worship to the goddess, and on the morrow the men began building the temple.

Demeter refuses to drink wine,[3] because wine, the sur-

[1] *Supra*, p. 239–242.

[2] 266: παῖδες Ἐλευσινίων πόλεμον καὶ φύλοπιν αἰνὴν
αἰὲν ἀλλήλοισι συνάξουσ' ἤματα πάντα.

[3] 207: οὐ γὰρ θεμιτόν οἱ ἔφασκε
πίνειν οἶνον ἐρυθρόν.

rogate of blood, was excluded from the non-animal sacrifice offered to cereal deities. The incident of Demophoön is invented to account for the common practice of passing children over a fire for purification and to make them thrive. The erection of the temple marks the transition of the cult of the Corn-Goddess from the hands of the women into those of the men. The shedding of Eleusinian blood by Eleusinians is introduced so awkwardly and gratuitously that its mention must be due to ritual reasons—to the necessity of accounting for this particular way of offering the worshipper's blood to the deity, *i.e.* by stoning each other (the *βαλλήτυς*).

301 *ad fin.* Demeter, in her resentment against Zeus, caused a famine, no crops grew, and no sacrifices could be offered to the gods. Nor did she relax her wrath, but sat apart from the other gods in her temple at Eleusis, until Zeus sent Hermes to bid Hades allow Persephone to be seen of her mother. Hades consented, but first set forth to Persephone the honour she gained by being his wife, and the authority she exercised over the dead to punish those who in their lifetime had neglected to do her worship. She was then restored to her mother at Eleusis; but, having been beguiled by Hades to eat, though only a pomegranate, she was still so far in his power that she would have to spend one-third of each year with him. Demeter then being reconciled with Zeus, allowed the crops once more to grow, and showed to Triptolemos, Diocles, Eumolpos, and Keleos the ritual with which they were henceforth to worship her. Then the two goddesses returned to Olympus; and blessed is the man who has seen what is to be seen in their sacred rites: wealth is his in this life and happiness in the next. Greatly blessed is the mortal whom they accept.

In the fully developed form of the Eleusinian mysteries, the last thing revealed and the highest revelation made to the worshipper was something which was visibly exhibited by the hierophant to the eyes of the worshipper. This revelation was the crown and consummation of the rites; and it was to this part of the mysteries that the taboo of silence pre-eminently applied. Herein the later mysteries did but faithfully adhere to the primitive agricultual ritual of Eleusis, for in the Homeric Hymn the same taboo of silence is solemnly imposed as to the sights revealed to the worshipper,[1] and it is the communion thus afforded rather than the sacramental *κυκεών* which is the crowning point of the ritual. When, then, we find that in later times an ear of corn was exhibited,[2] we may fairly infer that it was an ear of corn which was exhibited in the primitive agricultural rites, and that it was originally the embodiment of the Corn-Goddess.

[1] 477: *τά τ' οὔπως ἐστὶ παρεξέμεν οὔτε πυθέσθαι*
οὔτ' ἀχέειν· μέγα γάρ τι θεῶν ἅγος ἰσχάνει αὐδήν.
ὄλβιος, ὃς τάδ' ὄπωπεν ἐπιχθονίων ἀνθρώπων.

[2] *Philosophumena*, viii. 115, ed. Miller.

CHAPTER XXV

MONOTHEISM

If we accept the principle of evolution as applied to religion—and the many different forms of religion seem to be best accounted for by the theory of evolution—it seems to follow that monotheism was developed out of polytheism. The process of evolution is from the simple and homogeneous to the more complex and highly organised, from lower forms of life to the higher. The implements, the language, the science, the art, the social and political institutions of civilised man, have all been slowly evolved out of much simpler and more savage forms: our language has been traced back to the common speech out of which all Aryan tongues have been evolved; our institutions to the tribal customs of the wandering Teutons; we can see and handle the bronze and flint implements actually used by our own forefathers. Whether, therefore, we treat religion as an institution, and apply to it the same comparative method as to legal and political institutions; or examine it as belief, in the same way as we trace the slow growth of scientific conceptions of the universe; the presumption is that, here as everywhere else, the higher forms have been evolved out of lower forms, and that monotheism has been developed out of a previous polytheism. Religion is an organism which runs through its various stages, animism, totemism, polytheism, monotheism. The law of continuity links together the highest, lowest, and intermediate forms. The form of the religious idea is ever slowly changing, the content remains the same always.

The presumption thus raised by the general process of evolution, that monotheism is developed out of polytheism, is greatly strengthened by a survey of the general course of religion. Wherever we can trace its course, we find that every people which has risen above the most rudimentary stages has become polytheistic. This statement holds true of peoples in all quarters of the globe, in all stages of culture, in all ages of time. Since, then, all the peoples whose development is matter of direct observation have been polytheists, and since in the vast majority of cases we can directly observe the facts, the presumption, when we come to a people whose annals do not record a period of polytheism, is that the annals are, for whatever reason, faulty—not that the people is an exception to general law. The essence of the argument from induction is that it is an inference from cases which we can observe to others which are beyond our power of direct observation. Now there is only one people in this exceptional case—the Jewish people.

But we are not confined to mere presumptions—whether drawn from the general process of evolution or from the course of religious development in particular—to show that monotheism was developed out of polytheism. We have more direct evidence, of two kinds. First, in polytheism we can see forces at work which in more than one recorded case have brought it to the verge of monotheism. Next, in the Jewish monotheism we can trace apparent survivals of a previous polytheism.

The first step towards monotheism is taken when one deity is, as not unusually happens, conceived to be supreme over all the others, and the rest are but his vassals, his ministers or angels. This is due to the transference of the relations which obtain in human society to the community of the gods: they, like men, are supposed to have a king over them. The next step is the result of the constant tendency of the ancients to identify one god with another: Herodotus had no difficulty in recognising the gods of Greece under the names which the Egyptians gave to their own deities; Cæsar and Tacitus did not hesitate to identify the gods of Gaul and Germany with those of Rome. And this was the more easy and reasonable, because in many cases the gods in question were really the deification of some one and the same natural phenomenon—sun, moon, etc. But the most powerful impulse to the movement was given by metaphysical speculation: all real things are equally real, the reality of all is identical, there is only one reality—God. From this it followed that the various gods, believed by the vulgar to be different beings, were but different aspects or manifestation of one deity, in whom and in whose personality all met and were merged. As *The Book of the Dead*[1] puts it: "Osiris came to Mendes; there he met the soul of Ra; they embraced and became as one soul in two souls." The various forms in which the one real existence manifests himself are his own creation, whether they be material, human, or divine. Thus he, according to an expression of the Egyptian theologians, perpetually "creates his own members, which are the gods,"[2] or says, "I am the maker of heaven and of the earth. . . . It is I who have given to all the gods the soul which is within them. . . . I am Chepera in the morning, Ra at noon, Tmu in the evening."[3] But though maker of the earth, the one reality is "a spirit more spiritual than the gods; the holy soul which clothes itself with forms, but itself remains unknown."[4]

But while, on the one hand, we thus see polytheism approaching monotheism, on the other, we find among the monotheistic Jews survivals from a time when they apparently, like other Semites, were polytheists. The constant relapses of the mass of the people into idolatrous worship, as revealed by the denunciations in Scripture against such backsliding, seem to indicate a slow upward movement from polytheism, which was not yet complete, and so far as it was successful was due to the lifting power of a few great minds, striving to carry a reluctant people with them to the higher ground of monotheism. More conclusive, however, is the evidence afforded by the religious institutions of the Jews and by the ritual of Jehovah. Every god has some animal or other which and which alone it is proper to sacrifice to him. This close connection between a sacred animal and the god to whom it is sacred and is sacrificed points, as we have seen, to the ultimate identity of the god and the animal, and

[1] Ch. xvii., lines 42, 43. [2] D'Alviella, *Hibbert Lecture*, 214.
[3] Le Page Renouf, *Hibbert Lecture*, 221, 222.
[4] D'Alviella, *loc. cit.*, quoting Maspero, *Peuples de l'Orient*,[4] 279.

to an original totemism. From the nature of the sacrifice, therefore, *e.g.* whether animal or vegetable, we can infer something as to the origin of the god, whether he is descended from a plant or an animal totem. Further, if several kinds of animal are sacrificed, *e.g.* to Apollo, we can infer something as to the history of the god, namely, that under the one name, Apollo, several different gods have somehow come to be worshipped. When, then, we find that not only were animals sacrificed to Jehovah, but at the agricultural feast of Unleavened Bread a sheaf of corn played a prominent part, as in the agricultural rites at Eleusis; when we find that the Levitical law prescribed that oxen, sheep, goats, bread and wine should be offered at the sanctuary, the inference plainly seems to be that at the one altar a plurality of deities were worshipped, and the plural name "Elohim" used of the one God seems to add the evidence of language to that afforded by the comparative study of institutions.

Finally, the same causes which were at work elsewhere to evolve monotheism out of polytheism were in existence amongst the Jews. There was the same tendency to identify one god with another; and this tendency was considerably reinforced by the Semitic habit of applying general terms expressing lordship, *e.g.* Baal, to their gods; so that the difficulty would rather be to distinguish one Baal from another than to believe them the same god. Among the Jews, too, there would be the same tendency to project human relations on to things divine, to conceive the divine personality by what was known of the human, to imagine the community of the gods as reflecting the social relations of men. Hence the growth of the monarchy in the Jewish state would naturally be reflected by the development of the idea of one God, Lord and King of all. "In Greece and Rome the kingship fell before the aristocracy; in Asia the kingship held its own, till in the larger states it developed into despotism, or in the smaller ones it was crushed by a foreign despotism. This diversity of political fortune is reflected in the diversity of religious development. . . . The tendency of the West, where the kingship succumbed, was towards a divine aristocracy of many gods, only modified by a weak reminiscence of the old kingship in the not very effective sovereignty of Zeus; while in the East the national god tended to acquire a really monarchic sway. What is often described as the natural tendency of Semitic religion towards ethical monotheism, is in the main nothing more than a consequence of the alliance of religion with monarchy." [1]

Thus the hypothesis that monotheism was evolved out of polytheism has much to be said in its favour. There is the presumption afforded by the nature of evolution in general, and by the development of religion in particular; there is the improbability that the one doubtful case of the Jews should be an exception to a general law; there are the apparent survivals even in Jewish monotheism of a previous polytheism; there is the constant tendency of polytheisms to pass into monotheism, and the evidence for the existence of that tendency amongst the Jews themselves. But before we can accept the hypothesis, we must hear what, if anything, can be said against it.

We may, to begin with, admit that religion may advance from lower stages to higher; that Christianity is a higher form of religion than Judaism; that within the limits of the Old Testament itself a "progressive revelation" may be traced; and that, following the same line back, we may by the scientific use of the imagination conjecture in the unrecorded past a form of monotheism more rudimentary than any otherwise known to science. We may further admit the principle of evolution as applied to religion, but then we shall find that the argument from analogy tells rather against than for the hypothesis that monotheism is evolved from polytheism. If we are to treat religion as an organism and as subject to the same laws as govern the evolution of organisms, we must decline to take the two highest existing species and say that either is descended from the other; for that would be to repeat the vulgar error of imagining that men are supposed to be descended from apes. Indeed, if we base ourselves on evolutionary principles, we may safely say that, whatever be the genesis and history of monotheism, one thing is certain, namely, that it cannot have been developed

[1] Robertson Smith, *Religion of the Semites*, 74.

out of polytheism. Both species may be descended from a common ancestor, but not one from the other. Further, the original form out of which the two later varieties were developed must have so developed by a series of intermediate forms. We should therefore expect, if we could trace monotheism back through these intermediate forms, to find some of them of such a kind that it would be difficult to say whether, strictly speaking, they were forms of monotheism or not, though they clearly were not forms of polytheism. Thus the essence of monotheism is that in it the worshipper worships only one god. What then shall we say of the worshipper who worships one god alone, but believes that the gods worshipped by other tribes exist, and are really gods, though his own attitude towards them is one of hostility? It is obvious that his is a lower form of faith than that of the man who worships only one god, and believes that, as for the gods of the heathen, they are but idols. Yet though his is not the highest form of monotheism, to call it polytheism would be an abuse of language. But if several tribes, each holding this rudimentary form of monotheism, coalesced into one political whole, and combined their gods into a pantheon, each tribe worshipping the others' gods as well as its own, we should have polytheism; while another tribe, of the same stock, might remain faithful to its god and develop the higher forms of monotheism. Thus polytheism and monotheism would both be evolved out of one and the same rudimentary form and common ancestor.

It may be said that to argue thus is to derive polytheism from monotheism, which is just as erroneous as to derive monotheism from polytheism, or to argue that apes are descended from men. It becomes necessary, therefore, to insist on the plain fact that religion is not an organism: religion is not an animal, or a plant, that it must obey identically the same laws of growth and evolution. It may be that there are resemblances between religion as an organisation and an animal organism. It is certain that there are great differences. It may well be that the resemblances are sufficient to create an analogy between the two cases; but the differences make it inevitable that at some point or other the analogy should break down; and what that point is, where the line is to be drawn, is a question which cannot be settled *à priori* or by a consideration merely of the laws of animal life, but only by careful study of the facts and history of religion itself. We can say with certainty that a seed, if it is to become a full-grown tree, must pass through certain intermediate stages; that a butterfly must once have been a chrysalis. But we cannot, on the strength of these analogies from organic life, say that religion to reach monotheism must pass through a stage of polytheism; or that, if it grows at all, it must in all cases, however different they may be, run through the same successive forms.

We can infer with certainty on seeing an oak that it sprang from an acorn, because of the innumerable instances known in which acorns do develop into oaks. In the same way, if there were many instances known of the way in which monotheism grows up, we might infer with tolerable confidence that one particular instance, the history of which did not happen to be recorded, obeyed the same laws of growth as all the others. Even if monotheism sprang up in two independent peoples, and its history was fully known in one case and very imperfectly known in the other, we should naturally and reasonably employ our knowledge of the one to fill up the gaps in our knowledge of the other. But, as a matter of fact, not even this is the case. On the contrary, the monotheism of the Jews is a unique and solitary phenomenon in the history of religion. Nowhere else in the world has the development of religion culminated in monotheism. The reasonable inference from this patent and fundamental fact is, that nowhere else can religion have developed along the same lines as amongst the Jews. The very fact that all other nations have travelled along a line leading to polytheism, and that all have failed to get beyond it, constitutes a presumption that monotheism is not to be reached by the route that leads to polytheism. If it is possible to reach monotheism *via* polytheism, it is at least a remarkable fact that of all the peoples of the world no single one is known to have done so. It can hardly be alleged that it is by external, accidental circumstances that the consummation has been prevented. Had some one, some few peoples, only failed, their failure might be imputed to some accident due to their peculiar circumstances. But when the same experiment has been tried under the most diverse conditions of culture, clime, and time; when the circumstances have been varied to the utmost; when the seed has been sown in soils the most different and been developed under climatic conditions the most diverse, and yet has always refused to produce monotheism, or anything but polytheism; the inference seems to be that the refusal is due not to the circumstances being unfavourable, but to the seeds being of the wrong kind.

We can, however, go further than this, if we allow ourselves to be guided by the actual facts of religious history and not by the uncertain analogy drawn from the life-history of plant and animal organisms. What the actual polytheisms known to science pass into is either fetishism, as is the case with most African tribes,[1] or pantheism, as in Egypt; never monotheism. The tendencies which have been supposed in polytheism to make for monotheism have always been purely pantheistic—speculative rather than practical, metaphysical rather than religious; and, as being metaphysical speculations, have always been confined to the cultured few, and have never even leavened the polytheism of the masses. A god supreme over all the other members of the pantheon is very different from the one and only God of even the lowest form of monotheism; and the fact that Zeus lords it over the other gods, as a human king over his subjects, is no evidence or sign of any monotheistic tendency: it proceeds from no inner consciousness that the object of man's worship is one and indivisible, one and the same God always. It is scarcely a religious idea at all: it is not drawn from the spiritual depths of man's nature, it is a conception borrowed from politics, for the purpose not of unifying the multiplicity of gods, but of putting their multiplicity on an intelligible and permanent basis. On the other hand, the idea of a world-soul, a one reality of which all things animate or inanimate, human and divine, are the manifestations, does indeed reduce the multiplicity of the gods, amongst other things, to unity; but it is a metaphysical speculation, not a

[1] See for this, Chapter XIII. *supra*, "Fetishism."

fact of which the religious consciousness has direct intuition; and hence it is never, like a purely religious movement, propagated through the mass of average, unphilosophical mankind. They are not to be touched by complicated arguments; and the philosopher is not consumed by that zeal of the Lord which enables the religious reformer to fire his fellow-men. The prophets of Israel denounced the worship of false gods. The philosophers of Egypt found accommodation for them as manifestations of the one real existence. The belief that the one reality is equally real in all its forms, and that all its forms are equally unreal, is not a creed which leads to the breaking of idols, the destruction of groves and high places, or the denunciation of all worship save at the altar of the Lord. Pantheism is the philosophical complement of a pantheon; but the spirit which produced the monotheism of the Jews must have been something very different. Nor is it easy to see why among the Jews alone monarchy should have yielded monotheism. If monarchy, like monotheism, had been an institution peculiar to the Jews, there might be something in the argument. But monarchy has flourished amongst most peoples, much more successfully than among the Jews, and nowhere has it had monotheism for its concomitant. Even "the supposed monotheistic tendency of the Semitic as opposed to the Hellenic or Aryan system of religion," which "is in the main nothing more than a consequence of the alliance of religion with monarchy, . . . cannot in its natural development fairly be said to have come near to monotheism."[1] Amongst the Jews, alone of the Semites, did it follow a line other than that of "its natural development."

With syncretism—the practice of not merely identifying different gods, but of fusing their cults into one ritual—the case is somewhat different. On the one hand, it is probable that several gods have gone to the making up of, say, the one god Apollo, in whose worship the rites of all are united. On the other, it is certain that for the Greek of any recorded period the personality of Apollo was as individual as his own. But even if we were to admit that the ritual of Jehovah is to be accounted for in this way, we should be no

[1] Robertson Smith, *op. cit.* 74 and 75.

nearer to the desired conclusion that polytheism passes into monotheism; for, though syncretism on this theory terminates in monotheism, it does not start in polytheism. On the contrary, the analysis of the ritual even of polytheistic gods leads us back simply to inchoate monotheism. The earliest form of society, the clan, is not only a social community, it is also a religious society: fellow-tribesman and fellow-worshipper are convertible terms, because the members of the clan are united to one another, not only by the bond of kinship, but also by joint communion in the sacramental sacrifice of the totem-god. Hence changes in the social or political structure may react upon the cult of the community, and *vice versâ*. Thus, if two or more clans amalgamate, for any reason, their cults also will be amalgamated, for the ratification, or rather the very constitution of the political union, consists in the joint worship of the confederating clans at the same altar. When a tribe of the Fantis joins the confederation of the Ashantis, it does so by renouncing the worship of the Fanti god and joining that of the Ashanti confederation. Now, if the gods of the amalgamating clans have each a strongly marked individuality and a firm hold upon their worshippers, the result will be that each clan will worship the gods of the other clans—or the god of the clan which leads in the confederacy—without renouncing its own totem-god; and so the tribe which before amalgamation had but its own one god will after the amalgamation worship two or more gods. In this case, polytheism is the consequence of *synoikismos*, of political growth. But polytheism is not the consequence in all cases: syncretism is at first the more common consequence, because it is only by a slow process of development that gods acquire an individuality sufficiently well marked, and characteristics sufficiently specific, to prevent their being confused with other gods having a similar origin and the same ritual as themselves. At first the clan-god has not even a name of his own: he requires none, for the clan has no other god from whom he needs to be distinguished. For long, a general name or epithet suffices for all his needs. It is very late that he acquires a personal name, absolutely peculiar to himself. When, then, two or more clans, whose ideas of their gods are in this fluid state, amalgamate, it is almost inevitable that their gods should be unified: what is essential to their political union is that each should partake of the other's sacrifice and so become of one blood and one worship with each other; each therefore brings to a common altar its own animal-totem, each in turn dashes the blood of sacrifice on the same altar-stone, and each partakes of the other's victim. Thus the god of each passes into or manifests himself at the same altar and on the occasion of the same complex act of worship, and the identity of the altar and the unity of the ritual so add to the difficulty of mentally separating two nameless gods who have now nothing to distinguish them, that the very memory of their difference soon dies away. Even more rapid and complete is this process of syncretism, if one of the two gods has a personal name and the other has not; for the one with a name survives in the minds of men, and inherits altar and worship and all, whereas the nameless god is forgotten outright. In this way a god, whose worshippers were so vividly impressed with his personality as to appropriate to him a proper name, might, as his worshippers absorbed one tribe after another into their confederacy, come to inherit several different rituals: the various tribes might come to worship at his altar with their own rites and their own victims, but it would be at his altar and in his name. Thus, even if we admit that the complex sacrificial rites of the Levitical law are an instance of syncretism, inevitably consequent on the political process by which the Jews were formed into one state; still we are not thereby taken back from monotheism to previous polytheism, and we do gain an explanation not only of the ritual, but also of the backsliding which has been supposed to be a survival of polytheism; for some tribes doubtless would be reluctant to abandon their own gods entirely, and would seek to continue their worship concurrently with that of Jehovah.

The sacrifices offered to Jehovah point back, then, not to polytheism but to a low form of monotheism, in which each clan that offered sacrifice worshipped but one god, though that god was conceived in the form of the animal or plant which was sacrificed. This brings us to the question whether totemism, that lowest form of monotheism, is the earliest form of religion; and for the answer to the question we are reduced to conjecture. One certain fact, however, we have to go upon, if we accept the theory of evolution as applied to religion: it is that, then, the law of continuity must prevail throughout the history of religion, that is to say, there must be a *continuum* in religion, something which is common to all religions, so far as they are religious, and which, however much its forms may change in the course of evolution, underlies them all. This *continuum* is sometimes assumed to be animism. But though animism exercises great influence over religion in its early stages, directing its course and determining its various forms, it is not in itself a religious idea nor a product of the religious consciousness. It is the belief that all things which act, all agents, are personal agents; and this theory is a piece of primitive science, not of early religion. Not all personal agents are supernatural, nor are all supernatural powers gods.[1] Thus a specifically religious conception has to be imported into animism if it is to have any religious character at all. The religious element is no part of animism pure and simple. To make the personal agents of animism into supernatural agents or divine powers, there must be added some idea which is not contained in animism pure and simple; and that idea is a specifically religious idea, one which is apprehended directly or intuitively by the religious consciousness. The difference, whatever it may be, between human and divine personality is matter of direct, though internal, perception. Like other facts of consciousness, it may or may not, sometimes does and sometimes does not, arrest the attention of any given man. There are times, as Homer says, when all men have need of the gods, and when, in the words of Æschylus,[2] he prays and supplicates the gods who never believed in them before. That the gods have the power, sometimes the will, to save; that silent prayer to them is heard and direct answer given to the heart —all these are certainly parts of the religious idea, and as certainly are no part of animism pure and simple.

[1] *Supra*, pp. 22, 106, 107.

[2] *Persæ*, 497: θεοὺς δέ τις
τὸ πρὶν νομίζων οὐδαμοῦ τότ' εὔχετο
λιταῖσι.

That the divine personality does impress itself in these and other ways upon men, that it impresses itself unequally on different men, unequally on the same man at different times—these things are all matters of immediate consciousness, are direct perceptions. Whether these perceptions correspond to actual facts is not a question for the historian of religion to discuss: the eye of the soul may or may not be constituted, as the eye of the body is said to be, in such a way that from its very structure it cannot but be a false guide as to the light. The historian, however, has to recognise that these perceptions do exist; that—whether there exists anything objective corresponding to them or not—they are facts of consciousness; that they are universal, though they may play a little or a large part or no part at all in the life of this man or that; that they form part of the *continuum* in religious evolution; and that they are specifically religious, not animistic. In animism man projects his own personality on to external nature: in religion he is increasingly impressed by the divine personality; and, however faint or ill-attended to we may imagine this consciousness to have been in the early stages of the evolution of religion, it is in and by itself a higher form of religious thought than we get in animal-worship, in totemism. At first sight this may appear to settle the question: evolution proceeds by lower forms to higher, totemism is the lower and therefore the original form. But in reality the question is not settled quite so easily. It is true that the advance, in religion as in other things, from lower to higher is a process of evolution. It is not true that every process of evolution is an advance: decay is a form of evolution as much as growth. In art that form survives which is best adapted to the taste of the age—and the age may have no taste; or it may have worse taste than the previous age or better, and there will then be a decline or an improvement in art, as the case may be. But decline and improvement are equally part of the evolution in art, for in each case that form survives which is best fitted to survive under the given conditions, though it is not necessarily or always or commonly the highest form of art. In morals and in religion, evolution thus may follow a wavering course: first advance, then retrogression; then perhaps a fresh start is made by those who deviated, and they move in the right direction indeed, but not so accurately for the goal as those who never strayed; and everywhere it is the many who lapse, the few who hold right on—the progressive peoples of the earth are in the minority. Totemism, which is at least the worship of one god, declines into the worship of many gods; polytheism may in some few civilised peoples rise towards pantheism, but in most cases degenerates into fetishism; monotheism passes in one case from Judaism into Christianity, but in another into Mohammedanism; sacrifice degenerates from a sacrament into the making of gifts, and then, except in the case of Christianity, into mere magic used to constrain the gods to do the will of man.

It seems, then, that neither the course of evolution in general, nor that of religious evolution in particular, is so uniformly upward as to warrant the general proposition that of two related forms the higher must have been evolved out of the lower. Relapse is at least sufficiently common in the history of religion to make it conceivable that totemism was a degeneration from some simpler form of faith, for evolution does, though progress does not always, move from the simple to the complex, from less to more fully differentiated forms. Further, we have seen reason to believe [1] that the distinction between the natural and the supernatural has always been known to man; that it was only by slow degrees he came to attribute supernatural powers to the personal agents of animism; and later still, that he took an animal for his clan-god. Here, then, we have the stage in religious development out of which, on the one hand, a relatively higher form of monotheism was evolved, and, on the other, by a process of degeneration but still of evolution, totemism was developed.

That it was only amongst one people of the earth that this simple and amorphous monotheism was developed into something higher, and everywhere else degenerated into the grosser form of animal-worship, is a fact which will not surprise us when we reflect that, though evolution is universal, progress is exceptional. Progress in higher

[1] *Supra*, p. 18 ff.

matters is always due to the minority, to individual thinkers, discoverers, reformers. And there is no known law of the distribution of genius: in literature and art, for instance, the great names are as frequent B.C. as A.D. Progress does not multiply them or produce them: they initiate it. That in historic times progress in religion is due to individual teachers, prophets, and reformers, may be taken to be undoubted; and we may venture to infer that whatever progress was made in prehistoric times was made in the same way. The growth of civilisation seems to have no power to increase the number of geniuses born in a century; and it would be difficult to prove that it is impossible for a mind of the highest powers to be born of a race in a rude and semi-civilised or even uncivilised state. But it may perhaps be argued that a mind so born would fail to develop because of its unfavourable environment. Here, however, we must distinguish between the two kinds of knowledge, first the intuitive or immediate, and second that which is gained by means of inference, inductive or deductive. As regards the latter, a Newton might be born out of due season, in a race which knew no processes of mathematical inference, and so might fail, because he found no mental instruments, no mathematical methods, in existence, to do what otherwise he might have done. But this is not the case, or not so much so, with the knowledge which is intuitive: the artist of to-day has better means—materials and methods elaborated by his predecessors—for expressing himself, but he has not a more direct perception of the truth than had the prehistoric artist who has bequeathed to us his sketches of the reindeer and the mammoth. Now, the artist's source of truth is his direct perception of things external; but of spiritual things the knowledge comes by inward intuition, by direct perception of things not apprehended by the outward senses. In the degree of this knowledge men vary; and of old as at the present day "the million rose to learn, the one to teach." We may explain this as due to revelation or to greater powers of spiritual insight or in some other way, but the fact remains that men do thus vary, and that it is the minority who teach, who reform religion and impart to it its progress.

Religious progress moves wholly on one line, that of personality, and is the unveiling, revealing disclosure of what is implied therein. But the divine personality impresses itself unequally on different minds, and it is to those most impressed by it that religious progress is due: to them monotheism was disclosed, the divine personality was in their own belief revealed; and we cannot maintain it to be impossible or even improbable that such revelation may have been made even to primitive man.

CHAPTER XXVI

THE EVOLUTION OF BELIEF

BELIEFS are about facts—facts of external consciousness and internal consciousness—and are statements that facts are thus and thus. The ultimate test of a belief is whether the facts actually are as stated and believed to be—*i.e.* is the appeal to consciousness.

Differences of belief (which may be compared to the variations of organisms), so far as they are not due to erroneous logical processes, may be explained in one of two ways: (1) the *powers* of vision (spiritual, moral, æsthetic) may be supposed to vary from individual to individual, as do those of physical vision, and for the same (unexplained but not therefore supernatural) causes. This assumes that the facts are themselves always the same, but that one man, having better sight, sees them and their relations to each other better than other people, and therefore differently from other people. This accounts for the *origin* of different varieties of belief. The *perpetuation* of any variety depends solely on the conditions under which it occurs: whatever varieties of belief are not favoured by the conditions, by their environment, will perish—the rest will survive (the surviving belief will not necessarily be that of the keenest-sighted man, but that which accords with what the average sight can see of the facts). The survival of a new variety of belief implies harmony between the reformer's vision and the average man's view of the facts, on this theory; and therefore the theory fails to explain any advance—unless, indeed, we postulate that the new variety or "sport" at once alters the conditions and makes them favourable to itself and its own growth. Now this is what really takes place in the case of belief (bad ones propagate themselves thus as well as good), and it seems to be equally true of organisms, *e.g.* man has modified his environment to favour his own growth.

There is, of course, the possibility that the same causes which raise (or lower) the powers of vision in the individual at the same time raise them in different degrees in all the other members of the race; and in the same way it is conceivable that the same causes which produced an atmosphere such as the earth possesses also favoured the occurrence of forms of life such as would survive in that atmosphere. But here we are supplementing the negative method of exclusions, which is the essence of the "survival" theory, by a positive cause which does away with chance—the survival of one variety will not be due to the fact that it happened by chance to be the one which survived, whilst the ninety-nine perished (on the ground that of a hundred different varieties one must be more in harmony with the conditions than the ninety-nine), but to the fact that both the occurrence of the variety and the change in conditions necessary for its survival are the joint effects of one common cause (or collocation of causes or *causa causarum*).

That the change in conditions should synchronise with the first occurrence of the new variety, and should take place just in time to favour its development, rather fits in with the theory of design than with that of the accidental survival of the variety which happened to be best adapted to pre-existing conditions. In this connection note we have no evidence that forms of life incapable of surviving under conditions found on this planet ever *did* occur upon the earth: all we can say is that if they occurred, they would, *ex hypothesi*, perish. Note, too, there is nothing to compel us to believe that such radically unfit forms ever did occur. The position of the argument simply is that if we assume the existence of fit and unfit forms side by side, we need not call in the theory of design to account for the existence of forms specially adapted to the conditions under which they occur—we can explain their survival as due to the selective agency of the conditions (assumed to be constant).

It is only for the purpose of dispensing with the design theory that the occurrence of radically unfit forms is *necessary*. No argument can be drawn from the fact that of the numerous forms capable of existing for a longer or shorter time, some eventually perish—for they are, *ex hypothesi*, *not* radically unfit, but simply less fit than others.

If, then, we confine ourselves to the facts, the only forms we have experience of are forms fit in some measure or other: radically unfit forms are unproven—a mere hypothesis.

The one thing certain is that forms of life capable of surviving must have existed in the beginning. And granted that unfit forms also existed (or rather failed to exist), their existence (or failure to exist) throws no light either on the survival or on the origin of the forms which were capable of surviving. The fit survived because they were fit, not because others were fundamentally unfit.

But the absence of fundamentally unfit forms seems to indicate that the forms of life which first occurred on this planet were the outcome of the same causes as the conditions which favoured their development. And it seems fairly obvious that what favoured their growth might favour their origin (which is only the earliest period of growth).

And so generally throughout the course of development, the causes which bring about a change in the conditions would also produce a variation fit to survive in the new conditions and to take the place of the antiquated species.

(2) The other theory of the *origin* of varieties in belief, *i.e.* of the fact that one man sees (spiritually or morally) what another cannot see, is not that he has greater powers of vision, but that he has more revealed to him. On this theory the *survival* of a new variety must be due to the fact that a similar revelation is simultaneously or subsequently made to those who accept the new belief, so that to them also more is revealed than was known before. This would be in accordance with the view already set forth, that the same cause (not necessarily a *personal* cause) which produces a new variety also produces the conditions favourable to the survival of that variety.

On the other hand, this theory (1) would make *teaching* quite unnecessary, whereas, as a matter of fact, teaching seems to be an essential condition (perhaps not the only one) of any extension in the disciples' range of vision, and (2) would make the process of spiritual or moral reform purely mechanical, quite apart from the rest of man's nature and absolutely necessitarian.

As regards the last consideration, the "higher *power* of vision" theory is just as fatal to free will as the revelation theory.

Now, if the facts of the internal consciousness are realities in the same sense as the facts of the external consciousness, then they must be the same for all men, and equally available for all. And from the religious point of view it must be that all who seek can find them out, that the door will open to all who knock.

The latter consideration points to the rejection of necessitarianism: it implies that the truth can be perceived by anyone who chooses to look for it, that the facts are there all the time for those who will attend to them. This is not, however, inconsistent with the revelation theory as such; but it requires us to believe that as attention is a matter of personal will and choice, so the revelation of new facts is a matter of personal grace, invariably accorded but strictly conditional on the free exercise of the seeker's will. Thus the facts *are* equally open to all, and if not equally revealed are equally ready to reveal themselves. So, too, external facts have to be learnt by humble and patient watching for them.

This theory then will account for the two fundamental explicanda: (1) that differences in the *range* of vision do exist in different individuals; (2) that the facts, the reality, the truth are equally open to all minds.

The "greater power of vision" theory is then superfluous. And note that it is only a hypothesis, its only evidence is that it explains the facts. It is not capable of *independent* verification; and, as a matter of scientific psychology, the faculty theory has been discarded as an erroneous and misleading statement of the simple fact that different minds do behave in different ways. Some minds seek religious truth more earnestly than others, have a greater hunger and thirst for righteousness. Even to the reformer the greater measure of revelation is accorded because of his greater importunity.

Thus the ultimate reason for variety of belief seems to be

τὸ ὅτι, the fact that men in the exercise of their free will pay varying degrees of attention to the facts; and this is an ultimate fact, for which we are not in a position to assign a reason, any more than we can assign a reason for "sports" differing from the other individuals of the species, or for the fact that bodies tend towards one another in the manner formulated by the law of gravity. From it we can deduce things as they are; for it we can assign no scientific cause. Indeed, if we could assign a cause (other than the individual's own free choice) we should thereby deny the freedom of the will, and have to ask why the potter blames the pots for the flaws in them of his own making. Free will is the ultimate term to which we come when we look at the facts of "internal consciousness" in our endeavour to escape from the endless chain of scientific causation, just as a First Cause is the ultimate term and mode of escape when we look at the facts of "external consciousness." Personality is the concept which supplies the solution in both cases: the free will of a personal agent is the unifying principle of experience in both spheres.

But as the First Cause acts by laws which, though natural laws, are God's laws and the expression of His will, so the free will of the human agent acts with equal regularity, and in the same way under the same circumstances. No scientific account of nature or of man is possible save on this assumption, namely, that there is not only a uniformity of nature but a uniformity of human nature. But this latter uniformity is the expression of the free will of the human agent, just as the former is of God's will. It is from this point of view that we have to inquire why and how erroneous as well as correct beliefs originate and are evolved.

First, we must distinguish true and false belief. Beliefs are about facts, are statements about facts, statements that certain facts will be found to occur in a certain way or be of a certain kind. If the facts are found to be or occur as stated, the belief is correct; if not, not. The only final test is the actual facts—the test of immediate consciousness. Consciousness is a sphere, one half or hemisphere being "external consciousness," the other consisting of the internal facts of consciousness. That certain acids corrode certain things, is a statement the only test of whose truth is immediate observation, the presentation of the external fact to the consciousness. So, too, the statement that revenge is sweet. A belief is an inference, and as such is the work of the reason. The reason endeavours to anticipate the movement of facts; and the movement of reason is distinct from the movement of facts, for it may go wrong altogether, and leads us to expect something which, after all, does not happen.

At first sight it might appear that here we have the source of errors in religion: the human reason goes astray—and that doubtless is the reason of some religious errors. But if we put all the blame on the erring human reason, then in the case of correct beliefs we must assign it all the credit. In other words—to come back to our proper subject, the evolution of belief—the religious progress which admittedly has taken place will be purely intellectual—the religious sentiment has had no share in it.

But there is another source of mistaken belief besides mere intellectual errors of calculation, so to speak, from correct premisses: there is mal-observation of the facts on which the reasoning is based. It is possible under the influence of a preconception to overlook certain facts, and by leaving them out of consideration to make any right conclusion impossible, however correct the process of reasoning applied to the incomplete premisses. Again, it is possible to mistake one person for another, one thing for another, to be unable to perceive that a certain shade of colour is green not blue, dark purple not black, pale cream not white.

Thus religious progress may consist not only in the correction of intellectual errors by the intellect, but also in renewed and closer attention to the facts presented in or by the religious consciousness—in a finer sense of what is repugnant to religious feeling. Here there is no process of inference, but an appeal to the testimony of consciousness, just as the question whether a given thing is or is not of exactly the same shade of colour as another given thing, is one which can only be settled by an appeal to the consciousness. In both cases the test of truth consists in the facts of the case, and in immediate consciousness of them.

Again, between the conviction that everything has a cause, and ability to assign the cause of everything that happens, there is a great distance. Man started in the beginning with the former, and is yet a long way off the latter. So far as he has bridged the gap, he has done so simply by closer and closer attention to the facts of consciousness. Even the destruction of erroneous canons of reasoning, *e.g.* like produces like, has been effected simply by the process of verification.

But the conviction with which man started was neither the result of any process of reasoning (no satisfactory reasoning has even yet been found for its proof) nor could it have been the result of experience, in the beginning when man had as yet had no experience. It was a conviction, undemonstrated and unproved, if not incapable of proof, yet one without which science could have made not only no progress, but not even a beginning.

So, too, the conviction that changes not caused by man are yet due to will, was a similar form of thought, a mode in which man could not help thinking, and without which religion could have made no progress.

But just as the conviction that everything has a cause does not help us to determine whether A, B, or C is the cause of Z, and does not prevent us from selecting A, B, C, or D as the cause when it really is K, so the conviction that changes not caused by man are due to will did not enable man to identify the Being whose will it was, nor prevent him from ascribing that will to many erroneous sources.

That man should in the beginning make many mistakes, needs no explanation. But it would be an error to suppose that his mistaken inferences were automatically corrected by their discrepancy with actual facts. Scientific knowledge is the possession even now of but few: the vast majority have not learnt to correct their inferences or verify their conclusions by comparing them with facts. Even when facts force themselves on their notice, they are disregarded: we note and remember those which confirm our preconceived opinions, and set aside the rest. The same is true of religion. In fine, it is neither the origin nor the growth nor the survival of error that need surprise us (for error has its laws of growth and propagation), but that truth should ever supplant it.

Now, it is possible to look at a thing without seeing it—*e.g.* to look at a rock without seeing its resemblance to a human face or figure. And when once the thing has been pointed out by somebody else, it is impossible to look at it without seeing it. This is as true of spiritual and mental vision as it is of physical sight. The one thing needful for the spread and propagation of the true view is that there should be someone to point it out. After that, the convincing power of facts should suffice. The preconceptions, the wrong way of looking at the facts, the overlooking of them, stand in the way and require to be removed by the assistance of someone who sees what he wishes you to see. That it is God with whom the religious heart communes in prayer, is a fact of immediate consciousness—which is none the less a fact because another looks at it without seeing it, or is as unable to distinguish it from some other fact of consciousness, as he may be to distinguish dark purple from black, the personal ambition which really moves him from the patriotism which stirs him in part though not as completely as he thinks.

That a man who sees the fact is able to assist others to concentrate their attention until they also see it, is undoubted—it is the only means of spreading *any* teaching, scientific, æsthetic, or religious. It is the condition of the growth of a belief. Is it not the condition or a condition of the *origin* also? What the reformer first sees in his own mind and heart he sees in consequence of his communing with God and of His teaching. Be this as it may, the mode of propagation is that the learner learns to see facts which he did not see before: *ex hypothesi* at first he cannot see them, but he believes that he may come to have immediate consciousness of them, and he so believes because he has faith in his master. The reason he cannot see them is that preconceptions block his view or direct it amiss. These preconceptions, *ex hypothesi*, are erroneous conclusions reached by a reasoning process, or simple want of teaching how to use the eye of the mind and direct it to the proper quarter. To lay aside or cast off these preconceptions means giving up belief in them, admitting that they are wrong; and such an admission is only possible to the humble-minded: humility is the first condition of learning. The man who thinks he knows has no desire to learn; the man who is sure he is right cannot set about amending his ways.

The period of faith does not terminate, however, when the pupil has come to have immediate consciousness of the facts which at first he could not see: the new facts of consciousness have to be reconciled with other (real or apparent) facts, *e.g.* the all-powerfulness with the all-goodness of God, and such reconciliation may be beyond the reasoning power of the individual or of man; but faith persists that the belief will ultimately be found to be justified by the facts. Here note that faith is not something peculiar or confined to religion, but is interwoven with every act of reason, no matter what the subject-matter to which the reasoning process is applied. The object of reason is to infer facts. The facts of which we have immediate consciousness at any moment are relatively very few. But the reasoning processes enable us to judge what certain facts will be, which at the moment are not immediately present to consciousness. The only reason why we believe that any given process will enable us to anticipate correctly the movement of facts, is that in the past it has so enabled us, and was verified by the facts. Here we evidently assume that facts will in the future continue to move on the same lines as in the past, and not swerve off in some totally different direction—in a word, we assume that nature is uniform. Now this belief that facts will behave in the future as in the past, that fire, *e.g.*, will not cease to burn, is a piece of pure faith. The difference between this faith and religious faith is that no great effort of will is required for it—the reason of which is that facts apparently irreconcilable with it are not of frequent occurrence. The moment such facts are alleged, *e.g.* as in the case of the way in which material objects are alleged to behave at spiritualistic séances, an effort of will to maintain the faith in the uniformity of nature is stimulated, which in the case supposed takes the form sometimes of angry denunciations of the folly of human nature, or confident assertions that the alleged facts will be found on closer inspection to be no facts at all. In the case of religious faith, the apparently irreconcilable facts are of more frequent occurrence, *e.g.* the difficulty of reconciling much that happens in the world with the faith that all that happens is for the best. Such difficulties require an act of will, if faith is to reassert itself; and the energy thus stimulated may expend itself in renewed efforts to harmonise the apparently conflicting facts. The desire to unify our experience is a perennial need of human nature. The faith that it can be unified is not peculiar to religion, but is the base of all science. The track by which science has marched in its conquest of nature is marked by the ruins of abandoned hypotheses. One hypothesis is cast aside in favour of another which explains a greater number of facts; and though no hypothesis, not even evolution, accounts for all the facts of the physical universe (*i.e.* for all the external facts of consciousness), yet no man of science believes that the facts are incapable of explanation: on the contrary, he believes that they are only waiting for the right hypothesis, and that then they will all fall into line. In a word, as a man of science, in his scientific labours he walks by faith—by the faith that the universe is constructed on rational principles, on principles the rationality of which the human, or at anyrate the scientific, mind can comprehend. His faith is that the external facts of consciousness do form one consistent, harmonious whole, regulated by the laws of nature, and that we can more or less comprehend the system which the physical universe forms. The moral philosopher holds the same faith with regard to the facts of morality, that they too are consistent with one another and are all consistent with reason and with the moral aspirations of man rightly construed. The religious mind believes that these facts, all facts, external or internal, of which we have immediate consciousness, can be reconciled with one another, or rather actually are harmonious and consistent, if only we could see them as they are, instead of looking at them without seeing them. But this, the religious, faith which looks forward to the synthesis of all facts in a manner satisfying to the reason, to the moral and to the spiritual sense alike, covers a much larger area than either science or moral philosophy, and is much more liable to meet with facts apparently irreconcilable with it.

Hence the effort of will is a much more frequent and more marked feature of religious than of scientific faith.

Scientific investigations made by means of the microscope or telescope entail a considerable expenditure of will-power and a considerable exercise of scientific faith—of faith that the results will be worth the labour, and of will-power in the concentration of attention for long hours on what is presented to the eye. The attitude of the religious mind differs from that of the scientific, in that it is one not of critical observation but of trustful waiting and watching, and its faith is in a personal God, and not in natural laws conceived as working mechanically. But the religious mind equally with the scientific is engaged in the contemplation of facts of immediate consciousness, and as great concentration of attention is required in the one case as in the other. And once more it is only by an appeal to the facts of consciousness that the truth of any statement or of any process of reasoning can be demonstrated. But to observe with the exactitude which science requires is an art not acquired in a day: what the microscope presents to the eye of the trained observer is something very different from what is seen when the microscope is used for the first time. For one thing, the trained microscopist knows how to use his instrument, but, what is more important, he knows how to use his eye—a knowledge which is only obtained by habitual concentration of the attention upon what is presented to the eye. The fact that the untrained observer does not see something is no proof that the thing is not there to be seen. This consideration may serve to illustrate the proposition that though the same facts are present in the spiritual consciousness of all men, they are not equally discerned by all. Thus there is an *à priori* reason why the historian of religion should assume that man being man began with a spiritual consciousness of the same content as now. There is no reason why he should assume that man began by realising all that was contained in that consciousness. In this respect the "external consciousness" is the counterpart of the internal: the laws which science has discovered to pervade the facts of the physical universe, of external consciousness, were at work when man first appeared, but man was not then aware of them. But even then he was so far conscious of the uniformity of nature as to act upon it: once bitten, doubtless he was twice shy—else he would have soon perished. Even then, too, he acted on the belief that everything had a cause—but for him every cause was personal, every effect the effect of some will or other. This, however, was not a religious belief: the wills he assumed rivers and trees to have were in his eyes natural not supernatural, not superhuman, but like his own human will. They were inferences, immediate inferences, made by his reason from the facts of his external consciousness, and were an early piece of philosophy—just as to this day theism is a philosophical rather than a religious belief. That man from the beginning had some conception, some sentiment, of the supernatural, is not here denied. What is maintained is that that sentiment was not derived from the external facts of which he was conscious, but from his own heart: the sense of his dependence on a supernatural will, not his own, though personal like his own, was found by him in his inner consciousness—a fact of which he had no more doubt than he doubted that fire burns. That he should look for that supernatural will amongst the external, physical embodiments of will, such as plants, animals, rivers, clouds, etc., by which he was surrounded, was an inevitable consequence of the fact that he had as yet made little progress in the work of discriminating the contents of his consciousness, external and internal. But that the contemplation of such external objects could be the source of the sentiment of the supernatural, is impossible—that lay within him.

It is an established fact of psychology that every act, mental or physical, requires the concurrence, not only of the reason and the will, but of emotion: in any given act one of these three elements may predominate so much that the other two may easily be overlooked; but that they are present for all that, is agreed by all psychologists. That for the concentration of the attention on the facts of spiritual consciousness an effort of the will is required, we have already argued. Coleridge, indeed, said that it required the greatest effort that man could make. Be that as it may, no one will doubt that acts of worship are accompanied by emotion. Nor can there be any doubt as to the quality of that emotion: it is desirable, it has its own peculiar joy, peace, and blessedness; it is envied by those who think they cannot share it; it strengthens those who feel it in the habit and activity of faith. Now these are facts which cannot be overlooked when we come to consider that religion and worship are universal among mankind. It is true that the widest-spread forms of religious belief are the lowest, but the persistence of religion under conditions the most unfavourable for its survival is proof that even in those conditions it has not entirely lost its prerogative. We may therefore safely infer that from the beginning man not only recognised his dependence on a personal and supernatural will, but that he found a peculiar happiness in the recognition. To put it another way: as the laws of nature were in existence and in operation long before they were formulated by man, so before the truth was formulated that God is Love, His love was towards all His creatures; and as even primitive man acted on the conviction that nature is uniform, so his heart responded with love to the divine love, though he may have reasoned little or not at all on either point. Indeed, the reason of primitive man was *ex hypothesi* undeveloped; and, in any case, religious belief is not an inference reached by reason, but is the immediate consciousness of certain facts. Those facts, however, may be and are taken, like other facts of consciousness, as the basis for reasoning, and as the premisses from which to reach other facts not immediately present to consciousness. The motive for this process is the innate desire of man to harmonise the facts of his experience, to unite in one synthesis the facts of his external and his inner consciousness. The earliest attempt in this direction took the form of ascribing the external prosperity which befell a man to the action of the divine love of which he was conscious within himself; and the misfortunes which befell him to the wrath of the justly offended divine will. Man, being by nature religious, began by a religious explanation of nature. To assume, as is often done, that man had no religious consciousness to begin with, and that the misfortunes which befell him inspired him with fear, and fear led him to propitiate the malignant beings whom he imagined to be the causes of his suffering, fails to account for the very thing it is intended to explain, namely, the existence of religion. It might account for superstitious dread of malignant beings: it does not account for the grateful worship of benignant beings, nor for the universal satisfaction which man finds in that worship.

In the conviction that all events have will for their cause, and in the recognition, bringing with it its own delight, of man's dependence on that will, there was nothing to suggest to the mind of man more than one object of worship; and there is reason to believe that it is a psychological impossibility for the mind of man to seek communion with two objects of worship simultaneously. It is, however, certain that—with the (disputed) exception of the Hebrews—polytheism has been universal amongst mankind; and it is certain that man sought the God, of whose "everlasting power and divinity" from the beginning he was conscious in his heart, in external nature. And there can be no reasonable doubt that this was one of the consequences of his attempt to synthesize the external and internal facts of consciousness by a reasoning process: all external objects were conceived by him as personal, and he identified now one and now another of them with the will with which his heart prompted him to seek communion. If, as is maintained in this book, animals were the first of the external objects that thus came to be worshipped, and totemism was the first form of that worship, then for a long period man continued to have only one object of worship, namely, the totem or tribal god. It was not usually until one tribe united with another or several others to form a new political whole and a new religious community, that polytheism came into existence.

Polytheism presupposes totemism: its existence is in itself proof of the existence of totemism in a previous stage. The animal sacrifices offered to polytheistic gods, the animal forms in which those gods appear in mythology, the animals with which they are associated in art, find their only satisfactory explanation in the hypothesis that those gods were originally totem animals. Totemism, again, is an attempt to translate and express in outward action the union of the human will with the divine. In totemism that outward act took the form of animal sacrifice, because in that stage of intellectual development man sought to reconcile his internal and external experience by identifying the personal divine will, which manifested itself to his inner consciousness, with one of the personal agents in the external world that exercised an influence on his fortunes; and the personal agents which his immature reasoning led him to regard as exercising that influence were various species of animals. Having thus chosen as the seat of that influence an external agent, he necessarily adopted an external means of communion with it; and the only means which man in that stage of social development (the tribal) knew for effecting permanent union with anyone external to the tribe, was a blood-covenant. The covenant with the animal totem therefore took the form of participatiug in the blood of the animal totem. Animal sacrifice continued as an institution long after totemism was a thing of the forgotten past; but as a survival it points back to totemism, as totemism in its turn points to the previous conviction of the necessity and the comfort of union with the divine will.

It is a commonplace that no lie can circulate unless it contains some truth; that it is the element of truth in it which is seen to correspond to facts, and therefore is supposed to lend its countenance to the elements of error associated with it. So in religion, the notion that animal sacrifice was an essential condition of communion with God was an error; but it was an error which could neither have come into existence nor have continued to exist, unless there had been a desire for such communion—and the desire is inexplicable except on the assumption that its satisfaction was found, as a matter of immediate consciousness, to bring spiritual comfort. But it was the patent truth of the facts that floated the erroneous reasoning imposed upon them. The fact that some degree of spiritual communion—in proportion to the extent to which God was revealed to the particular worshipper—was attained after the offering of animal sacrifice, was fallaciously interpreted to imply that communion was the effect of animal sacrifice: *post hoc ergo propter hoc.* The truth that some external act of worship is necessary to the continued exercise of the habit of faith, may easily be made into an argument in favour of a mischievous rite. Errors may attach themselves to the truth, but the truth must first be there before they can do so. In this sense, that is to say logically, totemism, animal-worship, presupposes a stage in which man had not yet found, as he supposed, in the external world the source of his inner consciousness of the divine, and had not yet identified it, by a process of vain reasoning, with an animal species. The historical existence of this stage can only be matter of conjecture, and must rest mainly on the difficulty of supposing that man, the moment he was man, invented the idea of animal sacrifice — an idea which, whatever its origin, can hardly be regarded as innate or even as obvious.

The nature of religious belief in the pre-totemistic stage is also entirely matter of conjecture. That it was exclusively of the nature of fear is, however, improbable. Man did indeed find himself in the midst of a world of forces (conceived by him as personal agents) over which he had in the main no control, and by which his fortunes were affected, often disastrously. But these forces were not all of them inimical, that he should fear them. Again, love and gratitude are just as natural, just as much integral parts of the constitution of man, as fear and hatred. There is no probability in the idea that the only emotion early man felt or was capable of feeling was fear. Indeed, the fact that in the totemistic stage he selected now one and now another of the personal agents, which made up the world for him, as the embodiment of the Being after whom his heart instinctively sought peradventure it might find Him, is itself a presumption that he did not regard everything external with fear. In the same way the fact that in the stage of totemism the clan has but one totem, one tribal god, constitutes some presumption that man was conscious of but one God, before he identified Him with one or other of the forces of nature. So far belief in this stage may be termed monotheism; for, as already said, there is reason to believe that polytheism was developed out of totemism, and does not occur until a relatively late period in the evolution of society.

On the other hand, man's consciousness of God must, in

this early stage, have been so rudimentary, *ex hypothesi*, as to permit of His coming to be conceived, by a process of vain reasoning, as manifesting Himself in animal form. And this is in accordance with all that science teaches as to early man's undeveloped condition, material and mental, social and moral. Once more, we must remember that the facts of consciousness were the same for early as for civilised man; but they were not as yet discriminated They swam before man's untrained eye, and ran into one another. Even the fundamental division of objects into animate and inanimate had not been fixed. But even so, all was not irrational chaos for man. In the outer world of his experience, the laws of nature, which are God's laws, worked with the same regularity then as now. In the world of his inner experience, God was not far from him at any time. If he could not formulate the laws of nature, at least he had the key to their comprehension in the conviction, not expressed but acted on, that nature was uniform. If his spiritual vision was dim, his consciousness of God was at least so strong, to start with, that he has never since ceased seeking after Him. The law of continuity holds of religion as of other things.

Finally, sacrifice and the sacramental meal which followed on it are institutions which are or have been universal. The sacramental meal, wherever it exists, testifies to man's desire for the closest union with his god, and to his consciousness of the fact that it is upon such union alone that right social relations with his fellow-man can be set. But before there can be a sacramental meal there must be a sacrifice. That is to say, the whole human race for thousands of years has been educated to the conception that it was only through a divine sacrifice that perfect union with God was possible for man. At times the sacramental conception of sacrifice appeared to be about to degenerate entirely into the gift theory; but then, in the sixth century B.C., the sacramental conception woke into new life, this time in the form of a search for a perfect sacrifice—a search which led Clement[1] and Cyprian[2] to try all the mysteries of Greece in vain. But of

[1] Euseb. *Præpar. Evangel.* ii. 2.

[2] Foucart, *Associations Religieuses*, 76, note 2.

all the great religions of the world it is the Christian Church alone which is so far heir of all the ages as to fulfil the dumb, dim expectation of mankind: in it alone the sacramental meal commemorates by ordinance of its founder the divine sacrifice which is a propitiation for the sins of all mankind.

INDEX

E

G

H.

I

J

K

N

O

T

totem, 209; branch or plant carried in (sacramental) procession, *ib.*; dead buried in totem-tree, 210; tree appears in marriage-rite, *ib.*; plant-totems the source of domesticated plants, 210 ff.; plant-totems preserved, for their supernatural protection, from one year to the next, 211; and worshipped, 212; plant-totem anthropomorphised, 213; plant furnishes the sacramental meal, 214; seeds eaten *simpliciter*, 214, 215; made into a dough-doll, 215–6; use of dough-dolls spreads to non-cereal deities, 216; wafers take the place of the dolls, 218–9; blood extended from animal to plant-totems, 219, 220; two modes of communion with tree-totems, 220, by eating, *ib.*; and by incorporation of the worshipper with the object of his worship, 220–2; survival of original taboo on plant-totems as food, 222–3; importation into religion of the conception of "property," 223–4; consequent "gift theory" of sacrifice, 224–5; degradation of religion, 224; erroneous views of history of religion, 225; totem-gods absorbed by syncretism, 236; sex-totems, 239; how totem-gods were affected by polytheism, 242–3, 249; totemism, in India, 317; under what conditions alone it results in metempsychosis, 314–5; in Egypt in Græco-Roman times, 316; passes into polytheism, 395; the earliest form of religion known to science may be a relapse from an earlier and purer form, 395; totem-sacrifice aims at the union of man with the divine, 411–2; presupposes a previous stage in religious development, 413; a form of monotheism, *ib.*

Totonacs, dough and blood, 219

Tragedy, 352

Τράγοι, 351

Transformation, of men into beasts, amongst Jacoons, Bushmans, in Kirchhain, 16, 251, 253, 257, 259; posthumous transformation into totem-animal, 314–5, 325–6

Transformation Conflict, 355 ff.

Transmigration of Souls, 314–26; totemism does not always result in, 314; conditions under which alone it does so result, 315; in Egypt, 315–7; in India, 317–20; Buddhist revolt against Brahminist transmigration, 318–9; differences between Egyptian and Indian doctrines, 319, 320; Pythagoreanism, 320 ff.; its difference from the Indian doctrine, 321; its resemblances to the Egyptian, 322–3; its slight attachment to native Greek beliefs, 323–4; impossibility of its being native, 324–5; elements of the belief in a future state, 325; why their synthesis before 600 B.C. was unsatisfactory to the religious consciousness, 326

Travancore. *See* Veddahs

Trees, as totems, 207; dead buried in, 210; in marriage-rites, 210; human figure attached to, 215–6, 255; rags tied on, 221; hung with fruits (syncretism), 235; sacred, 242; clothed in human dress, 252

Tree-burial, 204, 210

Tree-gods, present in "lots," 289

Trenches, offerings made in, 51, 52

Triangle, totemistic, 127 ff.

Trouis, blood-offerings, 52

Troy, 304

Tscheremiss, feast the dead, 51; sacrificial meal, 150

Tscherkess, funeral feasts, 51; mutilation, 170

Tschuwasch, funeral feasts, 51

Tshi-speaking peoples, tempt the soul of the deceased to return, 45; funeral lamentations, 47; purify mourners, 57; vessels taboo, 63; cat fetish, 64; taboo-days, 65; taboo colours, 67; mother unclean after child-birth, 74, 75; purified, 75, 76; corpses taboo, 76; mourners, 77, 79; the god fights for his own people, 108; survival of totemism, 155; their deities, 163 ff.; paint for blood, 192; plant-totems, 207; functional deities, 247

Tuitonga, 66, 79, 223

Tumanang, 101

Tupai, 60

Tuppin Imbas, blood-guiltiness, 292; next life, 308

Turtle, as totem, 153, 243

Turtle-clan, 104; myth of origin, 251–2

Tycoon, 277

U

Uaaupés Valley, cannibalism, 202

Uliase Islands, cure for disease, 45

Umbrellas, to save the sun from being polluted by taboo persons, 60

Unclean things, transmit their taboo, 62; infect time, 65; unclean animal, 127; the unclean forbidden to communicate, 155; unclean animals make a more potent sacri-

PRINTED BY
MORRISON AND GIBB LIMITED, EDINBURGH.

A CATALOGUE OF BOOKS AND ANNOUNCEMENTS OF METHUEN AND COMPANY PUBLISHERS : LONDON 36 ESSEX STREET W.C.

CONTENTS

OCTOBER 1896

OCTOBER 1896.

MESSRS. METHUEN'S ANNOUNCEMENTS

Poetry

RUDYARD KIPLING

BALLADS. By RUDYARD KIPLING. *Crown 8vo.* 6*s*.

150 copies on hand-made paper. *Demy 8vo.* 21*s*.
30 copies on Japanese paper. *Demy 8vo.* 42*s*.

The enormous success of 'Barrack Room Ballads' justifies the expectation that this volume, so long postponed, will have an equal, if not a greater, success.

GEORGE WYNDHAM

SHAKESPEARE'S POEMS. Edited, with an Introduction and Notes, by GEORGE WYNDHAM, M.P. *Crown 8vo.* 3*s*. 6*d*.
[*English Classics.*

W. E. HENLEY

ENGLISH LYRICS. Selected and Edited by W. E. HENLEY. *Crown 8vo. Buckram.* 6*s*.

Also 15 copies on Japanese paper. *Demy 8vo.* £2, 2*s*.

Few announcements will be more welcome to lovers of English verse than the one that Mr. Henley is bringing together into one book the finest lyrics in our language. The volume will be produced with the same care that made 'Lyra Heroica' delightful to the hand and eye.

'Q'

POEMS AND BALLADS. By 'Q,' Author of 'Green Bays,' etc. *Crown 8vo. Buckram.* 3*s*. 6*d*.

25 copies on Japanese paper. *Demy 8vo.* 21*s*.

History, Biography, and Travel

CAPTAIN HINDE

THE FALL OF THE CONGO ARABS. By SIDNEY L. HINDE. With Portraits and Plans. *Demy 8vo.* 12*s*. 6*d*.

This volume deals with the recent Belgian Expedition to the Upper Congo, which developed into a war between the State forces and the Arab slave-raiders in Central Africa. Two white men only returned alive from the three years' war—Commandant Dhanis and the writer of this book, Captain Hinde. During the greater part of the time spent by Captain Hinde in the Congo he was amongst cannibal races in little-known regions, and, owing to the peculiar circumstances of his position, was enabled to see a side of native history shown to few Europeans. The war terminated in the complete defeat of the Arabs, seventy thousand of whom perished during the struggle.

S. BARING GOULD

THE LIFE OF NAPOLEON BONAPARTE. By S. BARING GOULD. With over 450 Illustrations in the Text and 13 Photogravure Plates. *Large quarto.* 36*s.*

This study of the most extraordinary life in history is written rather for the general reader than for the military student, and while following the main lines of Napoleon's career, is concerned chiefly with the development of his character and his personal qualities. Special stress is laid on his early life—the period in which his mind and character took their definite shape and direction.

The great feature of the book is its wealth of illustration. There are over 450 illustrations, large and small, in the text, and there are also more than a dozen full page photogravures. Every important incident of Napoleon's career has its illustration, while there are a large number of portraits of his contemporaries, reproductions of famous pictures, of contemporary caricatures, of his handwriting, etc. etc.

It is not too much to say that no such magnificent book on Napoleon has ever been published.

VICTOR HUGO

THE LETTERS OF VICTOR HUGO. Translated from the French by F. CLARKE, M.A. *In Two Volumes. Demy 8vo.* 10*s.* 6*d. each. Vol. I.*

This is the first volume of one of the most interesting and important collection of letters ever published in France. The correspondence dates from Victor Hugo's boyhood to his death, and none of the letters have been published before. The arrangement is chiefly chronological, but where there is an interesting set of letters to one person these are arranged together. The first volume contains, among others, (1) Letters to his father; (2) to his young wife; (3) to his confessor, Lamennais; (4) a very important set of about fifty letters to Sainte-Beuve; (5) letters about his early books and plays.

J. M. RIGG

ST. ANSELM OF CANTERBURY: A CHAPTER IN THE HISTORY OF RELIGION. By J. M. RIGG, of Lincoln's Inn, Barrister-at-Law. *Demy 8vo.* 7*s.* 6*d.*

This work gives for the first time in moderate compass a complete portrait of St. Anselm, exhibiting him in his intimate and interior as well as in his public life. Thus, while the great ecclesiastico-political struggle in which he played so prominent a part is fully dealt with, unusual prominence is given to the profound and subtle speculations by which he permanently influenced theological and metaphysical thought; while it will be a surprise to most readers to find him also appearing as the author of some of the most exquisite religious poetry in the Latin language.

EDWARD GIBBON

THE DECLINE AND FALL OF THE ROMAN EMPIRE. By EDWARD GIBBON. A New Edition, edited with Notes, Appendices, and Maps by J. B. BURY, M.A., Fellow of Trinity College, Dublin. *In Seven Volumes. Demy 8vo, gilt top.* 8*s.* 6*d. each. Crown 8vo.* 6*s. each. Vol. II.*

W. M. FLINDERS PETRIE

A HISTORY OF EGYPT, FROM THE EARLIEST TIMES TO THE PRESENT DAY. Edited by W. M. FLINDERS PETRIE, D.C.L., LL.D., Professor of Egyptology at University College. *Fully Illustrated. In Six Volumes. Crown 8vo. 6s. each.*

Vol. II. XVII.-XVIII. DYNASTIES. W. M. F. PETRIE.

'A history written in the spirit of scientific precision so worthily represented by Dr. Petrie and his school cannot but promote sound and accurate study, and supply a vacant place in the English literature of Egyptology.'—*Times.*

J. WELLS

A SHORT HISTORY OF ROME. By J. WELLS, M.A., Fellow and Tutor of Wadham Coll., Oxford. With 4 Maps. *Crown 8vo.* 3*s.* 6*d.* 350 *pp.*

This book is intended for the Middle and Upper Forms of Public Schools and for Pass Students at the Universities. It contains copious Tables, etc.

H. DE B. GIBBINS

THE HISTORY OF ENGLISH INDUSTRY. By H. DE B. GIBBINS, M.A. With 5 Maps. *Demy 8vo.* 10*s.* 6*d.* *Pp.* 450.

This book is written with the view of affording a clear view of the main facts of English Social and Industrial History placed in due perspective. Beginning with prehistoric times, it passes in review the growth and advance of industry up to the nineteenth century, showing its gradual development and progress. The author has endeavoured to place before his readers the history of industry as a connected whole in which all these developments have their proper place. The book is illustrated by Maps, Diagrams, and Tables, and aided by copious Footnotes.

MRS. OLIPHANT

THOMAS CHALMERS. By Mrs. OLIPHANT. *Second Edition. Crown 8vo.* 3*s.* 6*d.* [*Leaders of Religion.*

Naval and Military

DAVID HANNAY

A SHORT HISTORY OF THE ROYAL NAVY, FROM EARLY TIMES TO THE PRESENT DAY. By DAVID HANNAY. *Illustrated. Demy 8vo.* 15*s.*

This book aims at giving an account not only of the fighting we have done at sea, but of the growth of the service, of the part the Navy has played in the development of the Empire, and of its inner life. The author has endeavoured to avoid the mistake of sacrificing the earlier periods of naval history—the very interesting wars with Holland in the seventeenth century, for instance, or the American War of 1779-1783—to the later struggle with Revolutionary and Imperial France.

COL. COOPER KING

A SHORT HISTORY OF THE BRITISH ARMY. By Lieut.-Colonel COOPER KING, of the Staff College, Camberley. *Illustrated. Demy 8vo.* 7*s.* 6*d.*

This volume aims at describing the nature of the different armies that have been formed in Great Britain, and how from the early and feudal levies the present standing army came to be. The changes in tactics, uniform, and armament are briefly touched upon, and; the campaigns in which the army has shared have been so far followed as to explain the part played by British regiments in them.

G. W. STEEVENS

NAVAL POLICY: WITH A DESCRIPTION OF ENGLISH AND FOREIGN NAVIES. By G. W. STEEVENS. *Demy 8vo.* 6*s.*

This book is a description of the British and other more important navies of the world, with a sketch of the lines on which our naval policy might possibly be developed. It describes our recent naval policy, and shows what our naval force really is. A detailed but non-technical account is given of the instruments of modern warfare—guns, armour, engines, and the like—with a view to determine how far we are abreast of modern invention and modern requirements. An ideal policy is then sketched for the building and manning of our fleet; and the last chapter is devoted to docks, coaling-stations, and especially colonial defence.

Theology

F. B. JEVONS

AN INTRODUCTION TO THE HISTORY OF RELIGION. By F. B. JEVONS, M.A., Litt.D., Fellow of the University of Durham. *Demy 8vo.* 12*s.* 6*d.*

This is the third number of the series of 'Theological Handbooks' edited by Dr. Robertson of Durham, in which have already appeared Dr. Gibson's 'XXXIX. Articles' and Mr. Ottley's 'Incarnation.'

Mr. F. B. Jevons' 'Introduction to the History of Religion' treats of early religion, from the point of view of Anthropology and Folk-lore; and is the first attempt that has been made in any language to weave together the results of recent investigations into such topics as Sympathetic Magic, Taboo, Totemism, Fetishism, etc., so as to present a systematic account of the growth of primitive religion and the development of early religious institutions.

W. YORKE FAUSSETT

THE *DE CATECHIZANDIS RUDIBUS* OF ST. AUGUSTINE. Edited, with Introduction, Notes, etc., by W. YORKE FAUSSETT, M.A., late Scholar of Balliol Coll. *Crown 8vo.* 3*s.* 6*d.*

An edition of a Treatise on the Essentials of Christian Doctrine, and the best methods of impressing them on candidates for baptism. The editor bestows upon this patristic work the same care which a treatise of Cicero might claim. There is a general Introduction, a careful Analysis, a full Commentary, and other useful matter. No better introduction to the study of the Latin Fathers, their style and diction, could be found than this treatise, which also has no lack of modern interest.

General Literature

C. F. ANDREWS

CHRISTIANITY AND THE LABOUR QUESTION. By C. F. ANDREWS, B.A. *Crown 8vo.* 2*s.* 6*d.*

R. E. STEEL

MAGNETISM AND ELECTRICITY. By R. ELLIOTT STEEL, M.A., F.C.S. With Illustrations. *Crown 8vo.* 4*s.* 6*d.*

G. LOWES DICKINSON

THE GREEK VIEW OF LIFE. By G. L. DICKINSON, Fellow of King's College, Cambridge. *Crown 8vo.* 2*s.* 6*d.* [*University Extension Series.*

J. A. HOBSON

THE PROBLEM OF THE UNEMPLOYED. By J. A. HOBSON, B.A., Author of 'The Problems of Poverty.' *Crown 8vo.* 2*s.* 6*d.* [*Social Questions Series.*

S. E. BALLY

GERMAN COMMERCIAL CORRESPONDENCE. By S. E. BALLY, Assistant Master at the Manchester Grammar School. *Crown 8vo.* 2*s.* [*Commercial Series.*

L. F. PRICE

ECONOMIC ESSAYS. By L. F. PRICE, M.A., Fellow of Oriel College, Oxford. *Crown 8vo.* 6*s.*

This book consists of a number of Studies in Economics and Industrial and Social Problems.

Fiction

MARIE CORELLI'S ROMANCES

FIRST COMPLETE AND UNIFORM EDITION

Large crown 8vo. 6*s.*

MESSRS. METHUEN beg to announce that they have commenced the publication of a New and Uniform Edition of MARIE CORELLI'S Romances. This Edition is revised by the Author, and contains new Prefaces. The volumes are being issued at short intervals in the following order:—

1. A ROMANCE OF TWO WORLDS. 2. VENDETTA.
3. THELMA. 4. ARDATH.
5. THE SOUL OF LILITH. 6. WORMWOOD.
7. BARABBAS. 8. THE SORROWS OF SATAN.

BARING GOULD

DARTMOOR IDYLLS. By S. BARING GOULD. *Cr. 8vo.* 6*s.*

GUAVAS THE TINNER. By S. BARING GOULD, Author of 'Mehalah,' 'The Broom Squire,' etc. Illustrated. *Crown 8vo.* 6*s.*

THE PENNYCOMEQUICKS. By S. BARING GOULD. New Edition. *Crown 8vo.* 6*s.*

A new edition, uniform with the Author's other novels.

LUCAS MALET

THE CARISSIMA. By LUCAS MALET, Author of 'The Wages of Sin,' etc. *Crown 8vo.* 6*s.*

This is the first novel which Lucas Malet has written since her very powerful 'The Wages of Sin.'

ARTHUR MORRISON

A CHILD OF THE JAGO. By ARTHUR MORRISON. Author of 'Tales of Mean Streets.' *Crown 8vo.* 6*s.*

This, the first long story which Mr. Morrison has written, is like his remarkable 'Tales of Mean Streets,' a realistic study of East End life.

W. E. NORRIS

CLARISSA FURIOSA. By W. E. NORRIS, 'Author of 'The Rogue,' etc. *Crown 8vo.* 6*s.*

L. COPE CORNFORD

CAPTAIN JACOBUS: A ROMANCE OF HIGHWAYMEN. By L. COPE CORNFORD. Illustrated. *Crown 8vo.* 6*s.*

J. BLOUNDELLE BURTON

DENOUNCED. By J. BLOUNDELLE BURTON, Author of 'In the Day of Adversity,' etc. *Crown 8vo.* 6*s.*

J. MACLAREN COBBAN

WILT THOU HAVE THIS WOMAN? By J. M. COBBAN, Author of 'The King of Andaman.' *Crown 8vo.* 6*s.*

J. F. BREWER

THE SPECULATORS. By J. F. BREWER. *Crown 8vo.* 6*s.*

A. BALFOUR

BY STROKE OF SWORD. By ANDREW BALFOUR. *Crown 8vo.* 6*s.*

M. A. OWEN

THE DAUGHTER OF ALOUETTE. By MARY A. OWEN. *Crown 8vo.* 6*s.*

A story of life among the American Indians.

RONALD ROSS

THE SPIRIT OF STORM. By RONALD ROSS, Author of 'The Child of Ocean.' *Crown 8vo.* 6*s.*

A romance of the Sea.

J. A. BARRY

IN THE GREAT DEEP: TALES OF THE SEA. By J. A. BARRY. Author of 'Steve Brown's Bunyip.' *Crown 8vo.* 6*s.*

JAMES GORDON

THE VILLAGE AND THE DOCTOR. By JAMES GORDON. *Crown 8vo.* 6*s.*

BERTRAM MITFORD

THE SIGN OF THE SPIDER. By BERTRAM MITFORD. *Crown 8vo.* 3*s.* 6*d.*

A story of South Africa.

A. SHIELD

THE SQUIRE OF WANDALES. By A. SHIELD. *Crown 8vo.* 3*s.* 6*d.*

G. W. STEEVENS

MONOLOGUES OF THE DEAD. By G. W. STEEVENS. *Foolscap 8vo.* 3*s.* 6*d.*

A series of Soliloquies in which famous men of antiquity—Julius Cæsar, Nero, Alcibiades, etc., attempt to express themselves in the modes of thought and language of to-day.

S. GORDON

A HANDFUL OF EXOTICS. By S. GORDON. *Crown 8vo.* 3*s.* 6*d.*

A volume of stories of Jewish life in Russia.

P. NEUMANN

THE SUPPLANTER. By P. NEUMANN. *Crown 8vo.* 3*s.* 6*d.*

EVELYN DICKINSON

THE SIN OF ANGELS. By EVELYN DICKINSON. *Crown 8vo.* 3*s.* 6*d.*

H. A. KENNEDY

A MAN WITH BLACK EYELASHES. By H. A. KENNEDY. *Crown 8vo.* 3*s.* 6*d.*

A LIST OF

MESSRS. METHUEN'S PUBLICATIONS

Poetry

Rudyard Kipling. BARRACK-ROOM BALLADS; And Other Verses. By RUDYARD KIPLING. *Ninth Edition. Crown 8vo.* 6*s*.

'Mr. Kipling's verse is strong, vivid, full of character. . . . Unmistakable genius rings in every line.'—*Times.*

'"Barrack-Room Ballads" contains some of the best work that Mr. Kipling has ever done, which is saying a good deal. "Fuzzy-Wuzzy," "Gunga Din," and "Tommy," are, in our opinion, altogether superior to anything of the kind that English literature has hitherto produced.'—*Athenæum.*

'The ballads teem with imagination, they palpitate with emotion. We read them with laughter and tears; the metres throb in our pulses, the cunningly ordered words tingle with life; and if this be not poetry, what is?'—*Pall Mall Gazette.*

"Q." THE GOLDEN POMP: A Procession of English Lyrics from Surrey to Shirley, arranged by A. T. QUILLER COUCH. *Crown 8vo. Buckram.* 6*s*.

'A delightful volume: a really golden "Pomp."'—*Spectator.*

"Q." GREEN BAYS: Verses and Parodies. By "Q.," Author of 'Dead Man's Rock,' etc. *Second Edition. Crown 8vo.* 3*s*. 6*d*.

'The verses display a rare and versatile gift of parody, great command of metre, and a very pretty turn of humour.'—*Times.*

H. C. Beeching. LYRA SACRA: An Anthology of Sacred Verse. Edited by H. C. BEECHING, M.A. *Crown 8vo. Buckram.* 6*s*.

'An anthology of high excellence.'—*Athenæum.*

'A charming selection, which maintains a lofty standard of excellence.'—*Times.*

W. B. Yeats. AN ANTHOLOGY OF IRISH VERSE. Edited by W. B. YEATS. *Crown 8vo.* 3*s*. 6*d*.

'An attractive and catholic selection.'—*Times.*

'It is edited by the most original and most accomplished of modern Irish poets, and against his editing but a single objection can be brought, namely, that it excludes from the collection his own delicate lyrics.'—*Saturday Review.*

E. Mackay. A SONG OF THE SEA: MY LADY OF DREAMS, AND OTHER POEMS. By ERIC MACKAY, Author of 'The Love Letters of a Violinist.' *Second Edition. Fcap. 8vo, gilt top.* 5*s*.

'Everywhere Mr. Mackay displays himself the master of a style marked by all the characteristics of the best rhetoric. He has a keen sense of rhythm and of general balance; his verse is excellently sonorous.'—*Globe.*

'Throughout the book the poetic workmanship is fine.'—*Scotsman.*

Ibsen. BRAND. A Drama by HENRIK IBSEN. Translated by WILLIAM WILSON. *Second Edition. Crown 8vo.* 3s. 6d.

'The greatest world-poem of the nineteenth century next to "Faust." It is in the same set with "Agamemnon," with "Lear," with the literature that we now instinctively regard as high and holy.'—*Daily Chronicle.*

"A. G." VERSES TO ORDER. By "A. G." *Cr. 8vo.* 2s. 6d. *net.*

A small volume of verse by a writer whose initials are well known to Oxford men.

'A capital specimen of light academic poetry. These verses are very bright and engaging, easy and sufficiently witty.'—*St. James's Gazette.*

F. Langbridge. BALLADS OF THE BRAVE: Poems of Chivalry, Enterprise, Courage, and Constancy, from the Earliest Times to the Present Day. Edited, with Notes, by Rev. F. LANGBRIDGE. *Crown 8vo. Buckram.* 3s. 6d. *School Edition.* 2s. 6d.

'A very happy conception happily carried out. These "Ballads of the Brave" are intended to suit the real tastes of boys, and will suit the taste of the great majority.'—*Spectator.* 'The book is full of splendid things.'—*World.*

Lang and Craigie. THE POEMS OF ROBERT BURNS. Edited by ANDREW LANG and W. A. CRAIGIE. With Portrait. *Demy 8vo, gilt top.* 6s.

This edition contains a carefully collated Text, numerous Notes, critical and textual, a critical and biographical Introduction, and a Glossary.

'Among the editions in one volume, Mr. Andrew Lang's will take the place of authority.'—*Times.*

'To the general public the beauty of its type, and the fair proportions of its pages, as well as the excellent chronological arrangement of the poems, should make it acceptable enough. Mr. Lang and his publishers have certainly succeeded in producing an attractive popular edition of the poet, in which the brightly written biographical introduction is not the least notable feature.'—*Glasgow Herald.*

English Classics

Edited by W. E. HENLEY.

'Very dainty volumes are these; the paper, type, and light-green binding are all very agreeable to the eye. *Simplex munditiis* is the phrase that might be applied to them.'—*Globe.*

'The volumes are strongly bound in green buckram, are of a convenient size, and pleasant to look upon, so that whether on the shelf, or on the table, or in the hand the possessor is thoroughly content with them.'—*Guardian.*

'The paper, type, and binding of this edition are in excellent taste, and leave nothing to be desired by lovers of literature.'—*Standard.*

THE LIFE AND OPINIONS OF TRISTRAM SHANDY. By LAWRENCE STERNE. With an Introduction by CHARLES WHIBLEY, and a Portrait. *2 vols.* 7s.

THE COMEDIES OF WILLIAM CONGREVE. With an Introduction by G. S. STREET, and a Portrait. *2 vols.* 7s.

THE ADVENTURES OF HAJJI BABA OF ISPAHAN. By JAMES MORIER. With an Introduction by E. G. BROWNE, M.A., and a Portrait. *2 vols.* *7s.*

THE LIVES OF DONNE, WOTTON, HOOKER, HERBERT, AND SANDERSON. By IZAAK WALTON. With an Introduction by VERNON BLACKBURN, and a Portrait. *3s. 6d.*

THE LIVES OF THE ENGLISH POETS. By SAMUEL JOHNSON, LL.D. With an Introduction by J. H. MILLAR, and a Portrait. *3 vols.* *10s. 6d.*

Illustrated Books

Jane Barlow. THE BATTLE OF THE FROGS AND MICE, translated by JANE BARLOW, Author of 'Irish Idylls,' and pictured by F. D. BEDFORD. *Small 4to.* *6s. net.*

S. Baring Gould. A BOOK OF FAIRY TALES retold by S. BARING GOULD. With numerous illustrations and initial letters by ARTHUR J. GASKIN. *Second Edition.* *Crown 8vo.* *Buckram.* *6s.*

'Mr. Baring Gould has done a good deed, and is deserving of gratitude, in re-writing in honest, simple style the old stories that delighted the childhood of "our fathers and grandfathers." We do not think he has omitted any of our favourite stories, the stories that are commonly regarded as merely "old fashioned." As to the form of the book, and the printing, which is by Messrs. Constable, it were difficult to commend overmuch.—*Saturday Review.*

S. Baring Gould. OLD ENGLISH FAIRY TALES. Collected and edited by S. BARING GOULD. With Numerous Illustrations by F. D. BEDFORD. *Second Edition.* *Crown 8vo.* *Buckram.* *6s.*

'A charming volume, which children will be sure to appreciate. The stories have been selected with great ingenuity from various old ballads and folk-tales, and, having been somewhat altered and readjusted, now stand forth, clothed in Mr. Baring Gould's delightful English, to enchant youthful readers. All the tales are good.'—*Guardian.*

S. Baring Gould. A BOOK OF NURSERY SONGS AND RHYMES. Edited by S. BARING GOULD, and Illustrated by the Birmingham Art School. *Buckram, gilt top.* *Crown 8vo.* 6s.

'The volume is very complete in its way, as it contains nursery songs to the number of 77, game-rhymes, and jingles. To the student we commend the sensible introduction, and the explanatory notes. The volume is superbly printed on soft, thick paper, which it is a pleasure to touch; and the borders and pictures are, as we have said, among the very best specimens we have seen of the Gaskin school.' —*Birmingham Gazette.*

H. C. Beeching. A BOOK OF CHRISTMAS VERSE. Edited by H. C. BEECHING, M.A., and Illustrated by WALTER CRANE. *Crown 8vo, gilt top.* 5*s.*

A collection of the best verse inspired by the birth of Christ from the Middle Ages to the present day. A distinction of the book is the large number of poems it contains by modern authors, a few of which are here printed for the first time.

'An anthology which, from its unity of aim and high poetic excellence, has a better right to exist than most of its fellows.'—*Guardian.*

History

Gibbon. THE DECLINE AND FALL OF THE ROMAN EMPIRE. By EDWARD GIBBON. A New Edition, Edited with Notes, Appendices, and Maps, by J. B. BURY, M.A., Fellow of Trinity College, Dublin. *In Seven Volumes. Demy 8vo. Gilt top.* 8*s.* 6*d. each. Also crown 8vo.* 6*s. each. Vol. I.*

'The time has certainly arrived for a new edition of Gibbon's great work. . . . Professor Bury is the right man to undertake this task. His learning is amazing, both in extent and accuracy. The book is issued in a handy form, and at a moderate price, and it is admirably printed.'—*Times.*

'The edition is edited as a classic should be edited, removing nothing, yet indicating the value of the text, and bringing it up to date. It promises to be of the utmost value, and will be a welcome addition to many libraries.'—*Scotsman.*

'This edition, so far as one may judge from the first instalment, is a marvel of erudition and critical skill, and it is the very minimum of praise to predict that the seven volumes of it will supersede Dean Milman's as the standard edition of our great historical classic.'—*Glasgow Herald.*

'The beau-ideal Gibbon has arrived at last.'—*Sketch.*

'At last there is an adequate modern edition of Gibbon. . . . The best edition the nineteenth century could produce.'—*Manchester Guardian.*

Flinders Petrie. A HISTORY OF EGYPT, FROM THE EARLIEST TIMES TO THE PRESENT DAY. Edited by W. M. FLINDERS PETRIE, D.C.L., LL.D., Professor of Egyptology at University College. *Fully Illustrated. In Six Volumes. Crown 8vo.* 6*s. each.*

Vol. I. PREHISTORIC TIMES TO XVI. DYNASTY. W. M. F. Petrie. *Second Edition.*

'A history written in the spirit of scientific precision so worthily represented by Dr. Petrie and his school cannot but promote sound and accurate study, and supply a vacant place in the English literature of Egyptology.'—*Times.*

Flinders Petrie. EGYPTIAN TALES. Edited by W. M. FLINDERS PETRIE. Illustrated by TRISTRAM ELLIS. *In Two Volumes. Crown 8vo.* 3*s.* 6*d. each.*

'A valuable addition to the literature of comparative folk-lore. The drawings are really illustrations in the literal sense of the word.'—*Globe.*

'It has a scientific value to the student of history and archæology.'—*Scotsman.*

'Invaluable as a picture of life in Palestine and Egypt.'—*Daily News.*

Flinders Petrie. EGYPTIAN DECORATIVE ART. By W. M. FLINDERS PETRIE, D.C.L. With 120 Illustrations. *Crown 8vo.* 3s. 6d.

'Professor Flinders Petrie is not only a profound Egyptologist, but an accomplished student of comparative archæology. In these lectures, delivered at the Royal Institution, he displays both qualifications with rare skill in elucidating the development of decorative art in Egypt, and in tracing its influence on the art of other countries. Few experts can speak with higher authority and wider knowledge than the Professor himself, and in any case his treatment of his subject is full of learning and insight.'—*Times.*

S. Baring Gould. THE TRAGEDY OF THE CÆSARS. The Emperors of the Julian and Claudian Lines. With numerous Illustrations from Busts, Gems, Cameos, etc. By S. BARING GOULD, Author of 'Mehalah,' etc. *Third Edition. Royal 8vo.* 15s.

'A most splendid and fascinating book on a subject of undying interest. The great feature of the book is the use the author has made of the existing portraits of the Caesars, and the admirable critical subtlety he has exhibited in dealing with this line of research. It is brilliantly written, and the illustrations are supplied on a scale of profuse magnificence.'—*Daily Chronicle.*

'The volumes will in no sense disappoint the general reader. Indeed, in their way, there is nothing in any sense so good in English. . . . Mr. Baring Gould has presented his narrative in such a way as not to make one dull page.'—*Athenæum.*

A. Clark. THE COLLEGES OF OXFORD: Their History, their Traditions. By Members of the University. Edited by A. CLARK, M.A., Fellow and Tutor of Lincoln College. *8vo.* 12s. 6d.

'A work which will certainly be appealed to for many years as the standard book on the Colleges of Oxford.'—*Athenæum.*

Perrens. THE HISTORY OF FLORENCE FROM 1434 TO 1492. By F. T. PERRENS. Translated by HANNAH LYNCH. *8vo.* 12s. 6d.

A history of Florence under the domination of Cosimo, Piero, and Lorenzo de Medicis.

'This is a standard book by an honest and intelligent historian, who has deserved well of all who are interested in Italian history.'—*Manchester Guardian.*

E. L. S. Horsburgh. THE CAMPAIGN OF WATERLOO. By E. L. S. HORSBURGH, B.A. *With Plans. Crown 8vo.* 5s.

'A brilliant essay—simple, sound, and thorough.'—*Daily Chronicle.*

'A study, the most concise, the most lucid, the most critical that has been produced.'—*Birmingham Mercury.*

'A careful and precise study, a fair and impartial criticism, and an eminently readable book.'—*Admiralty and Horse Guards Gazette.*

H. B. George. BATTLES OF ENGLISH HISTORY. By H. B. GEORGE, M.A., Fellow of New College, Oxford. *With numerous Plans. Third Edition. Crown 8vo.* 6s.

'Mr. George has undertaken a very useful task—that of making military affairs intelligible and instructive to non-military readers—and has executed it with laudable intelligence and industry, and with a large measure of success.'—*Times.*

'This book is almost a revelation; and we heartily congratulate the author on his work and on the prospect of the reward he has well deserved for so much conscientious and sustained labour.'—*Daily Chronicle.*

O. Browning. A SHORT HISTORY OF MEDIÆVAL ITALY, A.D. 1250-1530. By OSCAR BROWNING, Fellow and Tutor of King's College, Cambridge. *Second Edition. In Two Volumes. Crown 8vo. 5s. each.*

VOL. I. 1250-1409.—Guelphs and Ghibellines.
VOL. II. 1409-1530.—The Age of the Condottieri.

'A vivid picture of mediæval Italy.'—*Standard.*

'Mr. Browning is to be congratulated on the production of a work of immense labour and learning.'—*Westminster Gazette.*

O'Grady. THE STORY OF IRELAND. By STANDISH O'GRADY, Author of 'Finn and his Companions.' *Cr. 8vo. 2s. 6d.*

'Most delightful, most stimulating. Its racy humour, its original imaginings, make it one of the freshest, breeziest volumes.'—*Methodist Times.*

'A survey at once graphic, acute, and quaintly written.'—*Times.*

Biography

R. L. Stevenson. VAILIMA LETTERS. By ROBERT LOUIS STEVENSON. With an Etched Portrait by WILLIAM STRANG, and other Illustrations. *Second Edition. Crown 8vo. Buckram. 7s. 6d.*

'The Vailima Letters are rich in all the varieties of that charm which have secured for Stevenson the affection of many others besides "journalists, fellow-novelists, and boys."'—*The Times.*

'Few publications have in our time been more eagerly awaited than these "Vailima Letters," giving the first fruits of the correspondence of Robert Louis Stevenson. But, high as the tide of expectation has run, no reader can possibly be disappointed in the result.'—*St. James's Gazette.*

'For the student of English literature these letters indeed are a treasure. They are more like "Scott's Journal" in kind than any other literary autobiography.' —*National Observer.*

F. W. Joyce. THE LIFE OF SIR FREDERICK GORE OUSELEY. By F. W. JOYCE, M.A. With Portraits and Illustrations. *Crown 8vo. 7s. 6d.*

'All the materials have been well digested, and the book gives us a complete picture of the life of one who will ever be held in loving remembrance by his personal friends, and who in the history of music in this country will always occupy a prominent position on account of the many services he rendered to the art.'—*Musical News.*

'This book has been undertaken in quite the right spirit, and written with sympathy, insight, and considerable literary skill.'—*Times.*

W. G. Collingwood. THE LIFE OF JOHN RUSKIN. By W. G. COLLINGWOOD, M.A., Editor of Mr. Ruskin's Poems. With numerous Portraits, and 13 Drawings by Mr. Ruskin. *Second Edition. 2 vols. 8vo. 32s.*

'No more magnificent volumes have been published for a long time.'—*Times.*

'It is long since we had a biography with such delights of substance and of form. Such a book is a pleasure for the day, and a joy for ever.'—*Daily Chronicle.*

'A noble monument of a noble subject. One of the most beautiful books about one of the noblest lives of our century.'—*Glasgow Herald.*

C. Waldstein. JOHN RUSKIN: a Study. By CHARLES WALDSTEIN, M.A., Fellow of King's College, Cambridge. With a Photogravure Portrait after Professor HERKOMER. *Post 8vo.* 5*s.*

'A thoughtful, impartial, well-written criticism of Ruskin's teaching, intended to separate what the author regards as valuable and permanent from what is transient and erroneous in the great master's writing.'—*Daily Chronicle.*

W. H. Hutton. THE LIFE OF SIR THOMAS MORE. By W. H. HUTTON, M.A., Author of 'William Laud.' *With Portraits. Crown 8vo.* 5*s.*

'The book lays good claim to high rank among our biographies. It is excellently, even lovingly, written.'—*Scotsman.*
'An excellent monograph.'—*Times.*
'A most complete presentation.'—*Daily Chronicle.*

M. Kaufmann. CHARLES KINGSLEY. By M. KAUFMANN, M.A. *Crown 8vo. Buckram.* 5*s.*

A biography of Kingsley, especially dealing with his achievements in social reform.
'The author has certainly gone about his work with conscientiousness and industry.—*Sheffield Daily Telegraph.*

A. F. Robbins. THE EARLY LIFE OF WILLIAM EWART GLADSTONE. By A. F. ROBBINS. *With Portraits. Crown 8vo.* 6*s.*

'Considerable labour and much skill of presentation have not oeen unworthily expended on this interesting work.'—*Times.*

Clark Russell. THE LIFE OF ADMIRAL LORD COLLINGWOOD. By W. CLARK RUSSELL, Author of 'The Wreck of the Grosvenor.' With Illustrations by F. BRANGWYN. *Third Edition. Crown 8vo.* 6*s.*

'A most excellent and wholesome book, which we should like to see in the hands of every boy in the country.'—*St. James's Gazette.*
'A really good book.'—*Saturday Review.*

Southey. ENGLISH SEAMEN (Howard, Clifford, Hawkins. Drake, Cavendish). By ROBERT SOUTHEY. Edited, with an Introduction, by DAVID HANNAY. *Second Edition. Crown 8vo.* 6*s.*

'Admirable and well-told stories of our naval history.'—*Army and Navy Gazette.*
'A brave, inspiriting book.'—*Black and White.*
'The work of a master of style, and delightful all through.'—*Daily Chronicle.*

General Literature

S. Baring Gould. OLD COUNTRY LIFE. By S. BARING GOULD, Author of 'Mehalah,' etc. With Sixty-seven Illustrations by W. PARKINSON, F. D. BEDFORD, and F. MASEY. *Large Crown 8vo.* 10*s.* 6*d.* *Fifth and Cheaper Edition.* 6*s.*

"Old Country Life," as healthy wholesome reading, full of breezy life and movement, full of quaint stories vigorously told, will not be excelled by any book to be published throughout the year. Sound, hearty, and English to the core.'—*World.*

S. Baring Gould. HISTORIC ODDITIES AND STRANGE EVENTS. By S. BARING GOULD. *Third Edition. Crown 8vo.* 6*s.*

'A collection of exciting and entertaining chapters. The whole volume is delightful reading.'—*Times.*

S. Baring Gould. FREAKS OF FANATICISM. By S. BARING GOULD. *Third Edition. Crown 8vo.* 6*s.*

'Mr. Baring Gould has a keen eye for colour and effect, and the subjects he has chosen give ample scope to his descriptive and analytic faculties. A perfectly fascinating book.'—*Scottish Leader.*

S. Baring Gould. A GARLAND OF COUNTRY SONG: English Folk Songs with their Traditional Melodies. Collected and arranged by S. BARING GOULD and H. FLEETWOOD SHEPPARD. *Demy 4to.* 6*s.*

S. Baring Gould. SONGS OF THE WEST: Traditional Ballads and Songs of the West of England, with their Traditional Melodies. Collected by S. BARING GOULD, M.A., and H. FLEETWOOD SHEPPARD, M.A. Arranged for Voice and Piano. In 4 Parts (containing 25 Songs each), *Parts I., II., III.,* 3*s. each. Part IV.,* 5*s. In one Vol., French morocco,* 15*s.*

'A rich collection of humour, pathos, grace, and poetic fancy.'—*Saturday Review.*

S. Baring Gould. YORKSHIRE ODDITIES AND STRANGE EVENTS. *Fourth Edition. Crown 8vo.* 6*s.*

S. Baring Gould. STRANGE SURVIVALS AND SUPERSTITIONS. With Illustrations. By S. BARING GOULD. *Crown 8vo. Second Edition.* 6*s.*

'We have read Mr. Baring Gould's book from beginning to end. It is full of quaint and various information, and there is not a dull page in it.'—*Notes and Queries.*

S. Baring Gould. THE DESERTS OF SOUTHERN FRANCE. By S. BARING-GOULD. With numerous Illustrations by F. D. BEDFORD, S. HUTTON, etc. 2 *vols. Demy 8vo.* 32*s.*

This book is the first serious attempt to describe the great barren tableland that extends to the south of Limousin in the Department of Aveyron, Lot, etc., a country of dolomite cliffs, and cañons, and subterranean rivers. The region is full of prehistoric and historic interest, relics of cave-dwellers, of mediæval robbers, and of the English domination and the Hundred Years' War.

'His two richly-illustrated volumes are full of matter of interest to the geologist, the archæologist, and the student of history and manners.'—*Scotsman.*

'It deals with its subject in a manner which rarely fails to arrest attention.'—*Times.*

R. S. Baden-Powell. THE DOWNFALL OF PREMPEH. A Diary of Life with the Native Levy in Ashanti, 1895. By Lieut.-Col. BADEN-POWELL. With 21 Illustrations, a Map, and a Special Chapter on the Political and Commercial Position of Ashanti by Sir GEORGE BADEN-POWELL, K.C.M.G., M.P. *Demy 8vo.* 10*s.* 6*d.*

'A compact, faithful, most readable record of the campaign.'—*Daily News.*
'A bluff and vigorous narrative.'—*Glasgow Herald.*
'A really interesting book.'—*Yorkshire Post.*

W. E. Gladstone. THE SPEECHES AND PUBLIC ADDRESSES OF THE RT. HON. W. E. GLADSTONE, M.P. Edited by A. W. HUTTON, M.A., and H. J. COHEN, M.A. With Portraits. *8vo. Vols. IX. and X.* *12s. 6d. each.*

Henley and Whibley. A BOOK OF ENGLISH PROSE. Collected by W. E. HENLEY and CHARLES WHIBLEY. *Cr. 8vo.* *6s.*

'A unique volume of extracts—an art gallery of early prose.'—*Birmingham Post.*
'An admirable companion to Mr. Henley's "Lyra Heroica."'—*Saturday Review.*
'Quite delightful. The choice made has been excellent, and the volume has been most admirably printed by Messrs. Constable. A greater treat for those not well acquainted with pre-Restoration prose could not be imagined.'—*Athenæum.*

J. Wells. OXFORD AND OXFORD LIFE. By Members of the University. Edited by J. WELLS, M.A., Fellow and Tutor of Wadham College. *Crown 8vo.* *3s. 6d.*

This work contains an account of life at Oxford—intellectual, social, and religious—a careful estimate of necessary expenses, a review of recent changes, a statement of the present position of the University, and chapters on Women's Education, aids to study, and University Extension.
'We congratulate Mr. Wells on the production of a readable and intelligent account of Oxford as it is at the present time, written by persons who are possessed of a close acquaintance with the system and life of the University.'—*Athenæum.*

W. M. Dixon. A PRIMER OF TENNYSON. By W. M. DIXON, M.A., Professor of English Literature at Mason College. *Crown 8vo.* *2s. 6d.*

'Much sound and well-expressed criticism and acute literary judgments. The bibliography is a boon.'—*Speaker.*
'No better estimate of the late Laureate's work has yet been published. His sketch of Tennyson's life contains everything essential; his bibliography is full and concise: his literary criticism is most interesting.'—*Glasgow Herald.*

W. A. Craigie. A PRIMER OF BURNS. By W. A. CRAIGIE. *Crown 8vo.* *2s. 6d.*

This book is planned on a method similar to the 'Primer of Tennyson.' It has also a glossary.
'A valuable addition to the literature of the poet.'—*Times.*
'An excellent short account.'—*Pall Mall Gazette.*
'An admirable introduction.'—*Globe.*

L. Whibley. GREEK OLIGARCHIES: THEIR ORGANISATION AND CHARACTER. By L. WHIBLEY, M.A., Fellow of Pembroke College, Cambridge. *Crown 8vo.* *6s.*

'An exceedingly useful handbook: a careful and well-arranged study of an obscure subject.'—*Times.*
'Mr. Whibley is never tedious or pedantic.'—*Pall Mall Gazette.*

W. B. Worsfold. SOUTH AFRICA: Its History and its Future. By W. BASIL WORSFOLD, M.A. *With a Map. Crown 8vo.* *6s.*

'An intensely interesting book.'—*Daily Chronicle.*
'A monumental work compressed into a very moderate compass.'—*World.*

C. H. Pearson. ESSAYS AND CRITICAL REVIEWS. By C. H. PEARSON, M.A., Author of 'National Life and Character.' Edited, with a Biographical Sketch, by H. A. STRONG, M.A., LL.D. With a Portrait. *Demy 8vo.* 10*s.* 6*d.*

'These fine essays illustrate the great breadth of his historical and literary sympathies and the remarkable variety of his intellectual interests.'—*Glasgow Herald.*

'Remarkable for careful handling, breadth of view, and thorough knowledge.'—*Scotsman.*

'Charming essays.'—*Spectator.*

Ouida. VIEWS AND OPINIONS. By OUIDA. *Crown 8vo. Second Edition.* 6*s.*

'Ouida is outspoken, and the reader of this book will not have a dull moment. The book is full of variety, and sparkles with entertaining matter.'—*Speaker.*

J. S. Shedlock. THE PIANOFORTE SONATA: Its Origin and Development. By J. S. SHEDLOCK. *Crown 8vo.* 5*s.*

'This work should be in the possession of every musician and amateur, for it not only embodies a concise and lucid history of the origin of one of the most important forms of musical composition, but, by reason of the painstaking research and accuracy of the author's statements, it is a very valuable work for reference.'—*Athenæum.*

E. M. Bowden. THE EXAMPLE OF BUDDHA: Being Quotations from Buddhist Literature for each Day in the Year. Compiled by E. M. BOWDEN. With Preface by Sir EDWIN ARNOLD. *Third Edition.* 16*mo.* 2*s.* 6*d.*

J. Beever. PRACTICAL FLY-FISHING, Founded on Nature, by JOHN BEEVER, late of the Thwaite House, Coniston. A New Edition, with a Memoir of the Author by W. G. COLLINGWOOD, M.A. *Crown 8vo.* 3*s.* 6*d.*

A little book on Fly-Fishing by an old friend of Mr. Ruskin.

Science

Freudenreich. DAIRY BACTERIOLOGY. A Short Manual for the Use of Students. By Dr. ED. VON FREUDENREICH. Translated from the German by J. R. AINSWORTH DAVIS, B.A., F.C.P. *Crown 8vo.* 2*s.* 6*d.*

Chalmers Mitchell. OUTLINES OF BIOLOGY. By P. CHALMERS MITCHELL, M.A., F.Z.S. *Fully Illustrated. Crown 8vo.* 6*s.*

A text-book designed to cover the new Schedule issued by the Royal College of Physicians and Surgeons.

G. Massee. A MONOGRAPH OF THE MYXOGASTRES. By GEORGE MASSEE. With 12 Coloured Plates. *Royal 8vo.* 18*s. net.*

'A work much in advance of any book in the language treating of this group of organisms. It is indispensable to every student of the Myxogastres. The coloured plates deserve high praise for their accuracy and execution.'—*Nature.*

Philosophy

L. T. Hobhouse. THE THEORY OF KNOWLEDGE. By L. T. HOBHOUSE, Fellow and Tutor of Corpus College, Oxford. *Demy 8vo. 21s.*

'The most important contribution to English philosophy since the publication of Mr. Bradley's "Appearance and Reality." Full of brilliant criticism and of positive theories which are models of lucid statement.'—*Glasgow Herald.*

An elaborate and often brilliantly written volume. The treatment is one of great freshness, and the illustrations are particularly numerous and apt.'—*Times.*

W. H. Fairbrother. THE PHILOSOPHY OF T. H. GREEN. By W. H. FAIRBROTHER, M.A., Lecturer at Lincoln College, Oxford. *Crown 8vo.* 3*s.* 6*d.*

This volume is expository, not critical, and is intended for senior students at the Universities and others, as a statement of Green's teaching, and an introduction to the study of Idealist Philosophy.

'In every way an admirable book. As an introduction to the writings of perhaps the most remarkable speculative thinker whom England has produced in the present century, nothing could be better than Mr. Fairbrother's exposition and criticism.'—*Glasgow Herald.*

F. W. Bussell. THE SCHOOL OF PLATO: its Origin and its Revival under the Roman Empire. By F. W. BUSSELL, M.A., Fellow and Tutor of Brasenose College, Oxford. *Demy 8vo. Two volumes. 7s. 6d. each. Vol. I.*

'A highly valuable contribution to the history of ancient thought.'—*Glasgow Herald.*

'A clever and stimulating book, provocative of thought and deserving careful reading.' —*Manchester Guardian.*

F. S. Granger. THE WORSHIP OF THE ROMANS. By F. S. GRANGER, M.A., Litt.D., Professor of Philosophy at University College, Nottingham. *Crown 8vo. 6s.*

The author has attempted to delineate that group of beliefs which stood in close connection with the Roman religion, and among the subjects treated are Dreams, Nature Worship, Roman Magic, Divination, Holy Places, Victims, etc. Thus the book is, apart from its immediate subject, a contribution to folk-lore and comparative psychology.

'A scholarly analysis of the religious ceremonies, beliefs, and superstitions of ancient Rome, conducted in the new instructive light of comparative anthropology.'—*Times.*

Theology

E. C. S. Gibson. THE XXXIX. ARTICLES OF THE CHURCH OF ENGLAND. Edited with an Introduction by E. C. S. GIBSON, D.D., Vicar of Leeds, late Principal of Wells Theological College. *In Two Volumes. Demy 8vo. 7s. 6d. each. Vol. I. Articles I.-VIII.*

'The tone maintained throughout is not that of the partial advocate, but the faithful exponent.'—*Scotsman.*

'There are ample proofs of clearness of expression, sobriety of judgment, and breadth of view. . . . The book will be welcome to all students of the subject, and its sound, definite, and loyal theology ought to be of great service.'—*National Observer.*

'So far from repelling the general reader, its orderly arrangement, lucid treatment, and felicity of diction invite and encourage his attention.'—*Yorkshire Post.*

R. L. Ottley. THE DOCTRINE OF THE INCARNATION. By R. L. OTTLEY, M.A., late fellow of Magdalen College, Oxon., Principal of Pusey House. *In Two Volumes. Demy 8vo.* 15*s.*

'Learned and reverent: lucid and well arranged.'—*Record.*

'Accurate, well ordered, and judicious.'—*National Observer.*

'A clear and remarkably full account of the main currents of speculation. Scholarly precision . . . genuine tolerance . . . intense interest in his subject—are Mr. Ottley's merits.'—*Guardian.*

S. R. Driver. SERMONS ON SUBJECTS CONNECTED WITH THE OLD TESTAMENT. By S. R. DRIVER, D.D., Canon of Christ Church, Regius Professor of Hebrew in the University of Oxford. *Crown 8vo. 6s.*

'A welcome companion to the author's famous 'Introduction.' No man can read these discourses without feeling that Dr. Driver is fully alive to the deeper teaching of the Old Testament.'—*Guardian.*

T. K. Cheyne. FOUNDERS OF OLD TESTAMENT CRITICISM: Biographical, Descriptive, and Critical Studies. By T. K. CHEYNE, D.D., Oriel Professor of the Interpretation of Holy Scripture at Oxford. *Large crown 8vo. 7s. 6d.*

This important book is a historical sketch of O. T. Criticism in the form of biographical studies from the days of Eichhorn to those of Driver and Robertson Smith. It is the only book of its kind in English.

'A very learned and instructive work.'—*Times.*

C. H. Prior. CAMBRIDGE SERMONS. Edited by C. H. PRIOR, M.A., Fellow and Tutor of Pembroke College. *Crown 8vo. 6s.*

A volume of sermons preached before the University of Cambridge by various preachers, including the Archbishop of Canterbury and Bishop Westcott.

'A representative collection. Bishop Westcott's is a noble sermon.'—*Guardian.*

H. C. Beeching. SERMONS TO SCHOOLBOYS. By H. C. BEECHING, M.A., Rector of Yattendon, Berks. With a Preface by Canon SCOTT HOLLAND. *Crown 8vo. 2s. 6d.*

Seven sermons preached before the boys of Bradfield College.

E. B. Layard. RELIGION IN BOYHOOD. Notes on the Religious Training of Boys. With a Preface by J. R. ILLINGWORTH. By E. B. LAYARD, M.A. *18mo.* *1s.*

Devotional Books.

With Full-page Illustrations. Fcap. 8vo. Buckram. 3s. 6d.
Padded morocco, 5s.

THE IMITATION OF CHRIST. By THOMAS À KEMPIS. With an Introduction by DEAN FARRAR. Illustrated by C. M. GERE, and printed in black and red. *Second Edition.*

'Amongst all the innumerable English editions of the "Imitation," there can have been few which were prettier than this one, printed in strong and handsome type by Messrs. Constable, with all the glory of red initials, and the comfort of buckram binding.'—*Glasgow Herald.*

THE CHRISTIAN YEAR. By JOHN KEBLE. With an Introduction and Notes by W. LOCK, M.A., Sub-Warden of Keble College, Ireland Professor at Oxford, Author of the 'Life of John Keble.' Illustrated by R. ANNING BELL.

'The present edition is annotated with all the care and insight to be expected from Mr. Lock. The progress and circumstances of its composition are detailed in the Introduction. There is an interesting Appendix on the MSS. of the "Christian Year," and another giving the order in which the poems were written. A "Short Analysis of the Thought" is prefixed to each, and any difficulty in the text is explained in a note.—*Guardian.*

'The most acceptable edition of this ever-popular work.'—*Globe.*

Leaders of Religion

Edited by H. C. BEECHING, M.A. *With Portraits, crown 8vo.*

A series of short biographies of the most prominent leaders of religious life and thought of all ages and countries. **3/6**

The following are ready—

CARDINAL NEWMAN. By R. H. HUTTON.

JOHN WESLEY. By J. H. OVERTON, M.A.

BISHOP WILBERFORCE. By G. W. DANIEL, M.A.

CARDINAL MANNING. By A. W. HUTTON, M.A.

CHARLES SIMEON. By H. C. G. MOULE, M.A.

JOHN KEBLE. By WALTER LOCK, M.A.

THOMAS CHALMERS. By Mrs. OLIPHANT.

LANCELOT ANDREWES. By R. L. OTTLEY, M.A.

AUGUSTINE OF CANTERBURY. By E. L. CUTTS, D.D.

WILLIAM LAUD. By W. H. HUTTON, M.A.

JOHN KNOX. By F. M'CUNN.

JOHN HOWE. By R. F. HORTON, D.D.

BISHOP KEN. By F. A. CLARKE, M.A.

GEORGE FOX, THE QUAKER. By T. HODGKIN, D.C.L.

Other volumes will be announced in due course.

Fiction

SIX SHILLING NOVELS

Marie Corelli's Novels

Crown 8vo. 6s. each.

A ROMANCE OF TWO WORLDS. *Fourteenth Edition.*

VENDETTA. *Eleventh Edition.*

THELMA. *Fourteenth Edition.*

ARDATH. *Tenth Edition.*

THE SOUL OF LILITH. *Ninth Edition.*

WORMWOOD. *Eighth Edition.*

BARABBAS: A DREAM OF THE WORLD'S TRAGEDY. *Twenty-fifth Edition.*

'The tender reverence of the treatment and the imaginative beauty of the writing have reconciled us to the daring of the conception, and the conviction is forced on us that even so exalted a subject cannot be made too familiar to us, provided it be presented in the true spirit of Christian faith. The amplifications of the Scripture narrative are often conceived with high poetic insight, and this "Dream of the World's Tragedy" is, despite some trifling incongruities, a lofty and not inadequate paraphrase of the supreme climax of the inspired narrative.'—*Dublin Review.*

THE SORROWS OF SATAN. *Twenty-ninth Edition.*

'A very powerful piece of work. . . . The conception is magnificent, and is likely to win an abiding place within the memory of man. . . . The author has immense command of language, and a limitless audacity. . . . This interesting and remarkable romance will live long after much of the ephemeral literature of the day is forgotten. . . . A literary phenomenon . . . novel, and even sublime.'—W. T. STEAD in the *Review of Reviews.*

Anthony Hope's Novels

Crown 8vo. 6s. each.

THE GOD IN THE CAR. *Seventh Edition.*

'A very remarkable book, deserving of critical analysis impossible within our limit; brilliant, but not superficial; well considered, but not elaborated; constructed with the proverbial art that conceals, but yet allows itself to be enjoyed by readers to whom fine literary method is a keen pleasure; true without cynicism, subtle without affectation, humorous without strain, witty without offence, inevitably sad, with an unmorose simplicity.'—*The World.*

A CHANGE OF AIR. *Fourth Edition.*

'A graceful, vivacious comedy, true to human nature. The characters are traced with a masterly hand.'—*Times.*

A MAN OF MARK. *Third Edition.*

'Of all Mr. Hope's books, "A Man of Mark" is the one which best compares with "The Prisoner of Zenda." The two romances are unmistakably the work of the same writer, and he possesses a style of narrative peculiarly seductive, piquant, comprehensive, and—his own.'—*National Observer.*

THE CHRONICLES OF COUNT ANTONIO. *Third Edition.*

'It is a perfectly enchanting story of love and chivalry, and pure romance. The outlawed Count is the most constant, desperate, and withal modest and tender of lovers, a peerless gentleman, an intrepid fighter, a very faithful friend, and a most magnanimous foe. In short, he is an altogether admirable, lovable, and delightful hero. There is not a word in the volume that can give offence to the most fastidious taste of man or woman, and there is not, either, a dull paragraph in it. The book is everywhere instinct with the most exhilarating spirit of adventure, and delicately perfumed with the sentiment of all heroic and honourable deeds of history and romance.'—*Guardian.*

S. Baring Gould's Novels

Crown 8vo. 6s. each.

'To say that a book is by the author of "Mehalah" is to imply that it contains a story cast on strong lines, containing dramatic possibilities, vivid and sympathetic descriptions of Nature, and a wealth of ingenious imagery.'—*Speaker.*

'That whatever Mr. Baring Gould writes is well worth reading, is a conclusion that may be very generally accepted. His views of life are fresh and vigorous, his language pointed and characteristic, the incidents of which he makes use are striking and original, his characters are life-like, and though somewhat exceptional people, are drawn and coloured with artistic force. Add to this that his descriptions of scenes and scenery are painted with the loving eyes and skilled hands of a master of his art, that he is always fresh and never dull, and under such conditions it is no wonder that readers have gained confidence both in his power of amusing and satisfying them, and that year by year his popularity widens.'—*Court Circular.*

ARMINELL: A Social Romance. *Fourth Edition.*

URITH: A Story of Dartmoor. *Fourth Edition.*

'The author is at his best.'—*Times.*

'He has nearly reached the high water-mark of "Mehalah."'—*National Observer.*

IN THE ROAR OF THE SEA. *Fifth Edition.*

'One of the best imagined and most enthralling stories the author has produced.' —*Saturday Review.*

MRS. CURGENVEN OF CURGENVEN. *Fourth Edition.*

'A novel of vigorous humour and sustained power.'—*Graphic.*
'The swing of the narrative is splendid.'—*Sussex Daily News*

CHEAP JACK ZITA. *Third Edition.*

'A powerful drama of human passion.'—*Westminster Gazette.*
'A story worthy the author.'—*National Observer.*

THE QUEEN OF LOVE. *Fourth Edition.*

'The scenery is admirable, and the dramatic incidents are most striking.'—*Glasgow Herald.*
'Strong, interesting, and clever.'—*Westminster Gazette.*
'You cannot put it down until you have finished it.'—*Punch.*
'Can be heartily recommended to all who care for cleanly, energetic, and interesting fiction.'—*Sussex Daily News.*

KITTY ALONE. *Fourth Edition.*

'A strong and original story, teeming with graphic description, stirring incident, and, above all, with vivid and enthralling human interest.'—*Daily Telegraph.*
'Brisk, clever, keen, healthy, humorous, and interesting.'—*National Observer.*
'Full of quaint and delightful studies of character.'—*Bristol Mercury.*

NOÉMI: A Romance of the Cave-Dwellers. Illustrated by R. CATON WOODVILLE. *Third Edition.*

'"Noémi" is as excellent a tale of fighting and adventure as one may wish to meet. All the characters that interfere in this exciting tale are marked with properties of their own. The narrative also runs clear and sharp as the Loire itself.'—*Pall Mall Gazette.*
'Mr. Baring Gould's powerful story is full of the strong lights and shadows and vivid colouring to which he has accustomed us.'—*Standard.*

THE BROOM-SQUIRE. Illustrated by FRANK DADD. *Third Edition.*

'A strain of tenderness is woven through the web of his tragic tale, and its atmosphere is sweetened by the nobility and sweetness of the heroine's character.'—*Daily News.*
'A story of exceptional interest that seems to us to be better than anything he has written of late.'—*Speaker.* 'A powerful and striking story.'—*Guardian.*
'A powerful piece of work.'—*Black and White.*

Gilbert Parker's Novels

Crown 8vo. 6s. each.

PIERRE AND HIS PEOPLE. *Third Edition.*

'Stories happily conceived and finely executed. There is strength and genius in Mr. Parker's style.'—*Daily Telegraph.*

MRS. FALCHION. *Third Edition.*

'A splendid study of character.'—*Athenæum.*

'But little behind anything that has been done by any writer of our time.'—*Pall Mall Gazette.*

'A very striking and admirable novel.'—*St. James's Gazette.*

THE TRANSLATION OF A SAVAGE.

'The plot is original and one difficult to work out; but Mr. Parker has done it with great skill and delicacy. The reader who is not interested in this original, fresh, and well-told tale must be a dull person indeed.'—*Daily Chronicle.*

'A strong and successful piece of workmanship. The portrait of Lali, strong, dignified, and pure, is exceptionally well drawn.'—*Manchester Guardian.*

THE TRAIL OF THE SWORD. *Fourth Edition.*

'Everybody with a soul for romance will thoroughly enjoy "The Trail of the Sword."'—*St. James's Gazette.*

'A rousing and dramatic tale. A book like this, in which swords flash, great surprises are undertaken, and daring deeds done, in which men and women live and love in the old straightforward passionate way, is a joy inexpressible to the reviewer, brain-weary of the domestic tragedies and psychological puzzles of everyday fiction; and we cannot but believe that to the reader it will bring refreshment as welcome and as keen.'—*Daily Chronicle.*

WHEN VALMOND CAME TO PONTIAC: The Story of a Lost Napoleon. *Third Edition.*

'Here we find romance—real, breathing, living romance, but it runs flush with our own times, level with our own feelings. Not here can we complain of lack of inevitableness or homogeneity. The character of Valmond is drawn unerringly; his career, brief as it is, is placed before us as convincingly as history itself. The book must be read, we may say re-read, for any one thoroughly to appreciate Mr. Parker's delicate touch and innate sympathy with humanity.'—*Pall Mall Gazette.*

'The one work of genius which 1895 has as yet produced.'—*New Age.*

AN ADVENTURER OF THE NORTH: The Last Adventures of 'Pretty Pierre.'

'The present book is full of fine and moving stories of the great North, and it will add to Mr. Parker's already high reputation.'—*Glasgow Herald.*

'The new book is very romantic and very entertaining—full of that peculiarly elegant spirit of adventure which is so characteristic of Mr. Parker, and of that poetic thrill which has given him warmer, if less numerous, admirers than even his romantic story-telling gift has done.'—*Sketch.*

THE SEATS OF THE MIGHTY. *Illustrated. Fourth Edition.*

'The best thing he has done; one of the best things that any one has done lately.'—*St. James's Gazette.*

'Mr. Parker seems to become stronger and easier with every serious novel that he attempts. . . . In "The Seats of the Mighty" he shows the matured power which his former novels have led us to expect, and has produced a really fine historical novel. . . . The great creation of the book is Doltaire. . . . His character is drawn with quite masterly strokes, for he is a villain who is not altogether a villain, and who attracts the reader, as he did the other characters, by the extraordinary brilliance of his gifts, and by the almost unconscious acts of nobility which he performs. . . . Most sincerely is Mr. Parker to be congratulated on the finest novel he has yet written.'—*Athenæum.*

"Mr. Parker's latest book places him in the front rank of living novelists. 'The Seats of the Mighty' is a great book."—*Black and White.*

"One of the strongest stories of historical interest and adventure that we have read for many a day. . . . Throughout all, Mr. Parker moves with an assured step, while in his treatment of his subject there is that happy blending of the [illegible] with the prosaic which has distinguished all his writings. A notable and successful book."—*Speaker.*

"The story is very [illegible] and dramatically told. . . . In none of his books has his imaginative faculty appeared to such splendid purpose as here. Captain Moray, Alixe, Gabord, Voltaire—above all, Doltaire—and, indeed, every person who takes part in the action of the story are clearly conceived and finely drawn and individualised."—*Scotsman.*

"An admirable romance. The glory of a romance is its plot, and this plot is crowded with fine sensations, which have no rest until the fall of the famous old city and the final vindication of love."—*Pall Mall Gazette.*

Conan Doyle. ROUND THE RED LAMP. By A. CONAN DOYLE, Author of "The White Company," "The Adventures of Sherlock Holmes," etc. *Fourth Edition. Crown 8vo.* 6s.

"The book is, indeed, composed of leaves from life, and is far and away the best view that has been vouchsafed us behind the scenes of the consulting-room. It is very superior to 'The Diary of a late Physician.'"—*Illustrated London News.*

Stanley Weyman. UNDER THE RED ROBE. By STANLEY WEYMAN, Author of "A Gentleman of France." With Twelve Illustrations by R. Caton Woodville. *Eighth Edition. Crown 8vo.* 6s.

"A book of which we have read every word for the sheer pleasure of reading, and which we put down with a pang that we cannot forget it all and start again."—*Westminster Gazette.*

"Every one who reads books at all must read this thrilling romance, from the first page of which to the last the breathless reader is haled along. An inspiration of 'manliness and courage.'"—*Daily Chronicle.*

"A delightful tale of chivalry and adventure, vivid and dramatic, with a wholesome modesty and reverence for the highest."—*Globe.*

Mrs. Clifford. A FLASH OF SUMMER. By MRS. W. K. CLIFFORD, Author of "Aunt Anne," etc. *Second Edition. Crown 8vo.* 6s.

"The story is a very sad and a very beautiful one, exquisitely told, and enriched with many subtle touches of wise and tender insight. It will, undoubtedly, add to its author's reputation—already high—in the ranks of novelists."—*Speaker.*

"We must congratulate Mrs. Clifford upon a very successful and interesting story, told throughout with finish and a delicate sense of proportion, qualities which, indeed, have always distinguished the best work of this very able writer."—*Manchester Guardian.*

Emily Lawless. HURRISH. By the Honble. EMILY LAWLESS, Author of "Maelcho," etc. *Fifth Edition. Crown 8vo.* 6s.

A reissue of Miss Lawless' most popular novel, uniform with "Maelcho."

Emily Lawless. MAELCHO: a Sixteenth Century Romance. By the Honble. EMILY LAWLESS, Author of "Grania," "Hurrish," etc. *Second Edition. Crown 8vo.* 6s.

"A really great book."—*Spectator.*

"There is no keener pleasure in life than the recognition of genius. Good work is commoner than it used to be, but the best is as rare as ever. All the more gladly, therefore, do we welcome in 'Maelcho' a piece of work of the first order, which we do not hesitate to describe as one of the most remarkable literary achievements of this generation. Miss Lawless is possessed of the very essence of historical genius."—*Manchester Guardian.*

J. H. Findlater. THE GREEN GRAVES OF BALGOWRIE. By JANE H. FINDLATER. *Third Edition. Crown 8vo.* 6s.

'A powerful and vivid story.'—*Standard.*

'A beautiful story, sad and strange as truth itself.'—*Vanity Fair.*

'A work of remarkable interest and originality.'—*National Observer.*

'A really original novel.'—*Journal of Education.*

'A very charming and pathetic tale.'—*Pall Mall Gazette.*

'A singularly original, clever, and beautiful story.'—*Guardian.*

'"The Green Graves of Balgowrie" reveals to us a new Scotch writer of undoubted faculty and reserve force.'—*Spectator.*

'An exquisite idyll, delicate, affecting, and beautiful.'—*Black and White.*

'Permeated with high and noble purpose. It is one of the most wholesome stories we have met with, and cannot fail to leave a deep and lasting impression.'—*Newsagent.*

E. F. Benson. DODO: A DETAIL OF THE DAY. By E. F. BENSON. *Sixteenth Edition. Crown 8vo.* 6s.

'A delightfully witty sketch of society.'—*Spectator.*

'A perpetual feast of epigram and paradox.'—*Speaker.*

'By a writer of quite exceptional ability.'—*Athenæum.*

'Brilliantly written.'—*World.*

E. F. Benson. THE RUBICON. By E. F. BENSON, Author of 'Dodo.' *Fifth Edition. Crown 8vo.* 6s.

'Well written, stimulating, unconventional, and, in a word, characteristic.'—*Birmingham Post.*

'An exceptional achievement; a notable advance on his previous work.'—*National Observer.*

M. M. Dowie. GALLIA. By MÉNIE MURIEL DOWIE, Author of 'A Girl in the Carpathians.' *Third Edition. Crown 8vo.* 6s.

'The style is generally admirable, the dialogue not seldom brilliant, the situations surprising in their freshness and originality, while the subsidiary as well as the principal characters live and move, and the story itself is readable from title-page to colophon.'—*Saturday Review.*

'A very notable book; a very sympathetically, at times delightfully written book.'—*Daily Graphic.*

Mrs. Oliphant. SIR ROBERT'S FORTUNE. By MRS. OLIPHANT. *Crown 8vo.* 6s.

'Full of her own peculiar charm of style and simple, subtle character-painting comes her new gift, the delightful story before us. The scene mostly lies in the moors, and at the touch of the authoress a Scotch moor becomes a living thing, strong, tender, beautiful, and changeful.'—*Pall Mall Gazette.*

Mrs. Oliphant. THE TWO MARYS. By MRS. OLIPHANT. *Second Edition. Crown 8vo.* 6s.

W. E. Norris. MATTHEW AUSTIN. By W. E. NORRIS, Author of 'Mademoiselle de Mersac,' etc. *Fourth Edition. Crown 8vo.* 6s.

'"Matthew Austin" may safely be pronounced one of the most intellectually satisfactory and morally bracing novels of the current year.'—*Daily Telegraph.*

W. E. Norris. HIS GRACE. By W. E. NORRIS. *Third Edition. Crown 8vo.* 6s.

'Mr. Norris has drawn a really fine character in the Duke of Hurstbourne, at once unconventional and very true to the conventionalities of life, weak and strong in a breath, capable of inane follies and heroic decisions, yet not so definitely portrayed as to relieve a reader of the necessity of study.'—*Athenæum.*

W. E. Norris. THE DESPOTIC LADY AND OTHERS. By W. E. NORRIS. *Crown 8vo.* 6*s.*

'A budget of good fiction of which no one will tire.'—*Scotsman.*

'An extremely entertaining volume—the sprightliest of holiday companions.'—*Daily Telegraph*

H. G. Wells. THE STOLEN BACILLUS, and other Stories. By H. G. WELLS, Author of 'The Time Machine.' *Crown 8vo.* 6*s.*

'The ordinary reader of fiction may be glad to know that these stories are eminently readable from one cover to the other, but they are more than that; they are the impressions of a very striking imagination, which, it would seem, has a great deal within its reach.'—*Saturday Review.*

Arthur Morrison. TALES OF MEAN STREETS. By ARTHUR MORRISON. *Fourth Edition. Crown 8vo.* 6*s.*

'Told with consummate art and extraordinary detail. He tells a plain, unvarnished tale, and the very truth of it makes for beauty. In the true humanity of the book lies its justification, the permanence of its interest, and its indubitable triumph.'—*Athenæum.*

'A great book. The author's method is amazingly effective, and produces a thrilling sense of reality. The writer lays upon us a master hand. The book is simply appalling and irresistible in its interest. It is humorous also; without humour it would not make the mark it is certain to make.'—*World.*

J. Maclaren Cobban. THE KING OF ANDAMAN: A Saviour of Society. By J. MACLAREN COBBAN, Author of 'The Red Sultan,' etc. *Crown 8vo.* 6*s.*

'An unquestionably interesting book. It would not surprise us if it turns out to be the most interesting novel of the season, for it contains one character, at least, who has in him the root of immortality, and the book itself is ever exhaling the sweet savour of the unexpected. . . . Plot is forgotten and incident fades, and only the really human endures, and throughout this book there stands out in bold and beautiful relief its high-souled and chivalric protagonist, James the Master of Hutcheon, the King of Andaman himself.'—*Pall Mall Gazette.*

'A most original and refreshing story. James Hutcheon is a personage whom it is good to know and impossible to forget. He is beautiful within and without, whichever way we take him.'—*Spectator.*

'"The King of Andaman," is a book which does credit not less to the heart than the head of its author.'—*Athenæum.*

'The fact that Her Majesty the Queen has been pleased to gracefully express to the author of "The King of Andaman" her interest in his work will doubtless find for it many readers.'—*Vanity Fair.*

H. Morrah. A SERIOUS COMEDY. By HERBERT MORRAH. *Crown 8vo.* 6*s.*

'There are many delightful places in this volume, which is well worthy of its title. The theme has seldom been presented with more freshness or more force.'—*Scotsman.*

L. B. Walford. SUCCESSORS TO THE TITLE. By MRS. WALFORD, Author of 'Mr. Smith,' etc. *Second Edition. Crown 8vo.* 6*s.*

'The story is fresh and healthy from beginning to finish; and our liking for the two simple people who are the successors to the title mounts steadily, and ends almost in respect.'—*Scotsman.*

'The book is quite worthy to be ranked with many clever predecessors. It is excellent reading.'—*Glasgow Herald.*

T. L. Paton. A HOME IN INVERESK. By T. L. PATON. *Crown 8vo.* 6*s.*

'A distinctly fresh and fascinating novel.'—*Montrose Standard.*
'A book which bears marks of considerable promise.'—*Scotsman.*
'A pleasant and well-written story.'—*Daily Chronicle.*

John Davidson. MISS ARMSTRONG'S AND OTHER CIRCUMSTANCES. By JOHN DAVIDSON. *Crown 8vo.* 6*s.*

'Throughout the volume there is a strong vein of originality, a strength in the handling, and a knowledge of human nature that are worthy of the highest praise.'—*Scotsman.*

J. B. Burton. IN THE DAY OF ADVERSITY. By J. BLOUNDELLE BURTON, Author of 'The Hispaniola Plate,' etc. *Crown 8vo.* 6*s.*

'Unusually interesting and full of highly dramatic situations.'—*Guardian.*
'A well-written story, drawn from that inexhaustible mine, the time of Louis XIV.—*Pall Mall Gazette.*

H. Johnston. DR. CONGALTON'S LEGACY. By HENRY JOHNSTON. *Crown 8vo.* 6*s.*

'The story is redolent of humour, pathos, and tenderness, while it is not without a touch of tragedy.'—*Scotsman.*
A worthy and permanent contribution to Scottish creative literature.'—*Glasgow Herald.*

Julian Corbett. A BUSINESS IN GREAT WATERS. By JULIAN CORBETT, Author of 'For God and Gold,' 'Kophetua XIIIth.,' etc. *Crown 8vo.* 6*s.*

'In this stirring story Mr. Julian Corbett has done excellent work, welcome alike for its distinctly literary flavour, and for the wholesome tone which pervades it. Mr. Corbett writes with immense spirit, and the book is a thoroughly enjoyable one in all respects. The salt of the ocean is in it, and the right heroic ring resounds through its gallant adventures.'—*Speaker.*

C. Phillips Woolley. THE QUEENSBERRY CUP. A Tale of Adventure. By CLIVE PHILLIPS WOOLLEY, Author of 'Snap,' Editor of 'Big Game Shooting.' *Illustrated. Crown 8vo.* 6*s.*

'A book which will delight boys: a book which upholds the healthy schoolboy code of morality.'—*Scotsman.*
'A brilliant book. Dick St. Clair, of Caithness, is an almost ideal character—a combination of the mediæval knight and the modern pugilist.'—*Admiralty and Horseguards Gazette.*

Robert Barr. IN THE MIDST OF ALARMS. By ROBERT BARR, Author of 'From Whose Bourne,' etc. *Third Edition. Crown 8vo.* 6*s.*

'A book which has abundantly satisfied us by its capital humour.'—*Daily Chronicle.*
'Mr. Barr has achieved a triumph whereof he has every reason to be proud.'—*Pall Mall Gazette.*

L. Daintrey. THE KING OF ALBERIA. A Romance of the Balkans. By LAURA DAINTREY. *Crown 8vo.* 6*s.*

Miss Daintrey seems to have an intimate acquaintance with the people and politics of the Balkan countries in which the scene of her lively and picturesque romance is laid. On almost every page we find clever touches of local colour which differentiate her book unmistakably from the ordinary novel of commerce. The story is briskly told, and well conceived.'—*Glasgow Herald.*

Mrs. Pinsent. CHILDREN OF THIS WORLD. By ELLEN F. PINSENT, Author of 'Jenny's Case.' *Crown 8vo.* 6*s.*

'Mrs. Pinsent's new novel has plenty of vigour, variety, and good writing. There are certainty of purpose, strength of touch, and clearness of vision.'—*Athenæum.*

Clark Russell. MY DANISH SWEETHEART. By W. CLARK RUSSELL, Author of 'The Wreck of the Grosvenor,' etc. *Illustrated. Fourth Edition. Crown 8vo.* 6*s.*

G. Manville Fenn. AN ELECTRIC SPARK. By G. MANVILLE FENN, Author of 'The Vicar's Wife,' 'A Double Knot,' etc. *Second Edition. Crown 8vo.* 6*s.*

'A simple and wholesome story.'—*Manchester Guardian.*

R. Pryce. TIME AND THE WOMAN. By RICHARD PRYCE, Author of 'Miss Maxwell's Affections,' 'The Quiet Mrs. Fleming,' etc. *Second Edition. Crown 8vo.* 6*s.*

'Mr. Pryce's work recalls the style of Octave Feuillet, by its clearness, conciseness, its literary reserve.'—*Athenæum.*

Mrs. Watson. THIS MAN'S DOMINION. By the Author of 'A High Little World.' *Second Edition. Crown 8vo.* 6*s.*

Marriott Watson. DIOGENES OF LONDON and other Sketches. By H. B. MARRIOTT WATSON, Author of 'The Web of the Spider.' *Crown 8vo. Buckram.* 6*s.*

'By all those who delight in the uses of words, who rate the exercise of prose above the exercise of verse, who rejoice in all proofs of its delicacy and its strength, who believe that English prose is chief among the moulds of thought, by these Mr. Marriott Watson's book will be welcomed.'—*National Observer.*

M. Gilchrist. THE STONE DRAGON. By MURRAY GILCHRIST. *Crown 8vo. Buckram.* 6*s.*

'The author's faults are atoned for by certain positive and admirable merits. The romances have not their counterpart in modern literature, and to read them is a unique experience.'—*National Observer.*

E. Dickinson. A VICAR'S WIFE. By EVELYN DICKINSON. *Crown 8vo.* 6*s.*

E. M. Gray. ELSA. By E. M'QUEEN GRAY. *Crown 8vo.* 6*s.*

THREE-AND-SIXPENNY NOVELS 3/6

Crown 8vo.

DERRICK VAUGHAN, NOVELIST. By EDNA LYALL.
MARGERY OF QUETHER. By S. BARING GOULD.
JACQUETTA. By S. BARING GOULD.
SUBJECT TO VANITY. By MARGARET BENSON.
THE MOVING FINGER. By MARY GAUNT.
JACO TRELOAR. By J. H. PEARCE.

AUT DIABOLUS AUT NIHIL. By X. L.

THE COMING OF CUCULAIN. A Romance of the Heroic Age of Ireland. By STANDISH O'GRADY. *Illustrated.*

THE GODS GIVE MY DONKEY WINGS. By ANGUS EVAN ABBOTT.

THE STAR GAZERS. By G. MANVILLE FENN.

THE POISON OF ASPS. By R. ORTON PROWSE.

THE QUIET MRS. FLEMING. By R. PRYCE.

THE PLAN OF CAMPAIGN. By F. MABEL ROBINSON.

DISENCHANTMENT. By F. MABEL ROBINSON.

MR. BUTLER'S WARD. By F. MABEL ROBINSON.

A LOST ILLUSION. By LESLIE KEITH.

A REVEREND GENTLEMAN. By J. M. COBBAN.

A DEPLORABLE AFFAIR. By W. E. NORRIS.

A CAVALIER'S LADYE. By Mrs. DICKER.

HALF-CROWN NOVELS 2/6

A Series of Novels by popular Authors.

1. HOVENDEN, V.C. By F. MABEL ROBINSON.
2. ELI'S CHILDREN. By G. MANVILLE FENN.
3. A DOUBLE KNOT. By G. MANVILLE FENN.
4. DISARMED. By M. BETHAM EDWARDS.
5. A MARRIAGE AT SEA. By W. CLARK RUSSELL.
6. IN TENT AND BUNGALOW. By the Author of 'Indian Idylls.'
7. MY STEWARDSHIP. By E. M'QUEEN GRAY.
8. JACK'S FATHER. By W. E. NORRIS.
9. JIM B.

Lynn Linton. THE TRUE HISTORY OF JOSHUA DAVIDSON, Christian and Communist. By E. LYNN LINTON. *Eleventh Edition. Post 8vo.* 1*s.*

Books for Boys and Girls 3/6

A Series of Books by well-known Authors, well illustrated.

1. THE ICELANDER'S SWORD. By S. BARING GOULD.
2. TWO LITTLE CHILDREN AND CHING. By EDITH E. CUTHELL.

3. TODDLEBEN'S HERO. By M. M. BLAKE.
4. ONLY A GUARD ROOM DOG. By EDITH E. CUTHELL.
5. THE DOCTOR OF THE JULIET. By HARRY COLLINGWOOD.
6. MASTER ROCKAFELLAR'S VOYAGE. By W. CLARK RUSSELL.
7. SYD BELTON: Or, The Boy who would not go to Sea. By G. MANVILLE FENN.

The Peacock Library

A Series of Books for Girls by well-known Authors, handsomely bound in blue and silver, and well illustrated. 3/6

1. A PINCH OF EXPERIENCE. By L. B. WALFORD.
2. THE RED GRANGE. By Mrs. MOLESWORTH.
3. THE SECRET OF MADAME DE MONLUC. By the Author of 'Mdle Mori.'
4. DUMPS. By Mrs. PARR, Author of 'Adam and Eve.'
5. OUT OF THE FASHION. By L. T. MEADE.
6. A GIRL OF THE PEOPLE. By L. T. MEADE.
7. HEPSY GIPSY. By L. T. MEADE. 2*s.* 6*d.*
8. THE HONOURABLE MISS. By L. T. MEADE.
9. MY LAND OF BEULAH. By Mrs. LEITH ADAMS.

University Extension Series

A series of books on historical, literary, and scientific subjects, suitable for extension students and home-reading circles. Each volume is complete in itself, and the subjects are treated by competent writers in a broad and philosophic spirit.

Edited by J. E. SYMES, M.A.,
Principal of University College, Nottingham.
Crown 8vo. Price (with some exceptions) 2*s.* 6*d.*
The following volumes are ready:—

THE INDUSTRIAL HISTORY OF ENGLAND. By H. DE B. GIBBINS, M.A., late Scholar of Wadham College, Oxon., Cobden Prizeman. *Fourth Edition. With Maps and Plans.* 3*s.*

'A compact and clear story of our ndustrial development. A study of this concise but luminous book cannot fail to give the reader a clear insight into the principal phenomena of our industrial history. The editor and publishers are to be congratulated on this first volume of their venture, and we shall look with expectant interest for the succeeding volumes of the series.'—*University Extension Journal.*

A HISTORY OF ENGLISH POLITICAL ECONOMY. By L. L. PRICE, M.A., Fellow of Oriel College, Oxon. *Second Edition.*

PROBLEMS OF POVERTY: An Inquiry into the Industrial Conditions of the Poor. By J. A. HOBSON, M.A. *Third Edition.*

VICTORIAN POETS. By A. SHARP.

THE FRENCH REVOLUTION. By J. E. SYMES, M.A.

PSYCHOLOGY. By F. S. GRANGER, M.A., Lecturer in Philosophy at University College, Nottingham.

THE EVOLUTION OF PLANT LIFE: Lower Forms. By G. MASSEE, Kew Gardens. *With Illustrations.*

AIR AND WATER. Professor V. B. LEWES, M.A. *Illustrated.*

THE CHEMISTRY OF LIFE AND HEALTH. By C. W. KIMMINS, M.A. Camb. *Illustrated.*

THE MECHANICS OF DAILY LIFE. By V. P. SELLS, M.A. *Illustrated.*

ENGLISH SOCIAL REFORMERS. H. DE B. GIBBINS, M.A.

ENGLISH TRADE AND FINANCE IN THE SEVENTEENTH CENTURY. By W. A. S. HEWINS, B.A.

THE CHEMISTRY OF FIRE. The Elementary Principles of Chemistry. By M. M. PATTISON MUIR, M.A. *Illustrated.*

A TEXT-BOOK OF AGRICULTURAL BOTANY. By M. C. POTTER, M.A., F.L.S. *Illustrated.* 3*s.* 6*d.*

THE VAULT OF HEAVEN. A Popular Introduction to Astronomy. By R. A. GREGORY. *With numerous Illustrations.*

METEOROLOGY. The Elements of Weather and Climate. By H. N. DICKSON, F.R.S.E., F.R. Met. Soc. *Illustrated.*

A MANUAL OF ELECTRICAL SCIENCE. By GEORGE J. BURCH, M.A. *With numerous Illustrations.* 3*s.*

THE EARTH. An Introduction to Physiography. By EVAN SMALL, M.A. *Illustrated.*

INSECT LIFE. By F. W. THEOBALD, M.A. *Illustrated.*

ENGLISH POETRY FROM BLAKE TO BROWNING. By W. M. DIXON, M.A.

ENGLISH LOCAL GOVERNMENT. By E. JENKS, M.A., Professor of Law at University College, Liverpool.

Social Questions of To-day

Edited by H. DE B. GIBBINS, M.A.

Crown 8vo. 2s. 6d.

2/6

A series of volumes upon those topics of social, economic, and industrial interest that are at the present moment foremost in the public mind. Each volume of the series is written by an author who is an acknowledged authority upon the subject with which he deals.

The following Volumes of the Series are ready:—

TRADE UNIONISM—NEW AND OLD. By G. HOWELL, Author of 'The Conflicts of Capital and Labour.' *Second Edition.*

THE CO-OPERATIVE MOVEMENT TO-DAY. By G. J. HOLYOAKE, Author of 'The History of Co-operation.' *Second Edition.*

MUTUAL THRIFT. By Rev. J. FROME WILKINSON, M.A., Author of 'The Friendly Society Movement.'

PROBLEMS OF POVERTY: An Inquiry into the Industrial Conditions of the Poor. By J. A. HOBSON, M.A. *Third Edition.*

THE COMMERCE OF NATIONS. By C. F. BASTABLE, M.A., Professor of Economics at Trinity College, Dublin.

THE ALIEN INVASION. By W. H. WILKINS, B.A., Secretary to the Society for Preventing the Immigration of Destitute Aliens.

THE RURAL EXODUS. By P. ANDERSON GRAHAM.

LAND NATIONALIZATION. By HAROLD COX, B.A.

A SHORTER WORKING DAY. By H. DE B. GIBBINS and R. A. HADFIELD, of the Hecla Works, Sheffield.

BACK TO THE LAND: An Inquiry into the Cure for Rural Depopulation. By H. E. MOORE.

TRUSTS, POOLS AND CORNERS: As affecting Commerce and Industry. By J. STEPHEN JEANS, M.R.I., F.S.S.

THE FACTORY SYSTEM. By R. COOKE TAYLOR.

THE STATE AND ITS CHILDREN. By GERTRUDE TUCKWELL.

WOMEN'S WORK. By LADY DILKE, MISS BULLEY, and MISS WHITLEY.

MUNICIPALITIES AT WORK. The Municipal Policy of Six Great Towns, and its Influence on their Social Welfare. By FREDERICK DOLMAN.

SOCIALISM AND MODERN THOUGHT. By M. KAUFMANN.

THE HOUSING OF THE WORKING CLASSES. By R. F. BOWMAKER.

MODERN CIVILISATION IN SOME OF ITS ECONOMIC ASPECTS. By W. CUNNINGHAM, D.D., Fellow of Trinity College, Cambridge.

Classical Translations

Edited by H. F. FOX, M.A., Fellow and Tutor of Brasenose College, Oxford.

Messrs. Methuen are issuing a New Series of Translations from the Greek and Latin Classics. They have enlisted the services of some of the best Oxford and Cambridge Scholars, and it is their intention that the Series shall be distinguished by literary excellence as well as by scholarly accuracy.

ÆSCHYLUS—Agamemnon, Chöephoroe, Eumenides. Translated by LEWIS CAMPBELL, LL.D., late Professor of Greek at St. Andrews. 5*s*.

CICERO—De Oratore I. Translated by E. N. P. MOOR, M.A., Assistant Master at Clifton. 3*s*. 6*d*.

CICERO—Select Orations (Pro Milone, Pro Murena, Philippic II., In Catilinam). Translated by H. E. D. BLAKISTON, M.A., Fellow and Tutor of Trinity College, Oxford. 5*s*.

CICERO—De Natura Deorum. Translated by F. BROOKS. M.A., late Scholar of Balliol College, Oxford. 3*s*. 6*d*.

LUCIAN—Six Dialogues (Nigrinus, Icaro-Menippus, The Cock, The Ship, The Parasite, The Lover of Falsehood). Translated by S. T. IRWIN, M.A., Assistant Master at Clifton; late Scholar of Exeter College, Oxford. 3*s*. 6*d*.

SOPHOCLES—Electra and Ajax. Translated by E. D. A. MORSHEAD, M.A., late Scholar of New College, Oxford; Assistant Master at Winchester. 2*s*. 6*d*.

TACITUS—Agricola and Germania. Translated by R. B. TOWNSHEND, late Scholar of Trinity College, Cambridge. 2*s*. 6*d*.

Educational Books

CLASSICAL

TACITI AGRICOLA. With Introduction, Notes, Map, etc. By R. F. DAVIS, M.A., Assistant Master at Weymouth College. *Crown 8vo.* 2*s.*

TACITI GERMANIA. By the same Editor. *Crown 8vo.* 2*s.*

HERODOTUS: EASY SELECTIONS. With Vocabulary. By A. C. LIDDELL, M.A., Assistant Master at Nottingham High School. *Fcap. 8vo.* 1*s.* 6*d.*

SELECTIONS FROM THE ODYSSEY. By E. D. STONE, M.A., late Assistant Master at Eton. *Fcap. 8vo.* 1*s.* 6*d.*

PLAUTUS: THE CAPTIVI. Adapted for Lower Forms by J. H. FREESE, M.A., late Fellow of St. John's, Cambridge. 1*s.* 6*d.*

DEMOSTHENES AGAINST CONON AND CALLICLES. Edited with Notes, and Vocabulary, by F. DARWIN SWIFT, M.A., formerly Scholar of Queen's College, Oxford; Assistant Master at Denstone College. *Fcap. 8vo.* 2*s.*

GERMAN

A COMPANION GERMAN GRAMMAR. By H. DE B. GIBBINS, M.A., Assistant Master at Nottingham High School. *Crown 8vo.* 1*s.* 6*d.*

GERMAN PASSAGES FOR UNSEEN TRANSLATION. By E. M'QUEEN GRAY. *Crown 8vo.* 2*s.* 6*d.*

SCIENCE

THE WORLD OF SCIENCE. Including Chemistry, Heat. Light, Sound, Magnetism, Electricity, Botany, Zoology, Physiology, Astronomy, and Geology. By R. ELLIOT STEEL, M.A., F.C.S. 147 Illustrations. *Second Edition.* *Crown 8vo.* 2*s.* 6*d.*

'Mr. Steel's Manual is admirable in many ways. The book is well calculated to attract and retain the attention of the young.'—*Saturday Review.*

'If Mr. Steel is to be placed second to any for this quality of lucidity, it is only to Huxley himself; and to be named in the same breath with this master of the craft of teaching is to be accredited with the clearness of style and simplicity of arrangement that belong to thorough mastery of a subject.'—*Parents' Review.*

ELEMENTARY LIGHT. By R. E. STEEL. With numerous Illustrations. *Crown 8vo.* 4*s.* 6*d.*

ENGLISH

ENGLISH RECORDS. A Companion to the History of England. By H. E. MALDEN, M.A. *Crown 8vo.* 3*s.* 6*d.*

A book which aims at concentrating information upon dates, genealogy, officials, constitutional documents, etc., which is usually found scattered in different volumes.

THE ENGLISH CITIZEN: HIS RIGHTS AND DUTIES. By H. E. MALDEN, M.A. 1*s.* 6*d.*

'The book goes over the same ground as is traversed in the school books on this subject written to satisfy the requirements of the Education code. It would serve admirably the purposes of a text-book, as it is well based in historical facts, and keeps quite clear of party matters.'—*Scotsman.*

METHUEN'S COMMERCIAL SERIES.

Edited by H. DE B. GIBBINS, M.A.

BRITISH COMMERCE AND COLONIES FROM ELIZABETH TO VICTORIA. By H. DE B. GIBBINS, M.A., Author of 'The Industrial History of England,' etc. etc. 2*s.*

COMMERCIAL EXAMINATION PAPERS. By H. DE B. GIBBINS, M.A. 1*s.* 6*d.*

THE ECONOMICS OF COMMERCE. By H. DE B. GIBBINS, M.A. 1*s.* 6*d.*

A MANUAL OF FRENCH COMMERCIAL CORRESPONDENCE. By S. E. BALLY, Modern Language Master at the Manchester Grammar School. 2*s.*

A FRENCH COMMERCIAL READER. By S. E. BALLY. 2*s.*

COMMERCIAL GEOGRAPHY, with special reference to Trade Routes, New Markets, and Manufacturing Districts. By L. W. LYDE, M.A., of the Academy, Glasgow. 2*s.*

A PRIMER OF BUSINESS. By S. JACKSON, M.A. 1*s.* 6*d.*

COMMERCIAL ARITHMETIC. By F. G. TAYLOR, M.A. 1*s.* 6*d.*

WORKS BY A. M. M. STEDMAN, M.A.

INITIA LATINA: Easy Lessons on Elementary Accidence. *Second Edition. Fcap.* 8*vo.* 1*s.*

FIRST LATIN LESSONS. *Fourth Edition. Crown* 8*vo.* 2*s.*

FIRST LATIN READER. With Notes adapted to the Shorter Latin Primer and Vocabulary. *Second Edition. Crown* 8*vo.* 1*s.* 6*d.*

EASY SELECTIONS FROM CAESAR. Part I. The Helvetian War. 18*mo.* 1*s.*

EASY SELECTIONS FROM LIVY. Part I. The Kings of Rome. 18*mo.* 1*s.* 6*d.*

EASY LATIN PASSAGES FOR UNSEEN TRANSLATION. *Third Edition. Fcap.* 8*vo.* 1*s.* 6*d.*

EXEMPLA LATINA. First Lessons in Latin Accidence. With Vocabulary. *Crown* 8*vo.* 1*s.*

EASY LATIN EXERCISES ON THE SYNTAX OF THE SHORTER AND REVISED LATIN PRIMER. With Vocabulary. *Fourth Edition. Crown* 8*vo.* 2*s.* 6*d.* Issued with the consent of Dr. Kennedy.

THE LATIN COMPOUND SENTENCE: Rules and Exercises. *Crown* 8*vo.* 1*s.* 6*d.* With Vocabulary. 2*s.*

NOTANDA QUAEDAM: Miscellaneous Latin Exercises on Common Rules and Idioms. *Second Edition. Fcap.* 8*vo.* 1*s.* 6*d.* With Vocabulary, 2s.

LATIN VOCABULARIES FOR REPETITION: Arranged according to Subjects. *Fourth Edition. Fcap.* 8*vo.* 1*s.* 6*d.*

A VOCABULARY OF LATIN IDIOMS AND PHRASES. 18*mo.* 1*s.*

STEPS TO GREEK. 18*mo.* 1*s.*

EASY GREEK PASSAGES FOR UNSEEN TRANSLATION. *Fcap.* 8*vo.* 1*s.* 6*d.*

GREEK VOCABULARIES FOR REPETITION. Arranged according to Subjects. *Second Edition. Fcap.* 8*vo.* 1*s.* 6*d.*

GREEK TESTAMENT SELECTIONS. For the use of Schools. *Third Edition.* With Introduction, Notes, and Vocabulary. *Fcap.* 8*vo.* 2*s.* 6*d.*

STEPS TO FRENCH. *18mo.* 8*d.*

FIRST FRENCH LESSONS. *Crown 8vo.* 1*s.*

EASY FRENCH PASSAGES FOR UNSEEN TRANSLATION. *Second Edition. Fcap. 8vo.* 1*s.* 6*d.*

EASY FRENCH EXERCISES ON ELEMENTARY SYNTAX. With Vocabulary. *Crown 8vo.* 2*s.* 6*d.*

FRENCH VOCABULARIES FOR REPETITION: Arranged according to Subjects. *Third Edition. Fcap. 8vo.* 1*s.*

SCHOOL EXAMINATION SERIES.

EDITED BY A. M. M. STEDMAN, M.A.

Crown 8vo. 2*s.* 6*d.*

FRENCH EXAMINATION PAPERS IN MISCELLANEOUS GRAMMAR AND IDIOMS. By A. M. M. STEDMAN, M.A. *Sixth Edition.*

A KEY, issued to Tutors and Private Students only, to be had on application to the Publishers. *Second Edition. Crown 8vo.* 6*s. net.*

LATIN EXAMINATION PAPERS IN MISCELLANEOUS GRAMMAR AND IDIOMS. By A. M. M. STEDMAN, M.A. *Fourth Edition.* KEY issued as above. 6*s. net.*

GREEK EXAMINATION PAPERS IN MISCELLANEOUS GRAMMAR AND IDIOMS. By A. M. M. STEDMAN, M.A. *Third Edition.* KEY issued as above. 6*s. net.*

GERMAN EXAMINATION PAPERS IN MISCELLANEOUS GRAMMAR AND IDIOMS. By R. J. MORICH, Manchester. *Third Edition.* KEY issued as above. 6*s. net.*

HISTORY AND GEOGRAPHY EXAMINATION PAPERS. By C. H. SPENCE, M.A., Clifton Coll.

SCIENCE EXAMINATION PAPERS. By R. E. STEEL, M.A., F.C.S., Chief Natural Science Master, Bradford Grammar School. *In two vols.* Part I. Chemistry; Part II. Physics.

GENERAL KNOWLEDGE EXAMINATION PAPERS. By A. M. M. STEDMAN, M.A. *Second Edition.* KEY issued as above. 7*s. net.*

Printed by T. and A. CONSTABLE, Printers to Her Majesty
at the Edinburgh University Press

www.ingramcontent.com/pod-product-compliance
Lightning Source LLC
Chambersburg PA
CBHW021427300426
44114CB00010B/678

* 9 7 8 3 3 3 7 1 3 0 2 3 7 *